The Sixties, Center Stage

The Sixties, Center Stage

*Mainstream and Popular Performances
in a Turbulent Decade*

Edited by

James M. Harding and Cindy Rosenthal

University of Michigan Press ANN ARBOR

Published in the United States of America by
The University of Michigan Press
Manufactured in the United States of America
♾ Printed on acid-free paper

2020   2019   2018   2017   4   3   2   1

A CIP catalog record for this book is available from the British Library.

ISBN 978-0-472-07336-8 (hardcover : alk. paper)
ISBN 978-0-472-05336-0 (paper : alk. paper)
ISBN 978-0-472-12260-8 (e-book)

Acknowledgments

No major project is finished without proper acknowledgment of those who have made it possible. When the project is an anthology like this one, acknowledgment has to begin with the contributors. As editors, we want to thank each of our authors not only for the important chapters they contributed to this volume and for the provocative insights they added to the larger debate that the volume initiates, but we also want to thank them for their patience as we brought this project to completion. In no uncertain terms, their individual contributions have made this a volume well worth the wait. In addition to the note of thanks to our contributors, we want to express our deep appreciation to Jeff Kaplan at the University of Maryland, who offered invaluable assistance in the final preparation of the manuscript for submission. We would also like to thank theater photographers Joan Marcus and Carol Rosegg for their advice and assistance on the book cover.

We also want to acknowledge those at the University of Michigan Press who have helped move this project into print. From start to finish, LeAnn Fields has believed in and supported this work. Many times in the past, we have expressed our gratitude to her for her support—not only of projects like this one, but also of scholarship in the field of theater and performance studies in general. But even at the risk of repeating a familiar refrain that comes from a large chorus of scholars, we want to thank her for being such a fierce advocate on behalf of the scholarship produced in our discipline. We also want to thank our anonymous reviewers who not only took the time to understand this anthology's core issues and contributions but who offered genuinely constructive suggestions. The anthology is stronger as a result of their careful reading of the manuscript. On the production side, we want to thank Marcia LaBrenz and the entire production staff at the University of Michigan Press for their hard work in preparing the manuscript for publication. We are absolutely delighted to publish with Michigan again.

Of course, none of the essays in this anthology would be possible were it not for the countless artists, practitioners and scholars whose work provides both the context and the substance for the discussions in the pages that follow. Fortunately, many of the key artists who are subjects in this volume are still with us. Much of the work here thus builds in part upon interviews that our contributors have conducted with artists who were kind enough to offer valuable reflections and perspectives on work that they and their fellow artists produced decades ago. We are grateful to them for the generosity they have shown in sharing their thoughts about the sixties, for the enduring commitment they continue to have to the arts, and, above all, for the multiple contributions they have made to the theater. Similar acknowledgments are warranted with regard to the scholars who preceded us, and in particular we want to express our gratitude to the editors of and contributors to journals like *TDR*, all of whom, regardless of aesthetic or political orientation, realized early on that the theater being produced in the 1960s was of major significance and needed careful documentation. We owe a great deal to that documentation and to early scholarly reflections on its significance. All of this said, the 1960s are now a half-century behind us, and we are painfully aware that many practitioners, artists and scholars of the period are no longer with us. We want to pay special tribute to artists like Judith Malina, Edward Albee, and Zelda Fichandler, who passed while this book was in progress.

We have a sincere recognition of and heartfelt appreciation for the day-to-day sacrifices and compromises made by Cindy's partner, Emanuel Levy, and James's partner, Friederike Eigler. We are both extremely lucky and grateful to have partners like Emanuel and Friederike, whose enduring support has eased the way to the completion of this anthology.

With one exception, the essays in this anthology are all new pieces. An earlier version of David Crespy's essay was published under the title "A Paradigm for New Play Development: The Albee Barr Wilder Playwrights Unit" in *Theatre History Studies* 26 (2006): 31-51.

In the long life of La MaMa Experimental Theatre Company, "La MaMa" has been printed and typeset many different ways. Following the preference of La MaMa's artistic leadership and the most common spelling at the time of publication we have opted for consistency sake to use "La MaMa" throughout this volume. However, it is worth noting that in the 1960s and 1970s this was less frequently used than "La Mama."

We hope you find this anthology as rewarding to read as we have experienced the process as editors.

James Harding and Cindy Rosenthal
Washington D.C. and New York City, 2016

Contents

INTRODUCTION

James M. Harding and Cindy Rosenthal

Pulling the Curtain on False Dichotomies

*The Importance of the Theatrical
Mainstream in the 1960s*

Historians commonly conceptualize the 1960s as a "long decade," even though that concept remains the subject of much debate. In many respects, the registers of that debate are perhaps more interesting than the actual question of whether one ought to conceptualize "the sixties" as the strict chronological marker of a particular decade or as an idea with roots deep in the 1950s and branches extending well into the 1970s. In 1984, for example, Fredric Jameson, Anders Stephanson, and Cornel West famously pointed to the Battle of Algiers, the launch of Sputnik and the independence of Ghana in 1957 as marking the beginning of the sixties and to the death of Mao Zedong in 1976 as the marker bringing them to a close.[1] These historical events, they openly admitted, were pivotal moments in "a very partial chronology." Jameson, in particular, locates the sixties, or at least the radical conception of them, in the anticolonial movements in the third world during the 1950s, suggesting that it hardly seems "controversial to mark the beginnings of what [. . . would] come to be called the 60s in the third world with the great movement of decolonialization in British and French Africa."[2] But if this is a noncontroversial claim, it is so in large part because Jameson frames it within a historiographical model that he specifically characterizes as "tentative and provisional" and because he readily acknowledges the "selectiveness" of his "historical narrative."[3] His is a historical narrative that, "without apology,"[4] openly serves a very specific political agenda and that, as a consequence, also openly justifies its admittedly selective focus. There is an important historiographical lesson in that openness even though the lesson in history that Jameson, Stephanson, and West provide is tendentious. In many respects, that is precisely the point.

For an anthology like this one, which focuses on mainstream and popular performances rather than on radical politics, Jameson's unapologetically selective narrative of the 1960s might seem an odd point of departure were it not for two major aspects of the periodization that he provides. First, his open acknowledgment of the selectiveness of his historical narrative is a clear reminder that the image of the radical sixties has always been a bit of a construct—and frequently a vague one at that. Andrew Hunt calls attention to that vagueness, for example, when he cites the easy and often uncritical slippage between terms like *the sixties* and *the movement*. "The sixties," he argues, "has become synonymous with 'the movement', a vague yet frequently used expression used to describe a cluster of mass protests, on local and national levels, typically originating from Civil Rights or Black Power struggles, the antiwar movement, the New Left, student power groups, feminism, and other political, cultural or minority activists."[5] However much those various movements may have coalesced into a more general notion of "the movement," they still provide a vague and partial image of "the sixties" more generally. It is worth recalling, for example, that the decade literally opened not only with the formation of the Student Nonviolent Coordinating Committee (SNCC) in 1960 at the historically black Shaw University in North Carolina but also with the formation of Young Americans for Freedom "at the family estate of [the] conservative ideologue William F. Buckley"[6] as well as with the evangelist Billy Graham's deeply conservative essay "The National Purpose" being read into the congressional record.[7] Indeed, the image of radicalism associated with the sixties is in no small part a consequence of the selective construction of histories of the period.

Despite popular myths to the contrary, narratives that cast the sixties primarily as a radical period traffic at best in half truths. Whether the registers of those narratives are political or cultural, they are like Jameson's own narrative: "partial," "tentative," and "selective," particularly in the United States, where the sixties were as much a period of unprecedented economic growth, American entrepreneurialism, "silent majorities," and Richard Nixon as they were a period of social unrest fueled by a courageous civil rights movement, a growing antiwar activism, and a blossoming youth-centered counterculture. That counterculture, we might add, as Thomas Frank brilliantly argues in *The Conquest of Cool: Business Culture, Counterculture, and the Rise of Hip Consumerism* (1997), was as much a product of a revolution in the commercial advertising industry as it was of youthful disenchantment with the establishment. In this respect, what Jameson achieves in the openly acknowledged selectiveness of his historical narrative is a subtle but important grounding of the sixties not so much as a period of unprecedented progressiveness and of liberal cultural advances but rather as a period of contestation and of struggles that have yet to be fully resolved even thirty-some years after Jameson's essay was published in 1984.

Sympathetic though one may be with the unapologetic politics of Jameson's narrative, it behooves us nonetheless to ask rather obvious questions not only about what such narratives leave out but also about the ends and costs of deliberate selectiveness in the writing of history. Every written history is the product of selectiveness. The question is, whose interests motivate and are served by that selectiveness? With Jameson, such questions are not particularly difficult to address since the primary focus of his essay is that of "periodizing the 60s" in terms of its progressive political struggles. But as one shifts the primary focus from politics to theater in the 1960s, things quickly become more complicated, murky, and vague. Certainly numerous practitioners during the period envisioned a theater that would have a vital role to play in political struggles. Yet there has been a surprising selectiveness among theater historians not with regard to politics per se but rather with regard to the kind of theatrical practice that they associate with it.

In many respects, written histories of theater practice in the 1960s could easily serve as a showcase for Alan Woods's now classic critique of the undue privileging of avant-garde performance in theater histories,[8] particularly since there is a tendency among theater historians writing on the 1960s to equate the experimental with the politically progressive and radical—a tendency, in short, to assume that radical and innovative performance aesthetics are the exclusive domain of experimental theaters (like those of off-off-Broadway) and, more importantly, are somehow more directly at the forefront of political change than other, seemingly more conventional theatrical forms. A case in point is our own earlier anthology, *Restaging the Sixties: Radical Theaters and Their Legacies* (2006), which, by focusing entirely on experimental and avant-garde theaters like the Living Theatre, Bread and Puppet, and the Open Theatre, implicitly equates them with "the sixties" as a concept as well as implies that, among theater practitioners, the experimental aesthetics that they applied to politics were the primary embodiment of the progressive political currents of the period. But time has a way of stripping away the blinders of established perception and, contrary to Richard Schechner's 1995 claim in *The Future of Ritual* that the avant-garde has devolved into a mere "style,"[9] we would suggest that, when it comes to innovation and to politics—especially in the realms of theatrical and performance practices in the 1960s—the postwar Western avant-garde was always already a bit of a style: one sphere of political and aesthetic innovation among many. In this regard, a serious look at the innovative and provocative political underpinnings of mainstream and popular performances of the period is not only overdue. It is, we would argue, also a crucial aspect of understanding the 1960s as a period, particularly if one follows Jameson's example and adopts a long-decade view of the sixties.

At some level, a more systematic examination of mainstream and popular performances from the period seems to be such an obvious avenue of scholarly inquiry that the governing assumptions of works like *Restaging the Sixties* ought to be an anomaly rather than merely one of the more recent examples of a larger, established scholarly trend—a trend that includes works like Arthur Sainer's *New Radical Theatre Notebook* (1975; revised edition, 2000), Theodore Shank's *Beyond the Boundaries: American Alternative Theatre* (1988; revised edition, 2002), and Stephen Bottoms's *Playing Underground: A Critical History of the 1960s Off-Off-Broadway Movement* (2006). But inasmuch as *Restaging the Sixties*, continued the kind of institutionalized proclivity that Alan Woods lamented more generally in the late 1980s, it is worth asking where such trends originated or at least where the institutionalization of them began. On that note, one could do far worse than to look at the profound influence of a journal like *TDR* on the legacy of 1960s theater simply as a consequence of the significant commitment it has made over the past fifty years to publishing scholarship on—as well as documents from—avant-garde theater and performance from the period. Indeed, that commitment arguably originated at a decisive moment in the 1960s themselves, when the journal, under the new editorship of Richard Schechner, began its evolution from the *Tulane Drama Review* into *The Drama Review* and ultimately into *TDR: The Journal of Performance Studies*.

On the face of things, that evolution was the product of Schechner's move from Tulane University to NYU in 1967, but at a conceptual level it arguably began almost immediately after Schechner took the reins of the journal as editor in 1962 and inaugurated what was to become a signature of his tenure as editor: the *TDR* Comment. From the very beginning, the provocative tone of Schechner's editorials not only announced new directions for the journal but also aimed—quite effectively—at steering the entire profession down new paths. One could cite any number of instances over the past five decades where Schechner has prodded theater scholarship in specific directions by admonishing *TDR*'s readers to make tough choices, but it is worth recalling that this rhetorical strategy was already in place in 1963 when he published what was only his second editorial. Entitled "Intentions, Problems, Proposals," that editorial ended with a blunt choice that signaled a very clear course for the journal in terms of the kind of theater that Schechner would champion and, by default, in the kind of scholarship that the journal would cultivate and publish under his editorship. Schechner presented readers with an either/or proposition and told them in no uncertain terms,

> You choose Broadway and I'll choose an experimental theatre. There are many roads to truth. But neither of us can choose *both* Broadway and an experimental theatre. That's a contradiction in intention.[10]

Coming as it did from the new editor, this broad rejection of commercial theater was nothing short of an implicit mission statement for the journal itself, and as *TDR* began to flourish under Schechner's leadership, so too did the influence of this unofficial policy.

Schechner was certainly not the first to question the priorities of commercial theater nor the only one to do so in the 1960s, but the choice that he posited in this early editorial did more than define the course that *TDR* would take. Arguably, it also had a profound impact on subsequent scholarship on theater in the 1960s more generally. Given the prominent position of *TDR* within the profession, many scholars carefully attended to its path. Moreover, the choice Schechner presented was not limited to readers and contributors to *TDR*. It reverberated beyond the pages of the journal itself, playing no small part in encouraging theater and performance historians writing on the sixties not only to privilege the values of experimentation, anticonsumerism, and, by extension, counterculturalism but also to assume that these values were by definition antithetical to mainstream theatrical practice. It is one thing to espouse such values as central to what constitutes genuinely significant, aesthetically interesting, and socially relevant theater in the 1960s. It is another thing altogether to assume that these values were fundamentally irreconcilable with Broadway and the mainstream or that their origins were not to be found there as frequently as in the fringe or elsewhere.

The problem is that, however influential this early provocation from Schechner might have been, it was largely based upon a false dichotomy. While experimentation and anticonsumerism were immensely important and sociopolitically significant parts of theatrical practice during the 1960s, the privileging of this focus in *TDR* and in other scholarly explorations of sixties theater produced a skewed image of what was actually happening among performance practitioners. Despite assumptions to the contrary, historical evidence clearly indicates that experimentation and anticonsumerism moved throughout the 1960s with great fluidity, traveling back and forth between the margins and the mainstream. Indeed, as the essays in this anthology amply demonstrate, not only were the lines between Broadway and experimental theater never as clearly drawn as Schechner's polemic suggested, but Broadway itself was a much more complex and nuanced environment—both aesthetically and politically—than his categorical dismissal of it implied. Broadway frequently engaged with some of the most pressing political issues of the period, and it also was the site of numerous innovations worthy of note. Combined with a subtle political undercurrent, those innovations were significant enough, in fact, that one of the single most overlooked aspects of theater in the 1960s is what, in the absence of a critical term for it, we would call "the mainstream experimental," a designation that is consciously calculated as an intervention and counter to Schechner's influential dichotomy.

That the mainstream experimental initially sounds a bit like an oxymoron or a "contradiction in intention" is itself a testament to just how ingrained Schechner's Broadway/experimental binary is as a conceptual frame for writing the history of sixties theater. If nothing else, the term mainstream experimental serves as a reminder that the choice Schechner posited in that binary encouraged a highly selective vision of theatrical practice. Ironically enough, mainstream experimental also carries an anti-institutional undercurrent, for insofar as the selective vision Schechner advocated became institutionalized as implicit editorial policy in *TDR*, it curtailed serious exploration of the rich tensions, dialogues, and exchanges that took place between the theatrical mainstream and the experimental performative avant-gardes during one of the most socially turbulent periods of the late twentieth century.

At the heart of this anthology is an exploration of that profoundly important and at times deeply nuanced richness: an exploration that highlights the innovativeness, the political engagement, and the attention to process and craft in mainstream and popular performances in the 1960s. One of the best examples of the mainstream experimental can be found in the work of the legendary avant-garde scenic designer Boris Aronson, whose designs for *The Diary of Anne Frank* (1955), *Fiddler on the Roof* (1964), and *Cabaret* (1966), as Alisa Solomon notes in her contribution to this anthology, mark not only the emergence of scenic abstraction on the main stage but also what Solomon describes as the "snaking lines of aesthetic innovation and of new Jewish assertion as they intersected in the 1960s" with mainstream and popular performance. Aronson is no anomaly in this regard.

Beneath the surface of the turbulent decade that was the 1960s, the dividing lines between radicals and conservatives, between older and younger generations, or between commercialism and countercultures were not as clearly drawn in the theater as popular conceptions of the 1960s might suggest. At some level, even *TDR* evinced some deep awareness of this, particularly with regard to theater like Peter Brook's Royal Shakespeare Company (RSC) production of *Marat/Sade*, which opened in England in 1964 and arrived to much acclaim on Broadway in 1965. The commercial and critical success of the production bled into *TDR*. Advertisements for production memorabilia like the album soundtrack to *Marat/Sade* populate the pages of numerous issues of *TDR* during the period. In his contribution to this anthology, Marvin Carlson not only cites the RSC production of *Marat/Sade* as "one of the major offerings of the 1960s" but also rightly identifies Brook as being "widely regarded [in the late 1960s] as the most imaginative and innovative director in the English-speaking world." His work was then and arguably continued to be for many years the quintessential example of the mainstream experimental, skirting the fence between avant-garde and mainstream performances in productions like *Marat/Sade* as well as in subsequent antiwar pieces like *US*. As Harding notes in his essay in this volume, Brook defied categorization consistently enough that in 1999 Schechner ultimately placed him, along with Robert Wilson and Ariane Mnouchkine, in a separate category altogether, situated at the intersection of avant-garde and mainstream theatrical practice.

Much of the material in this anthology attests to the fact that that intersection had already been a major thoroughfare long before Schechner acknowledged it in 1999. Neil Blackadder and Kate Bredeson, for example, provide ample evidence that the traffic moving through the intersection of the mainstream and the experimental was often part of broad international cultural exchange, and it was an exchange moving in both directions. Following the flow from Europe to the United States, Blackadder explores the exceptionally strong support that Broadway and off-Broadway venues gave to the translated work of major European playwrights like Ionesco, Genet, Dürrenmatt, Brecht, and Beckett. He specifically cites the long-running off-Broadway production of Genet's *The Blacks*, noting how it calls into question Schechner's assertion in "Intentions, Problems, Proposals" that a work like Genet's *The Balcony* could fare "well [on] off-Broadway only because it was presented in a Broadway-influenced, impure manner." Controversial though the thesis of *The Blacks* might have been, its 1961 off-Broadway production, Blackadder notes, broke significant ground both politically and aesthetically, as well as providing significant acting opportunities, during its run of fourteen hundred performances at St. Mark's Playhouse, to black actors like James Earl Jones, Louis Gossett Jr., Cicely Tyson, and Maya Angelou (among others). In a complimentary way, Kate Bredeson follows the international flow of theatrical practice in the opposite direction and argues that significant productions of the American avant-gardes were canonized in no small part as a consequence of the success that they enjoyed on tour, playing to enthusiastic mainstream audiences across Europe. Indeed, she argues that in France, the "kind of American theater . . . considered 'alternative' in the United States found great critical attention, wide press coverage, [and] large audiences." The work of artists and groups like "William Carlos Williams, El Teatro Campesino, Firehouse Theater, Jack Gelber, Bread and Puppet, and the Living Theatre—all considered to be in opposition to the Broadway/off-Broadway model, or 'experimental' in their home country," were celebrated in mainstream theatrical venues in France and Europe more generally. But there were even more pronounced ways in which the mainstream experimental was a part of the cultural landscape of the 1960s.

Schechner and Theodore Hoffman admitted as much in "TDR—1963?," the editorial that they coauthored in late 1963. Much in their editorial is relevant to the arguments of this introduction, but suffice it for now to note that Schechner and Hoffman's discussions of U.S. regional theaters repeatedly blur the lines separating the experimental and the mainstream. Looking beyond New York, for example, Schechner and Hoffman cite the Guthrie in Minneapolis and the Arena Stage in Washington, D.C. (and ten other theaters across the country) as being separate from "commodity theatre" and part of "a movement toward resident professional theatre on the verge of engaging the core of America's theatrical imagination."[11] As Donatella Galella notes in her investigation of Zelda Fichandler's significant track record at the helm of Arena Theatre in Washington, D.C., this "movement" hardly fit into the dichotomy that Schechner had posited earlier that same year. Galella specifically draws attention to how "political works, for example those by or indebted to Brecht, were often economic and artistic hits with audiences in the sixties." The success stories of experimental and political works with the Arena Stage audiences emerged season after season, and that success ran counter to the assumption that producing new, edgy, and avant-garde plays would be detrimental to the economic well-being of resident theaters.

Fichandler modeled the Arena Stage on European theater companies in her choice to maintain a resident acting company and to produce a rotating repertory that included a solid mix of reimagined classics, new plays, and works from the European avant-garde. "Moreover," Galella argues, "institutionalizing, professionalizing, and maintaining a balanced budget did not necessarily mean reducing artistic standards and experiments." Similar developments and outcomes also mark the history of the Guthrie. As Suzanne Engstrom argues in her essay on Twin Cities theater in the 1960s, the Guthrie, too, produced epic classical works, developed new plays with U.S. playwrights, and presented experimental pieces by Samuel Beckett and Brendan Behan. In contrast to Galella, however, Engstrom observes that "at times the demands of nonprofit professionalism seemed to stymie the theater's overall goals, minimizing risk taking and depth of artistic production," and, she explains, there were instances when "the Guthrie prioritized survival rather than art." Interestingly enough, that priority had little to do with the presumed divide between mainstream and experimental theater. The other theater at the center of Engstrom's inquiry, the Twin Cities' avant-garde Firehouse Theater, also struggled to find a balance between its mission and "the necessities of professionalism." Even the radical political commitments of the Living Theatre did not exempt it from the basic struggle, a point driven home by the playwright Jack Gelber in his 1986 *TDR* article "Julian Beck, Business Man."[12]

Such struggles had significant financial implications for theaters across the spectrum from experimental to mainstream, and they frequently sought external support from nonprofit organizations. In this respect, the Guthrie and Firehouse were typical of theaters across the United States. Indeed, this is precisely the focus of Dorothy Chansky's contribution to this anthology. Her essay spotlights the vast assortment of theater industry acronyms that came into being in the 1960s and the impact the corresponding institutionalizing and professionalizing explosion had on the field. Digging beneath the basic opposition between mainstream and experimental theaters, her analysis challenges the solidity of the profit/nonprofit binary: "Many nonprofit theaters aspire to and succeed in sending plays to Broadway," Chansky observes. The celebrated and lucrative transfer of Arena Stage's production of Howard Sackler's *The Great White Hope* (1967–68) to Broadway is but one case in point, and Chansky notes that "of the thirty-five Pulitzer Prizes awarded in drama since 1965, thirty have gone to works that originated in an NEA-supported nonprofit theater." Such support went in all directions and literally bankrolled all sorts of experimentation in mainstream and avant-garde theaters.

If Peter Brook's work with the RSC; the broad international exchanges catalogued by Blackadder, Bredeson, Galella and Engstrom; and support by organizations like the NEA all provide examples of a particular type of the mainstream experimental in clearly defined theater communities, at the opposite end of the spectrum we find examples of the mainstream experimental in the realms of popular cultural performances as well. In his contribution to this volume, Graham White carefully reads the cultural contexts of the Beatles' exploration in "the abortive recordings [that] came to be known as the *Get Back* sessions" of "how far experimental practices might operate in the mainstream." Those experiments, White argues, are evidence of how "the many roads to truth" in Schechner's dichotomy were consistently "being rerouted during the 1960s." In this respect White reminds us that the real problem with Schechner's argument is not the binary itself—which served an important rhetorical purpose in its own historical context—but rather its seeming absolutism as a fixed roadmap for a cultural and political terrain that was rapidly changing. At a conceptual level, White's argument about that rerouting finds a powerful echo in Kimberly Jannarone's provocative rethinking of the demonstrations that occurred in the streets of Chicago during the 1968 Democratic National Convention. There the dividing lines between what she describes as the "orderly, commercial performance" of the Democratic convention and the "experimental, participatory mass performance" unfolding outside in the Chicago city streets blurred into a composite public spectacle that amounted to what we would identify as one of the most politically significant examples of the mainstream experimental of the late 1960s.

Such blurring has important implications for the history of theater and performance in the 1960s. Indeed, there is an important reworking of our understanding of the very notion of "theater in the streets" in that blurring—one that challenges the presumed historical parallels between experimental theater and artistically inspired political activism. As Jannarone's essay reminds us, the streets leading to the Democratic convention were in a very literal sense main streets. If her arguments were not compelling enough to force a rethinking of how events like those surrounding the 1968 convention were always already an amalgam of the popular and the experimental, one need look no further than Stephen Bottoms's contribution to this volume—and in particular to his discussion of Jacques Levy—for concrete evidence further supporting Jannarone's claims.

Much of that evidence comes in Bottoms's detailed discussion of the constant traffic moving back and forth between off-off-Broadway and Broadway at the time of the New York productions of *Hair* (1968) and *Oh! Calcutta!* (1969). Levy had close ties, for example, with the Open Theatre, directing its production of Jean-Claude Van Itallie's *America Hurrah* in 1966. But at the time that he was working on *Oh! Calcutta!*, he was deeply involved with the Yippies and, as Bottoms notes, he was "helping to conceive and delivering the 'guerrilla theater' tactics of Abbie Hoffman's radical Yippie organization (including their notorious interventions at the 1968 Chicago Democratic Convention)." There was, in short, a direct tie between the radical streets of Chicago and that main street of theatrical main streets, Broadway. Moreover, the avenues of exchange between European drama and mainstream theater played out in *Oh! Calcutta!* as well. In his discussions of Levy's work on the production, Bottoms notes that Levy made major alterations to the script and even included Beckett's short play *Breath* at the beginning of the show.

The musicals *Hair* and *Oh! Calcutta!* carried the 1960s well into the 1970s. Like *Oh! Calcutta!*, *Hair*'s initial run on Broadway continued until 1972, but concurrent and touring productions continued both nationally and internationally. Also, like *Oh! Calcutta*, *Hair* was situated at the intersection of the experimental and the mainstream. As Bottoms notes, "Both of these productions . . . stood squarely upon foundations laid by the Open Theatre—the experimental acting ensemble that Gerome Ragni [who cowrote *Hair* with James Rado] had helped to found." Both productions were also directed by figures from New York's avant-garde. Jacques Levy was not the only director with avant-garde theater credentials. The director of *Hair*, Tom O'Horgan, had established ties to off-off-Broadway as well, especially to Ellen Stewart's Café La MaMa, where he had been directing shows since the mid-1960s. The point here is not that directors like Levy or O'Horgan were selling out but rather, as Bottoms convincingly argues, that the counterculture was making itself known across the spectrum of theatrical practice, in terms of both its aesthetics and its politics.

When it came to aesthetics and politics, *Hair* itself was a showcase of the mainstream experimental. Bottoms recounts, for example, that in his *Village Voice* review of the musical's Broadway opening Michael Smith argued that *Hair*'s importance was as an experimental piece, "not in 'anything it says about hippies, [but in] the plain fact that O'Horgan has blown up Broadway.'" While *Hair* certainly brought a new aesthetic to Broadway shows, it also brought what was perhaps the most widely disseminated antiwar piece of the decade. Rather than being derivative of off-off-Broadway pieces like Megan Terry's *Viet Rock*, *Hair*, Bottoms argues, was in fact a response to Terry's play. In this respect, *Hair* is a striking example of the ongoing dialogue that took place among theater practitioners in the 1960s—a dialogue that was less concerned with whether the venue was experimental or mainstream than it was with how theater practitioners and artists might effectively counter the escalating war in Vietnam more generally. Here the choice was less between Broadway and experimental theater than it was a more general question of how one might use whatever opportunities were available to further the antiwar movement—regardless of whether those opportunities were to be found in off-off-Broadway venues like La MaMa (e.g., *Viet Rock*), off-Broadway venues like the Public Theater (e.g., *The Basic Training of Pavlo Hummel*), or Broadway venues like the Biltmore Theatre (e.g., *Hair*).

As the essays in this anthology demonstrate, the lines of division so frequently conceptualized in theory by scholars like Schechner were often difficult to identify in actual theatrical practice. Time and again in the 1960s, Broadway musicals, mainstream dramas, and experimental performances all participated in a complex dialogue about politics, society, and culture. That dialogue began on the main stage as often as it did in off-off-Broadway venues, and here the evidence from theater in the 1960s clearly echoes Alan Woods's claims that "not all experimental work rejects the entertainment world from which it comes" and that "traditional entertainment forms provide the base from which avant-garde work springs in a positive sense as well."[13] In the 1960s there was perhaps no better example of the tendency Woods describes than the Playwright's Unit, which, as David Crespy reminds us in his contribution to this volume, "would have never existed without the unique partnership of its off- and on-Broadway producers Richard Barr and Clinton Wilder and the playwright Edward Albee." Ironically, in the same year that Schechner told readers to choose between experimental theater and Broadway, Barr, Wilder, and Albee founded the Playwrights Unit, which famously provided opportunities for young playwrights like Sam Shepard, Doric Wilson, Megan Terry, Jean-Claude van Itallie, Lanford Wilson, Adrienne Kennedy, and Amiri Baraka (to name only a few) to have their early work staged and developed. The Playwrights Unit became "a kind of halfway house between the café scene and commercial theatre, by using a roster of recognized professional actors and directors who volunteered their services free of charge."[14] Indeed, in *Playing Underground*, Stephen Bottoms argues that "the Unit was less an Off Off Broadway venture than an instance, as Doric Wilson puts it, of 'non-commercial Off Broadway.'"[15]

Of course, the real irony here was not merely that the Playwrights Unit occupied the space of a "non-commercial Off Broadway" theater that was unaccounted for in Schechner's stark dichotomous choice between experimental theater and Broadway. It was that Schechner had so roundly denounced Albee a few months earlier in the very first editorial that he penned after taking over the editorship of the *Tulane Drama Review*. Roughly a half of a decade before the 1969 Stonewall riots would inaugurate a full-fledged gay rights movement, Schechner infamously dismissed Albee as a peddler of "morbidity and sexual perversity which are there only to titillate an impotent and homosexual theatre and audience."[16] Stephen Bottoms has written at length on the homophobic legacy of those comments.[17] Concurrent with the publication of his editorial, which was entitled "Who's Afraid of Edward Albee," Schechner also published Alan Schneider's rebuttal, "Why So Afraid?"[18] But the larger point is that the gay community, which included Albee, Barr, and Wilder, was never committed to an experimental/commercial binary, and the history of the Playwrights Unit points precisely to this fact. Elsewhere David Crespy has noted that "Albarwild, Inc. was one of the few producing organizations operating on Broadway in the 1960s with gay men as the principal partners."[19] But even beyond the not so latent homophobia in Schechner's dismissal of Albee, the Playwrights Unit disrupted the binary that Schechner had posited in "Intentions, Problems, Proposals" because it answered Schechner's calls both to situate the playwright as "the cornerstone of our emerging theatre"[20] and "to accommodate an idea based on the validity of experimentation."[21] As Crespy notes in his contribution to this volume, given "Albee's enormous influence on theater at the time," the Playwrights Unit "made it possible for the experimentation of noncommercial radical theater to organically influence and, ultimately," not to succumb to but rather "to transform the commercial mainstream theater." There is in Crespy's argument about Albee an important resonance with Bottoms's argument that directors like Jacques Levy and Tom O'Horgan in their work later in the decade on shows like *Oh! Calcutta!* and *Hair* were not so much "'selling out' to commercial interests" as they were "seeking to 'buy in' to the counterculture."

While Albee, as an immensely successful playwright, had the financial means to help facilitate such transformations, his director and cofounder of the Playwrights Unit, Richard Barr—who at the end of the decade would produce *The Boys in the Band*—had deep interests, as Crespy notes, in the "absurdist work of European authors, including Beckett, Genet, Ionesco, and Arrabal." Seen through the examples of the Playwrights Unit and the work of directors like Levy and O'Horgan, the sixties were thus a period when the whole of the theatrical landscape was radically changing, when commercial and experimental theaters were engaged in meaningful dialogue and exchange with each other, and when the dialogue was as much between a theater broadly defined and the public more generally as it was between mainstream and experimental theaters.

In that dialogue with the public, frequently it was Broadway that was ahead of the curve, and interestingly enough this brings us to the second way in which Jameson's periodization of the sixties figures into the objectives of this anthology. By working from a long-decade model, with the conceptual bookends of the era in the fifties and seventies, Jameson encourages scholars and critics to frame the sixties in a like manner. The question is how theater historians might follow suit. Interestingly enough, there are hints, if not altogether decisive cues, in Jameson's own argument. Jameson suggests that the radical politics of the 1960s in first world countries like the United States and France were deeply indebted to "the great movement of decolonization in British and French Africa" in the 1950s. Generally speaking, "a first world 60s," Jameson argues, "owed much to third-worldism in terms of [its] politicocultural models." In the United States, he adds,

> the one significant exception to all this is in many ways the most important first world political movement of all—the new black politics and the civil rights movement, which must be dated not from the Supreme Court decision of 1954, but rather from the first sit-ins in Greensboro, North Carolina, in February of 1960. Yet it might be argued that this was also a movement of decolonization, and in any case the constant exchange and mutual influences between the American black movements and the various African and Caribbean ones are continuous and incalculable throughout the period.[22]

In terms of the politics of theater, Jameson's allusion to the Greensboro sit-ins provides an important point of reference for what might legitimately be called the beginning of the sixties. If nothing else, what is striking about this specific allusion—at least within the objectives of this anthology—is the coincidental echo that Jameson's argument about the Greensboro sit-ins quickly found in the writings of Amiri Baraka in the 1980s. But as was often the case with Baraka, the echo carried an unexpected and added resonance.

Not long after Jameson published his article "Periodizing the 60s" in 1984, Baraka, in a 1986 *Washington Post* article, drew parallels between the Woolworth sit-ins in North Carolina in 1960 and the opening of Lorraine Hansberry's *A Raisin in the Sun* roughly a year earlier, in March 1959, at Broadway's Ethel Barrymore Theatre. Baraka's essay was originally published to mark the twenty-fifth anniversary of that opening, and Baraka used that opportunity to reassess his earlier dismissals of the play as "middle class." In his now famous essay, Baraka confesses that he had earlier "missed the essence of the work—that Hansberry had created a family on the cutting edge of the same class and ideological struggles as existed in the movement itself and among the people." The 1959 production of *A Raisin in the Sun* was, according to Baraka, nothing short of "the accurate telling and stunning vision of the real struggle."[23] In terms of both its social and its theater politics, that "real struggle" was a struggle for mainstream acceptance.

Baraka's reassessment of Hansberry subtly but effectively upended many of the governing assumptions about the flow of ideas in the theater: in particular, the assumption that ideas emerge within the vanguard and flow back to the mainstream. Indeed, in a 2009 interview with Tracy Heather Strain, Baraka argued something quite to the contrary of that assumption, suggesting that *A Raisin in the Sun*—and its Broadway production—"actually opened the whole sixties so that the whole Black Arts Movement, Black Theatre Movement, flows naturally" out of the impact that it, along with Baldwin's *Blues for Mister Charlie*, had on black artists.[24] Baldwin himself, speaking about the significance of *A Raisin in the Sun*, recalled, "I had never in my life seen so many black people in the theatre," as Harvey Young notes in his contribution to this anthology.[25] The play's "ability," Young notes, "to draw nontraditional theater audiences, essentially folks whose interests were previously ignored by theater producers, was noticeable." If Broadway was its own neighborhood, new folks were moving in, sitting, so to speak, at its diner counters, and demanding the seat at the front of its bus that they had previously been denied.

It is worth pausing momentarily to consider the contrast between Broadway and experimental theater at that precise historical moment when Hansberry's play was in the midst of its politically significant run on Broadway in 1959. It had opened in the spring, and in October of that same year (about the time that *Raisin* was moving from the Ethel Barrymore Theatre to the Belasco Theatre) one of the most widely celebrated performances in the history of the American avant-gardes was staged for small audiences of art aficionados at the Ruben Gallery on Fourth Street, not far from Washington Square Park. It was there that Allan Kaprow performed *18 Happenings in Six Parts*, perhaps the single most important work in the formation of what six years later in the pages of *TDR* Michael Kirby would celebrate as "The New Theatre."[26] However innovative Kaprow's piece might have been artistically, there was something undeniably insular about it and its audiences compared to what was happening at the Ethel Barrymore Theatre. Indeed, there is a profound contrast between the "nontraditional theater audiences" that Young identifies as being drawn to *A Raisin in the Sun* and the strikingly predictable whiteness of Kaprow's audiences.

In the larger context of the civil rights movement, the overwhelming whiteness of Kaprow's audiences is perhaps less disconcerting than the awkwardness of his piece's racial politics—an awkwardness that surfaced again when André Lepecki restaged *18 Happenings in Six Parts* at Munich's Haus der Kunst in 2006. In the research that Lepecki did in preparation for that restaging, he too laments the more general "lack of *visibility* of black women in avant-garde circles of New York" in the late 1950s.[27] But that lament is a lesson in history. More troubling still is how *18 Happenings* perpetuated that invisibility in the actual substance of the piece itself. In this respect, the most telling aspect of Lepecki's comments on his restaging of *18 Happenings* is his strained effort to account for the presence not only of a mechanical dancing black sambo doll but also of a fetishized image of the black female body (via a black woman in black leotards). Lepecki's efforts notwithstanding, there is no dancing around the ugly residues of racism popping up in what is widely reputed to be one of the most generative performance pieces in the American avant-gardes. While such issues are not key to Alan Woods's assertion that "the happenings of the 1960s loom far larger in theatre history than one would expect,"[28] they do add weight to his call for scholars to reconsider their historiographical priorities. Simply put, there is little dispute that the racial politics of a generative work like *18 Happenings* were decisively in the rearguard of the precedent being set simultaneously on Broadway by Hansberry's *A Raisin in the Sun*. If there is a choice here between Broadway and experimental theater—a choice not merely about theater and the civil rights movement but about where the sixties began—then we would suggest that the choice should be Broadway.

The issue raised by the Broadway production of Hansberry's *A Raisin in the Sun* concerns more than the countless Clybourne Parks across the United States that still maintain their unofficial boundaries more than a half century after the premier of Hansberry's play. Within the context of theater history, the issue is really about who historically has had the luxury of choice in the dichotomy Schechner constructed when he asked readers to choose between Broadway and experimental theater. It concerns the difference between those who choose to join the fringe and those who dwell there not by choice but by oppressive marginalization. When all is said and done, the choice between

Broadway and experimental theater is open only to those who have access to Broadway in the first place and who thus have the luxury of walking away. Baraka notes that at the most basic level Hansberry's play is about a family "buying a house and moving into [a] 'white folks' neighborhood,'" an act that he places at "the essence of black people's striving and the will to defeat segregation, discrimination and national oppression" and that he argues challenges the racist underpinnings of the very notion of a "white neighborhood" as such.[29] Similarly, the production history of Hansberry's play is about opportunities on Broadway for playwrights, for producers, and, as Harvey Young notes in his contribution to this anthology, for actors. In this respect, *A Raisin in the Sun* belongs to a whole line of Broadway productions that from the late 1950s into the 1960s displayed the courage to enter the mainstream, to borrow and recode the language of Broadway, and to challenge white entitlement—an entitlement, we would suggest, that was subtly but certainly maintained in the choice that was taken for granted in the categorical rejection of Broadway in favor of experimental theaters.

Problematic though its casting obviously was, the 1957 Broadway production of *West Side Story* might be seen as a precursor to this very tendency and as a precursor to the sixties as well, particularly if one reads its evolution from *East Side Story* to *West Side Story*—as Brian Herrera does—as a reflection of the precarious situations of multiple immigrant communities striving to find their place within resistant and bigoted white neighborhoods. In his recent essay "Compiling *West Side Story*'s Parahistories, 1949–2009," for example, Herrera acknowledges the deeply problematic representations that have led critics like Frances Negrón-Muntaner and David Román to describe *West Side Story* as a kind of "Puerto Rican *Birth of the Nation*" and as a show that has ignited "Latino ire" because of its "casting of non-Latinos in Latino roles" amid its simultaneous "perpetuation of Latino stereotypes as criminal and primitive."[30] But at the same time Herrera reminds us of the importance of understanding the way works like *West Side Story* address "uncertainty among 1950s observers regarding how the new Puerto Rican arrivals in New York should be understood, especially with regard to existing racial structures."[31] There is something profoundly American in that uncertainty, and it is embedded deeply in the history of the musical and in Jerome Robbins's original conception of it as an East Side story of conflict between Catholics and Jews "'at the coincidence of Easter-Passover celebrations', when [as Robbins argued] feelings would be running 'high.'"[32] There is little mistaking the coded reference in Robbins's description. His mention of feelings "running high" was a not so subtle allusion to the anti-Semitism that motivated the Jets' hatred of the Emeralds (who later became the Puerto Rican Sharks).

If, in the transition from an *East Side Story* to a *West Side Story*, the uncertainty that mainstream audiences had about immigrant and American Jewish communities was abandoned as those groups were subsequently replaced with a Puerto Rican "Other," that original uncertainty was later given a more thorough hearing when the sixties were in full swing and the musicals *Fiddler on the Roof* (1964) and *Cabaret* (1966) premiered on Broadway. Both of these works figure prominently in the essays that Alisa Solomon and Stacy Wolf have contributed to this anthology, and in a very literal sense there is a direct line connecting the 1957 production of *West Side Story* with these two major shows from the mid-1960s. The producer Harold Prince was involved in all three productions, and, as Solomon notes, he was already working on what was to become *Cabaret* prior to taking "up the producing reins of *Fiddler*." Solomon argues that both of these latter works owe much to Prince's sense—amid the civil rights, student, antiwar, and women's liberation movements—that "the commercial theater, could—and should—come to grips with the exigencies of the day." If nothing else, the innovative Broadway production of *Cabaret*—which as a transformative and precedent-setting amalgam of avant-garde and mainstream theatrical techniques is yet another example of the mainstream experimental— presented audiences with a compelling historical allegory that looked back to what Solomon describes as "the decadent milieu of Weimar Germany, where the people of Berlin partied on while fascists tromped to power." The moral argument here, she suggests, is that people cannot "stand by as evil gains ground," whether that evil is the bigotry of anti-Semitism, the denial of civil rights, or the "escalating Vietnam War." But the larger point here is clear. By the mid-point of the decade, politically and aesthetically innovative theater was already well-established practice in the mainstream, and like Harold Prince, numerous practitioners who were moving with great fluidity between experimental and mainstream venues were actively engaged in challenging public opinion wherever they mounted shows.

Such was also arguably the case with the Broadway production of *Fiddler on the Roof*, which, while perhaps not as innovative as *Cabaret*, not only had Prince as its producer but also had the Russian avant-gardist Boris Aronson as its stage designer. (It was Aronson who designed the Chagall-inspired set for the show, and his work is the focus of Solomon's contribution to this volume.) The immensely successful production of *Fiddler* literally bridged the 1960s and the 1970s, running as it did consecutively from 1964 until 1972. The reasons for this success were numerous, and the broad appeal of *Fiddler* has to be counted among them. Its appeal even extended to politically conservative audiences. *Fiddler* certainly played well into the ideologies of the Cold War, especially if one recalls its concluding images of Tevye and his family immigrating to what was presumably a more welcoming and tolerant United States in their flight from the Russian pogroms that have driven them from their home. If there is an argument by analogy here, it is one of mainstreaming Judaism in the United States through a calculated portrayal of the contrast between the presumed openness of America and the repressiveness of Russia (and by extension the Soviet Union). In this respect, *Fiddler on the Roof* is a prime example of what Stacy Wolf, in her contribution to this volume, describes as the ways in which "Broadway musicals of the 1960s are performative archives of their era." But there were also other politics at play in this production that coincided more locally with Prince's belief that commercial theater could "come to grips with the exigencies of the day."

A key aspect of those exigencies was second-wave feminism, which historians generally argue began with the publication of Betty Friedan's *The Feminine Mystique* and which carried the sixties into the 1970s, well beyond the ill-fated attempt to pass the Equal Rights Amendment starting in 1972 and the Supreme Court decision in *Roe v. Wade* in 1973. There is a strong case to be made that *Fiddler* is a performative archive of this era as well. This, in fact, is at the core of Wolf's argument in this volume. While *Fiddler on the Roof* certainly helped to mainstream Judaism, Wolf argues that unlike the original character from Sholem Aleichem's tales, the Tevye of the Broadway musical was very much "a man of the mid-1960s grappling with breathtaking changes around him," particularly with regard to the changing roles of women in society. Indeed, Wolf argues, "*Fiddler* navigates the politics of gender as much as ethnicity." Placing its Broadway premier against the backdrop of the 1963 publication of *The Feminine Mystique*, Wolf suggests that "as the Cossacks force Tevye out of Anatevka, feminism pushes him out of his village mind-set." Much of Tevye's transformation results, Wolf argues, from his having to come to terms with his daughters' growing sense of independence, and on this note Wolf provides a powerfully developed echo of Raymond Knapp's earlier arguments that in "its treatment of feminist themes of self-determination," *Fiddler* offers "a seeming response to the emergent feminism of the 1960s."[33] At some level, that response once again put the mainstream if not in advance of then at least on a parallel track with off-off-Broadway. But it would also seem to bring us full circle with regard to the stark choice between experimental and commercial theater that Schechner posited in the summer of 1963.

With the advantage of hindsight, it is possible to see the choice mapped out in *TDR* as the product of a concatenation of quickly articulated and fundamentally related binaries that not only have had a lasting influence on how scholars understand theater in the 1960s but also are profoundly gendered in their conceptualization. The choice between experimental theater and Broadway was the culmi-nation of three binaries that not only shunned Broadway but also conceptualized its commercialism as a decidedly unmasculine and dubiously effeminate form. Seen in isolation, the choice that Schechner offered in his second *TDR* editorial appears as a simple, albeit stark, contrast between noncommercial and commer-cial theaters. But placed in the context of his first editorial—that now infamous polemic against Albee—the simplicity of the second editorial begins to fade against a more complicated and problematic agenda. For in that first editorial, Schechner stereotypically characterized commercial Broadway theater like Al-bee's as something decidedly unmasculine: something "impotent and homosex-ual." The problematic rhetoric behind this characterization implicitly suggested that mainstream theater was effeminate and thus a theater to be shunned in favor of an experimental, noncommercial theater that was somehow more masculine and therefore worthy of being championed. There is nothing experimental or pathbreaking in that sense of entitlement.

Such implicit suggestions were hardly one-off moments in the logic of male privilege. By the end of 1963, Schechner (along with Theodore Hoffman) con-ceded that "there will always be a commodity theatre, but the real work," they argued, "gets done elsewhere."[34] The gendered underpinnings of this notion of "real work" are evident in the clear echo between the reference to theater labor in "*TDR*—1963?" and Schechner's inauguration of the *TDR* Comment section of the journal a year earlier, where he likened commercial theater to the dubi-ous commerce of prostitution. (It was a poor comparison, since women work-ing in the theater had long endured their reputations being sullied by similar accusations.) In the preface that he wrote introducing the addition of *TDR* Comment to the journal, Schechner framed the contrast between noncommer-cial and commercial theaters in the clichéd image of the virgin and the whore, and he positioned *TDR* as a kind of high-minded cavalier who would rescue and restore a fallen theater's virtue. Schechner explained that the "*TDR Com-ment* is frankly an editorial section presenting as forcefully as we know how our views on the theatre." The justification for a new editorial section in *TDR* was simple, he continued,

The American theatre is in a state of flux, and it lacks significant leadership. Hopefully TDR COMMENT will provide this leadership and be a rallying point for those young and eager theatre-workers who are dedicated to an art which has been, in our country, too long the call-girl of money and ambi-tion. In some sense we hope to restore virginity to the theatre, and purpose to theatre-workers.[35]

Some fifty years later, it is difficult to fathom precisely what the metaphor of restoring "virginity to the theatre" actually means as a stated goal. But for the women back in 1963 who found inspiration in the publication of Betty Friedan's *The Feminine Mystique*, the notion of restoring virginity as a cure for something conceptualized as the "call-girl" syndrome of theater probably sounded like the typical condescending patriarchal rhetoric from which they and ultimately theater itself both needed liberation. In this regard, perhaps Tevye's daughters were doing real work after all each night on Broadway, encouraging middle-class women to assert control over their own lives by the staged example of defying "tradition."

In the larger context of the history of 1960s theater, perhaps such moments of defying tradition also encourage theater historians to consider the implications of dichotomous choices between noncommercial and commercial theater that lend themselves so easily to being framed in narratives about virgins and call girls. Perhaps it suffices as a conclusion to state emphatically that it is finally time to close the curtain on those false dichotomies and open the stage of the 1960s to its own broad spectrum of vibrant theatrical forms and to a scholarly assessment that gives it the long overdue hearing it deserves. For whatever its entertainment value, there was real work being done in the 1960s on Broadway and in mainstream and popular theatrical venues—work that was attentive to and seriously engaged with the most important social, political, and cultural currents of the period.

NOTES

1. Fredric Jameson, Anders Stephanson, and Cornel West, "A Very Partial Chronology," *Social Text* 9–10 (1984): 210–15.

2. Fredric Jameson, "Periodizing the 60s," *Social Text* 9–10 (1984): 180.

3. Ibid., 178, 179.

4. The phrase "without apology" comes from the special issue of *Social Text* "The 60's without Apology," where Jameson's article first appeared in 1984.

5. Andrew Hunt, "'When Did the Sixties Happen?' Searching for New Directions," *Journal of Social History* 33.1 (1999): 147.

6. Brian Ward, *The 1960s: A Documentary Reader* (Malden, MA: Wiley-Blackwell, 2010), 151.

7. See ibid., 147.

8. See Alan Woods, "Emphasizing the Avant-Garde: An Exploration in Theatre Historiography," in *Interpreting the Theatrical Past: Essays in the Historiography of Performance*, ed. Thomas Postlewait and Bruce A. McConachie (Iowa City: University of Iowa Press, 1989).166–76.

9. Richard Schechner, *The Future of Ritual* (New York: Routledge, 1995), 8.

10. Richard Schechner, "Intentions, Problems, Proposals," *Tulane Drama Review* 7.4 (1963): 21.

11. Richard Schechner and Theodore Hoffman, "*TDR*—1963?," *Tulane Drama Review* 8.2 (1963): 9.

12. Jack Gelber, "Julian Beck, Businessman," *TDR* 30.2 (1986): 6–29.

13. Woods, "Emphasizing the Avant-Garde," 170.

14. Stephen Bottoms, *Playing Underground* (Ann Arbor: University of Michigan Press, 2006), 84.

15. Ibid.

16. Richard Schechner, "Who's Afraid of Edward Albee," *Tulane Drama Review* 7.3 (1963): 9.

17. See Stephen Bottoms, "The Efficacy/Effeminacy Braid: Unpacking the Performance Studies/Theatre Studics Dichotomy," *Theatre Topics* 13.2 (2003): 173–87.

18. Alan Schneider, "Why So Afraid?," *Tulane Drama Review* 7.3 (1963): 10–13.

19. David Crespy, "Richard Barr (1917—1989)," in *GLBTQ: An Encyclopedia of Gay, Lesbian, Transgender & Queer Culture*, http://www.glbtqarchive.com/arts/barr_r_A.pdf.

20. Schechner, "Intentions, Problems, Proposals," 16.

21. Ibid., 19.

22. Jameson, "Periodizing the 60s," 180.

23. Amiri Baraka, "A Critical Reevaluation: *A Raisin in the Sun*'s Enduring Passion," in *"A Raisin in the Sun" and "The Sign in Sidney Brustein's Window,"* edited by Robert Nemiroff (New York: Vintage Books, 1995), 18–19.

24. "Amiri Baraka on the Impact of Lorraine Hansberry and James Baldwin," interview by Tracy Heather Strain, YouTube, https://www.youtube.com/watch?v=tM9Bk093u68.

25. Adrienne Macki Braconi, "African American Women Dramatists, 1930–1960," in *The Cambridge Companion to African American Theatre*, ed. Harvey Young (Cambridge: Cambridge University Press, 2013), 120.

26. Michael Kirby, "The New Theatre," *Tulane Drama Review* 10.2 (1965): 23–43.

27. André Lepecki, "Redoing '18 Happenings in 6 Parts,'" *MAP: Media, Archive, Performance* 1 (2009), http://www.perfomap.de/map1/iii.-kuenstlerische-praxis-als-forschung/redoing-201c18-happenings-in-6-parts201d.

28. Woods, "Emphasizing the Avant-Garde," 168.

29. Baraka, "Critical Reevaluation," 19–20.

30. Negrón-Muntaner and Román qtd. in Brian Eugenio Herrera, "Compiling *West Side Story*'s Parahistories, 1949–2009," *Theatre Journal* 64.2 (2012): 233.

31. Ibid., 240.

32. Ibid., 234.

33. Raymond Knapp, *The American Musical and the Formation of National Identity* (Princeton, NJ: Princeton University Press, 2005), 219.

34. Schechner and Hoffman, "*TDR*—1963?," 9.

35. Richard Schechner, TDR Comment, *Tulane Drama Review* 7.2 (1962): 8.

PART I
RE-VISIONING BROADWAY

Stacy Wolf

The Feminine Mystique Goes to Broadway

Housewives in 1960s Musical Theater

Betty Friedan's *The Feminine Mystique*—the book that effectively launched the Women's Liberation Movement—was published on February 19, 1963, during a lively season for Broadway musicals. *Oliver!*; *Stop the World I Want to Get Off*, with Anthony Newly; *Mr. President*, with Nanette Fabray; Richard Rodgers's *No Strings*, with Richard Kiley and Diahann Carroll; and Stephen Sondheim's *A Funny Thing Happened on the Way to the Forum* were all then playing to enthusiastic audiences. Though the second wave of feminism might seem far removed from Broadway musical theater, in fact, the women who were Friedan's intended readers were the same women who not only attended Broadway musicals but likely selected the shows that they and their husbands would see after his long week at the office and hers at home with the children. Broadway's theaters in the early 1960s were filled with Manhattan residents and "bridge-and-tunnel" suburbanites from New Jersey, Connecticut, and New York—gray-flannel-suited men and their well-coiffed wives to whom *The Feminist Mystique* was addressed. After a day spent doing laundry in a washing machine and dryer, making a casserole with Campbell's cream of mushroom soup, baking dessert from a Betty Crocker cake mix, and driving children from school to music lessons in a station wagon, these white, middle-class suburban housewives had the luxury of taking the train into Manhattan to meet their husbands for drinks, dinner, and a show.[1] They no doubt recognized themselves in the opening words of Friedan's book:

> The problem lay buried, unspoken, for many years in the minds of American women. It was a strange stirring, a sense of dissatisfaction, a yearning. . . . Each suburban wife struggled with it alone. As she made the beds,

shopped for groceries, matched slipcover material, ate peanut butter sandwiches with her children, chauffeured Cub Scouts and Brownies, lay beside her husband at night—she was afraid to ask even of herself the silent question—"Is this All?"[2]

Friedan wrote the book based on a survey and follow-up interviews that she conducted with two hundred of her Smith College classmates, in which she found that the happiest women had jobs and activities outside the home and those discontented with their lives were traditional housewives and mothers. Her first article, "Are Women Wasting Their Time in College?," was rejected by *McCall's* and by *Redbook*, whose male editor sent it back to her agent saying that Friedan "must be going off her rocker. Only the most neurotic housewife will identify with this."[3] Many publishers passed on the book before W. W. Norton eventually bought it in 1959. *Good Housekeeping* published Friedan's article "Women Are People Too" in 1960 and was joined by *McCall's* to release excerpts from the book to close to thirty-six million readers.[4] Norton agreed to an initial printing of only two thousand copies of *The Feminine Mystique*, in part because the Book-of-the-Month Club refused it. The book was an immediate commercial success, remaining on the *New York Times* best seller list for six weeks and selling three million copies in the first three years. The paperback edition, published a year later, sold 1.4 million copies. Ninety percent of the thousands of readers who wrote to Friedan in response to the book thanked her and agreed with its argument,[5] and its title soon entered the lexicon as shorthand for the frustrations felt by many women.[6]

The female Broadway theatergoer might have related to Friedan's scathing observation that "American women are suffering, quite simply, a massive sickness of sex without self" because she had heard it before.[7] Articles in late 1950s women's magazines noted signs of discontent in "The Mother Who Ran Away" and "Why Young Mothers Feel Trapped."[8] At the same time, though, women were bombarded with messages about the value of domesticity, the importance of submissiveness for a successful marriage, and the centrality of motherhood to a woman's natural role. A 1957 manual advised women to drop out of school for the "PhT degree": "Putting husband Through" to feel the "joy of being a part of her husband's preparation for a career,"[9] and a *McCall's* questionnaire in 1960, "Look Before You Leap," quizzed women to confirm that they could cook, clean, and take care of a house the way their mate desired. "Has he pointed out things about you that he doesn't like, and have you changed because of what he's said?" it asked, presuming an affirmative response.[10] Television featured happy housewives like Donna Reed, Harriet Nelson, and June Cleaver.

In 1960, three years before the publication of *The Feminine Mystique*, two musicals set in their contemporary moment opened on Broadway and presented female characters who wanted precisely what Friedan reviled: to quit their jobs and become housewives with well-employed, white-collar husbands, houses in the suburbs, and children. These were *Bye Bye Birdie* and *How to Succeed in Business without Really Trying*, the latter of which was still playing when *The Feminine Mystique* was published.

This essay investigates how Broadway musical theater—and specifically its representation of the housewife—was in conversation with *The Feminine Mystique*. To answer this question, I'll look at those two musicals, which opened before the publication of *The Feminine Mystique*, and then two musicals that premiered shortly after the book's release: *Fiddler on the Roof* and *I Do! I Do!* While I'm not arguing for a direct, cause-and-effect connection between *The Feminine Mystique* and Broadway musical theater, then, as now, the Broadway musical was a commercial enterprise that depended on ticket sales to ensure its profitability. With few exceptions, Broadway musicals were open-ended, designed to run until ticket sales failed to cover daily production costs. While marketing and critics' views influenced audiences' perceptions of a show, a successful musical—as these four were—had to resonate with the social and historical context, with the zeitgeist. In the early to mid-1960s, Friedan's ideas were a part of that zeitgeist.

The Broadway musical was in its "Golden Age" and occupied a visible and viable place in popular culture at the time. Songs played on the radio, people collected LP cast albums, and actors frequently appeared on the *Ed Sullivan Show*. Stylistically, musicals of this period tended to follow the conventions of the formally integrated book musical, which Rodgers and Hammerstein developed starting with *Oklahoma!* in 1943. The book (or story or script or libretto) organized the show's architecture, and realist spoken scenes alternated with vibrant, emotion-laden musical numbers. Musical numbers came "naturally" from the story, whether to express emotions too big for a character to speak, to propel the story forward, or to provide an aurally and visually (through dance) rich pause for audiences to contemplate what had just happened. Composers and lyricists wrote songs from each character's perspective, with music and lyrics expressing that character's background and psyche. Moreover, the artists created a total theatrical world—held together by musical tropes and motives that repeated across numbers, by lyrics that captured the vocabulary of the characters, by character-appropriate movement, and by mimetic set, lighting, and costume designs—a believable reality, even in its excessive, admittedly unrealistic emotional display.

In terms of gender, most female principals in the 1940s and 1950s were feisty ingénues, from Julie Jordan in *Carousel* (1945) to Marion in *The Music Man*

(1956) to Eliza in *My Fair Lady* (1956), who typically longed for romance but resisted the male principal whom the audience knew she would eventually marry. Most musicals of this era are structured by a romance plot that tracks obstacles to the marriage but then culminates in its celebration, and *Bye Bye Birdie* and *How to Succeed* also conclude with a marriage. Unlike women of the preceding decades, though, their female leads are motivated not by romance but by wanting the life of a housewife. Smart and able working women, they don't sing about being in love but about marriage and a middle-class life in the suburbs, which the man must provide. The leading men, similarly unromantic, are preoccupied by their careers; only a climactic revelation transforms them into husbands. These pre–*Feminine Mystique* musicals are parodic and cartoonish, self-aware as they poke fun at cultural trends but also reinforce certain mores and values.

BYE BYE BIRDIE

Bye Bye Birdie, which opened on April 14, 1960, joined the young team of composer Charles Strouse and lyricist Lee Adams with librettist Michael Stewart and Gower Champion in his first assignment as director- choreographer.[11] The show assembled a cast of better-known women—Chita Rivera, who created the role of Anita in *West Side Story*, and established comedian Kay Medford (who later played Fanny Brice's mother in *Funny Girl* [1964, film 1968])—with a then-little-known Dick Van Dyke (who won the role with a sensational audition), and what began as a musical theater trifle came a big hit.[12] The musical's catchy pop and pseudo–rock and roll score jammed together brightly charming musical numbers, cartoonish supporting teenage and adult characters, and plenty of one-line jokes and shtick. Tonally, *Birdie* hearkened back to an "old style" musical comedy, with a vaudeville feeling and the book and numbers arranged in a "mosaic-like way."[13] The show satirized the generation gap and was the first Broadway musical to represent youth culture's fascination with Elvis Presley, which it did, in the words of critic Kenneth Tynan, with "affectionate freshness."[14] Brooks Atkinson panned the show in the *New York Times*, but every other reviewer loved it.[15] *Birdie* ran for 607 performances, launched several touring companies and a London production, and to this day it's among the most popular musicals performed by high school and community theaters.

Rose Alvarez (played by Rivera), the singing and dancing star of the show, is Albert's secretary and fiancée, whose superobjective in the show never wavers: she wants to marry Albert and become a suburban housewife. Her housewife fantasies anticipate how Friedan would describe married women's lives a few years later. Throughout the show, Rose is charming, appealing, smart, and correct. Her songs reveal different sides of a remarkably well-rounded character, as she sings a range of musical styles in eight songs, either solo, in duets with Kim and with Albert, or with the company. The role features considerable dancing, too, as Champion created four numbers for the virtuosic Rivera. Though she occupies the most stage space in *Bye Bye Birdie*, Rose—both the character and the performer who plays her—oscillates between passivity and activity, between housewife desires and irrepressible sexiness.

Rose dominates *Bye Bye Birdie*'s first scene, as she threatens to leave Albert and then sings her first number, "An English Teacher." This quiet, wistful tune serves as the character's conventional "I am/I want" song, and Rose sings the song standing still—the only one in the show in which she's not dancing. Focused entirely on the man, she longs to be "Mrs. Peterson, Mrs. Albert Peterson, Mrs. Phi Beta Kappa Peterson, the English teacher's wife," which she sings in a simple melody, much of it sustained on a few notes.[16] Rose had envisioned a bright future for Albert that began with his own plan (or so she says) to be an intellectual and a poet, not a songwriting "music business bum."[17] When she begins to picture her fantasy life, triplets emerge in the rhythm to create a sense of excitement: "We'd have a little apartment in Queens, / You'd get a summer vacation, / And we would know what life means!"[18] Rose has no ambitions for herself because she would benefit from her husband's success. In Friedan's view—which would be widely publicized three years after *Birdie*'s premiere—the life Rose desires, which the musical presents as perfectly reasonable, will be stultifying for the active, intelligent woman the musical shows her to be.

Tinged with loss, the lyrics of Rose's first song are written in a past subjunctive tense: "If only you'd been an English teacher!"[19] Rose enunciates a dream that is already past, it's already too late, and she missed her chance to be a housewife: "A man who's got his masters, / Is really someone! / How proud I'd be if / You had become one!"[20] The song ends mournfully, and the musical introduces Rose as disappointed about the life she hasn't had and, as a woman, can't fix. As it turns out, though, by the end of *Bye Bye Birdie* Albert becomes the very man Rose describes. In her first number, then, she outlines his future, and though she sounds pathetically passive, she accurately articulates Albert's trajectory to masculinity and their happy matrimonial conclusion.

Rose's first number, then, at once bespeaks her desires sincerely but also gives a false impression of her submissiveness. In the very next scene, it's clear that while she officially works as Albert's secretary, in truth she is the brains and the active force of the business and Albert is a talented songwriter but just a mama's boy. Determined to make Albert into the man she wants, Rose cleverly masterminds a publicity scheme for him to write "One Last Kiss" for rock star Conrad Birdie to serenade and kiss a lucky girl as his grand army send-off.

Rose proposes that Conrad will leave, and Albert will be rich and can cut his ties to his mother and the music company, free to fulfill his higher ideals.[21] She not only contrives the plan but takes the lead in spinning Conrad's fictitious innocent past for the press and stages the entire scene for the television cameras.

Still, Albert fails to rise to her challenge, and act 2 begins the same as act 1, with Rosie threatening to leave him. She takes a different course this time, electing to remake herself instead of him. She sings the fast and furious "What Did I Ever See in Him?" with notes rapidly rising in every line to a series of frantic triplets and then a belted repeat of the title line. She caps the song with, "That's right, the hell with you! From now on, it's just going to be me, Rosie, on the town, singing, dancing, having a ball, making up for eight years of being in love with a Mama-clutching, aspirin-splitting six foot tower of Jello!"[22] Rose's payback is not to plan her own career or marry someone else, but to act wild, sexual, and free; that is, to behave as an anti-housewife.

Rose takes her revenge on Albert in "The Shriner's Ballet," a number that highlights Rivera's dancing prowess even as it portrays the character's misguided route toward independence. She gets drunk in a bar and then sneaks into a Shriners' meeting. Set to a vaguely middle eastern melody and with vaguely "Turkish," "genie-in-a-bottle" choreography (consistent with the Shriners' iconography, with which 1960 audiences would be familiar), the number builds, as the stage directions describe it, "From tassel-twirling to tickling, from tickling to a few kicks, from kicks to grinds, and from grinds to bumps, until Rosie begins turning the quiet meeting into a sort of Midwestern version of a Turkish orgy."[23] The men are "shocked at first" but "gradually warm up," loosen their ties, and untuck their shirts.[24] The dance is choreographed around, on, and under a long meeting table, and the number climaxes with a visual joke: "The Shriners have gone wilder than Rosie imagined as they toss her from one to another as they whirl like dervishes finally disappearing under the table once again. Finally a crash of music, a hand comes up, Rosie is yanked down with them. Blackout."[25] Rosie enters in the next scene, coming "limply out the door, wearing a red fez. She collapses on box next to garbage can as Hugo comes in."[26] Although the scene is meant to be humorous and show the men's weakness, it's in essence a staged rape, brought on by a woman determined to use her sexual attractiveness to avenge a man who's not there. It reveals how few choices women have: her threats are self-destructive; when she goes out on the town, she behaves ridiculously; and it's not what she wants anyway. The number affirms the correctness of her housewife desires. And yet, ironically, the dance was a star-making performance feat for Rivera and one that she repeated on numerous TV variety shows over the years: the performer's charismatic physicality contradicted the female character's weakness.[27]

Rose's brush with sexual violence jolts Albert to action and the plot moves swiftly toward its matrimonial resolution, but not before Rose's eleven o'clock number, "Spanish Rose." This penultimate song in a Broadway musical conventionally functions to bring the house down, to give the audience one last musical and emotional lift before the show's finale, and to reveal the character's most intense and sincere feelings. Surprisingly, though, Rose's is a silly charm song in which she playfully performs a false identity. When Albert finally quits the company, sends his mother off, and proposes to Rose, that is, when he exclaims, "I'm a new man, Rose!" she sees her housewife future.[28] "Call me Mrs. Peterson," she snaps at Albert's mother and launches into the victory dance that parodies all things Latino/a, even though, as she quips, "I'm from Allentown, PA." Tongue in cheek, she promises that she will be Spanish Rose, will eat tacos and enchiladas, will dance with a fan and click castanets: "I will be so Spanish it will make you sick!"[29] The melody is simple and repetitive, an imitation of a Spanish children's song, with jokes landing on every rhyme. While the song was designed as a show-stopping performance opportunity for the Latina bombshell Rivera, it sends up the very identity she embodies and highlights (again) Rose's clever self-consciousness and her understanding of identity as performative, as a role she can put on or take off.[30]

The end of *Bye Bye Birdie* follows 1950s musical theater's conventions: charismatic Rose becomes a housewife. The musical's last song—the show's only love duet—sounds as corny as any song Albert would write for Conrad, not a soaring harmonic melody but a sweet little ditty that suggests a companionate marriage and a pleasant life in the suburbs. "Now my life is Rosie," he croons in a simple sing-song tune. He puns on her name and the flower rose, and they lightly kiss and walk off arm in arm.

Rose's trajectory in the musical is rife with contradictions. The physical exuberance and linguistic humor in her star-turn dances are buttoned down by marriage's inevitability and the housewife position that she desires. Her first song of frustration portrays her as passive and submissive, which is untrue; then, as she approaches the housewife future she wants (in Ohio!), her final number expresses her happiness in a clever, self-conscious parody of her ethnicity. This last song captures her wit and high spirits but is a completely false expression; it's an image in which no one is invested, a purely performative charm song. The housewife narrative contains her even as the form of the musical allows her to shine.

Rose gets what she wants at the end: a simple life as an English teacher's wife in the Midwest (which could land her a bigger house than in Queens). And while the musical lampoons rock star idolatry, mama's-boy passivity, and every American family's obsession with television fame, it takes housewife desires perfectly seriously. Except for her brief drunken adventures with the Shriners, which ultimately prove that she should be a housewife and not a single girl, Rose's desires are not a source of humor in the show. In the end, Rose/Rivera is contained along the lines of Betty Friedan's housewives—by choice. But where will she be in a few short years?

HOW TO SUCCEED

How to Succeed in Business without Really Trying brought together an experienced and successful artistic team in the award-winning composer and lyricist Frank Loesser (*Guys and Dolls*, *Most Happy Fella*) with book writers Abe Burrows, Jack Weinstock, and Willie Gilbert to adapt Shepherd Mead's best-selling self-help satire of corporate life. Veteran director Burrows directed, and Bob Fosse replaced the show's first choreographer and earned billing as "musical staging by," though many of his hallmark moves, such as the office workers who become falling dominoes during "Coffee Break," are inseparable from the show itself. A grinning and gap-toothed Robert Morse starred as the young, ambitious, cipher Finch, and Bonnie Scott (who later played Marlo Thomas's neighbor Judy on *That Girl*) originated the role of Rosemary, one of the few characters who didn't appear in Mead's book.[31]

The show opened on October 14, 1961, to rave reviews and ran for 1,417 performances. It won seven Tony Awards, the New York Drama Critics' Circle Award, and the 1962 Pulitzer Prize for Drama. Walter Kerr called it "crafty, conniving, sneaky, cynical, irreverent, impertinent, sly, malicious, and lovely, just lovely," and Howard Taubman declared that "it stings mischievously and laughs uproariously."[32]

How to Succeed, like its source material, is clever, self-conscious, and painted in broad strokes and bright colors. No character escapes judgment, and all resonate with then-obvious types and stereotypes. Fosse used a stop-action technique to convey the cartoonish style, as the actors freeze for an instant to create a tableau that looks like one frame from a comic strip.[33]

The female principal, Rosemary, is a secretary in the World Wide Wicket corporation where J. Pierpont Finch sets his ambitious eye. The musical is built around Finch's rise to the top and his use and abuse of everyone on the corporate ladder on his way up. Rosemary, then, is just a cog in his machinery, but because musical theater's conventions require a romance and a female romantic lead, she has more of a stage and vocal presence than a plot summary of *How to Succeed* suggests.

Like Rose in *Bye Bye Birdie*, Rosemary is employed as a secretary who possesses considerable knowledge of the business world, but she wants to be a housewife. And like Rose's first "I am/I want" number, Rosemary's musical introduction, "Happy to Keep His Dinner Warm," expresses those housewife desires through a fantasy of a man not yet formed. While both Rose and Rosemary are eager to give up their jobs for the satisfaction of taking care of their future husbands, Rosemary imagines J. Pierpont as a rich businessman, "my darling tycoon," with a wealthier lifestyle than Albert's humble and poetic intellectual English teacher. Rose's "little apartment in Queens"[34] is Rosemary's "mansion [in] New Rochelle."[35] And Rose's idea that "you'll have a summer vacation / And we will know what life means"[36] translates for Rosemary to "waiting . . .'til he comes wearily home from downtown."[37] Both Rose and Rosemary clearly envision the men they want, but they face opposite challenges. Rose and Albert have been together for eight years; they know and love each other, but she has hit the breaking point because he's unable to move forward professionally and matrimonially. Rosemary, on the other hand, has just met Ponty and doesn't know him at all beyond the clear signs of his relentless ambition, the very trait that marks him as "the darling, bright, young man / I've picked out for marrying me."[38]

"Happy to Keep His Dinner Warm" is the quintessential song of early 1960s housewife desires. It combines a sweet melody with a dance rhythm and determined march, and Rosemary, too, wears these qualities of charming naïveté and sheer willfulness. The song opens with the words *New Rochelle*, as Rosemary's fantasy is thoroughly tied to the suburbs, the site of her future life as a housewife. The verse goes on in clever rhymes to describe how "he'll do well / I can tell / So it isn't a moment too soon / To plan on my life in New Rochelle / The wife of my darling tycoon." Smitty, who's been listening to this elaborate fantasy, chimes in, speaking, "Honey, you'll be in New Rochelle and your darling tycoon will be here at the office." Rosemary sings her reply in the chorus: "I'll be so happy to keep his dinner warm," with an upwardly soaring phrase that captures her expansive feeling and thoroughly contradicts the victim-laden lyrics she sings. When she sings of his action—"While he moves onward and upward"—the rhythm shifts to a march. Rosemary welcomes the emotional coldness of such an ambitious chap, as she sings, "Waiting until his mind is clear, / While he looks through me, right through me." Then she imagines herself as "wearing the wifely uniform"—in this case, both an apron and an undemanding attitude—and then, announcing her pregnancy nonchalantly. She doesn't want romance or even attention; it's "such heaven" to get her identity from him, "to belong in the aura / Of his frown, darling busy frown" and "to bask in the glow / Of his perfectly understandable neglect."[39] As an over-the-top enunciation of a housewife's masochistic desires, the song is crafty, and Burrows described it as "a pathetic, masochistic love song."[40] The musical is aware of the problems women face, which Friedan will soon enunciate, but here Rosemary longs for them as her future.[41]

Although Rosemary and Ponty are on opposite ends of the marriage spectrum through much of the show—it's only what she wants and it distracts from what he wants—the two characters are actually equally focused on "how to succeed" within late-1950s gender roles. For him, success means rising in the company and becoming an executive. For her, success means leaving her job in the steno pool to become the executive's wife. Separately, they respond identically to obstacles, undaunted: "I'm prepared for exactly this sort of thing," Ponty says to Rosemary when they meet, and she repeats the line to Smitty.[42] For women, though, success depends on the man—both his ability to move up the corporate ladder and his desire for her to be his wife. Rosemary's self-abnegation is so extreme that it seems silly, and yet she desires precisely what Betty Friedan would characterize as the housewife's situation a few years later.

That Rosemary and Rose want to be housewives wasn't surprising in a culture and moment that valued marriage for women above a career. These characters came of age during the late 1950s, when most women married around the age of twenty.[43] In 1960 *Look* magazine warned that women were "likely to get stranded" if they didn't marry by the time they were twenty-four, after which "it's a downhill slide."[44] In a frequently cited 1962 poll, "The American Woman: Her Attitudes on Family, Sex, Religion and Society," when asked, "At any time since your marriage, have you ever wondered—even for a moment—whether you would have not been better off to have become a career woman instead of getting married?" only 37 percent of women answered yes.[45] Ninety-six percent of married women said they were either fairly happy or extremely happy; most weren't interested in being equal in business or politics but felt that the "chief purpose of her life is motherhood."[46] Still, it was up to the woman to attract and marry a man by way of "good looks, personality and cheerful subservience."[47] Rosemary and Rose accept what Friedan describes as "the new mystique [of] housewife-mothers," "the model for all women [that] presupposes that history has reached a final and glorious end in the here and now as far as women are concerned."[48]

Moreover, good jobs were hard for women to come by. Help-wanted ads were divided by gender, and female jobs included secretaries, girl Fridays, and receptionists, but not accountants, attorneys, or management trainees.[49] The most important skill for a woman to possess was typing.[50] Although many women worked—in fact, from 1940 to 1960, the percentage of women who worked doubled from 15 to 30 percent, and by 1955 more women worked than during World War II—by 1961, they made only sixty cents to a man's dollar.[51] Seventy-five percent of women who worked were in all-female service professions, and almost no women occupied high-status positions like doctors, lawyers, politicians, or college professors. Many institutions, including university clubs and the National Press Club, were all male or didn't allow women to speak.[52]

Rose and Rosemary's occupation as secretaries, one of the few viable occupations for unmarried white women, signaled that they were biding time until marriage. Except for the television character of Ann Southern, the decisively single working woman in the enormously popular CBS series *Private Secretary* (1952–57) and *The Ann Southern Show* (1958–61), the steno pool was a temporary stop on the way to marriage. Secretaries were in demand in the late 1950s, when businesses suffered a severe shortage and advertised boldly that the office was a place to meet a husband, specifying the ratio of men to women and highlighting the opportunity to meet clients.[53] In a 1955 *New York Times Magazine* article, one secretary, speaking "frankly," said, "A girl can get a job easily these days; it's much tougher to get a man. A girl's main purpose when she takes a job is not to prepare herself for a career but to tide herself over until the right man comes along."[54]

The Feminine Mystique didn't take on the politics of women's labor or even the topic of women as full-time workers. Rather, Friedan presumed that a (white, middle-class, heterosexual) woman would marry, have children, and take primary responsibility for the household. The "problem with no name," as Friedan called it, was that women had nothing else—no hobbies, interests, part-time work; their identities were fully shaped in their roles as housewives and mothers, which simply wasn't enough to satisfy an intelligent, educated woman. Furthermore, she argued, if women did develop activities outside of the house, it would make them happier people and so better wives and mothers and more desirable mates. As she said in a 1963 interview, "Don't be an appliance, a vegetable or a service station. How will you get a man? If you find yourself first you won't need any trickery. He'll find you and he'll have plenty of competition."[55]

By its February 1963 publication, many theater-going women would already have read excerpts from Friedan's book in *McCall's* or *Ladies Home Journal*. However, none of them would read a *New York Times* review until April, as *The Feminine Mystique* was published during a 114-day newspaper strike in New York City.[56] (As a side note, the February 19, 1963, western edition of the *New York Times* also contained an article about studies on a birth control pill and how it was 100 percent effective, with no side effects.) When a review finally did appear on April 7, 1963, it was lukewarm, three scant paragraphs buried at the end of a section that summarized fifty books that had been published during the strike.[57] This was an inauspicious beginning for a book that would go on to be considered among the most influential books of the century.[58]

Without the typical advertising outlets, publisher W. W. Norton sent Friedan on a tour, which was then a new way to promote a book, and she spoke at colleges and bookstores and frequently on television talk shows.[59] The media response was huge; numerous publications, including women's magazines, *Harper's*, and *TV Guide* included articles by or about Friedan.[60] By the end of the year, hers was a household name and the term *feminine mystique* was already making its way into everyday speech.

Why did *The Feminine Mystique* grab women so forcefully? First, it relied on many familiar formal and rhetorical devices typical of women's magazines at the time: "the professional voice of the advice columnist, the anecdotal and other 'proofs' of non-fiction articles . . . and the epiphanies that routinely climaxed romantic fiction," as well as Friedan's "didactic tone."[61] As in other contemporaneous books of social criticism—*The Organization Man* and *The Man in the Grey Flannel Suit*—Friedan focused on individual solutions, ending with a series of "small but achievable steps" that the reader could follow to improve her life. According to historian Patricia Bradley, "Friedan reflected the merging of the traditional self-help articles of the magazines with the postwar popularization of psychology."[62]

Second, Friedan put a name, and a sexy one at that, on a condition that many women felt but few could articulate. The original title of the book was *The Togetherness Woman* (to confront *McCall's* 1954 "togetherness" family campaign), but the word *mystique* was perfect for the time, conveying a "vague exoticism" and resonating with the Red menace and other mysterious threats to the American way of life.[63] In this way, Friedan connected feminism to anxieties that were already roiling under the surface of a prosperous white, middle-class America: fear of the Bomb, of new ideas about sexuality, of new rock music.[64]

Third, the book was published in the same year as two others that examined the status of women in the United States: the widely read report of the President's Commission on the Status of Women, which criticized women's lack of financial and legal independence (but still maintained the view that being a housewife and mother was a woman's key identity), and *The Employed Mother in America*, a well-respected academic sociological study of gender, which stated that "working mothers are happy mothers" and that there are "no negative psychological differences between children of employed and stay-at-home mothers."[65]

Fourth, though powerfully argued, Friedan's polemic wasn't all that radical but rather firmly liberal and humanist. She didn't urge women to leave their families or to work full-time but to take classes or volunteer and then later return to work. The book was about individual women making changes, not about women joining to make social change, and not even about men helping with housework. Friedan argued, as historian Stephanie Coontz summarizes, that women should "develop a life plan that would give meaning to the years after their children left home." Furthermore, Friedan did not bash men but rather blamed women for their situation.[66] And she stressed that having a more meaningful life would make them better housewives and mothers.

Thousands of women wrote to Friedan to express their gratitude; for example, "I feel, today, as though I had been filled with helium and turned loose!" "Like light bulbs going off again and again." "I understood what I was feeling and felt validated!"[67] In her 2012 book *A Strange Stirring*, Coontz interviewed hundreds of women again to ask about the effects of the book, and most remembered well how they had felt almost fifty years earlier: "'The Feminine Mystique' left me breathless." "I finally realized I wasn't crazy." "It literally changed (and perhaps saved) my life." "Something clicked." "It slammed me in the face." "A bolt of lightning." "A revelation." "A bombshell."[68]

By 1964 the Broadway musical was starting to shift. Economically, it became harder to make a profit on a hands-on, labor-intensive enterprise with ever-rising production expenses. Broadway melodies no longer carried the airwaves, and the romantic sensibility of the Broadway musical didn't jibe with the Civil Rights Movement, protests against the war in Vietnam, or early Women's Lib. A number of Broadway musicals from the mid-1960s conceive of marriage in a new way and represent marriage differently than had earlier musicals, and they also start to revise the conventions of the form so thoroughly dominated by the work of Rodgers and Hammerstein until 1960. *Fiddler on the Roof* (1964) and *I Do! I Do!* (1966) are about the institution of marriage and both look well past the wedding. *Fiddler* presents a synchronic model, examining several marriages over a short period of time, while *I Do! I Do!* presents one marriage diachronically over a forty-year period. In the wake of *The Feminine Mystique*, *Fiddler* and *I Do! I Do!* offer optimistic but not romantic views of marriage. While *Fiddler* and *I Do! I Do!* present marriage more complexly, their female characters are only housewives; we don't see them employed or having another identity at all.

FIDDLER ON THE ROOF

Jerry Bock and Sheldon Harnick's *Fiddler on the Roof* opened on September 22, 1964, surpassing *My Fair Lady* as the longest-running Broadway musical when it played until July 1972, for a total of 3,242 performances. It won nine Tony Awards, including Best Musical, Best Score, and Best Director, and Maria Karnilova (Golde) won for Best Featured Actress in a Musical. Enormously successful in spite of skyrocketing production costs and rock music's takeover of the airwaves in the mid-1960s, *Fiddler* is often considered the last musical of Broadway's "golden age." Formally, it exhibits the qualities of an integrated musical, with all of the musical numbers growing out of the story, smooth transitions between songs and dialogue, and character-specific music and lyrics. It also contains characteristics of what would come to be labeled the "concept musical," including a self-consciously performative, introductory "welcome-to-my-world" ensemble number, numerous small plots, and an idea—"tradition"— unifying the show more than plot.[69]

Fiddler opened a year after Friedan's book was published. Though the musical achieved fame because of its representation of Jews, *Fiddler* navigates the politics of gender as much as ethnicity. Tevye the dairyman is Sholem Aleichem's creation, but in Bock, Harnick, librettist Joseph Stein, and director and choreographer Jerome Robbins's version, he's a man of the mid-1960s grappling with breathtaking changes around him. As the Cossacks force Tevye out of Anatevka, feminism pushes him out of his village mind-set; the musical traces a transformation of the social order via gender. When it opened the *Vogue* magazine reviewer disliked the "ruthless commercialization of the [original] stories" but noted that "the marriages of Tevye's five daughters is [*sic*] the substance of the plot."[70] *Fiddler* intertwines the political, generational, and personal changes that reshaped the United States in the mid-1960s, presenting them as ambivalent, challenging, and inevitable. Unlike *Bye Bye Birdie* and *How to Succeed*, which feature the single female principal who sings of her housewife desires and gets married by the end of the show, *Fiddler* presents several women at different stages of their marriages. In this way, it opens a synchronic examination of housewives' desires, linking the housewife to a larger social sphere and community organization.

Fiddler multiples the marriage plot by three. As each daughter finds her own way to marriage, she increasingly threatens the father's authority. Tzeitl, the eldest daughter, chooses her husband rather than agreeing to the arranged marriage with the old, rich man that Tevye brokered for her. Hodel goes one step further and marries a man who becomes a revolutionary and is arrested in Siberia; she then leaves to join him. Chava defies the faith by marrying a non-Jew. Tevye initially finds each match "unthinkable" and "preposterous," but only Chava's choice severs her from the family, seemingly irreparably.[71] And yet, near the end of the show, as the family prepares to leave Anatevka, Chava appears and Tevye acknowledges her. His love for his daughter takes precedence over his commitment to tradition. Raymond Knapp points to the musical's feminization of Jews and how *Fiddler*'s "key events emasculate [Tevye] from both within and without."[72] He observes "its treatment of feminist themes of self-determination, a seeming response to the emergent feminism of the 1960s."[73]

"Matchmaker, Matchmaker," one of the musical's first numbers, is a lively trio of the oldest daughters, their collective "I am/I want" song that conveys their primary objective, to be married. The rousing waltz seems to emerge spontaneously after the daughters see Yente the matchmaker visit their house. Somehow naïve about the real power Yente has over their lives, the younger two sing a verse, hoping for "a scholar," a man "rich as a king," someone "handsome" with a ring to "make me the envy of all I see."[74] Tzeitl, the eldest and already involved with Motel the tailor, perfectly impersonates Yente in a playful scenario in the middle of the song and offers her sisters one old and ugly man and another who is an alcoholic abuser.

The song maintains a regular waltz rhythm with the feeling of a dance-based game. The song's melody repeats and its lyrics take the three on an emotional journey from girlhood to womanhood, as they together imagine possible futures and teach each other about the consequences of Yente's actions. After Tzeitl plays out the possible horrors of Yente's choice, given that the girls have "no money, no dowry, no family background," she blares, "Be glad you have a match!"[75] The younger two retract their wishes in the B-section in a soaring melody, "Dear Yente, See that he's gentle / Remember you were also a bride," and then they confess, "It's not that I'm sentimental / it's just that I'm terrified!"[76] The song tracks their feelings, from enthusiastic and eager to cautious and nervous, as they become aware that they are vulnerable to the whims of Yente and their father. "I could get stuck for good," they sing, and conclude, more slowly, "I'm in no rush / Maybe I've learned / Playing with matches a girl can get burned," and they hope that Yente will "please take your time" and only bring "a matchless match."[77] Raymond Knapp observes that they "move through three phases: romantic idealizing, more realistic projection, and the beginnings of a sensibility that will support their eventual individual self-actualizations."[78]

Though the daughters sing of their obedience, their vibrant singing, dancing, and playacting—choreographed by Robbins with mops and pails, everyday objects found in the house—tell the audience that these three are unlikely to let a man be chosen for them. They seem girlish, but the lyrically clever, punning song (verb and noun forms of groom, find, and catch; double meaning of "match"—both mate and fire starter) hints that these young women are unlikely to abide by the matchmaker's rules. The musical goes on to show them as active makers of their marriages, but still, they only want to be housewives.

And yet, while *Fiddler*'s narrative approves that the daughters choose their own husbands, the score doesn't ultimately value their point of view. In the mode that musical theater values—songs—they have little to do after "Matchmaker."[79] In contrast, the two Jewish fiancés, Model and Perchik, each sing a solo to celebrate the successful engagement. *Fiddler* locates the joy of imminent marriage with the men and not in a romantic love duet. In this way, it contradicts its textual message, which says that the women have power; when the men sing, their women are objects they've acquired. Only Hodel's solo, "Far from the Home I Love," a haunting, wrenching song of farewell to her father, gives a female character a unique voice, but it comes very near the end of the show.

As a more insidious undermining of the daughters' independence, their music is tied to the "tradition" motive that threads through *Fiddler's* score. Although "Matchmaker" doesn't have an especially "Jewish" sound,[80] the first two notes repeat the same interval of the first two notes of the *Fiddler's* theme that opens the show, as well as the second and third note of "Tradition" (on the syllables *di* and *tion*), the first two notes of "Sabbath Prayer," of "Sunrise, Sunset," and of "Do You Love Me?"[81] However the daughters seem to assert their independence by selecting their own husbands, they're still musically tied to the old ways.

Fiddler's synchronic exploration of marriage eschews the wedding scene that typically concludes a musical. Two weddings are performed: one that Tevye creates in his "dream" and the other immediately followed by a pogrom that concludes the act. Moreover, the show is equally concerned with what happens to marriage after the wedding, including Motel's acquisition of a sewing machine, Perchik's arrest in Siberia, and Chava's departure with the non-Jewish Fyedka. It thus engages with Friedan's project to analyze women's lives after their wedding day.

Marriage's long-term consequences are crystallized in Tevye and Golde's act 2 duet, "Do You Love Me?" Unlike their daughters, Tevye and Golde had an arranged marriage and first met, as Tevye sings, "on our wedding day." Each chimes in a bit of the story, underlining how in sync they've become:

TEVYE: I was scared
GOLDE: I was shy
TEVYE: I was nervous
GOLDE: So was I.[82]

The sweetly comic song shows Golde as eminently practical and theatrically hilarious. Tevye asks conversationally, "Do you love me?" And she replies with a surprising melodic upward leap and alarming shriek, "Do I what?"[83] Then she perfectly articulates the housewife's situation: "For twenty-five years I've washed your clothes, cooked your meals, cleaned your house, given you children, milked the cow, after twenty-five years, why talk about love right now?"[84] The three-minute song doesn't resolve a single melodic phrase until the very end, when they agree they do "suppose" they love each other and they harmonize easily in a typical downward phrase, "after twenty-five years, it's nice to know."[85] The song presents a satisfactory marriage, and it allows the housewife to think about what being a wife and mother has meant to her. Unlike in *Bye Bye Birdie* and *How to Succeed*, the details of this experience aren't presented as a single woman's fantasy for her future but as a middle-aged woman's description of her past.

In the end, *Fiddler* performs ambivalence about the power, status, and agency of women that would have resonated with the 1960s context. And finally, what is the daughters' revolution? They marry whom they choose, but there is no indication that they might do anything other than be housewives. To be sure, they serve dramaturgically for the audience to see how their matrimonial independence affects Tevye and how he must adapt. But in terms of gender politics, their radical acts don't change their housewife destinies.

I DO! I DO!

On December 5, 1966, *I Do! I Do!*, Tom Jones and Harvey Schmidt's musical two-hander about fifty years of a couple's marriage, opened at the 46th Street Theatre. Based on Jan de Hartog's 1951 nonmusical hit *The Fourposter*, which starred Hume Cronyn and Jessica Tandy, *I Do! I Do!* was invented as a vehicle for the imitable Mary Martin, the fifty-two-year-old star of *South Pacific* (1949), *Peter Pan* (1954), and *The Sound of Music* (1959), who had just completed a run in *Hello, Dolly!*[86] The show became a perfectly balanced duet of a musical after Robert Preston (*The Music Man*, 1956) agreed to play the husband, Michael, for which he won a Tony. A David Merrick production, the top-notch creative team included Gower Champion as director-choreographer, still aglow from his successful productions of *Carnival* (1961) and the blockbuster *Hello, Dolly!* (1964), and the well-established designers Oliver Smith (set) and Freddy Wittop (costumes).

The show garnered positive and some ecstatic reviews, especially for the stars. "Charming, tuneful, warm-hearted and delightful!" wrote Richard Watts Jr. in the *New York Post*.[87] Water Kerr was less enthused about the show but appreciated Martin, whose voice had "mellow sounds that come from her throat like red wine at room temperature," and Preston, "at his untouchable best when the show asks him to be pompous, and blissfully obtuse."[88] After almost two years on Broadway, Preston and Martin took the show on a year-long national tour, which ended a month early when Martin became ill.[89] It was nominated for six additional Tony Awards, though Martin lost Best Actress in a Musical (as did Lotte Lenya in *Cabaret*) to Barbara Harris in her three different roles in *The Apple Tree*. The show ran for 561 performances, cut short by an Actors' Equity strike in 1968.

I Do! I Do!, in its diachronic representation of one marriage over fifty years, takes a completely different tack than *Fiddler*, with its synchronic framework. It begins with the wedding and traces one marriage as a process, through pregnancy, children, conflict, and reconciliation. *I Do! I Do!* is *about* marriage. As opposed to Rose in *Bye Bye Birdie*, Rosemary in *How to Succeed*, and the daughters in *Fiddler*, Agnes is introduced on the cusp of marriage and housewifery. She doesn't express housewife desires because her given circumstances locate her as a housewife-to-be from the start.

I Do! I Do! sought a balance between the specific and the general. The characters are named "He" and "She" in the script. Wittop's numerous costumes, many of which the actors had to change with alarming speed, tracked the musical's historical setting from the 1910s to the 1950s, and Smith captured the generalized location and the passage of time through props and only a few set pieces, including a large bed center stage. The production was overt about its theatricality—the actors applied makeup on stage as they aged, and the orchestra was lit and visible behind the cyclorama at the opening of act 2—and aimed to create intimacy with the audience.[90] As Long describes it, the set's "sketchiness suggested less a particular bedroom and marriage than the idea of a universal marital experience. *I Do! I Do!* was thus very close to being, if not actually, a concept musical."[91]

The show also sought a balance between the two characters. Most of the numbers—eleven of the seventeen songs of the score—are duets. Each song consists of sections sung in unison, for example, in the opening number, in which the melody echoes wedding bells, they're both terrified of "the strange new world that you enter when you say 'I do.'"[92] In the first song after they're married—a piece that alternates between an anxious and tentative conversation and a lullaby—they're both sexually "innocent," as Agnes sings, though she admits it first. In the early years of their marriage, they express mutual devotion in the "countryish waltz" "My Cup Runneth Over."[93]

Each duet also contains verses that particularize the man's and the woman's point of view, balanced between them and stereotypically gendered. Preceding the birth of their children, Michael wants a boy to play sports and Agnes hopes for a girl to dress in ribbons and lace. Then, a few years later, in the bouncy, hilarious number of mutual fury "Nobody's Perfect," Michael accuses Agnes of always being late, of being overdrawn in her checking account, and of wearing cold cream to bed. She accuses him of grinding his teeth at night, of yelling for his lost socks when he's wearing them, and of beating her to the punch line of her jokes. Since Michael and Agnes mostly sing together or sing the same thing, the show emerges as an extended duet.

Key character differences emerge via gender, though. The show is built around marriage and the home, yet Michael is a writer who refers to his work several times. The fact that his novel sells three hundred thousand copies launches them into wealth and propels a hearty fight because he's supremely vain and condescending, has been having an affair, and is contemplating leaving the marriage.

HE: Agnes, Agnes, Agnes, I'm famous. Can't you understand? I've changed. Can't you see how I've changed?
SHE: No.[94]

The musical can't conceive of a man without a career, an activity outside the home that defines his identity, but she is only a housewife and mother. In fact, when she tries to throw him out, he reminds her that he owns the house.[95]

Each character also sings three solos, again balanced to develop a gendered point of view in the marriage, and Agnes's solos throughout the show illustrate her maturation as a housewife and mother. Even though the show is historically specific, as the costumes reflect, the representation of marriage and of her status as a housewife and mother is completely ahistorical. In act 1 she sings "Something Has Happened," about the emotional intensity of being pregnant and anticipating motherhood.[96]

"Flaming Agnes," her musical high point in the show, near the end of the act, imagines her revenge against Michael's affair and is a brassy, belting number rife with contradictions. Constructed of three sections, the song opens with Agnes's recitative-like telling of the story of the "eighty-five dollar hat" that she's "hid . . . at the foot of the bed / Right here in this very same room." She concludes with a seductive threat: "If I am going to go to pot / This pot is gonna be hot," which the orchestration echoes with a vamp. In the verse, each line moves up the scale, exploding with her belting, "flaming Agnes!" The B-section finds her mapping out her fantasy of retribution in more detail, housewife-turned-seductress, with each line, again, slowly climbing teasingly up the scale. Rather than seeing herself as a victim "once her husband up and left her," she imagines an "emancipated lady," a "pale, available matron / Underneath the peacock's tail." She vows to leave her former self—"mousy housewife was her name"—who was "up to here in Cream of Wheat." The last section modulates to raise the pitch and raise the stakes, celebrating that "while he slaves to pay the alimony," "she flames from night till early morning."[97]

The song is pure fantasy. Agnes may own the hat but she will never become the temptress she imagines. She can only enhance her sexual desirability through commodities, while Michael sings to a charming soft-shoe, "a man is more attractive / The older that he grows."[98] In terms of power, the woman simply can't compete. However, the burlesque-style number is a fantastic performance opportunity for the actor playing Agnes, whether Martin, Carol Lawrence, or the countless women who have taken on the role since 1966. She dances, prances, taunts, shimmies, and belts, her partner a glorious bird of a hat. In the end, she sings in a vavoom way, but it's fully contained in the marriage and in what a middle-aged woman can really do.

In act 2, then, once their children get married and Agnes is unsure of her role, she sings "What Is a Woman," an unnerving little melody that concludes with "A woman is only / Alive when in love."[99] Feeling that she's had no life of her own, Agnes threatens to leave and tells Michael that she no longer loves him: "I can't die behind the stove like a domestic animal!"[100] She asserts, "You wouldn't understand. You're a man. You'll be able to do what you like until you're seventy. . . . Today I stopped being a mother. In a few years' time, perhaps next year, even—I'll stop being a woman—"[101] Her words echo Betty Friedan's:

> They thought all they had to do was get that man at nineteen and that would take care of the rest of their life, and then they woke up at twenty-five or thirty-five or forty-five with four children, the house, and the husband, and realized they had to face a future ahead in which they would not be able to live through others.[102]

With some tenderness but not much effort, Michael convinces her to stay, reminding her that he needs her support, her encouragement, and her critique of his work. The musical ends with them quietly together, looking out to old age as a pair. Though Agnes never moves beyond her housewife role, the musical gives her the brief moment to express a frustration that would have been familiar to many women in the 46th Street Theatre in 1966.

Nineteen sixties Broadway musical theater didn't foment political change or lead the feminist movement, but neither was it escapist or out of step with its time. In fact, its mainstream status and its tendency to align with dominant mores and values—a necessity of commercial theater—render the Broadway musical a strikingly useful document of the period. Because of the centrality of gender, romance, and marriage to the structure and narratives of Broadway musicals, they necessarily conversed with Betty Friedan's *The Feminist Mystique*, albeit obliquely. The musicals that preceded the book's publication coexisted in its zeitgeist and teetered between parody and sincerity, irony and earnestness; those that followed presented marriage beyond the wedding and women beyond their housewife desires. The creators of 1960s musicals crafted the genre's aesthetic tools of music, lyrics, dance, dialogue, and design to provide an evening of entertainment but not escapism, seduction but not stupor. The very ways that musicals grab audiences—musical pleasure, visual stimulation, kinesthetic engagement—and the requisite clarity, humor, emotional connection, and accessible meanings situate them historically, socially, and politically. Like *The Feminine Mystique*, Broadway musicals of the 1960s are performative archives of their era.

NOTES

Many thanks to Liza Gennaro, Ray Knapp, George Reddick, Liz Wollman, to Linda Oppenheim at Princeton University's Firestone Library for research help, to Judah Cohen and Jill Dolan for reading drafts of this essay, and to Cindy Rosenthal and James Harding for their superb editing work.

1. See Glenna Matthews, *Just a Housewife: The Rise and Fall of Domesticity in America* (New York: Oxford University Press, 1987), 212.

2. Betty Friedan, *The Feminine Mystique* (1963; repr., New York: Dell, 1974), 11.

3. Qtd. in Peter Dreier, "*The Feminine Mystique* and Women's Equality—50 Years Later," *Huffington Post*, February 18, 2001, http://www.huffingtonpost.com/peter-dreier/the-feminine-mystique-betty-friedan_b_2712355.html.

4. Stephanie Coontz, *A Strange Stirring: "The Feminine Mystique" and American Women at the Dawn of the 1960s* (New York: Basic Books, 2011), xxi.

5. Rebecca Jo Plant, *Mom: The Transformation of Motherhood in Modern America* (Chicago: University of Chicago Press, 2010), 147.

6. Helen Gurley Brown's *Sex and the Single Girl* was published shortly before Friedan's book. Addressed to single working women, it also became a sensation, selling two million copies in three weeks. For an analysis of "the single girl" in 1960s Broadway musicals in conversation with Brown's argument, see Stacy Wolf, *Changed for Good: A Feminist History of the Broadway Musical* (New York: Oxford University Press, 2011), 53–90.

On Friedan's writings about theater and her performance of self in writing and in public appearances, see Dorothy Chansky, "Usable Performance Feminism for Our Time: Reconsidering Betty Friedan," *Theatre Journal* 60.3 (October 2008): 341–64.

In 2013 many articles appeared that assessed the influence of *The Feminine Mystique* fifty years after its publication. See, for example, Gail Collins, "'The Feminine Mystique' at Fifty," *New York Times*, January 23, 2013, http://www.nytimes.com/2013/01/27/magazine/the-feminine-mystique-at-50.html?pagewanted=all; Jennifer Schuessler, "Criticisms of a Classic Abound," *New York Times*, February 18, 2012; Janet Maslin, "Critic's Notebook: Looking Back at a Domestic Cri de Coeur," *New York Times*, February 18, 2013, http://www.nytimes.com/2013/02/19/books/betty-friedans-feminine-mystique-50-years-later.html?pagewanted=all; Ashley Fetters, "The Skeptical Early Reviews of Betty Friedan's 'The Feminine Mystique,'" *Atlantic*, February 13, 2013, http://www.theatlantic.com/sexes/archive/2013/02/the-skeptical-early-reviews-of-betty-friedans-the-feminine-mystique/272659/; Dreier, "*The Feminine Mystique* and Women's Equality."

7. Friedan, *Feminine Mystique*, 321.

8. Coontz, *Strange Stirring*, 22.

9. Qtd. in ibid., 109.

10. Ibid., 15.

11. See Jackson R. Bryer and Richard A. Davison, "Charles Strouse," in *The Art of the American Musical: Conversations with the Creators* (New Brunswick, NJ: Rutgers University Press, 2005), 224–37.

12. Herbert H. Keyser, *Geniuses of the American Musical Theatre* (New York: Applause, 2009), 205.

13. David Payne-Carter, *Gower Champion: Dance and the American Musical Theatre*, ed. Brooks McNamara and Steve Nelson (Westport, CT: Greenwood Press, 1999), 106.

14. Tynan qtd. in John Lahr, "Can't Stop the Beat," *New Yorker*, October 26, 2009, http://www.newyorker.com/arts/critics/theatre/2009/10/26/091026crth_theatre_lahr.

15. Keyser, *Geniuses*, 205.

16. Michael Stewart, Lee Adams, and Charles Strouse, *Bye Bye Birdie* (New York: DBS, 1958), 9.

17. Ibid., 7.

18. Ibid., 8.

19. Ibid.

20. Ibid.

21. Ibid., 40–41.

22. Ibid., 87.

23. Ibid., 117.

24. Ibid.

25. Ibid., 118.

26. Ibid., 119.

27. See "Chita Rivera recreates 'Shriners' Ballet' on *The Best of Broadway with the American Dance Machine* (aired on 5/24/85)," BlueGoBo, http://www.bluegobo.com/show/119147/video/10425. Many musicals of the 1960s presented this contradiction between character and performer. See Wolf, *Changed for Good*, 55.

28. Stewart, Adams, and Strouse, *Bye Bye Birdie*, 126.

29. Ibid., 134.

30. The creation of "Spanish Rose" underlines the practical exigencies of Broadway musical theater in the mid-twentieth century. First, Rose was originally written as Polish but her ethnicity was changed to Spanish after Rivera was cast. During tryouts in Philadelphia, Champion observed that the well-known and captivating Rivera didn't have a big enough role, the second act wasn't playing well, and he needed a strong eleven o'clock number. The entire song was written, staged, and performed in less than two days. Payne-Carter, *Gower Champion*, 71–73. On Rivera, see David Román, *Performance in America: Contemporary U.S. Culture and the Performing Arts* (Durham, NC: Duke University Press, 2005).

31. Thomas L. Riis, *Frank Loesser* (New Haven, CT: Yale University Press, 2008), 167, 171.

32. Stephen Suskin, *Opening Nights on Broadway: A Critical Quotebook of the Golden Era of the Musical Theatre* (New York: Schrimmer Books, 1990), 325; Howard Taubman, "Musical Comedy Seen at 46th Street Theatre," *New York Times*, October 16, 1961, 34.

33. Robert Emmet Long, *Broadway, the Golden Years: Jerome Robbins and the Great Choreographer-Directors, 1940 to the Present* (New York: Continuum, 2002), 157.

34. Stewart, Adams, and Strouse, *Bye Bye Birdie*, 8.

35. Abe Burrows, Jack Weinstock, Willie Gilbert, and Frank Loesser, *How to Succeed in Business without Really Trying* (London: Frank Music Co., 1963), 11.

36. Stewart, Adams, and Strouse, *Bye Bye Birdie*, 9.

37. Burrows et al., *How to Succeed*, 11.

38. Ibid.

39. Ibid., 12–13.

40. Qtd. in Riis, *Frank Loesser*, 172.

41. For twenty-first-century cultural critics, the question remains whether the witty musical ultimately critiques or reinforces the negative images it perpetuates. For contrasting interpretations of Rosemary's agency, see Scott Miller, "How to Succeed in Business without Really Trying," in *From "Assassins" to "West Side Story": The Director's Guide to Musical Theatre* (Portsmouth NH: Heinemann, 1996), 95–108; and Stuart J. Hecht, *Transposing Broadway: Jews, Assimilation, and the American Musical* (New York: Palgrave, 2011), 89–92. Both readings are, I think, entirely persuasive, and a production team would need to choose which angle to stress to find ways to give Rosemary power and choice.

42. Burrows et al., *How to Succeed*, 5, 11.

43. Jessica Weiss, *To Have and to Hold: Marriage, the Baby Boom, and Social Change* (Chicago: University of Chicago Press, 2000), 17.

44. Katherine J. Lehman, *Those Girls: Single Women in Sixties and Seventies Popular Culture* (Lawrence: University Press of Kansas, 2011), 20.

45. "Attitudes of American Women," June 1962, iPOLL Databank, Roper Center for Public Opinion Research, Cornell University https://ropercenter.cornell.edu/attitudes-american-women-1962/.

46. Qtd. in Alice Kessler-Harris, *Out to Work: A History of Wage-Earning Women in the United States* (New York: Oxford University Press, 1982), 302.

47. Qtd. in Elaine Tyler May, *Homeward Bound: American Families in the Cold War Era* (New York: Basic Books, 1988), 98.

48. Friedan, *Feminine Mystique*, 37.

49. Coontz, *Strange Stirring*, 9.

50. Ibid., 9.

51. Lehman, *Those Girls*, 20.

52. The professions listed were dominated by men, at 95 percent, 97 percent, 97 percent, and 78 percent, respectively. Louis Menand, "Books as Bombs: Why the Women's Movement Needed 'The Feminine Mystique,'" *New Yorker*, January 24, 2011, http://www.newyorker.com/arts/critics/books/2011/01/24/110124crbo_books_menand.

53. Lisa Parks, "Watching the 'Working Gals': Fifties Sitcoms and the Repositioning of Women in Postwar American Culture," *Critical Matrix* 11.2 (June 30, 1999): 8. Also see Lynn Peril, *Swimming in the Steno Pool: A Retro Guide to Making It in the Office* (New York: Norton, 2011).

54. Qtd. in Parks, "Watching," 8.

55. Janann Sherman, ed., *Interviews with Betty Friedan* (Jackson: University Press of Mississippi, 2002), 6. First published as Jane Howard, "Betty Friedan's Pet Pique: The Feminine Mystique—Angry Battler for her Sex," *Life*, November 1, 1963, 84–88.

56. Scott Sherman, "The Long Good-Bye," *Vanity Fair*, November 30, 2012, http://www.vanityfair.com/culture/2012/11/1963-newspaper-strike-bertram-powers.

57. Review by Lucy Freeman, *New York Times*, April 7, 1963.

58. Later scholars have critiqued Friedan's not entirely accurate account of the mass media and her somewhat fictionalized representation of herself and her life. Still, they agree that the book is an important and fascinating document of its historical moment. See, for example, Joanne Meyerowitz, "Beyond the Feminine Mystique: A Reassessment of Postwar Mass Culture, 1946–1958," in *Not June Cleaver: Women and Gender in Postwar America, 1945–1960*, ed. Joanne Meyerowitz (Philadelphia: Temple University Press, 1994), 229–62; Daniel Horowitz, *Betty Friedan and the Making of "The Feminine Mystique": The American Left, the Cold War, and Modern Feminism* (Amherst: University of Massachusetts Press, 2000); Hasia Diner, Shira Kohn, and Rachel Kranson, eds., *A Jewish Feminine Mystique?: Jewish Women in Postwar America* (New Brunswick, NJ: Rutgers University Press, 2010); Alice Echols, "Nothing Distant about It: Women's Liberation and Sixties Radicalism," in *The Sixties from Memory to History*, ed. David Farber (Chapel Hill: University of North Carolina Press, 1994), 149–74; Weiss, *To Have and to Hold*, 54–61.

59. Menand, "Books as Bombs"; Patricia Bradley, *Mass Media and the Shaping of American Feminism, 1963–1975* (Jackson: University Press of Mississippi, 2003), 11–13.

60. Matthews, *Just a Housewife*, 219.

61. Bradley, *Mass Media*, 11.

62. Ibid.

63. Ibid., 13.

64. Ibid.

65. Coontz, *Strange Stirring*, 5–6; Weiss, *To Have and to Hold*, 49, 62.

66. Coontz, *Strange Stirring*, 5–6. Plant argues that in fact Friedan added to the damaging anti-Mom attitudes that began in the 1960s, becoming a strange bedfellow with conservative writers like Philip Wylie.

67. Qtd. in Menand, "Books as Bombs."

68. Coontz, *Strange Stirring*, 32–33; qtd. in Menand, "Books as Bombs."

69. In the story about *Fiddler*'s creation that is repeated in virtually every interview, article, and scholarly account of the musical, Jerome Robbins fretted about what the musical was "about." The other creators would offer plot summaries ("It's about a poor dairyman whose daughters get married"), but Robbins was searching for the musical's theme, its concept, an image that would unify the whole, which was, ultimately "tradition." See, for example, Thomas S. Hischak, *Boy Loses Girl: Broadway's Librettists* (New York: Scarecrow Press, 2002), 192; Philip Lambert, *To Broadway, To Life! The Musical Theater of Bock and Harnick* (New York: Oxford University Press, 2011), 170; Richard Altman *The Making of a Musical: "Fiddler on the Roof,"* with Mervyn Kaufman (New York: Crown, 1971). Also see "Sheldon Harnick," in Bryer and Davison, *Art of the American Musical*, 73–94.

70. Elizabeth Hardwick, "Theatre: 'Fiddler on the Roof'/'Traveller without Luggage,'" *Vogue*, November 1, 1964, 66.

71. Joseph Stein, Jerry Bock, and Sheldon Harnick, *Fiddler on the Roof* (New York: Music Theatre International, 1964), 67.

72. Raymond Knapp, *The American Musical and the Formation of National Identity* (Princeton, NJ: Princeton University Press, 2005), 219.

73. Ibid.

74. Stein, Bock, and Harnick, *Fiddler on the Roof*, 17–18.

75. Ibid., 19.

76. Ibid., 20.

77. Ibid., 19–20.

78. Knapp, *American Musical*, 223.

79. In addition, what started as an extended ballet for Chava was eventually cut to the "brief but moving" little song "Chavaleh," which Tevye sings while the daughters, their husbands, Golde, and the Fiddler do a little pantomime "memory ballet" behind the scrim. Altman, *Making of a Musical*, 55.

80. Knapp, *American Musical*, 219.

81. Lambert, *To Broadway*, 160.

82. Stein, Bock, and Harnick, *Fiddler on the Roof*, 116.

83. Lambert, *To Broadway*, 159.

84. Stein, Bock, and Harnick, *Fiddler on the Roof*, 116.

85. Ibid., 118; Lambert, *To Broadway*, 159.

86. Ronald L. Davis, *Mary Martin: Broadway Legend* (Norman: University of Oklahoma Press, 2008), 236.

87. Qtd. in Tom Jones, introduction to *I Do! I Do! Director's Stage Guide* (New York: Music Theatre International, 1966), n.p.

88. Walter Kerr, "Theatre: Musical *I Do! I Do!* Arrives," *New York Times*, December 6, 1966, 58.

89. This was Martin's last musical. Davis, *Mary Martin*, 237.

90 Ibid., 238.

91. Long, *Broadway*, 202.

92. Tom Jones and Harvey Schmidt, *I Do! I Do!* (New York: Music Theatre International, 1966), I-2.

93. Steven Suskin, *Show Tunes*, 3rd ed. (New York: Oxford University Press, 2000), 307.

94. Jones and Schmidt, *I Do! I Do!*, I-55.

95. Ibid., I-63.

96. Ibid., I-21.

97. Ibid., I-58–59.

98. Ibid., I-56.

99. Ibid., II-24.

100 Ibid., II-26.

101. Ibid.

102. Qtd. in Weiss, *To Have and to Hold*, 61.

Harvey Young

The Long Shadow of *A Raisin in the Sun*

A sense of exhaustion, a deep—to the bones—tiredness, fills the opening moments of Lorraine Hansberry's *A Raisin in the Sun*. As the lights rise on the set, a tenement apartment in the Chicago area, it is immediately evident that both its residents and even their furniture are nearly worn out. "Weariness has, in fact, won in this room. . . . All pretenses but living itself have long since vanished from the very atmosphere," writes Hansberry.[1] The Youngers, who once were lively and happy, and even their furniture, formerly new, are now overworked. They are worn and stretched thin by the stress and strain of everyday life. A glimmer of hope enters this dismal setting through death. The recent passing of the family patriarch and the imminent arrival of his insurance money offer the promise of escape from the Youngers' hardships. Unfortunately, the life insurance check, when it arrives, will be insufficient to cover the costs associated with helping all of the Youngers to achieve their dreams. Choices will have to be made and, undoubtedly, more than one dream will be deferred.

A Raisin in the Sun premiered in New Haven, Connecticut, in January 1959, the first of a series of pre-Broadway "tryout" performances followed by stints in Philadelphia and Chicago before the opening in New York City on March 11, 1959. Moving from city to city, the production garnered increasingly positive reviews from critics, who praised the play for its ability to capture the struggle of working-class life and for its presentation of easily identifiable characters. Audiences understood Walter Lee, a chauffeur, and sympathized with his struggles with his mother, Lena; felt for his long-suffering wife, Ruth; and marveled at his sister Beneatha's joie de vivre. This identification is particularly noteworthy considering that the Youngers are African American. More than one critic praised Hansberry, a first-time professional playwright, for her ability to write black characters who were relatable to nonblack audiences. Reviewers frequently asserted that *A Raisin in the Sun* was not about the particular experiences of African Americans even though a pivotal moment in the play hinges on how the Youngers' complexions threaten the realization of their dream to move to a newer and bigger house.

Much has been written about *A Raisin in the Sun*, the first drama on Broadway penned by a black woman and directed by an African American. It has been noted that the play retells Hansberry's experience of living in Chicago and being one of the first families to legally challenge racial restriction of neighborhoods. It has been argued that the free-spirited character Beneatha *is* Hansberry. Scholars have looked at draft versions of the play, originally preserved by the executor of Hansberry's estate (and the playwright's ex-husband), Robert Nemiroff, and have explored how the tone of *A Raisin in the Sun* evolved throughout rehearsals and, later, the tryout performances.

This chapter centers on the connection that *A Raisin in the Sun* has with the theater of the 1960s. It chronicles how the play demonstrated to producers that a mainstream white audience as well as a sizable black audience would welcome a nearly all-black production. It points to the many careers that were launched by the 1959 play and contends that the success of *A Raisin in the Sun* enabled the development of black theater over the next decade. It is difficult to identify a major African American theater artist from the 1960s whose own career and professional identity were not touched by the long shadow of Hansberry's play. This chapter concludes by situating the play temporally among a series of artistic and political movements: the British New Wave, African independence movements, and the Black Arts Movement.

BROADWAY BOUND

A Raisin in the Sun introduces a topic that was familiar to most theater audiences in the 1950s: housing segregation. Despite the fact that the Supreme Court had struck down racial segregation within public schools a few years earlier, in 1955, integration elsewhere would occur *slowly* over subsequent decades. In 1956 the Montgomery Bus Boycott, a coordinated campaign sponsored by the Montgomery Improvement Association and triggered by the arrest and incarceration of a young social worker and case investigator who actively chose to sit in a racially restricted section of a public bus, brought national attention to the topic of racial segregation and, ultimately, succeeded in ending the practice within public transportation systems. In 1958, as William O'Ree, the first black professional hockey player, broke the color barrier in his sport, newspapers were reporting that film actor Sidney Poitier was determined to bring a play by a twenty-seven-year-old playwright to Broadway later that year. Although the "Great White Way," as the theater district was known, for its bright white lights that illuminated the streets in the evening, had a long history of featuring African American performers, the presence of black artists on its stages had noticeably declined within recent decades as the perceived appeal of black musicals had waned and, perhaps, as some producers may have sensed a lack of interest among white theatergoers in witnessing stories about the black experience. Although the occasional all-black or mostly black production would appear on Broadway, interest in presenting such plays had fallen since the 1930s and 1940s.

Early newspaper articles make it abundantly clear that the initial draw of this new Broadway-bound production, *A Raisin in the Sun*, was actor Sidney Poitier. By the early 1950s, the actor had won acclaim and wide recognition for appearing in such films as *The Blackboard Jungle, Edge of the City*, and most recently, *The Defiant Ones*. His attachment to the project proved instrumental in attracting the attention of both the press and, later, audiences. An April 26, 1958, article in the *New York Herald-Tribune*, published almost a year before the play would open on Broadway, led with the following headline: "Poitier Is Returning to Broadway to Play in 'A Raisin in the Sun.'"[2] Similarly, the *New York Times* had reported two weeks earlier that

> Sidney Poitier intends to return next season to Broadway in "A Raisin in the Sun," written by a 27-year-old Negro playwright Lorraine Hansberry. Lloyd Richards is to be the director. Philip Rose, the producer.[3]

At that time Sidney Poitier was the *only* actor linked to the production, and therefore the play was seen as a star vehicle for him.

The press coverage of the play in preproduction rarely provides a glimpse of the difficulties and challenges of bringing the story of the Younger family to a Broadway stage. With one exception, articles announce Poitier's intention without offering any way of gauging the likelihood of the film star realizing it. The *New York Herald-Tribune*, speaking of Poitier, notes that "the actor began his stage career in 1946 in 'Lysistrata,' which ran for four performances."[4] Certainly the lack of success of that production cast a cloud over *A Raisin in the Sun*. It raised a series of questions. Would the play succeed? In light of Poitier's previous failure on Broadway, could the actor—now a celebrity—find success with a play by a little-known playwright? In other coverage, newspapers presumably repeat assurances by the core production team that *A Raisin in the Sun* would appear on Broadway. Indeed, the inevitability of the production, which promised to break the metaphorical racial glass ceiling in the arts, was mentioned in the press. Lewis Funke, writing for the *New York Times*, contends, "Available information, for instance, indicates that it will be the first play on Broadway written by a Negro woman. . . . Also, Mr. Rose has engaged Lloyd Richards to direct and Mr. Richards, it appears, would be the first Negro to guide a Broadway product."[5] The transformative potential of the play was recognized before casting had been completed and rehearsals begun.

The play's steady march to Broadway was covered by the press. In mid-September 1958, the *New York Herald-Tribune* reported that rehearsals were scheduled to begin on December 15. The following month the *Chicago Defender* outlined the play's production schedule: "The show opens in January in New Haven for a week, followed by appearances in Boston, Philadelphia and Broadway in late January."[6] In early December the *Herald-Tribune* noted that the production schedule was slightly delayed—"will start rehearsals Dec. 27"—and that it "is due here [on Broadway] the week of February 8th, after stops in New Haven and Philadelphia."[7] Within these articles were updates on the casting of the show—the hiring of Claudia McNeil "for a leading role" and of Ruby Dee, who "played Poitier's wife in *Edge of the City*," Louis Gossett Jr., and Diana Sands.[8]

Despite the press attention, newspapers did not report on the specific plot points in Poitier's new play. There is no mention of the Younger family's battle against housing segregation or reference to the emotional toll that race relations has on their lives. This omission, likely encouraged by the production team, probably sought to distance the play from the racial tensions that were occurring within society at large. Surely people would assume that a play featuring Poitier, written by a black playwright, costarring an almost all-black cast, and directed by a black director would tackle issues related to the African American experience. In April 1958 the *New York Times* offered the following description of *A Raisin in the Sun*: "The drama about a Chicago Negro family's struggle to achieve middle-class living standards will be performed by a Negro and white cast."[9] This summary, which spotlights the presence of an integrated cast, hints at housing segregation. The *Herald-Tribune*, in articles appearing in both November and December of the same year, described the play as being "about a middle-class Negro family in Chicago with social aspirations."[10] The similar language that appeared in different newspapers over an eight-month period of time likely was inspired by press material made available to reporters by the production team. If that is the case, then it is clear that producers viewed—or at least promoted—the play as being about class and not strictly about race. It was a story about the possibilities of class ascendance and not necessarily about racial equality. Later reviews of the production, perhaps adopting the analytical frame provided by these early reports, would similarly note that the play was about realizing the American Dream of upward class mobility and that the central characters in this play *just happened* to be black. This marketing approach was a savvy move to downplay the centrality of race in a production that was still recruiting investors and paving a path to Broadway.

Despite the positive reviews its premiere in New Haven earned, the possibility of the show moving to Broadway appeared to be in question. The *Chicago Defender* reported, on January 27, 1959, that "though a [Broadway] theatre has not yet been secured in New York, 'A Raisin in the Sun' is expected to make its debut on the Big Street about mid-February."[11] Interestingly, on the same day, the *Chicago Daily Tribune* referred to Hansberry's play as "now on tryout tour" and announced that the production would soon arrive in Chicago for "a 3-week engagement in the Blackstone Theater, opening Feb. 8 or 9."[12] Indeed, the play would open at the Blackstone during the week that it was supposed to have premiered on the "Great White Way." For the first time since the play was announced ten months earlier, there appeared to be some doubt about the likelihood of a Broadway theater being made available for the production. It is possible that this challenge could have been prompted by postopening awareness of the play's handling of racial themes. It might have been the initially slow ticket sales for the original New Haven production, which eventually became a best seller thanks to positive word of mouth. It may have been the warm but not necessarily glowing critical reviews, which noted the play's potential but added that it still required revision and edits. It certainly could be attributed to the challenges associated with raising sufficient funds to finance a Broadway show. The production's three-week residency in Chicago provided an opportunity to respond to these stalling elements, allowing it to attract new investors, to revise the play, and to collect more (and more positive) reviews. The Chicago production met these goals and, in response to the resulting critical acclaim and strong ticket sales, a Broadway theater was made available for *A Raisin in the Sun*. The production opened on March 11, 1959, at the Barrymore Theatre, where it ran for over a year and more than five hundred performances.

A Raisin in the Sun was celebrated for its many firsts. It also was praised for offering a glimpse into the life of an African American family to whom audiences could relate. Critics, perhaps influenced by press materials, were quick to highlight Hansberry's ability to script a social drama about the travails of individuals without overly emphasizing race politics. The *New Haven Evening Register* noted that the play "involves its people deeply in the currents of today's Negro living but never sacrifices their individuality to politics or social symbolism."[13] Claudia Cassiday, writing for the *Chicago Daily Tribune*, told her readers, "You care about these people from the first scene." She described Walter Lee Younger, the character played by Poitier, "as the angry young man who happens to be a Negro."[14] Reviewing the same Chicago production, Darcy DeMille, reporting for the *Los Angeles Sentinel,* asserted that the "family could in fact be Italian, Jewish or Polish. The time and place could be Anywhere, U.S.A."[15] Brooks Atkinson, commenting on the Broadway production, praised it for its honesty and aligned it with a theatrical classic: "You might, in fact, regard 'A Raisin in the Sun' as a Negro 'The Cherry Orchard.'"[16]

A LAUNCHING PAD

The success of *A Raisin the Sun,* which won the New York Drama Critics' Circle award for Best American Play, significantly enhanced the careers of its core ensemble. Whereas Sidney Poitier originally was viewed as the only bankable star in the production, the majority of the company became recognizable names within the world of professional theater in the 1960s. The play either launched or improved the careers of Sidney Poitier, Ruby Dee (Ruth), Ossie Davis (who assumed the role of Walter Lee after Poitier), Douglas Turner Ward (moving man), Diana Sands (Beneatha), Louis Gossett Jr. (George Murchison), and Lloyd Richards.

Poitier's "halo effect," lending his celebrity to help raise public awareness about the production, proved crucial to the play's success. While the play was in production and playing in New Haven, Philadelphia, and Chicago, Philip Rose was still actively recruiting small investors. In the end, 150 people would help finance the production. The fundraising drive had to have been made easier by the fact that Rose's lead actor was enjoying tremendous success with his latest film, *The Defiant Ones* (1958), costarring Tony Curtis. Poitier's performance won wide acclaim among critical and popular audiences and earned him an Academy Award nomination. When Poitier stood onstage at the Barrymore Theatre on Broadway in March 1959, he had become a bankable film star whose box-office appeal succeeded in attracting unconventional theater audiences. African American spectators purchased tickets both to be in the presence of a popular film actor but also to witness a story that, through word of mouth, they realized concerned their lived experience. The production of *A Raisin in the Sun* presented a variety of firsts for audiences who, only a few years after the Supreme Court ruling banning segregation in public schools, likely understood that the society within which they lived was changing. The Broadway stage offered a glimpse at the shifts that would occur over the next decade.

Poitier's career in the 1960s reveals the dramatic social changes occurring. As Aram Goudsouzian observes in his biography of the actor, Poitier "had become American popular culture's foremost expression of racial possibilities."[17] In 1961 Poitier reprised the role of Walter Lee with a mostly reunited company, including producer Philip Rose, for the film version of *A Raisin in the Sun*. The film, which was sparingly distributed within southern movie houses out of concern that it would create racial unrest, received warm praise and garnered Golden Globe acting awards for Poitier and Claudia McNeil. Although the cinematic adaptation did not succeed in becoming the hit that the stage play was, it captured the power of the original production and exposed it to new audiences across the globe. The film was even screened at the Cannes Film Festival.

By the early 1960s, Sidney Poitier was actively and visibly involved in the U.S. civil rights movement. During the March on Washington, the film star stood at the Lincoln Memorial as Dr. Martin Luther King Jr. delivered his "I Have a Dream" speech. In one widely circulated image from that event, he stands alongside Harry Belafonte and Charlton Heston. The following year, 1964, Poitier became the first African American to win an Academy Award as a lead actor in a motion picture for *Lilies in the Field*. Media mogul Oprah Winfrey recalls the importance of his celebrity in the early 1960s:

> I am 10 years old, black people are still "colored"—and colored folks don't ride in limousines unless their kinfolk have just died. I press my knees into the cold linoleum and stare into our RCA black-and-white TV. My mouth falls open as a towering Sidney Poitier steps from a limo and into the Academy Awards. Awe. Freeze. Thaw. Run. "Everybody, come see: A colored man is in a limo—and nobody's died!" The next day—the next moment—I see myself in an entirely new way.[18]

Sidney Poitier, the only mainstream African American film star, helped African Americans to envision their own possibilities. For the remainder of the decade the celebrity starred in film after film, and by 1967 he had become the most commercially successful actor of any race working in the film industry. Poitier's global celebrity made him and his films veritable lightning rods for criticism. Was he a fighter for black equality or, as his detractors had labeled him, was he an "Uncle Tom"? Poitier, reflecting on the period following the 1968 assassination of Martin Luther King Jr., recalls "people turning on [him]."

> It was painful for a couple years. . . . I was the most successful black actor in the history of the country. I was not in control of the kinds of films I would be offered, but I was totally in control of the kinds of films I would do. So I came to the mix with that power—the power to say, "No, I will not do that." I did that from the beginning. Back then, Hollywood was a place in which there had never been a *To Sir, With Love*, *The Defiant Ones*, *In the Heat of the Night* or *Guess Who's Coming to Dinner*. Nothing like it. What the name-

callers missed was that the films I did were designed not just for blacks but for the mainstream. I was in concert with maybe a half-dozen filmmakers, and they were all white. And they chose to make films that would make a statement to a mainstream audience about the awful nature of racism.[19]

The critiques that Poitier received closely resembled those that would be levied against *A Raisin in the Sun* toward the end of the decade. By the late 1960s the integrationist vision of the 1950s increasingly was dismissed as being assimilationist. Against the backdrop of a Black Arts aesthetic that demanded the creation of black art for black people, the seemingly token blackness in Poitier's films became the antithesis of everything that the younger, newer generation of black artists were seeking to develop. Sidney Poitier and his oeuvre, including *A Raisin in the Sun*, were not revolutionary and certainly no longer progressive to this new audience. By the early 1970s both the play and its most famous actor were heavily critiqued and outright shunned. Poitier eventually retreated into a self-imposed exile before reemerging, several years later, as a film director who specialized in mainstream films that frequently featured a black protagonist and commented on contemporary race relations through the comedy genre.

Whereas Poitier frequently was challenged and called upon to defend his blackness despite his contributions to the civil rights movement, Ossie Davis and Ruby Dee found their embrace within black communities, particularly black theater communities, to be long held. The couple, who had married in the late 1940s and toward the end of the Broadway run of *A Raisin in the Sun* had played the roles of Walter Lee and Ruth, continued to actively work in the world of professional theater and film, with the majority of their projects targeting an African American audience. Ruby Dee, describing her professional career during this period as "busy," notes that neither she nor her husband had attained the heights of celebrity reached by their more famous friends, such as actor-singer Harry Belafonte, and had to support themselves through a series of "odd jobs" within the performing arts.[20] They assumed roles onstage and on the television screen, directed and starred in short films, and in general, lived the lives of working actors.

Ruby Dee's simple description—"odd jobs"—understates how active and high profile she and her husband were in the early 1960s. One year after *A Raisin in the Sun* closed on Broadway, the couple were back on the Great White Way in a play penned by Davis. *Purlie Victorious*, buoyed by audiences' desire to see Dee and Davis together again and, perhaps, to witness the next Broadway hit featuring a majority black cast, ran for nine months and more than 250 performances. Despite not being a smashing commercial success like Hansberry's play, it ran longer than two of the four plays nominated for a Tony Award that year—Paddy Chayefsky's *Gideon* and Harold Pinter's *The Caretaker*—and nearly as long as a third nominee, Tennessee Williams's *Night of the Iguana*.[21] Similar to *A Raisin in the Sun*, the play was adapted into a film, *Gone Are the Days* (1963). At the close of the decade, *Purlie Victorious* was adapted into a musical (*Purlie*, 1970) that ran on Broadway for two years. The production, produced by Philip Rose, likely inspired Robert Nemiroff to create a musical version of *A Raisin in the Sun*. *Raisin* (1973), the musical, similarly was more successful than the original. Major critics frequently observed that it might be "even better than the play."[22] Despite the tremendous success that Dee and Davis achieved onstage, they never reached the star status of screen icons like Poitier, Lena Horne, or Harry Belafonte.

In a way, their comparatively lower wattage celebrity coupled with their sustained work in the New York theater community protected them from the negative backlash that Poitier received. Not having to worry about their mainstream image, particularly their appeal to white audiences, they could be even more active and vocal in the movement for civil rights. The two actively supported the social change efforts of both Martin Luther King Jr. and Malcolm X. In 1963 they served as emcees at the March on Washington. The couple befriended Malcolm X through Dee's brother, whom she describes as a "devotee of Malcolm."[23] Following the assassination of Malcolm X in 1965, the slain leader's legacy would be defined, in part, by Ossie Davis, who delivered the eulogy. As Keith Byron Kirk asserts, a eulogy can be understood as an "ordering factor" that selects and places emphasis on particular episodes in a person's life with the aim of giving context to the life lived and structuring how others will remember the deceased following the funeral ceremony.[24] Davis's eulogy did this. He proclaimed,

> It is not in the memory of man that this beleaguered, unfortunate, but nonetheless proud community has found a braver, more gallant young champion than this Afro-American who lies before us—unconquered still. I say the word again, as he would want me to: Afro-American—Afro-American Malcolm, who was a master, was most meticulous in his use of words. Nobody knew better than he the power words have over minds of men. Malcolm had stopped being a "Negro" years ago. It had become too small, too puny, too weak a word for him. Malcolm was bigger than that. Malcolm had become an Afro-American and he wanted—so desperately—that we, that all his people, would become Afro-Americans too.[25]

With these words, Davis not only pronounced Malcolm X to be a "champion," thus defending his legacy against critics, but also gave a sense of renewed urgency to the leader's efforts to reappropriate the image of blackness and infuse it with a sense of beauty, strength, and indeed, possibility. Davis and Dee's close relationship with Malcolm X would insulate them from the type of backlash that was directed toward Sidney Poitier. Older than the relatively youthful leaders of the Black Arts Movement, they widely were viewed as respected elders, as evidenced in Woodie King Jr.'s documentary film *Black Theater: The Making of a Movement* (1978).[26]

Douglas Turner Ward, an actor and playwright, was catapulted from relative obscurity in the aftermath of *A Raisin in the Sun* and by the end of the 1960s proved to be an outspoken—and often cited—champion of black theater. His one-act plays *Happy Ending* and *Day of Absence* (1965) were two of the more significant plays of the Black Arts Movement. Both call attention to the vital contributions that African Americans make to everyday life. In *Day of Absence*, Ward asks what would happen if every black person in society disappeared. Waking up one morning to discover that all blacks are gone, white Americans are forced to realize that everything on which they depend requires the labor of African Americans. Without black folks, society cannot function, and chaos results. In *Happy Ending*, he points out the hypocrisy of younger folks who critique their parents for working in service industries and, perhaps, associate that work as being akin to plantation-era servitude by noting that that labor has financially supported black families and therefore deserves acknowledgment and respect.

Ward's most significant contribution to American theater, particularly in the 1960s, was his advocacy for the development of community theaters. Having witnessed the struggle to raise sufficient capital to bring *A Raisin in the Sun* to Broadway and to convince theater owners to make their stages available, the actor-playwright urged the creation of smaller scale productions in local communities. He essentially agreed with theater critic Harold Clurman that "a theater which depends entirely on the production of immediate smash hits is doomed."[27] Ward was particularly critical of Broadway-like venues, which he described in 1966 as "a pretentious theatre elevating the narrow preoccupations of restricted class interests to inflated universal significance, tacitly assuming that its middle-class, affluent-oriented assumptions are central to the dominant human condition."[28] The playwright urged artists to create theater where they lived. Cecil Smith, summarizing a conversation with Ward, writes in a 1967 *Los Angeles Times* article, "The hope is, he said, that the 'ghetto' theater will spread, these people will march into the center of the city and re-shape the American theater into the institution it ought to be."[29] In support of black theater, Ward cofounded the Negro Ensemble Company (NEC) in 1967. The NEC, recipient of a special Tony Award in 1969, has served as the incubator of new black playwriting for five decades. It existed (and still exists) as a theatrical home for a wide range of African Americans, whose achievements on stage and screen have revised the popular representation of blackness. NEC alumni include Al Freeman Jr., Sherman Helmsley, Cleavon Little, Esther Rolle, and Denzel Washington. The company has served as the model for numerous black theater organizations, including Chicago's Black Ensemble Theatre and Congo Square Theatre Company.[30]

The careers of other company members similarly prospered in the years following the Broadway run of *A Raisin in the Sun*. Although a couple unsuccessful Broadway productions in the 1960s temporarily stalled Richards's directing career on the Great White Way, he was widely celebrated and revered for his ability to identify and nurture talent in others. This role of artistic mentor led to his nearly thirty-year (1968–98) residency as artistic director of the National Playwright's Conference at the Eugene O'Neill Theater Center and his twelve years (1979–91) of service as dean of Yale Drama School. It was during his tenure at the O'Neill and Yale that he identified a promising new playwright named August Wilson and directed that playwright's first six plays on Broadway. In 1987 he won a Tony Award for his direction of Wilson's *Fences*.

Diana Sands worked continuously until her untimely death in 1973. In 1962 she originated the role of Sarah in Adrienne Kennedy's *Funnyhouse of a Negro* in a workshop production directed by Edward Albee. The following year she appeared opposite Alan Alda, who had also appeared in both the play and film versions of *Purlie Victorious*, in *The Owl and the Pussycat*. Although the casting of an interracial couple initially was deemed controversial, the production ran for a year and earned Sands a Tony Award nomination. She would receive another nomination for her performance in James Baldwin's *Blues for Mister Charlie* (1965). For the remainder of her short career, she steadily worked onstage, in television, and in film. In 1970 she reteamed with Louis Gossett Jr. in the film *Landlord*.

Louis Gossett Jr., who, at the age of twenty-three, was the second youngest person in the *A Raisin in the Sun* company, had previously experienced Broadway success six years earlier in Louis Peterson's *Take a Giant Step*. He viewed this most recent opportunity to work alongside Poitier as an extended mentorship.

> I idolized the man so much that all I wanted was to be him. . . . I adored his style, his panache. He was a self-made man, the kind I have always respected. I knew that he and Harry Belafonte were friends, and to me that was the way black men should be. They were stars, as well as clean, handsome, talented, responsible, and funny men.[31]

This opportunity to closely observe and emulate Poitier would help Gossett to become one of the most accomplished black actors of the latter half of the twentieth century. In the 1970s he appeared in the television miniseries *Roots* and won an Emmy Award for his portrayal of Fiddler, the character who helps Kunta Kinte transition into slave life. In the early 1980s he won an Academy Award for Best Supporting Actor for playing a drill sergeant in *An Officer and a Gentleman*. When Gossett won the Academy Award, he was the third black actor to win the award and the first since Poitier received it twenty-five years earlier.

AHEAD OF THE TIMES, ALSO BEHIND

In 1958, when the press was announcing Poitier's plans to return to Broadway in a vehicle penned by a "27-year-old Negro playwright," another playwright, the same age as Hansberry, also captured critical attention. John Osborne, the English dramatist, had earned a Tony Award nomination for his play *Look Back in Anger* (1956). Osborne would lose to Dore Schary, a playwright who was his elder by twenty-four years, but the younger playwright's emergence signaled a generational shift within contemporary theater. He, alongside a crop of "angry young" British artists, cast a critical eye on the operations of class within British society and captured the malaise and frustration of their generation. Although Hansberry writes from a different cultural, national, racial, and gendered perspective, she allies with this group of revolutionary artists in her ability to reflect upon her lived experiences with an undisguised resentment, and even anger. From this particular vantage point, *A Raisin in the Sun* might be thought to exist somewhere between the impulses of the British New Wave and the Black Arts Movement.

Dan Rebellato opens *1956 and All That* with a summary of how critics often talk about the significance of Osborne's *Look Back in Anger*. The description resembles the words often employed to describe the achievement that was *A Raisin in the Sun*—with age substituting for race. He writes,

> New, youthful audiences flocked to the Royal Court Theatre to hear Jimmy Porter express their own hopes and fears. At a stroke, the old well-made dramatists were shown up as stale and cobwebbed.[32]

Rebellato, without disputing the significance of Osborne's arrival, urges a consideration of the many events of the period that supported a cultural shift sometimes *solely* attributed to Osborne. The same could be said for *A Raisin in the Sun*. It is not solely responsible for the embrace of black theater in the 1960s or the incorporation of sociopolitical themes in produced dramas. In addition to political protests and juridical pronouncements, the ability to talk about the experience of race on stage was made possible by other works of art. The tremendous success of the calypso musical *Jamaica* (1957), which had been playing on Broadway for more than a year when newspapers announced Poitier's intentions to stage *A Raisin in the Sun*, offered evidence of the potential box office draw of productions featuring majority black casts. The success of Hansberry's play can be attributed to audiences' proven thirst for a newer style of playwriting reflecting subjective experiences, a renewed interest in stories about black folk, and a desire to witness a dramatic narrative anchored in present-day sociopolitical concerns.

The truth of the experience portrayed on the stage contributed to the wide appeal of *A Raisin in the Sun* on Broadway. The play's ability to draw nontraditional theater audiences, essentially folks whose interests were previously ignored by theater producers, was noticeable and, occasionally, merited comment. James Baldwin, reflecting on the play's success, recalls, "I had never in my life seen so many black people in the theatre."[33] The play was both relevant and timely, as theater scholar Margaret Wilkerson has observed: "Rosa Parks' sudden refusal to move to the back of the bus, which became the catalyst for the historic Montgomery Bus Boycott, was mirrored in Lena Younger's political decision to live in Clybourne Park."[34] The success of the production demonstrated the desire to see black life—and the social and political realities faced by African Americans. This was noted in the positive reviews that the play received. Brooks Atkinson, writing for the *New York Times*, observed, "The play is honest. [Hansberry] has told the inner as well as the outer truth about a Negro family on the southside of Chicago at the present time."[35] Atkinson's comment echoes the earlier *New Haven Evening Register* review that praised the play for placing a spotlight on characters "deeply in the currents of today's Negro living."

Hansberry's centering on present-day political realities also appears in her representation of "Africa." As Sandra G. Shannon has observed, "In the early 1950s, Lorraine Hansberry was embroiled in a campaign to lessen the huge cultural gulf that separated the *African* and the *African-American*."[36] In the play, Beneatha, Walter Lee's younger sister, is courted by two men: George Murchison, a financially secure young man who is indifferent to politics, and Joseph Asagai, a Nigerian student with an infectious passion for black politics and culture. While the two men symbolize choices available to African Americans living in the 1950s—either integrate into society and risk losing one's blackness or celebrate an ancestral Africanness that lingers in the blood in order to preserve it, they more concretely offer Beneatha an opportunity to visualize two contrasting futures. She can embrace Africa and, in so doing, engage in sophisticated sociopolitical discourse or she can reject it. Certainly, Hansberry's politics, and arguably the influence of the "angry young" British playwrights, result in the fashioning of Asagai as a decidedly more appealing choice. The character introduces Beneatha to radical politics and the concept of social revolution: "I will teach and work and things will happen, slowly and swiftly. At times it will seem that nothing changes at all . . . and then again the sudden dramatic events which make history leap into the future."[37] Indeed, his influence is so significant within the play that playwright Kwame Kwei Armah felt compelled to write *Beneatha's Place* (2013), in which several scenes imagine an older Beneatha wed to Asagai and living in Lagos, Nigeria, in the 1960s.

Theater audiences likely were familiar with the colonial independence campaigns that were occurring in Africa. From the time that production plans for *A Raisin in the Sun* were first announced in April 1958 to the release of the film version of the stage play in 1961, twenty African countries had achieved independence. An additional twelve countries would become independent by the end of the 1960s. The development of an increasingly postcolonial Africa attracted the attention of African Americans not only because the campaigns invited parallels with the civil rights movement within the United States but also because the focus on African politics brought into view the cultural achievements of Africans across the massive continent. In the 1960s African American artists increasingly began to travel to the newly independent countries to learn about their histories and cultures and then to bring back the newly acquired performance vocabularies to share with American artists. For example, the vibrant African theater and dance scene that currently exists in Chicago roots itself in the 1960s travels of artists such as Darlene Blackburn, among others, who employed their bodies as bridges to span differing continental arts cultures.[38] *A Raisin in the Sun* anticipates this later exchange and literally stages the appeal of continental African history and culture for African Americans. Even Walter Lee, in an inebriated moment, gets caught up in his own fantasy of Africa.

African independence movements inspired select black nationalist leaders, such as Stokely Carmichael, who either traveled to the continent or frequently made reference to political events there in writings. In a 1966 article Carmichael noted, "The reality of black men ruling their own nations gives blacks elsewhere a sense of possibility, of power, which they do not now have."[39] Certainly the image of revolutionaries demanding freedom was appealing, perhaps especially to a younger generation of activists who would contend that nonviolent demonstrations were inadequate to respond to the murders of Medgar Evers and Martin Luther King Jr.

In the late 1950s, when nonviolent tactics were producing considerable social change and Evers and King were alive and actively working in support of civil rights, Lorraine Hansberry succeeded in scripting a play that hinted at the capacity of African Americans to enact more aggressive forms of protests. Margaret Wilkerson notes, "Black militancy born of anger, frustration and deferred dreams was captured in the explosive and desperate Walter Lee."[40] Economic exploitation and racial oppression are related for Hansberry's protagonist. He works as a chauffeur who drives a comparatively better resourced white businessman around. His frustration anchors itself in the fact that there is nothing that he can do to elevate his social standing without outside assistance (such as the death of his father and the arrival of the insurance money). He does not espouse violence. However, the severity of the swings in his mood, from the joy of believing that his entrepreneurial desires will be realized to the low of learning that he (along with his family) has been swindled, showcases the psychological strain attached to exploitation and oppression and hints at the animus of revolutionary spirit.

A decade after its premiere, the play was critiqued for being decidedly behind the times. *A Raisin in the Sun* represented everything that the new Black Arts Movement sought not to be. It was perceived to champion integration over blackness. It was a Broadway vehicle produced by a white lead producer rather than a play developed within and financed by (black) community theaters. The character of Lena Younger was dismissed by some as being mammy-like. Furthermore, the narrative structure of the play, which resembles the naturalistic style of late nineteenth- and early twentieth-century writers, was out of step with the more experimental forms of the decade, particularly the poetic and sometimes dreamlike approaches of Adrienne Kennedy and Amiri Baraka, among others. The criticism that *A Raisin in the Sun* received can be attributed to the relatively quick developments in the civil rights movement and to the reality that expressed politics cannot be held as being timeless. In 1945 the army was segregated; in 1955 the Supreme Court essentially declared all segregation to be illegal; in 1963 the March on Washington occurred; and in 1968 Martin Luther King Jr. was assassinated and the future direction of the civil rights movement was uncertain. Hansberry wrote *A Raisin in the Sun* in the shadow of Eugene O'Neill and Clifford Odets, before the emergence of Edward Albee and Adrienne Kennedy, and before experiencing the 1961 Broadway production of Jean Genet's *The Blacks*. Her play captures the societal mood at the dawn of the 1960s.

Nevertheless, the influence of *A Raisin the Sun* can be felt throughout the work of the Black Arts Movement. Margaret Wilkerson writes,

The Black Arts Movement of the 1960s seemed to burst on the American theatrical scene with no warning. The plays of LeRoi Jones (now Amiri Baraka), Ed Bullins, and others appeared, it seemed, from nowhere, called forth from hidden reserves of anger deep within the black community. Few had recognized the strains of militance in the earlier voice of Lorraine Hansberry.[41]

With these words, Wilkerson, anticipating Rebellato's caution, asserts that movements neither magically appear not sprout completely formed from a single source. The intervention that the esteemed scholar makes is to ground the Black Arts Movement, which is historically identified as masculinist, in the writings of a woman from the previous decade. To further push Wilkerson's intervention, it could be said that those "reserves of anger" might signal Hansberry's position as an artist who temporally worked between the British New Wave and the Black Arts Movement and whose dramaturgy reveals strains of both.

Traces of the influence of *A Raisin in the Sun* exists across several notable plays of the 1960s. Despite the fact that Amiri Baraka openly critiqued the play, only to revise his assessment later, there is a faint resemblance between George Murchison and the character Clay in *Dutchman*. Like George, Clay represents the integrated and assimilated black man. The difference, of course, is that Baraka scripts a character, Lula Lula, who harasses Clay about his race to the extent that a buried or suppressed anger emerges in the forefront. In a way, a similar emotional change occurs in *A Raisin in the Sun*, not in Clay but in Walter Lee, when Karl Lindner, the representative of the neighborhood where the Youngers are heading, tells the family that their blackness is objectionable to their future neighbors. Lindner aims to eliminate the threat of race by offering to buy back the home—which is a more peaceful form of race control than the option enacted in Baraka's play.

To a degree, Ward's *Happy Ending* and *Day of Absence* could be understood as a defense of *A Raisin in the Sun*. The backlash against Hansberry's drama frequently was directed against Lena Younger, who was memorably satirized by George C. Wolfe in his "Mama on the Couch" scene in *The Colored Museum* (1986). Wilkerson observes, "The perception of Lena Younger as a conservative, retarding force has been a difficult one to shed."[42] The concerns about Mama, a character imagined as deriving from the South, is that she, for some audiences, too closely resembles stereotypes of black women. Lena was a mammy. She is southern, sexless (perhaps as a result of her widowhood), religious, and domineering. What Ward demonstrates in both of his plays is that women like Lena Younger play a vital role both within society and within their own households.

Others thrive because of their hard work. Indeed, *A Raisin in the Sun* teaches that lesson. It is Lena Younger who loses her husband, opens her too small home to her children and grandchild, and, ultimately, travels (presumably alone) to a white neighborhood to look at and eventually to purchase a home.

A Raisin in the Sun is a play that looks back upon Hansberry's personal experiences with housing segregation in the 1930s and represents her memories in a manner than connects with the lived reality of theatrical audiences in the 1950s. In assessing the play, it is evident that its influence neither ended nor faded with the arrival a new decade. Although the political realities of the 1960s differed from those of the previous decade, both the play and its playwright cast a long shadow. A significant number of artists were affected by *A Raisin in the Sun*. Even those who critiqued the play, such as Amiri Baraka, still felt compelled to reconsider how their dramaturgy and politics resembled Hansberry's. For her part, Hansberry remained in the spotlight until her death in 1965, at the age of thirty-four. "An activist artist, she spoke at Civil Rights rallies and writers' conferences, and she confronted the U.S. Attorney General Robert Kennedy in a controversial meeting with black leaders about the role of the FBI in the Deep South," notes Wilkerson.[43] Her radical voice and activist politics are preserved in *A Raisin in the Sun*.

NOTES

1. Lorraine Hansberry, *A Raisin in the Sun*, in *Call & Response: The Riverside Anthology of the African American Literary Tradition*, ed. Patricia Liggins Hill with Bernard W. Bell, Trudier Harris, William J. Harris, R. Baxter Miller, Sonora A. O'Neal, and Horace A. Porter (New York: Houghton Mifflin, 1998), 1217.

2. "Poitier Is Returning to Broadway to Play in 'A Raisin in the Sun,'" *New York Herald Tribune*, April 26, 1958, 9.

3. Thomas M. Pryor, "Columbia May Develop Film of 'Seasaw,'" *New York Times*, April 12, 1958, 13.

4. "Poitier Is Returning," 9.

5. Lewis Funke, "News and Gossip of the Rialto," *New York Times*, April 27, 1958, xi.

6. "Poitier Set for Broadway Casting," *Chicago Daily Defender*, October 20, 1958, 19.

7. "'Raisin in the Sun' Rehearsals Set Dec. 27th," *New York Herald Tribune*, December 5, 1958, 15.

8. "First Revue of B'Way Season Opens Tonight at Royale Theater," *New York Herald Tribune*, November 11, 1958, 14; "'Raisin in the Sun' Rehearsals," 15; "Three Shows Add to Casts," *New York Times*, January 20, 1959, 20.

9. Pryor, "Columbia May Develop Film," 13.

10. "First Revue," 14; "'Raisin in the Sun' Rehearsals," 15.

11. "New Englanders Hail 'A Raisin in the Sun,'" *Chicago Daily Defender*, January 27, 1959, 18.

12. "Stage Note," *Chicago Daily Tribune*, January 27, 1959, A4.

13. Quoted in "New Englanders," 18.

14. Claudia Cassidy, "Warm Heart, Backbone, Funnybone in Blackstone Play and Cast," *Chicago Daily Tribune*, February 11, 1959, B1.

15. Darcy DeMille, "Says Negro Playwright Is a Genius," *Los Angeles Sentinel*, February 19, 1959, A7.

16. Brooks Atkinson, "A Raisin in the Sun," *New York Times*, March 12, 1959, 27.

17. Aram Goudsouzian, *Sidney Poitier: Man, Icon, Actor* (Chapel Hill: University of North Carolina Press, 2003), 188.

18. Oprah Winfrey, "Oprah Talks to Sidney Poitier," *O, the Oprah Magazine*, October 2000, http://www.oprah.com/omagazine/Oprah-Interviews-Sidney-Poitier.

19. Ibid.

20. "Ruby Dee," Archive of American Television, http://www.emmytvlegends.org/interviews/people/ruby-dee.

21. For number of performances, see Playbill Vault, http://www.playbillvault.com. The fourth nominee was Robert Bolt's *A Man for All Seasons*.

22. Clive Barnes, "'Raisin' in Musical Form," *New York Times*, October 19, 1973, 59.

23. "Ruby Dee."

24. Keith Bryon Kirk, "Eulogy as Mass Mobilization Narrative: Performing Commemorative Discourse in African American Civil Rights Funerals" (PhD diss., Northwestern University, 2013).

25. Ossie Davis, "Eulogy Delivered by Ossie Davis at the Funeral of Malcolm X," MalcolmX.com, http://www.malcolmx.com/eulogy/.

26. Woodie King Jr., *Black Theater: The Making of a Movement* (San Francisco: California Newsreel, 1978).

27. Harold Clurman, "Where Are the New Playwrights?," *New York Times*, June 7, 1964, SM26.

28. Douglas Turner Ward, "American Theater: For Whites Only?," *New York Times*, August 14, 1966, 93.

29. Cecil Smith, "Study of Negro in American Theater," *Los Angeles Times*, July 18, 1967, C8.

30. Harvey Young and Queen Meccasia Zabriskie, *Black Theater Is Black Life: An Oral History of Chicago Theater and Dance* (Evanston, IL: Northwestern University Press, 2014), 90, 110.

31. Louis Gossett Jr. and Phyllis Karas, *An Actor and a Gentleman* (Hoboken, NJ: John Wiley & Sons, 2010), 87.

32. Dan Rebellato, *1956 and All That: The Making of Modern British Drama* (London: Routledge, 1999), 1.

33. Adrienne Macki Braconi, "African American Women Dramatists, 1930–1960," in *The Cambridge Companion to African American Theatre*, ed. Harvey Young (Cambridge: Cambridge University Press, 2013), 120.

34. Margaret Wilkerson, "Anniversary of an American Classic," *Theatre Journal* 8.4 (1986): 444.

35. Atkinson, "A Raisin in the Sun," 27.

36. Sandra G. Shannon, "Women Who Cross Cultural Borders," in Young, *Cambridge Companion*, 224.

37. Hansberry, *Raisin in the Sun*, 1260–61.

38. Young and Zabriskie, *Black Theater*, 183, 191–221.

39. Stokely Carmichael, "What We Want," *New York Review of Books*, September 22, 1966, 5.

40. Wilkerson, "Anniversary," 444.

41. Margaret Wilkerson, "The Sighted Eyes and Feeling Heart of Lorraine Hansberry," *Black American Literature Forum* 17.1 (1983): 8.

42. Wilkerson, "Anniversary," 448.

43. Wilkerson, "Sighted Eyes," 8.

Stephen Bottoms

Selling the Ensemble

Hair, Oh! Calcutta!, *and Commercial Theater in the Late 1960s*

In American theater, as in the nation at large, the 1960s was a decade of cultural melting and blurring in which received distinctions between commercial and avant-garde, popular and experimental, high and low culture were thrown into question. "It was a period of integration," stresses director Tom O'Horgan, "in the sense that all things integrate, all aspects of life and all aspects of art. So much of what we were involved with was trying to meld this together."[1] There is an irony, then, in the fact that theater histories of the period tend to reinstate clear demarcation lines between that which is deemed politically or aesthetically progressive and that which is seen as mere "show business." Asked why his own accomplishments have been comparatively overlooked by posterity (when considered alongside the work of other experimental directors of the period, such as Joseph Chaikin, Judith Malina, or Richard Schechner), O'Horgan smiles wryly and replies, "Well of course, I made the big mistake of going to Broadway and being successful."

This chapter reexamines two of the most commercially successful stage shows of the late 1960s, both of which drew directly on the highly physicalized, ensemble-based staging methods also being explored within underground, avant-garde contexts. O'Horgan's production of the hippie musical *Hair*, by Gerome Ragni and James Rado, opened at Broadway's Biltmore Theatre in April 1968 and eventually ran for 1,750 performances, spawning simultaneous productions around the United States and worldwide. In 1969 its soundtrack (scored by Galt McDermot) spent thirteen weeks at the top of the album charts. That year also saw the opening of the erotic revue *Oh! Calcutta!*, which built directly on *Hair*'s controversial use of nudity. Though technically an off-Broadway show, opening in the East Village at the newly refurbished Eden

Theater, the venue's seating capacity of around twelve hundred was on par with the major Broadway houses. *Oh! Calcutta!* ran for 1,314 performances, closing in 1972, but four years later was remounted on Broadway by its original director, Jacques Levy. The revival played for an eye-watering 5,959 performances at the Edison Theatre before finally closing in 1989. As of 2016, it remained the seventh-longest-running show in Broadway history.

Both of these productions, as we will see, stood squarely upon foundations laid by the Open Theatre—the experimental acting ensemble that Gerome Ragni had helped to found (some say he christened it) and with which Jacques Levy had been an associate director. There is an irony here, insofar that the Open Theatre's inspirational leader, actor-director Joseph Chaikin, was deeply mistrustful of commercial theater and its lures. For some of his colleagues, however, this was an arena in which to reach wider audiences than could ever be accessed within the intimate spaces of the alternative, off-off-Broadway theater movement from which the Open Theatre had developed. In what follows, I will argue that both *Hair* and *Oh! Calcutta!* sought—albeit in very different ways—to capitalize on but also to challenge the commercial values of their production contexts, and to ask certain questions of their paying audiences. Although the politically progressive aspects of these performances became somewhat obscured by their sensationalized media treatment, I want to suggest that—far from merely "selling out" to commercial interests—these shows epitomize a moment in the late 1960s when the mainstream was seeking to "buy in" to the counterculture.

KEEP TIGHTLY CLOSED IN A COOL, DARK PLACE

The off-off-Broadway movement of the 1960s emerged less by design than by necessity, in order to give emerging theater artists a platform and context in which to develop their work.[2] Commercial producers, facing intense competition for entertainment dollars in the postwar period, had become highly risk averse, and so—lacking other opportunities—young writers and directors began mounting makeshift productions in the unpromising, unfunded context of Greenwich Village cafés, lofts, and church halls. Making a virtue of necessity, however, these artists quickly discovered that these settings afforded them a freedom from commercial imperatives that allowed them to experiment with form, content, and method. It was in this context that the Open Theatre was established in 1963, initially as an acting workshop with no production ambitions. The open-access group was composed of collaborating actors, directors, and playwrights and was given early impetus by Joseph Chaikin's attempts to develop improvisational acting techniques (building on the work of Viola Spolin and Nola Chilton) that would emphasize both the immediate, physical reality of the actors' presence on stage and their codependent relationships with each other. Eschewing the earnest psychologism of the dominant Method acting approach, Chaikin sought to foster a new kind of openness, playfulness, and physical self-awareness among performers. The Open Theatre's approach was thus typified by improvisatory games such as the "transformation exercise," in which performers might respond to each other's prompts by spontaneously shifting role and physical attitude within a scene. This might include adopting the physicality of, say, an animal or a machine, according to the felt demands of the moment.[3] "All exercises must start from and return to the body in motion," Chaikin later wrote. "In America many people live in their bodies like in abandoned houses, haunted with memories of when they were occupied."[4]

The Open Theatre ensemble eventually began to experiment with these developing techniques in performance, often using short, sketch-like plays by resident writers, including Jean-Claude van Itallie and Megan Terry. By May 1966 the company had developed their first, fully collaborative work in *Viet Rock*—which Terry scripted and directed in response to workshops with company members, and which premiered at Café La MaMa. But the pivotal moment in the company's history came in the fall of that year, when van Itallie persuaded Chaikin—against his own better judgment—to collaborate on a commercial, off-Broadway production of *America Hurrah*. By van Itallie's own admission, mounting this triptych of short plays was a kind of vanity project on his part: "I thought my God, I'm nearly thirty, I haven't had any public exposure, I've been writing for little lofts and dark corners, and in terms of my parents' ethic I'm a total failure. Let me at least try once!"[5] Van Itallie raised most of the starting capital himself, but his risk paid off in spades. *America Hurrah* became, in the words of critic William Coco, "the watershed play of the sixties."[6]

Prior to this moment, it had been generally assumed that an innovative play needed at least to ground itself in the conventions of realism if it was to achieve mainstream credibility (see, for example, Edward Albee's Broadway breakthrough with *Who's Afraid of Virginia Woolf?* in 1962). Yet each of van Itallie's plays adopted a very different form. The first, *Interview*, featured the contrapuntal interplay of multiple voices in multiple settings, in an attempt to evoke the hectic yet machine-like quality of urban life. The third, *Motel*, featured two life-size automata systematically trashing a soulless, rented room to the accompanying voiceover of ever-more-assaultive noise effects. *America Hurrah* thus brought to wider attention some of the richly theatrical experimentation that had been developing in downtown obscurity during the previous few years.

As a harbinger of countercultural crossover, *America Hurrah* was hailed as "a whisper in the wind"[7] by influential *New York Times* critic Walter Kerr—an endorsement that helped it to run for over a year.

Van Itallie's challenging plays were rendered accessible and engaging by the newly physicalized, fiercely precise stage language developed by the Open Theatre. The company provided four of the eight cast members and two directors: Chaikin himself handled *Interview*, which van Itallie had written with his approach in mind, while Levy oversaw *TV* and *Motel*. Yet the very success of the production also threatened to destroy the Open Theatre itself. Tensions and rivalries were fueled by the fact that, even as *America Hurrah* took off, a commercial production of *Viet Rock*—which opened at almost the same moment, using other actors from the company—met a much swifter demise. Kerr's damning *Times* review drew a direct comparison between the two shows, suggesting that "*Viet Rock* makes all of the same sounds [as *America Hurrah*], except the clear sound of talent. Here the distribution of voices and bodies remains mere random distribution, without a vortex to draw us down and in."[8]

For Chaikin, the brutal competitiveness of such comparisons reinforced all his misgivings about the commercial theater arena, but so too did the effects of *America Hurrah*'s long run (the production eventually clocked up 634 performances). The very state of fixity and repetition demanded of the actors, night after night, prevented the company, Chaikin felt, from evolving further as an ensemble: "There was no impetus left to do anything else, to do any research. We were being processed as a 'success.' . . . If you define yourself in these outside terms, you have only one course, to continue on that path you are on."[9] Following *America Hurrah*, Chaikin swore off ever again being involved in a commercial production, and the Open Theatre focused instead on laboratory experimentation, performing only occasionally in their own loft or in guest appearances at colleges and festivals. "Starting from the beginning," Chaikin later wrote of this reconstituted workshop group, "we had a utopian community."[10] The new, handpicked Open Theatre ensemble went on to develop acclaimed work such as *The Serpent* (1968) and *Terminal* (1970). Untainted by commercial pressures, the group's survival nonetheless depended in part on the emerging availability of state and foundation grant funding—initial access to which was greatly aided by the renown of *America Hurrah*.

TRIBAL INTERESTS

If Chaikin eschewed commercialism in search of a "utopian community," his erstwhile Open Theatre colleague Gerome Ragni had begun to believe that such idealistic collectivity might equally well be expressed squarely in the middle of the commercial arena. In collaboration with fellow actor James Rado, whom he had met in 1964 (both were cast members in the short-lived off-Broadway play *Hang Down Your Head and Die*), Ragni conceived a musical that would theatricalize the burgeoning hippie culture of the East Village by presenting flower children as an ecstatic "tribe." Although *Hair* was always intended as a vehicle for their own performance talents (despite both being in their thirties at the time, Ragni and Rado originated the central roles of hippie teenagers Berger and Claude), this was a show in which the principals were also very much members of the ensemble. Indeed, the collective, choral presence of the tribe is far more central to the show's impact than the ostensible plot of its "nonbook book" (the narrative thread of which is so tenuous that, when Milos Forman came to make the film version in the 1970s, playwright Michael Weller was hired to build a new storyline virtually from scratch).

The Open Theatre's foundational imprint on *Hair* is clear from the musical's published script.[11] Much emphasis is placed, for example, on the fact that the show takes place in the onstage present rather than in some fictional elsewhere and on a "bare stage, totally exposed, no wing masking."[12] As in the Open Theatre's workshop presentations, "all elements of this production are contained within the stage area from the outset and are manipulated in full view of the audience as the play progresses."[13] Members of the cast/tribe regularly acknowledge the audience's presence, even in the midst of ostensibly fictional scenes, and all the action seamlessly morphs from one song or set piece into the next without breaks or scene changes. As in Chaikin's transformation exercises, moreover, the characters' behavior is governed by a kind of spontaneous, lateral logic: for example, during the sequence in which Berger is expelled from school by a tribe member multi-roling as "Principal MacNamara," their oppositional dynamic is variously expressed as growling lion (Berger) versus whip-wielding lion tamer and then as "cheerleader" (Berger) versus "Nazi."[14]

"Jerry [Ragni] took some of the stuff we were working on and he popularized it," notes van Itallie, "which is a completely legitimate thing to do."[15] More than that, though, Ragni and Rado invested what had been developed as an anti-illusionistic acting approach with self-conscious cultural content: if the kids in the tribe "know they are on a stage in a theatre, performing for an audience," it is because they are (ostensibly) staging a kind of sit-in. They are, the stage directions note, "demonstrating their way of life . . . in order to persuade those who watch of their intentions, to perhaps gain greater understanding, support, and tolerance, and thus perhaps expand their horizons of active participation toward a better, saner, peace-full, love-full world."[16] The repetition of *perhaps* acknowledges necessary circumspection here, but it is clear that Ragni and Rado intended *Hair* to present a utopian community, whose idealism would be embodied and expressed in the onstage moment through their sheer, life-affirming exuberance ("I GOT LIFE"). This was to stand as an antidote to, and rebuttal of, the death-dealing realities of mainstream America, then prosecuting a war in Vietnam.

Indeed, *Hair* can be considered as a reaction of sorts to *Viet Rock*, in which Ragni performed during 1966, even as he was developing the new script with Rado. Megan Terry's play addresses the war primarily by presenting imagined scenes of conflict on the ground in Vietnam. This was despite the fact that nobody involved in the production had any firsthand experience on which to base their depictions. In *Hair*, Ragni and Rado instead presented the hippie dropouts of the East Village as a home front counterstatement to the war effort. Moreover, while the soundtrack to which *Viet Rock*'s title alludes was in fact more folk than rock, consisting of protest songs by Marianne de Pury played on a single acoustic guitar, Ragni and Rado wanted *Hair* to take advantage of the amplified, ecstatic potential of rock music as a celebration of the present, performed moment. By collaborating with the Grammy Award–winning composer Galt McDermot, Ragni and Rado found the musical uplift that their project vitally needed.

Hair's premiere was scheduled for the fall of 1967, as the inaugural production at the new, foundation-funded Public Theater on Astor Place. Legend has it that this unlikely collaboration with New York Shakespeare Festival impresario Joseph Papp came about because Ragni met him on a train in the fall of 1966 and handed him a draft script. (Both were traveling back from Yale, where the new dean of drama, Robert Brustein, had coordinated a series of debates and presentations on new theater practice—including a guest performance of *Viet Rock*.) It remains something of a mystery why Papp chose to launch his flagship venue with an untested musical by first-time writers, but it seems that—in that watershed season of 1966–67—Papp sensed that the underground was moving overground and wanted a piece of the action. He hedged his bets by assigning Gerald Freedman, an established and experienced director, to bring *Hair* to the stage, but Freedman's more traditional theater background gave him little natural affinity with Ragni and Rado's evolving vision for the show. The rehearsal process for the premiere was fraught with tensions and disagreements, and the eventual results were—to judge from Howard Taubman's inadvertently condescending *New York Times* review—suspended awkwardly between 1960s counterculture and 1920s revue. "Whatever the reservations one may have about *Hair*," Taubman wrote, "one is constantly disarmed by the youngsters' engaging high spirits, which is exactly how the youngsters in *The Grand Street Follies* and *The Garrick Gaieties* made their audiences feel."[17] With the Public's production limited to an eight-week run, Ragni and Rado invited Tom O'Horgan to see the show with a view to re-directing it for Broadway. "So I saw the piece," he recalls. "Don't know what I saw! A very weird piece and totally miscast, with people who were like very glossy, printed models. I couldn't grasp what I had seen."

O'Horgan was an off-off-Broadway director with a fast-rising reputation. With the guidance and encouragement of Ellen Stewart, the inspirational founder of the East Village's Café La MaMa venue, he had since 1965 been developing a physically dynamic, ensemble-based aesthetic of his own with an acting group that had become known as La MaMa Troupe (some of whom were former Open Theatre actors). O'Horgan had been Ragni and Rado's first choice to direct *Hair*, but he had been unavailable: La MaMa Troupe had painstakingly developed a touring reputation in Europe, and they were overseas throughout the summer and early fall of 1967. Ragni and Rado's fondness for O'Horgan's work, however, is apparent even in the pre-Broadway script. The second act's hallucinogenic trip through America's history of military and racial conflicts—with Berger as George Washington and other tribe members posing as Ulysses S. Grant, General Custer, Teddy Roosevelt, and John Wilkes Booth—reads as an homage to O'Horgan's work on Paul Foster's play *Tom Paine*, the first act of which presents a whistlestop reenactment of the American Revolutionary War. Indeed, Ragni and Rado's stage direction specifying that their historical figures should "dance a minuet" before being "attacked from behind"[18] is a direct steal from Foster's play, which had been written with the physical and musical capabilities of La MaMa Troupe very much in mind.[19] *Tom Paine* was first presented at La MaMa in the spring of 1967, before stealing the show at that summer's Edinburgh International Festival.

O'Horgan's background was as a musician and improvisatory comedian, and his approach to directing involved devising highly physicalized movement sequences that illustrated or counterpointed the words of a play's text. Actors were encouraged to be spontaneous in their physicality, within the confines of an underpinning structure in which particular sequences would begin and end on prespecified beats of music or lines of text. O'Horgan's aesthetic was thus characterized by a kind of raw, Dionysian energy that some compared unfavorably with the more restrained precision characteristic of Joseph Chaikin's work—not realizing that it was, in its own way, just as rigorously crafted. Both directors, Ross Wetzsteon noted in the *Village Voice*, were primarily concerned with staging "the disciplined conjunction of bodies—over and over, in the work of both, one sees stage images formed through a kind of visual kinetics: moving circles, Laocoon writhings, chains and piles of bodies, leanings and fallings and carryings."[20]

O'Horgan's ensemble-based aesthetic required immense trust, discipline, and cooperation among performers, and in agreeing to re-direct *Hair* for

Broadway, he insisted both on selecting his own performers and on securing sufficient rehearsal time to have them gel as a unit. A series of auditions was held in the hopes of finding actors with whom O'Horgan felt an affinity, and who seemed more authentically "hippie" than those Freedman had used. The youngest Broadway cast member, for example, was Walter Harris, who initially attended auditions simply to accompany a friend on guitar, but whom O'Horgan spotted and asked to try out. Just sixteen at the time, Harris was nonetheless known to O'Horgan, having been directed by him in a 1966 La MaMa production of Paul Foster's *The Madonna in the Orchard*. Harris's entire family were well known as enthusiastic participants in the off-off-Broadway scene, and O'Horgan clearly felt he could be trusted to "do it right."

The company's base for their extended rehearsal period of two and a half months (between January and April 1968) was the Ukrainian National Home on Second Avenue in the East Village, not far from La MaMa. "We didn't even start working on the script until two or three weeks into the rehearsal process," Harris recalls, "because Tom would spend most of his time just working with us, doing the trust exercises and building a sense of a tribal community, getting ourselves physically comfortable with each other so that he could form his kind of kinetic sculpture."[21] When work with the text finally began, O'Horgan set about stripping out much of what little plot and dialogue Ragni and Rado had written, collapsing songs and scenes into each other to create an ongoing fusion of music, spectacle, and action. Far from being affronted by this, Ragni and Rado participated enthusiastically in the collaborative re-creation process and worked with McDermot to write a whole series of new songs to help develop the show's feel and flow. Michael Smith's *Village Voice* review of the Broadway opening pointedly compared the results of this overhaul with *Hair*'s earlier incarnation at the Public: "Instead of being a patronizing portrait of hippies, *Hair* is now a direct freak-out. Never has a show been so chock full of shock effects, so manic in its pursuit of novelty." Its importance, Smith argued, lay not in "anything it says about hippies, [but in] the plain fact that O'Horgan has blown up Broadway."[22]

There were many, including some of O'Horgan's erstwhile admirers, who found the "manic novelty" of the production too glibly theatrical, and certainly there were moments in *Hair* that served no other purpose than to be gleefully silly—as when, for example, the three female performers singing "White Boys" as a kind of Supremes pastiche suddenly pulled apart and away from their shared microphone to reveal that their three floor-length gowns were in fact one, constructed from a single piece of concertina-like fabric. What the detractors perhaps missed, though, was that glee and silliness were integral components in Ragni and Rado's vision, now realized by O'Horgan as "a storyless contrast of values" between the tribe's liveliness and the state's death drive.[23]

In other moments that contrast was realized through poignancy rather than delirium. Walter Harris recalls how, midway through rehearsals, he and Ronald Dyson were handed the just-written music for a duet based on Hamlet's "what a piece of work is a man" soliloquy (which had appeared simply as spoken text in earlier versions of the script). This was to be placed in the show directly after the mayhem of the American history "trip,"

> and it stood out because of its simplicity. All these people had been fighting—there were special effects and strobe lights and machine guns and [self-immolating] monks and tomahawks and all that stuff, and suddenly everybody's dead, lying on the stage. And right in the middle of all this carnage, Ronnie and I would come down from the scaffold and stand on the stage and sing this lovely little ballad.

For Harris, the various skits, tableaux, and juxtapositions of mood were all engineered to move *Hair* toward its final reveal, "which sort of nailed people to their seats." In this moment, Claude is discovered lying dead in his military fatigues, hair shorn. (Drafted into the war against his will, he has died in Vietnam.) The tribe gather around him to sing "Let the Sun Shine In"—a redeveloped and recontextualized version of "The Flesh Failures," a song that had originally appeared in *Hair*'s first act. Heard in isolation, this song is easy to misunderstand as a simple, upbeat celebration, yet in this stage moment it acquires peculiar force as both a plea and a rebuke. The juxtaposition of image, music, and lyric, later reworked to similarly spine-tingling effect in Milos Forman's film version, epitomizes O'Horgan's contribution to *Hair*'s (re-)development.

It is worth stressing, though, that the sense of diametrically opposed values captured in this concluding tableau is also troubled and complicated by some of *Hair*'s underlying threads. As the charismatic leader of the peace-loving tribe, for example, Berger is on occasion guilty of a capricious violence of his own. In the pre-Broadway version of the script, this is expressed most directly in a scripted sequence in which, the stage directions stress, Berger symbolically *rapes* Sheila, the female lead.[24] O'Horgan, however, dispensed with this troublingly misjudged gesture and instead had Berger (Ragni) abruptly tear up a yellow shirt Sheila has given to him as a gift. This moment, sufficient to indicate Berger's careless narcissism, is then given a commentary through Sheila's song "Easy to Be Hard" (again, new for the Broadway version).

Counterbalancing Berger is the more reflective Claude, who expresses some ambivalence about the sustainability of their acid-fueled hippie lifestyle from *Hair*'s outset: "Now that I've dropped out," he sings, "why is life dreary dreary / Answer my weary query / Timothy Leary dearie."[25] Moreover, where Berger is casually gung-ho about resisting the draft, Claude proves far more hesitant—torn as he is between pacifism and patriotism ("Crazy for the Blue, White and Red"). The brutal choice between potential jail time, for burning his draft card, or potential death in Vietnam is reflected in Claude's plaintive solo "Where Do I Go?" at the act 1 climax ("will I ever / discover why / I live and die").[26] The undercurrent of youthful uncertainty and confusion that runs throughout *Hair*, and is epitomized by Claude, was arguably as important in connecting with audiences as the blazing, upbeat energies in its foreground. "Behind the sensationalism and glib inventiveness of *Hair*," Ross Wetzsteon wrote, "is an astonishing amount of . . . experimentation both bold and tentative, a combination which characterizes inquiry at its most serious. . . . O'Horgan didn't trick up *Hair* but found and expressed its essence, not its draft-card plot but its exuberant lifestyle, its hostilities and evasions as well as its challenges and humor."[27]

A very different critic, Charles Marowitz, made a similar point more succinctly: "O'Horgan has discarded the representation of states-of-being for the states-of-being themselves. This is what puts *Hair* into a class of its own."[28] That notion of "being" rather than merely "representing" had been central to Ragni and Rado's conception of the show from the outset, but O'Horgan faced particular challenges when the company moved uptown from their East Village rehearsal base. "When we first went up to Broadway I thought well this is ridiculous," he recalls. "We'll be up there for about twelve seconds and that will be that. I looked on it as a kind of sit-in." The architectural apparatus of a traditional Broadway theater, with its fixed demarcation lines between proscenium frame and auditorium, was alien territory to a director who had cut his teeth in the improvised, shared performance spaces of the downtown scene ("I'd never dealt with a stage!"), and O'Horgan sought actively for ways to bring the audience themselves within the circle of the performance. He deployed tribe members in costume on the street and in the lobby before the show started, joking and handing out flowers. Then, "as the house lights began to dim and the band began warming up," Walter Harris recalls,

> we were all fanned throughout the house and the balcony, and interacting with individual audience members in kind of a spacy, very earnest slow motion mode. We had worked with Tom a lot on that. We might touch somebody's face or play with a follicle of their hair or just touch their shoulder in passing, and then make our way toward the centre of the stage. All of this took about five minutes.

Conversely, at the show's climax, O'Horgan recalls, he had the cast "just step off the stage, and walk on the arms of the chairs, holding hands, right over the audience." There was in such gestures a deliberate challenge to the established norms of conduct in "legitimate" theater, but it was precisely in the breaking down of these barriers that *Hair* opened the door to a new, youthful audience demographic. "Once the show opened," O'Horgan recalls, "people just came from everywhere, you couldn't stop them. The audience spirit was just extraordinary. People came up on stage at the end of the play and danced. Nobody told them to do it, they just did it."

The appeal of *Hair* seems to have been multilayered. On the one hand, many young people found in it an energy and sentiment that they could identify with directly. On the other hand, the show's rock score had enough in common with, as Clive Barnes put it, the "soothing overtones of Broadway melody," that it appealed also to more traditional audiences.[29] "*Hair* served as a mirror but also a map," notes the show's official historian, Eric Grode. "It offered the older generation a fairly benign glimpse into the thoughts and actions of the hippie generation without sugarcoating it beyond what that generation would find palatable—never an easy combination."[30] Of course, the other factor often cited as exciting audience interest was the notorious nude scene, simply because it broke new ground on Broadway. In the original script, the only person to strip was Berger—as a gesture protesting the state's right to impose moral laws ("indecent exposure") while prosecuting immoral wars. O'Horgan, however, redeveloped the moment so that, in the aftermath of Claude's "Where Do I Go?," the tribe would collectively appear naked, facing forward in choral defiance of convention, as if stripped to their essential mortality. "It actually wasn't intended to be a big deal," Walter Harris recalls. "It was a color in the director's palette, something that Tom was actually quite comfortable and quite familiar with, and it was his notion that it would be part of a statement of openness and honesty as the tribe are trying to be close to Claude on his last night." Cast members were never required to strip if they were uncomfortable with the moment, and indeed participation would vary from night to night depending on mood.

According to Eric Grode, however, producer Michael Butler was sufficiently concerned with the commercial appeal of this moment that he eventually incentivized participation by offering an additional $1.50 per performance to those who stripped.[31] Crass as this strategy might initially appear, for Butler the nude scene was an exploitative means to a worthy end. "I have to thank the nude scene for getting a lot of people into the theatre," he explained. "That was the end of the first act, and then we had them for the second act, which is when the anti-war message is really laid out."[32] Butler's commitment to that "message" is beyond question. A wealthy playboy with no previous theatrical production experience, he was so taken with *Hair*'s impassioned stance when he saw the initial, Public Theater, version that he decided to put his ambitions for political office on hold in order to champion the show as producer and angel. Despite the refusal of most Broadway theater owners to countenance even the idea of hosting *Hair*, Butler persisted—putting O'Horgan's company into rehearsal before he even had a confirmed venue. "Michael had to play the role of the businessman," Walter Harris recalls, "because theater is an expensive business, especially when it involves a cast of twenty, and a band. But he put his career, put his friends, put his reputation at risk because what he saw in *Hair* was a political play, a play that had a chance to make a potent political statement."

BODIES IN MOTION

The erotic stage review *Oh! Calcutta!* was also conceived, self-consciously, as a statement by its creators—as throwing down the gauntlet to cultural convention. Picking up where *Hair*'s nude scene had left off, it focused unapologetically on displaying the body. The maverick theater critic Kenneth Tynan wanted to create a space in the "legitimate" theater for sexuality to be explored frankly and openly, without hiding behind ulterior justifications: "It occurred to me that there was no place for a civilized man to take a civilized woman to spend an evening of civilized erotic stimulation. At one end there's burlesque, at the other, an expensive night club, but no place in between."[33] Where *Hair* had caused ripples by importing countercultural mores into a mainstream context, Tynan seems to have been concerned with extending the sexual revolution to the existing, middle-class theatergoer.

Tynan first conceived the idea for *Oh! Calcutta!* in 1966, taking his title from a painting by the French artist Clovis Trouille, which depicts at its center a perfectly formed female bottom. (Trouille's pun was on the French words "Oh! Quel cul t'as!") In inviting writers to submit sketches for his proposed revue, Tynan was clear that there was to be "no crap about art or redeeming literary merit: this show will be expressly designed to titillate, in the most elegant and outré way."[34] Yet Tynan was strikingly traditionalist in his notions about titillation. He imagined a performance in which eight to ten female dancers would display their bodies in varying degrees of undress, while four male comics would provide jokes and commentary.

The director he eventually recruited to coordinate these proceedings was Jacques Levy, whose work on *America Hurrah* Tynan had been impressed with during the show's guest run at London's Royal Court Theatre in the summer of 1967. According to his wife, Kathleen, Tynan was particularly taken with Levy's work on *Motel*, for "its non-orgiastic style, its extreme cool."[35] This was, indeed, how Levy saw himself—as a "cool" director whose work contrasted markedly with the "heat" of peers such as Tom O'Horgan. His version of *Motel* had consciously reworked the approach adopted in its previous, La MaMa, production, for which director Michael Kahn had dressed the actors playing Man and Woman in monstrously oversized papier-mâché heads and bodies, designed by Robert Wilson (his very first theatrical engagement). Levy opted instead for clear plastic masks, closer to life-size: "It was the difference between Frankenstein, which is very 'hot,' and Dracula, which I think of as very cool."[36] Levy delivered fully on van Itallie's requirement for mounting sensory overload as the play moves toward its climax. Yet amid the blinding lights and deafening rock music, the masked figures trashing the motel room were instructed to be utterly methodical and emotionless: "Little by little they tore the place apart, but they never did it at a fast pace. The notes I would always give them were take your time, don't rush, just keep on doing what you're doing."

Presumably Tynan imagined that the application of Levy's chillingly cool aesthetic to his erotic fantasia would result in a show avoiding the nudge-and-wink smuttiness characteristic of much British discourse on sex. Levy, however, did not share Tynan's peccadilloes: "I was flattered to be asked. But what Ken had in mind was that it would all be set within a kind of tasteful, Victorian framework. A bit of underwear here and there. Now why he would choose me for that is anybody's guess." Levy's interest in *Oh! Calcutta!* was less concerned with its potential for erotic tease than with its capacity for political provocation. Indeed, it is worth noting that throughout the time he worked on *Oh! Calcutta!*, he was also involved in helping to conceive and deliver the "guerrilla theater" tactics of Abbie Hoffman's radical Yippie organization (including their notorious interventions at the 1968 Chicago Democratic Convention). For Levy, if the objective of Tynan's show was to challenge stage censorship, then the freedom of expression issue had to be front and center. His cast, both male and female, would need to be naked in plain sight: "I had in mind from the beginning that we really had to go for it. I didn't just want peekaboo."

Although Levy needed Tynan's contacts and celebrity to make the show happen, clashes over creative direction were always likely. Levy thus secured an important degree of artistic control when, in the autumn of 1968, plans for *Oh! Calcutta!*'s opening shifted from London to New York. The switch was partly thanks to Levy having found a producer, his friend Hilly Elkins, who would commit to securing the $125,000 starting capital needed. Moreover, with *Hair* having blazed a trail, it was felt that the cultural climate in America might prove less censorious than in the UK. Nevertheless, Levy's plan to use mobile, full-frontal nudity quite deliberately broke existing New York laws. *Hair* had carefully skirted prosecution by exploiting a legal loophole that deemed nudity acceptable provided it was in the form of static, sculptural tableaux. O'Horgan adhered closely to this regulation: at the crucial moment, a large scrim cloth would be pulled over the tribe, allowing them to disrobe beneath it, and they then simply stood up through holes in the cloth—as static, singing figures. Conversely, in touring their anarchist be-in *Paradise Now* to the city in 1968, the Living Theatre cast had worn bikini-style underwear rather than stripping naked, as they did in some other locations. Such precedents, however, prompted Levy to believe that the time was right for an explicit challenge to the law. Before opening night, he recalls, "the head pornographer for the mayor came to see it. He said please let me arrest you, don't make a fuss about it, and we'll let the judges work it out in court. And we said absolutely not, if you try to arrest us, we'll make a big fuss about it, because it's a first amendment issue!" At the risk of making the law itself appear ridiculous (if *Hair* had been allowed and this production was not), the city opted to turn a blind eye and the opening went ahead.

Oh! Calcutta! was important not just for the fact of its nudity but also for the way in which it was handled. Building on his experiences with the Open Theatre, Levy was committed to developing an ensemble-based dynamic and ensured a three-month rehearsal period (longer still than *Hair*'s), allowing the performers time to develop a sense of collective creativity and responsibility. There was no pretense here, however, that the actors were a "tribe": there was at all times a recognition of commercial theater realities, that people were being paid to do a particular job, not adopt a lifestyle. Levy instead came up with a team sports metaphor as a means of bonding the company. They wore uniform sweat tops and bottoms during scene work, and to formalize the potentially awkward work on nude scenes, they wore boxer-style robes with the words *Oh! Calcutta!* printed on the back like a team logo. "When people came into the theater," Levy explains,

> they each had a locker, and they would hang up their clothes and put on these robes. Then they'd come back on stage for the first rehearsal. We would start with these Open Theatre exercises that were getting at touching, feeling, etcetera, and then as this gradually became a mosh pit, the robes became a little unnecessary. . . . We kept working on this for days and days, and eventually it was just OK, but I never allowed anybody to be naked unless it was needed in a scene.

The "all in this together" egalitarianism of the ensemble approach meant that almost all nudity in the show was group nudity—avoiding the objectification and fetishization of individual bodies. By the same token, though, no individuals in the company were to accrue special benefits via the uninhibited physicality of the show itself. Levy insisted on what became known as the "NFL," or "No Fucking Law," which prohibited the fraternization of cast members outside the theater.

Perhaps most significantly, the ensemble approach made few distinctions between male and female performers. At the show's outset, the entire company of five men and five women would walk downstage in their robes, accompanied by an insistent, repetitive piece of bass-heavy rock music (the only lyrics were "Oh! Calcutta!" mysteriously sung at low pitch over and over again), and conduct a mocking, ironic striptease. The actors would show off a shoulder here, a buttock there, before abruptly revealing all, then pulling the robe back on and starting all over again: "They are going through a routine," state the stage directions in the published text, "not selling, a little bit tough, take it or leave it."[37] This routine was repeated until every member of the company had been introduced via projected slide and video images that individualized them as persons rather than as objects. Finally, having disrobed completely, the line of performers would then march off upstage, "proud as bullfighters, and exit where they came from."[38] In this equation, presumably, the robe is the bullfighter's cape and the audience is the bull, their horny expectations deftly swiped aside. As Clive Barnes observed in his *New York Times* review, "It is curious how anti-erotic public nudity, as opposed to private nudity, is. There is a clinical lack of mystery about it."[39]

Inverting Tynan's idea for the show to function as an extended tease, Levy ensured that the audience had seen everything there was to see at the outset and then presented the performers fully dressed for most of what remained. The show was bookended at its conclusion, however, by another all-nude, group-devised scene. The company would walk onstage in street clothes, chatting with and over each other like actors outside an audition room, voicing various comical anxieties about trying out for this show: "When they talk about the size of your part, they really mean it."[40] As music kicked in, they would then throw off their clothes with the innocent abandon of children going skinny-dipping and form a series of nude tableaux, fully lit against a backdrop of giant mirrors. The reflections ensured that the audience saw not only the performers but themselves watching the performers—even as the actors' words gave voice not to their own thoughts but to the unspoken thoughts of imagined spectators: "I wonder what the cast parties are like"; "My God, that's my daughter up there"; "All the men are circumcised. Must be a Jewish show."[41] The comic banality of these interjections operated to beg implied questions of the actual audience as to why they were present and what they were looking at. Finally, the performers would line up together in profile, swaying hips back and forth as if in some domino-effect orgy of humping—even though it was perfectly clear from the smiles and laughter of the group that nothing of the sort was happening. Their nudity proved, finally, to be no big deal (just as *Hair*'s was intended to be).

The London-based Tynan was not present during most of the rehearsal period, and when he arrived in New York late in the process, he was appalled by what he saw: "What we have now is not an erotic show," he protested to producer Elkins, "but a flesh show. There are ways of concealing this failure, by means of the running order [but] unless my feelings about 'my' show are respected, . . . I shall have to . . . pull out, not with a whimper but with a resounding bang."[42] Tynan was eventually talked down from this threat to publicly disown the show, but Levy always protested the implications of Tynan's "flesh show" judgment: "It wasn't just beautiful people. Bill Macy [another veteran of *America Hurrah*] was in that show—almost fifty, a bit of a belly. So it wasn't a skin show in that sense." Indeed, it is striking, watching video footage of the show (shot a year into its run in 1970, with most of the original cast), just how ordinary and unglossy these bodies are. Unlike the decidedly mixed-race cast of *Hair*, however, the bodies are all white—perhaps a calculated reflection of the show's anticipated middle-class audience.

As Tynan's discomfort over the "running order" indicates, Levy's concern to mirror and confront the audience was also apparent in his selection and sequencing of *Oh! Calcutta!*'s written sketches. Levy's editing skills were in fact a key part of his creative arsenal. (For his Open Theatre production of Michael Smith's *The Next Thing* [1966], for example, he had taken Smith's three chronologically arranged scenes and broken them into eleven shorter scenes, sequenced entirely out of chronological order.)[43] Potential sketches for *Oh! Calcutta!* had been gathered from both European and American writers over the course of two years, but Levy summarily dispensed with those that functioned solely to titillate. The published text contains, at the back, a number of "plays not in final production," such as "The Empress's New Clothes" (a male-narrated disquisition on the history of "knickers, knickers") and "St. Dominic's, 1917" (set in a boarding school dormitory, with four teenagers repeatedly changing clothes between various "kinds of schoolgirl *dishabille*").[44] Disregarding such material, Levy chose instead to wrongfoot audience expectations as far as possible. As the prologue to *Oh! Calcutta!*, preceding even the "Taking Off the Robe" matador sequence, he chose Samuel Beckett's thirty-five-second-long playlet *Breath*, in its world premiere outing. Levy placed a strategically positioned naked body among Beckett's pile of garbage but otherwise left this brief encapsulation of life and death, in a single inhalation and exhalation of breath, to play out as written: "So people came in for this supposedly hot skin show," he recalls, "and they all sat down, and you have *Breath*! And then the lights go up, and people are like, 'what just happened?'"

Tynan's invitation to sketch writers had specified that "you can either (i) create your own sexual fantasy or (ii) make a comment—satirical or ironic—on eroticism."[45] Levy selected material very much from the latter camp, and indeed in the case of Tynan's own sketch, "Suite for Five Letters," he shifted the tone toward the satirical. Where the stage directions call for this medley of "letters to the editor" expressing personal sexual kinks, to be sung "with serious purity of tone and a limpid nostalgic sweetness,"[46] Levy coached his actors to perform with the fixed smiles and hard edge of a Brecht-Weill song. At the scene's close, Tynan asks the performers to articulate "whatever sexual fantasy pops into their minds . . . it is very important [that these] be fresh improvisations each performance."[47] Levy, however, saved his actors from potential awkwardness by orchestrating a distinctly unspontaneous climax of brittle, pop-art porn: "I smothered his cock with cream cheese and then I stuck a bagel on the end of it."[48]

Just as Levy's Yippie colleagues famously hurled dollar bills onto the floor of the New York Stock Exchange, prompting traders to scramble like ill-disciplined children for these paltry rewards, so Levy's sketch choices seem to have aimed at a mocking interrogation of the expected audience's bourgeois sexual mores. In both "Dick and Jane" and "Will Answer All Sincere Replies," for example (few of the sketches can confidently be attributed to specific authors, because a policy was maintained of not attributing sections to individuals), the familiar, journalistic injunction to "spice up" a tired sex life is taken to farcical extremes. In the former, Dick wheels in an ever more bizarre succession of theatrical sex aids (much to Jane's mounting alarm). In the latter, a middle-class couple take the adventurous step of advertising to find another couple to "swing" with: "This is the age of the sex revolution," Dale assures his wife, Sue Ellen, "it's the wave of the future."[49] They are discomfited, however, when the couple coming to their home in response to their ad turn out to be somewhat more "common" than they had in mind—and the man is wearing a grotesque, full-arm plaster cast. It also transpires that Dale and Sue Ellen's "imaginative" sex games are far from original: "If the truth were known," Cherie informs them, deflatingly, "half the action in cocktail lounges is husbands pickin' up their *own* wives."[50]

Gender dynamics, as well as class, were held up for implicit scrutiny by Levy's sketch choices. In a disturbing scene titled "Jack and Jill," for example, the stereotypical notion that the male is the active sexual partner and the female his passive object of desire was explored by dressing two adults in scaled-up, antiquated children's clothing (boy in knickerbockers, girl in frills), and setting them to play amid a landscape of giant alphabet blocks. The scene involves a version of "I'll show you mine if you show me yours," but Jack is very much the insinuating, predatory male and Jill his innocent victim. She is eventually reduced to a kind of catatonic death trance after he figuratively rapes her. Conversely, in "Was It Good For You Too?" a young man volunteers to participate in a scientific experiment examining the "straight Hetero-Norm Coital set-up,"[51] only to discover that his assigned female partner is so disconcertingly passive as to appear bored. This scene, functioning as *Oh! Calcutta!*'s first act (anti-)climax, involves the first nudity since "Taking Off the Robe," but the naked couple are wired up to electrodes, poked and prodded at by a series of demented doctors and nurses during their simulated copulation. Choreographed with manic intensity, bleeps, and hooters by Levy ("If Brecht was doing Marx," he quips, "we were doing the Marx Brothers"), the scene actively undermined its own pornographic premise. Tynan reportedly found it "crude beyond words."[52]

The counterpoint to *Oh! Calcutta!*'s various satirical swipes lay at its temporal heart—immediately after intermission—when a new mood of Edenic innocence was introduced through music, dance, and an innovative use of color film footage to suggest green spaces outdoors. First as a group, and then gradually dividing into couples (with one or two lonely figures left poignantly forgotten), the naked performers would "touch one other innocently, carefully. . . . The mood of this exploration of sensuality is slow and tender."[53] Eventually the stage would clear to leave choreographer Margo Sappington to dance a nude pas de deux with actor George Welbes. Even on video, this sequence remains both striking and moving: very much a dance of mutuality, there is a grace and gentleness about the couple's touching, arching, and lifting that is genuinely sensual rather than merely titillating. Indeed, the fact of the performers' nudity becomes almost incidental to the emotive quality of the movement. As the more experienced dancer, moreover, it is Sappington who leads and who seems to express herself more fully through the extensions of her movement—thereby creating a strong sense of empowered, female eroticism.

Presumably it was these movement-based sequences in particular, at the start of act 2, that prompted *New York Times* critic Clive Barnes to declare that "there is no more innocent show in town." Far from making *Hair* look like *The Sound of Music*, he quipped (in response to one of the imagined "audience member" thoughts in the closing sequence), "*Oh! Calcutta!* makes *The Sound of Music* seem like *Hair* . . . . Innocent it is completely."[54] With hindsight, this might appear the greatest compliment Barnes could have paid the show—to suggest that a production consciously breaking cultural taboos around sex could also succeed in sweeping away acculturated perversions (through mockery) and restoring a freshness to the subject. The theater in which *Oh! Calcutta!* was appearing had, after all, been renamed the Eden in its honor. Barnes, however, proved unable to untangle his response to what he had seen from preshow expectations fueled by Tynan's press statements: "I thought we were to be offered a little pleasant erotic dramatic literature and a few neatly turned bawdy jokes, [but] this is the kind of show to give pornography a bad name."[55] Conversely, the *New York Post*'s Emily Genauer found *Oh! Calcutta!* to be "the most pornographic, brutalizing, degrading, shocking, tedious, witless . . . concoction" she had ever seen—but added, rather curiously, that it was also "the most shatteringly effective."[56] This general critical confusion about the show did nothing, however, to damage its box office potential. Sex sells, even when the seller is quietly asking what it is you think you're buying.

END OF AN ERA

Reviewing its last-ever New York performance in 1989, *Times* critic Frank Rich noted that "*Oh! Calcutta!* must have done something right. A theatrical production doesn't run off and on for 20 years at Broadway ticket prices, well into the era of video porn, simply by exposing a few breasts, buttocks and penises."[57] Yet Rich remained as much at a loss as his predecessors to explain the peculiar alchemy of the show's appeal. Both *Hair* and *Oh! Calcutta!* were restaged around the globe, but the mystery of what exactly made them so successful meant that they provided no template or model to be readily replicated by commercial producers. (*Oh! Calcutta!* had exploitative imitators such as *Let My People Come* [1974], but there was nothing approaching its longevity.) Investing in these shows' creators also proved to be a risky move. In 1972 the largest house on Broadway—the 1,788-seat Broadway Theatre—underwent internal reconstruction in order that Gerome Ragni's *Dude*, the long-awaited follow-up to *Hair* (with score by McDermot, but no Rado), could be presented "environmentally," with a stage in the center of the auditorium. "They completely gutted the place," recalls O'Horgan, "but the problem with Jerry is that you have to nail his feet down because otherwise he'll just keep going until he doesn't remember what the idea was to start with." O'Horgan was drafted in to attempt a last-minute resuscitation of the drifting *Dude* during previews, but it eventually closed after just sixteen performances, with losses of around $900,000.

The counterexample to *Dude*'s spectacular failure was the astonishing (and still continuing) success of the musical *A Chorus Line*, which won almost every theatrical award available after its 1975 opening. Following the fortunes of seventeen Broadway hopefuls, it is distinguished by its emphasis on ensemble rather than stars. Both Jean-Claude van Itallie and Jacques Levy felt (they told me in interviews) that it owed clear structural debts to, respectively, *America Hurrah* (*Interview*) and *Oh! Calcutta!* Perhaps still more crucial as a precursor, however, was *Hair*. Joseph Papp wanted to find another commercial hit whose profits, like *Hair*'s, could be used to underwrite other, less populist ventures. He thus threw the Public Theater's full support behind choreographer Michael Bennett (former mentor to Margo Sappington) in developing *A Chorus Line*.

The 1970s also saw the rise of Andrew Lloyd Webber as a major force in musicals—thanks in no small part to Tom O'Horgan's directorial work on the Broadway premiere of *Jesus Christ Superstar* (1971): "I still like that show, it holds up very well," O'Horgan notes, even while dismissing the formulaic scores of Lloyd Webber's 1980s megamusicals such as *Cats* and *Phantom of the Opera*. The commoditization and slavish reproduction of these shows, identically franchised around the world, were anathema to O'Horgan, who had directed seven different productions of *Hair* around the United States and in London but had insisted on tailoring each one to its particular context: "We always built it out of the town where we did it, the people there. So the Chicago *Hair* was about as different from the San Francisco *Hair* as New York was different." The fact that Michael Butler encouraged and enabled O'Horgan in this endeavor is further testament to the producer's passion for his project. Yet the more calculating logic of capitalism demands reproducible product that is not dependent on the energies, whims, and availability of individual artists. Hence O'Horgan's nickname for his erstwhile collaborator, "Android Webber."

If the commercial theater sector has become ever more robotically formulaic since the 1960s, experimental artists have simultaneously become less dependent on it, thanks to the emergence of a not-for-profit theater sector funded from a variety of sources, including state and federal arts grants, corporate and foundation sponsorship, and audience subscription schemes. Yet this separation of American theater into (at least) two distinct cultures has permitted the perpetuation—particularly in academic circles—of a reflexive prejudice against the "merely" commercial. Thus, while it seemed natural enough for a 1960s critic like Ross Wetzsteon to compare and contrast Chaikin's *The Serpent* and O'Horgan's *Hair* (as in the *Village Voice* article cited in this essay), despite their radically different scales and budgets, such comparisons feel curiously counterintuitive today. Moreover, in an economic context in which even experimental artists have had to become highly adept at self-marketing in order to attract corporate support (O'Horgan refers witheringly to "the yuppie avant-garde"), it is difficult to imagine mavericks such as Ragni, O'Horgan, or Levy even catching a break. These were outsider artists whose successes depended on the unexpected opportunities created by the cultural melting pot of the 1960s—yet by the mid-1970s, they were having to seek other arenas in which to express themselves. Jacques Levy, for instance, gravitated toward music, collaborating with the Byrds' Roger McGuinn and coauthoring Bob Dylan's legendary 1976 album *Desire*—still notable for its story-songs of outlaws and outsiders. "We just love outlaws," Levy notes wryly of the American folk tradition, "it's that love of the person beyond the bounds of society and tradition. At the end of the story, they have to be killed, because that's part of the bond you make with society, right? But while you're with them, they're fun to be with."

In Memoriam: This chapter makes use of material from unpublished interviews that I conducted with Tom O'Horgan and Jacques Levy in, respectively, 1995 and 2002. Although I have referred to them both, throughout, in the present tense in which I encountered them, both men have since passed away. Levy died in 2004, and O'Horgan in 2009. I salute them both for their generosity, wit, and insight. Two very different artists, two remarkable men.

NOTES

1. Tom O'Horgan, interview by the author, New York, NY, September 14, 1995. Subsequent quotations from O'Horgan are taken from this interview, unless otherwise indicated.

2. See Stephen Bottoms, *Playing Underground: A Critical History of the 1960s Off-Off-Broadway Movement* (Ann Arbor: University of Michigan Press, 2004), 177–78.

3. See Robert Pasolli, *A Book on the Open Theatre*, (New York: Avon, 1970) 20–22.

4. Joseph Chaikin, *The Presence of the Actor* (New York: TCG, 1991), 15–16.

5. Interview with van Itallie, in Stephen Bottoms, *Playing Underground*, 182.

6. Bill Coco, introduction to *America Hurrah and Other Plays*, by Jean-Claude van Itallie (New York: Grove Press, 2001), ix.

7. Walter Kerr, "Theater: A Whisper in the Wind," *New York Times,* November 7, 1966, 66.

8. Walter Kerr, "One Succeeds, the Other Fails. Why?," *New York Times*, November, 1966, 2.1.

9. Chaikin, *Presence of the Actor*, 106.

10. Ibid.

11. Gerome Ragni and James Rado, *Hair: The American Tribal Love-Rock Musical* (New York: Pocket Books, 1969). Please note that, although printed in 1969, this edition presents an earlier, pre-Broadway version of Ragni and Rado's text (presumably because they had not, at that point, worked up a new, "definitive" version).

12. Ibid., v.

13. Ibid., vi.

14. Ibid., 28–33.

15. Interview with van Itallie, Bottoms, *Playing Underground*, 182.

16. Ragni and Rado, *Hair*, ix.

17. Howard Taubman, "*Hair* and the 20's," *New York Times*, November 14, 1967, L50.

18. Ragni and Rado, *Hair*, 153.

19. Paul Foster, *Tom Paine* (London: Calder, 1967), 23.

20. Ross Wetzsteon, "Theatre Journal," *Village Voice*, March 6, 1969. 44.

21. Walter Michael Harris, interview by the author, by Skype from Seattle, April 12, 2013. Subsequent quotations taken from this interview.

22. Michael Smith, "Theatre Journal," *Village Voice*, May 2, 1968, [unpaginated clipping].

23. Wetzsteon, "Theatre Journal."

24. Ragni and Rado, *Hair*, 77–79.

25. Ibid., 5.

26. Ibid., 119.

27. Wetzsteon, "Theatre Journal."

28. Charles Marowitz, "Dateline London: Existential Thunder," *Village Voice*, February 20, 1969, [unpaginated clipping].

29. Clive Barnes, "Theater: *Hair*—It's Fresh and Frank," *New York Times*, April 30, 1968, 40.

30. Eric Grode, *Hair: The Story of the Show That Defined a Generation* (London: Carlton, 2010), 88.

31. Ibid., 73.

32. Michael Butler quoted in Ibid., 70.

33. Kenneth Tynan, quoted on the back cover of the published text of *Oh! Calcutta!: An Entertainment with Music*, devised by Kenneth Tynan and directed by Jacques Levy (New York: Grove Press, 1969).

34. Kenneth Tynan qtd. in Kathleen Tynan, *The Life of Kenneth Tynan* (London: Methuen, 1988), 279.

35. Ibid.

36. Jacques Levy, interview by the author, New York, NY, February 18, 2002. Subsequent quotations from this source unless otherwise stated.

37. *Oh! Calcutta!*, 11.

38. Ibid., 15.

39. Clive Barnes, "Theater: *Oh, Calcutta!* a Most Innocent Dirty Show," *New York Times*, June 18, 1969, [unpaginated clipping].

40. *Oh! Calcutta!*, 119.

41. Ibid., 124.

42. Tynan qtd. in Tynan, *Life of Kenneth Tynan*, 283–84.

43. For a full discussion, see Bottoms, *Playing Underground*, 177–78.

44. *Oh! Calcutta!*, 148.

45. Tynan, *Life of Kenneth Tynan*.

46. *Oh! Calcutta!*, 25.

47. Ibid., 31.

48. Transcribed from Revelation Films DVD of *Oh! Calcutta!*.

49. *Oh! Calcutta!*, 35.

50. Ibid., 39.

51. Ibid., 72.

52. Tynan, *Life of Kenneth Tynan*.

53. *Oh! Calcutta!*, 86.

54. Barnes, "Theater: *Oh, Calcutta!*"

55. Ibid.

56. Qtd. in Tynan, *Life of Kenneth Tynan*, 284–85.

57. Frank Rich, "Critic's Notebook: The Asterisks of *Oh! Calcutta!*," *New York Times*, August 8, 1989, http://www.nytimes.com/1989/08/08/theater/critic-s-notebook-the-asterisks-of-oh-calcutta.html.

PART II

THEATER ARTISTS' TRANSFORMATIONS AND INNOVATIONS

STAGECRAFT, PLAYWRITING, AND ACTING IN THE 1960s

Alisa Solomon

Boris Aronson, the Jewish Avant-Garde, and the Transition to Broadway

"By the time I was 14," the late scenic designer Boris Aronson liked to say, "I was past crying over *The Cherry Orchard* and no longer cared whether the three sisters arrived safely in Moscow."[1] It's the brash sort of statement one might imagine hearing from a theatrical innovator who had come of age amid the experimental fervor of the 1960s, decrying the drawing-room realism that dominated so much of the American theater for so many years. Boris Aronson, however, was fourteen in 1912.[2] His experimentalism was forged in the Russian and European avant-gardes of the early twentieth century. The pioneering work that he created for Broadway in the sixties—and that helped shape the way we have come to think of scenic innovation in that period—originated not in the trickle-up from the downtown lofts, churches, and black-box theaters of the period but in the Constructivist and Cubo-Futurist studios and stages of the early Soviet Union. His illustrious career makes a particularly strong case for challenging a rigid dichotomy between experimental and commercial theater in mid-twentieth-century America and for challenging the consecration of the sixties as the sole source of nonillusionistic theatricalism. Aronson was Broadway's sturdiest bridge to the earlier avant-garde.

At the same time, Aronson's rise to fame in the 1960s reveals how ideas of American ethnic identity—specifically Jewish American identity—were changing in the context of the Cold War and the growing civil rights movement. Aronson designed the midcentury productions that did the most to represent, and shape, a popular understanding of Jewish history. In the very look of his designs for *The Diary of Anne Frank* (1955), *Fiddler on the Roof* (1964), and *Cabaret* (1966) one can see Broadway's evolving acceptance of scenic abstraction as well as a shift in popular engagement with Holocaust remembrance, as the works move from documentary to elegy to metaphor. To trace Aronson's work, then, is to follow the thick, snaking lines of aesthetic innovation and of new Jewish assertion as they intersected in the 1960s, with blockbuster results on the Great White Way.

A PRIOR AVANT-GARDE / A YIDDISH AVANT-GARDE

Aronson was one of a steady flow of theater artists who immigrated to the United States after coming of age amid the heady artistic experiments of Russia and Europe in the nineteen teens and twenties and brought new styles and ideas into America's commercial realm. He was among the earliest to arrive in the United States—he came from Russia, via Berlin, in 1923—and the one who stuck most loyally to the theater. (He had occasion to work with many of the others over the years, among them George Balanchine, Vernon Duke, Rouben Mamoulian, and Kurt Weill.)[3] Aronson was also the most artistically radical of that group.

His rebellious, questioning spirit emerged early. Born in Kiev, he broke away from his religious family's expectations and insisted on pursuing art, only to chafe against the strictures of the French realism that dominated the painting curriculum he had to follow as a young student. Eventually he found more inspiring instruction in Alexandra Exter's Kiev studio, a gathering place for the creative elite of the thriving city. (The poets Anna Akhmatova and Osip Mandelstam were among the frequent visitors.) Exter had studied in Paris and she brought back news of Cubism, Futurism, and other avant-garde perspectives. She became the chief designer for Alexander Tairov at his daring Kamerny Theater in Moscow and created acclaimed settings for his 1920 production of *Romeo and Juliet*; the abstract design famously incorporated mirrors and also gave actors multiple, intersecting angular playing spaces of varying heights (observing Tairov's dictum that flat floors made for flat productions—a principle that Aronson would carry into midtown Manhattan more than four decades later).[4] Aronson assisted Exter on the costumes and stage models. Soon he moved to Moscow and reveled in the burgeoning theatrical culture, working amid the postrevolutionary ardor of artists like Vsevolod Meyerhold, Yevgeny Vakhtangov, and, at the Moscow State Yiddish Theater, the director Alexander Granovsky and the painters and designers (and Aronson's friends) Natan Altman and Marc Chagall. (Aronson wrote a monograph about the latter a couple of years later.)

Despite the fervent exploration in the theater, Aronson sensed an impending damping-down of artistic freedom and set out for New York (spending about eighteen months in Berlin along the way). "All human doubt officially disappeared,"[5] he later explained, and he anticipated he'd enjoy more liberty in the United States. When he arrived, he found his first jobs in the Yiddish theater, and not only because his English was not yet functional. The Yiddish fringe was the only sphere of American theater that appreciated his Constructivist, Cubo-Futurist sensibility and artistic restlessness.

While the fourth wall was growing ever more impregnable on the English-language commercial stage, Aronson was devising abstract, symbolic, or fanciful settings for productions at the Unzer Theater in the Bronx (later called the Schildkraut Theater when the acclaimed actor Rudolf Schildkraut took it over): an open platform and background of oddly shaped wall fragments for an Ansky play, *Day and Night* (1924); tall geometric chunks—buildings—with a flashing electric sign at the top for the urban street where the last act of Dovid Pinski's *The Final Balance* takes place (1925); and for Osip Dymov's *Bronx Express* (1925), in which a button maker drifts off to sleep on his commute and dreams of the glories suggested by the advertisements on the train, a tropical resort's palm trees, pink and turquoise wallpaper, and a beachscape, all enclosed under the arched ceiling of a subway car, with its suspended loops for standing passengers to hang on to always in view. With each of these designs, Aronson began anew, inspired by the material of the play, never from any formula. "In order to surprise the audience," he liked to say, "you must be able to surprise yourself."[6]

As he had hoped, Aronson moved on to Maurice Schwartz's Yiddish Art Theater, where the scope and budgets of his assignments expanded. For the multi-set *Tenth Commandment* (1926), for instance, for which he also designed the costumes, Aronson rendered the opening scene—a house in the woods—as an asymmetrical shack with cockeyed windows; for the next scene, played indoors, he unfolded its sides, like the flaps of a cardboard takeout container, to reveal an interior of stenciled walls, windows still atilt. Later scenes took place in heaven—ornate boxes at the opera—and hell—shadowy, red-tinged scaffolding erected within a giant profile of a man's head. Writing in *Theatre Arts Monthly*, John Mason Brown declared this work "the bravest experiments in scenic design that the present season has disclosed." In place of the "quiet, everyday theater of parlors and kitchens" Aronson brought "a welcome vigor and originality."[7]

Such qualities found little welcome in New York's mainstream theater, however, as the designer Lee Simonson noted in an article for the *Nation*. Reviewing a 1929 catalogue that accompanied an exhibit of Aronson's designs, he wrote—somewhat caustically—of the mismatch between Aronson's affinity for Constructivism and the everyday realism being eagerly pursued by American dramatists of the day. That incompatibility, Simonson argued, left Aronson's work "an exotic and transplanted thing," which would not find solid footing on U.S. stages until American playwrights found their own symbolic theatrical language.[8]

Nonetheless, Aronson scored his first Broadway assignment in 1932 (by then he was speaking English), a musical revue by Yip Harburg, Vernon Duke, and S. J. Perleman called *Walk a Little Faster*. He created a series of elegant settings featuring low-key mechanical devices inspired by American gizmos: a huge, proscenium-filling camera shutter that irised in on a romantic scene, a gargantuan piano roll painted with images of well-dressed people who scrolled by as it turned, a show curtain made of streamers—a couple dozen enormous zippers. His career was off and running. As he was tapped for major projects, he was increasingly called upon to make some of those kitchens and parlors, but always inflected by his penchant for asymmetry. Aronson established a close, fond working relationship with Harold Clurman, though he found that the Group Theater "wasn't theatrical enough for me."[9] And he worked repeatedly, too, with Elia Kazan. "In the Yiddish theater most of the settings were either Heaven or Hell," he once quipped. "On Broadway, I had to get down to earth—Coney Island, Ozone Park."[10]

As an immigrant, Aronson brought an outsider's sharply observant view to the everyday settings. To design Odets's *Awake and Sing* (1935) he needed a field trip: he went with the actor Julius (John) Garfield to visit his parents in the Bronx, to see what Jewish American homes looked and felt like. To prepare for *Three Men on a Horse* (1935), a George Abbott farce, he followed a woman around a five-and-dime store in Queens, buying the same items she bought. Working backward, he designed the living room where some of the action takes place, from the bric-a-brac up.

Aronson always rose to the occasion of realistic settings but itched for more opportunities to let his imagination break free. That day was long in coming. Its seemingly sudden arrival in the sixties evinces how quickly mainstream audiences were primed for visual innovation by the self-consciously theatrical, minimalist, and/or antipictorial settings that were part of the off-Broadway explosion. But it is the realm of sociopolitical change—specifically, in Aronson's case, in the Jewish sphere—that gave rise to the particular productions that would allow him freer artistic range.

Truly a cosmopolitan—he regarded himself as "European"—Aronson was not a religious man (though his father had been the grand rabbi of Kiev). Still, his direct, unselfconscious knowledge of Ashkenazi culture and Jewish urbanity—in all their variation and complexity—enabled him to engage *The Diary*, *Fiddler*, and *Cabaret* without sentimentality or bathos.

THE DIARY AS DOCUMENTARY

In theatrical style and in its reflection of the state of Jewish anxiety about assimilation, *The Diary of Anne Frank* is very much a work of the 1950s, and thus a revealing standard against which to measure the momentousness of the changes that would come within a decade.

To design *The Diary*, Aronson saw that he needed to work against his instinctive aesthetic inclinations. "My preference as a designer . . . is toward stage conceptions which permit me to capture the mood and essence of a locale rather than the literal reproduction of it," he noted. "As an artist I am strongly attracted by the 'intangible' rather than the photographic quality of a design. In my setting for the plays of Arthur Miller and Tennessee Williams, for example, I was attempting to find a synthesis between stage realism and a more epic or heroic approach to theatre design." *The Diary* was, for Aronson, a deliberate and important exception. He placed the play "in the tradition of documentary realism," believing that its "whole impact is based on this 'reality.'"[11]

Aronson's assignment for *The Diary* was set in motion some two decades earlier when he met Garson Kanin. Kanin was serving at the time as assistant director to George Abbott for *Three Men on a Horse*. Aronson, as Kanin recalled, had criticisms of the play but was insecure about speaking English, so he stood at the back of the theater muttering to himself in Yiddish. Kanin was impressed by how trenchant Aronson's remarks were and told him so—in Yiddish. It was the beginning of many long discussions in the mother tongue.[12]

In 1954, when Kanin was getting started on directing *The Diary*, he determined right away—even though the playwrights had already been working with another designer and Kanin himself had relied for his last string of Broadway shows on Donald Oenslager—that "there was only one man in the world to do [the scenery] if he could be interested and that was Boris Aronson."[13] A thoroughly secular Jew, Kanin regarded *The Diary* not as just another play but as "a religious experience" and told Aronson "how thrilled I am to be associated with you particularly on such a noble venture."[14] The play, after all, as Edna Nahshon has put it, was "a watershed event: it marked the first time that the mainstream American theater presented a play whose plot focused on the Holocaust."[15]

Aronson, too, recognized its unusual status. It was based on a document written not by a playwright, he noted, but by a young girl, and a document whose very existence he considered a "miracle."[16] As such, he thought one had to be careful to treat the material with a sober directness. In design terms, that didn't mean trying absolutely to replicate the back of the Annex at 263 Prisengracht Street in Amsterdam—which would have been impossible anyway, given that the relatively vast stage space at the Cort Theater had to be filled. Rather, he had to be true to the emotion and kinesthetic impression and to the specific physical conditions that produced them. Reaching back to his own boyhood memories of hiding during pogroms in Kiev, he recalled how disturbing it was never to have a chance to be alone. He wanted to capture the sense of claustrophobia and, especially, of the lack of privacy, taking his cue not from a floor plan but from "the nature of the material, what is it trying to say, what does it stand for."[17] Aronson had to invent a setting that *felt* like a replica of the Annex, even though it wasn't one.

Kanin agreed, as he put it, that "the actual set-up would be impractical for stage purposes, and a completely creative approach is required" (he insisted, for example, on making the entrance a trapdoor) but felt that knowing the specific locale would help him create a production that was properly authentic. Along with the playwrights, the married couple Frances Goodrich and Albert Hackett, he took a research trip to Amsterdam and even stayed overnight at the Annex to discover to what extent noises from the street seeped into the space. "Could you really hear a truck go by?" he wanted to know.[18] Sound became an important element in the production to help establish the sense of a world going on beyond the hiding place. Dutch children's songs, trams, and other local hubbub that Kanin collected on his trip were incorporated into Saki Oura's sound design.

Kanin hired a photographer to shoot every inch of the Annex and he sent to Aronson, by airmail, five envelopes of images of its interior and exterior, plus a package of books about Amsterdam and several shipments of postcards. "Needless to say," he reassured Aronson, "they have been sent to you only as a general guide."[19]

When Kanin rejected the designer from whom the Hacketts had commissioned some early ideas, he rejected, with him, a plan that entailed more than a dozen separate settings; all those scene changes, the director felt, would impede the flow of the story. Apart from Aronson's affinity for the material, Kanin also thought he was the one designer who could best figure out how to create what the director required: "a single unit set that would live the whole time, not with some areas going dead and some live, but leave the whole thing living the whole time."[20]

In an era in which placing a family's dwelling place on the stage in faithful detail had long been a given—to Aronson, even a cliché—Aronson's suspicion of realism helped make his design successful: verisimilitude was not a habit for him and he approached the work with fresh eyes and energy. He studied the photographs Kanin had sent in order to furnish the Annex with meticulous fidelity—stove, beds, sink, cots, cupboards, table, even the moldings and doorknobs. But in arranging the space, his guide was the atmosphere he wanted to conjure. He called it "organized clutter"[21]—a series of small compartments delineated within the single space, with each area identified with a specific character. And yet, with no doors or curtains to separate these areas from each other, the residents were always in each other's view. "Anne walks around from place to place," Aronson noted, "and can never for one second in any human fashion be alone."[22] Even as the spaces seemed to become more "homelike" as the play progressed, the sense of constant exposure grew sharper. So did the crush of their confinement. Consulting all those books and photos and postcards Kanin had sent, Aronson painted the skyline of Amsterdam on a cyclorama. In shadowy sepia and deep blue tones—the colors of Rembrandt, Aronson said—the city's gabled houses rose above the attic's jagged rooftop, invisible to the Frank family inside. Along with Kanin's soundtrack, the image of the city kept the context in view: life continued normally for other people. Aronson's was a dynamic realism; the space seemed alive.

Kanin had egged Aronson on in this direction, noting that their unit set should seem to have ten settings "since each time we see the rooms, some change has taken place. Furniture shifted, furniture added, furniture painted or repainted, a chair covered, perhaps later on, instead of blackout curtains being drawn, one section of a window has been painted out."[23] These small changes would convey the sense of time's passage, both reassuring (the concealed Jews have made it through another day)—and foreboding (how long can they endure?). The audience, of course, already knows the terrible answer before the action shows it.

True to its period, there was nothing particularly "experimental" about this setting—and certainly not about the conventional dramatic style of *The Diary of Anne Frank*. But Aronson made the space more than merely a locale; it played a part in the action—and, especially, in the all-important assertion of the diary's veracity. Like the diary itself on which it was based, the play's success depended on the historical fact of Anne's fate and her chronicling of it. The play's 717-performance run, and its winning of the Tony Award and the Pulitzer Prize in 1956, show how in tune *The Diary* was with sentiments of that decade, deriving its abiding power and poignancy from its status as an authentic record of an adolescent girl's last twenty-five months of life (despite the redactions to the diary scholars have unearthed in relatively recent years).[24] Aronson's design underscored this assertion.

That the playwrights fudged a number of facts far beyond what dramaturgical machinery may have called for tells volumes about the strange balancing act American Jews were attempting between blending in as full Americans and maintaining a sense of distinctiveness. Audiences, of course, had to understand that Anne and her cohabitants were pursued and died for one reason only, and the play, on the one hand, heightened the saturation level of the Franks' Jewish identification, transforming a line in Anne's diary about a St. Nicholas Day celebration into a Chanukah observance that brings the first-act curtain down on a song. On the other hand, the authors and producers worried about going too far in suggesting that Jews suffered uniquely, and the play took pains to "universalize" the story.[25]

Counterfactual as that impulse seems, it reflected the contours of Jewish communal concerns in the mid-1950s, when Jews were enjoying unprecedented access to the political, social, and economic mainstream. Anti-Semitism was declining, according to every postwar poll that measured popular attitudes, and Jews were increasingly being accepted, in the words of the historian Edward Shapiro, as "no longer an exotic ethnic and religious minority, but an integral part of American culture."[26] Will Herberg's influential book *Catholic, Protestant, Jew*—published the same year as *The Diary* opened—argued that *having* a religion was more important to being American than *which* religion one had. Herberg's emphasis on faith as the salient defining characteristic of Jewish difference reflected the community's profound, postgenocide suspicion of racial or ethnic categories.[27]

At the same time, stressing religion distinguished the United States from its Cold War adversary the godless Soviet Union and bound Americans of all faiths more tightly together in this confrontation, as Shapiro contends.[28] Jews had special reason to accentuate this point: the demagogic association between Jews and Communism that droned like an ominous ostinato of McCarthyism. America's major Jewish communal organizations labored mightily to show themselves free of any Red taint—they purged leftists from their payrolls and urged community centers not to book radical speakers; they ran ad campaigns asserting that Jews did not support Communism and that the Soviet Union was particularly hostile to Jews. The American Jewish Committee openly supported the execution of the Rosenbergs.[29]

Just months before *The Diary* premiered, the eight-month-long national observance of the Tercentenary of Jewish Settlement in America concluded its series of lectures, commemorations, and civic events celebrating, as its official theme put it, "Man's Opportunities and Responsibilities under Freedom." The aim of the programs was to honor the "American heritage of religious and civil liberty" and demonstrate "the strength of the American people's commitment to the principles of democracy in our struggle against communism and other forms of totalitarianism of our day," according to the tercentenary's initiating statement. President Eisenhower was the featured speaker at the opening banquet in October 1954.[30] The early multicultural theorist Horace Kallen criticized this Jewish celebration for barely mentioning anything Jewish. But that was its purpose: to pay tribute to the *Americanness* of the community and to its *lack* of difference. While the action of *The Diary* transpires in Amsterdam, this dominating spirit of Jewish sameness suffuses the American play, making Anne and her cohabitants universally relatable, recognizable as Jews only because they celebrate Chanukah.

At the same time, the play (and the diary before it) made presenting the Holocaust palatable less than a decade after the devastation: astonishingly, it produced a feeling of uplift in its viewers. Such a reaction is possible precisely because Anne did not write about violence or the camps or even much about persecution. Spectators encounter a creative, reflective adolescent concerned with a middle-class teenager's typical dilemmas. Those problems may be made more urgent by the close quarters and omnipresent threat, but Anne does not ask audiences to look at anything that is hard to take in. Nazis don't even appear. In his review for the *New York Times*, Walter Kerr praised the play exactly for this characteristic: "The precise quality of the new play at the Cort is the quality of glowing, ineradicable life—life in its warmth, its wonder, its spasms of anguish, and its wild and flaring humor." In the *New York World Telegram and Sun*, William Hawkins went even further: "One leaves the theater exhilarated, proud to be a human being."[31] In 1955 this was the way in which commercial theater was ready to represent, and audiences were ready to take in, one of the most horrific events in modern human history.

THE SIXTIES SURGE: JEWISH PARTICULARISM AND *FIDDLER ON THE ROOF*

In less than a decade, American Jewry was feeling the impact of postwar transformation: the end of quotas limiting the number of Jewish students in elite universities, the large-scale shift of Jewish populations from cities to suburbs (a majority of Jews had left urban centers by the mid-1960s), and most significantly in the cultural realm, the end of the blacklist. If a lingering effect of McCarthyism (present to this day) was a wariness of expressing radical politics in popular entertainment, the Jewish fear of guilt by association had been lifted: there was no more reason to hide. Midcentury liberalism, pressing the ideal of tolerance while extolling the virtues of bootstrap tenacity and individual freedoms, corresponded with the dominant Jewish American narrative and provided an arena for political engagement that bore no blot of Communism.

Anxiety about flaunting particularism—being "too Jewish"—had hardly evaporated. But as Jews gained in social, political, and economic standing—the striving second generation having the good fortune to come of age as America was booming—the idea that characters (and the people who create them) might "just happen to be Jewish" gained an easy currency. The authors of *Fiddler on the Roof*—Jerry Bock (music), Sheldon Harnick (lyrics), and Joseph Stein (book)—thought just that way about Tevye and the other characters who charmed them when, in search of material for a new musical, they re-read Sholem Aleichem's stories.[32] The show, which opened on Broadway in the fall of 1964, preceded—and advanced—the countercultural, back-to-one's-roots craze and the proud ethnic particularism that went with it (and that eventually took on a conservative valence as well). Unlike the creators of *The Diary of Anne Frank*, the makers of *Fiddler* had no sense that they were involved in anything holy—their project was not "religious" or "noble," as Kanin had described his play. They simply loved the material and were excellent showmen. Much to their surprise, the show touched Jewish Americans with special force, representing for the first time in mass popular culture the life of the Ashkenazi Old Country that they could proudly embrace as their heritage.

Meanwhile, in the intervening years, with Broadway absorbing some of the waves of experiment, Aronson enjoyed more opportunities to create more abstract, symbolic, and dynamic stage spaces—a sprawling circus tent for Archibald MacLeish's *J.B.* in 1958, a series of collages and a show curtain displaying a gigantic jukebox for *Do Re Mi* in 1960. And he still was offered plenty of living-room plays, works that lacked the urgency and the justification for scenographic veracity that he had discerned in *The Diary of Anne Frank*. But he was "tired of doing kitchens," as he put it.[33] When he turned down an invitation to design Gertrude Berg's *A Majority of One*, he wittily dismissed it as a comedy in which "the whole Jewish problem is solved because she could make gefilte fish for a Japanese fellow." (Donald Oenslager took the job.)[34]

In 1963, by which point he had designed more than ninety productions in the United States, Aronson caught wind that a musical based on Sholem Aleichem's Tevye stories was to be directed by Jerome Robbins, and for the first time in his thirty-year Broadway career, Aronson went after the job. Robbins had wanted to hire Chagall, but even before the artist wired Robbins from Paris to say no thank you, Robbins was on the phone with Aronson. The designer knew that, given his background, he was the most qualified man for the job.

Of course, there is no reference to the Holocaust in the story of Tevye the dairyman and his marriageable daughters living in the Pale of Settlement in 1905. But the topic floats over the action like an ethereal Chagall figure: the show—explicitly on Robbins's part—was meant to memorialize a world whose vestiges were obliterated in the Nazi slaughter. Spectators know what will happen to the residents of Anatevka who don't, at the end, leave the continent. That Tevye, Golde, and their youngest children are headed to New York is a significant change from the Sholem Aleichem stories on which the musical was based and one of many aspects of its timely Americanization. As families leaving religious persecution for the welcoming shores of a new world, the Anatevkans are figured as Pilgrims, Seth Wolitz has argued. [35] And, at a time when America's immigration policy was at last shifting away from the quotas enshrined in laws dating back to the 1920s that restricted all but Western and Northern Europeans, the mid-1960s saw a change in the locus for the nation's origin narrative: from, as Matthew Frye Jacobson has put it, Plymouth Rock to Ellis Island.[36]

A sentimental trope of the "vanished world" of "the shtetl," materially poor but spiritually rich, had been cemented in the postwar era in photographs, books, plays, and artworks and was well established as a mode of remembrance when Robbins joined Bock, Harnick, and Stein in 1963 to develop the musical. He both accessed and resisted this trope, seeking to make his representation of the shtetl gutsier and less sentimental than depictions that had come before. (Indeed, for all the mawkishness some people associate with *Fiddler* today, it is far tougher-minded than the adaptations of the Tevye stories presented in the 1950s on the nationally syndicated Jewish radio program *The Eternal Light*, for example, and in off-Broadway and touring dramas written by Arnold Perl.) Robbins, it's important to note in this context, was a crossover artist in more ways than one. Apart from thriving in the worlds of elite dance and of popular Broadway musicals, he was also engaged in experimental theater, going to see work of all kinds. (He hired the costume designer Patricia Zipprodt for several projects—including *Fiddler*—because he admired her work for the ground-shifting 1961 production of Genet's *The Blacks*.) Robbins directed the off-Broadway premiere of Arthur Kopit's *Oh Dad, Poor Dad, Momma's Hung You in the Closet and I'm Feeling So Sad* (eventually transferring it to Broadway) and tried to bring to Broadway audiences works by downtown luminaries like Bertolt Brecht and Maria Irene Fornes. For two years in the mid-1960s he presided over the experimental American Laboratory Theater, in which he sought to devise works combining theater, music, and new forms of dance. Robbins knew better than anyone how to construct, oil, and polish the machinery of a commercial musical, but his sensibility could not be fixed as "uptown" or "downtown." Robust imaginations like his (and like that of *Fiddler*'s star, Zero Mostel, an off-Broadway sensation in Ionesco's *Rhinoceros*) did not recognize such borders.

Robbins hit on a guiding metaphor for *Fiddler*: the circle—an ancient folk form that defined the community. He would establish it in the opening number, "Tradition," and make it dissipate in the closing one, "Anatevka." Aronson responded to the idea in the very floor of the stage. He embedded into it a large turntable and placed a smaller one asymmetrically within it. "Sholom

Aleichem, in his tales of Tevye the Milkman, describes him and his family as forming a circle within the circle of his friends in Anatevka, the town," Aronson wrote in some notes on the production. "I used this image as the key to my design of the musical: a small revolving stage inside of a large one. . . . On these turntables moved the people of Anatevka and their ramshackle dwellings . . . always against backdrops of delicately colored skies or trees. Even within poverty, there was natural beauty. . . . A glow coming from life itself."[37]

On the turntable Aronson placed Tevye's house, and like earlier dwellings he'd made for the Yiddish theater—*The Tenth Commandment, Stempenyu*—this house shifted from exterior to interior as it pivoted to an open position. Aronson made the stuff of everyday life realistic: hooks for hanging pots in the kitchen, little cubby shelves built into the walls. He'd seen them in research materials like the 1928 Soviet film *Laughter through Tears*, which adapted some Sholem Aleichem stories set in a prerevolutionary shtetl. Though the film meant to emphasize the benightedness of shtetl Jews—and thus suggest how the revolution would gust in and enlighten them—Robbins saw a gritty realism in its images. Stills of dozens of the film's frames were made by a professional photographer for Aronson to consult.

But outside the house (or train station or other specific settings), Aronson's work was fanciful: painted backdrops with thickly swirling moons, drawings of little houses that somersaulted across the proscenium arch, impressionist hay fields shimmering on a drop. "It was the emotion of Chagall's paintings I tried to incorporate," he said of these elements, but he did not want to copy Chagall directly. "The show needed to be solved in terms of its own problems."[38]

The mix of the fanciful with the earthy in Aronson's design helped give *Fiddler* its elegiac feel. In visual terms, the show recovers the lost world by dint of the detailed specificity indicated by the realistic elements, while producing a tender, affectionate tone through its dreamier, even whimsical imagery. (This is precisely the balance that was inevitably lost in the film version of *Fiddler*, which was shot, of course, in real settings.) *Fiddler* thus participated in what Barbara Kirshenblatt-Gimblett has called the "popular arts of ethnography" that were involved in post-Holocaust salvage.[39] It staged for fond remembrance a world that was no more. With its ongoing global popularity on community, scholastic, and professional stages (along with the extended reach of the movie), *Fiddler on the Roof*, historical inaccuracies notwithstanding, has played no small part in shaping how people imagine what the life of Eastern European Jews was like before their annihilation.

The show was embraced also for its keen engagement with the present: it understands the past through a lens trained on pressing concerns of the 1960s. It is, after all, a show about the parental generation trying to hold on to tradition in the face of their children's radical new ideas and the gale forces of history. The correlation between the Eastern European past and the American moment comes to the fore early in the show. Immediately after the opening number, in which "tradition" is asserted as the community's binding agent (despite some hints of cacophony and conflict), we see the eldest daughter, Tzeitl, urging her beloved tailor, Motel, to defy custom and ask Tevye for her hand. In "Matchmaker, Matchmaker" (an inversion of a standard "I want" song), the daughters learn what they *don't* want: to be "stuck for good," as a lyric puts it, in a confining marriage: an echo of what Betty Friedan had just controversially called, in her trailblazing, bestselling 1963 book *The Feminine Mystique,* "a comfortable concentration camp."[40] In the following scene, the revolutionary Perchik arrives and challenges the complacency of the men in the community. Asked where he has come from, he tells them: the university in Kiev. As if Perchik had blown in fresh from drafting the Port Huron Statement with founders of the rising radical student movement, an Anatevkan replies, "Aha! The university. Is that where you learned to criticize your elders?" Perchik is even so bold as to declare, "Girls are people, too!"

More associatively, the show responded to the rising currents of the civil rights movement (which resonated, too, for Jewish audiences; Jewish youth and clergy participated at rates disproportional to other whites, often citing the ethical imperatives of Judaism and/or of Jewish historical experience). Robbins consciously drew this connection in some attempted rehearsal exercises, asking actors to improvise some scenes of Jim Crow racism as a means of getting them in touch with what discrimination feels like. If clumsy as a rehearsal device, the analogy between Eastern European anti-Semitism and American racism was a powerful emotional current in *Fiddler,* framing not only the depiction of Jewish repression in the Pale but also Tevye's own inability to accept the choice of husband his third daughter, Chava, makes: "If I bend that far, I'll break," Tevye finally concludes when she runs off to marry Fyedka, a non-Jew. When the pair come to say goodbye in *Fiddler's* final scene, nobly claiming that they are leaving, too, because they cannot live among people who would do such things to Jews, Tevye ignores them, prompting Fyedka to challenge him: "Do you feel about us the way they feel about you?" and thereby making one of the show's most drastic changes from the original Sholem Aleichem stories to a midsixties American sensibility. Where the problem in the Yiddish stories is Chava's apostasy, her abandonment of her faith and her people, now the problem is Tevye's apparent bigotry. Not that Fyedka speaks for the show itself—audiences see other layers and viewpoints, too—but at the very least, through his decency and solidarity, a contemporary liberal American understanding resounds in the scene.

It rang loud and true for segments of the Jewish community where the issue of intermarriage took center stage in the 1960s. As anti-Semitic threats from malice outside the community subsided, Jewish America now saw its primary peril as coming, surprisingly, from hard-won tolerance: how would their children stay Jewish—especially now that there were no (or hardly any) impediments to their attending any university, pursuing any career, living in any neighborhood? In the fall of 1963 the annual statistical survey the *American Jewish Yearbook* reported with alarm on rising rates of interfaith marriages, noting most ominously that Jews who went to college were more than twice as likely to choose non-Jewish spouses as those who did not.[41] Months later, as *Fiddler* was about to begin rehearsals, the mainstream press picked up on the issue: *Look* magazine ran a cover story called "The Vanishing American Jew," addressing the communal anxiety that Jews would intermarry themselves out of existence.[42] Some prominent Jewish leaders blamed liberalism for the conundrum and questioned whether Jewish support for civil rights and sexual liberation was counterproductive. Jerry Robbins, meanwhile, clipped the *Look* story for his *Fiddler* research file.

THE TWENTIES MEET THE SIXTIES: *CABARET*

In retrospect, that blaming of liberalism in 1963 can be seen as an early eruption of Jewish neoconservatism, which would quickly claim a good deal of media attention over the next several years, even if it did not win large swaths of adherents in the Jewish community. The volume rose at that end of the spectrum in response to rising militancy on the left as liberalism's limitations became clearer: tolerance was not the issue; equality—equality of power—was. Along with Black Power, the rhetoric and activities of the student, antiwar, and Women's Liberation movements heated up, too, and as the experimental and noncommercial theater blatantly addressed such issues, the Broadway producer Hal Prince sensed that his medium, the commercial theater, could—and should—come to grips with the exigencies of the day as well.

Before he had taken up the producing reins of *Fiddler*, Prince had been at work on a musical adaptation of Christopher Isherwood's *Berlin Stories*. To pen a libretto, he had hired Joseph Masteroff, who had written the book for *She Loves Me*, the Bock and Harnick musical Prince had also produced. But work on the Isherwood project stalled, not only because *Fiddler* seized Prince's attention. The producer-director was having a hard time finding a way to convey what interested him most about the material: not the kooky, charismatic character of Sally Bowles (emphasized in John van Druten's nonmusical dramatization *I Am a Camera* in 1952—not least because of the young Julie Harris's breakthrough performance) so much as the decadent milieu of Weimar Germany, where the people of Berlin partied on while fascists tromped to power. Something about it felt familiar to Prince in America's mid-1960s—not the literal historical circumstances, but the sense of moral predicament for people who merely stand by as evil gains ground. In polarized America of the mid-1960s, people couldn't stay neutral, and, especially in the face of the escalating Vietnam War, they couldn't stay quiet. But Prince could not grab hold of a way to bring the Weimar atmosphere theatrically to life. Though by the summer of 1966 the script had been through a few drafts (including one in which the show ended with projected film footage of civil rights demonstrations in the South) and Kander and Ebb's score was largely in place, Prince postponed the production and took a trip. It changed everything.[43]

Prince traveled to Russia in the summer of 1966 and, with help from the American embassy after a snafu over his ticket reservation, snagged a last-row balcony seat for *Ten Days That Shook the World* at the Taganka Theater in Moscow. It shook *his* world with "the techniques, the vitality, the imagination to make every minute surprising, involving yet consistent with a concept."[44] Though Prince recognized many flaws in the revue based on John Reed's book about the October Revolution and had certainly seen and admired experimental work before (he claimed Meyerhold and Erwin Piscator as influences), he was simply bowled over. He loved the use of black velour drapes in place of painted drops, especially appreciating how they made various expressionistic illusions possible—"Paintings on the wall spoke, inanimate objects were animated, disembodied hands, feet, and faces washed across the stage."[45] Most of all, he was impressed by the "curtain of light" produced by lamps sunk into the covered-over orchestra pit and masking set changes going on behind it. As soon as he returned to New York, he asked his lighting designer, Jean Rosenthal, to create one of her own. The technique was impossible on the much larger Broadway stage, even for a genius like Rosenthal. But the idea led to Prince's plan to partition the play's world into the "real" settings—the vestibule in Sally's rooming house, her bedroom, the train, the cabaret—and a "limbo" area where some of the Emcee's numbers commenting on the action were performed, "illustrating changes in the German mind."[46] The division not only opened the show to a space of campy artifice (which, while echoing decadent Weimar cabaret, also bore some resemblance to, and likely also influenced, the glitter drag and "ridiculous" troupes of the period), it also emphasized the falseness of the separation between the political and private realms: history was impinging whether people accepted that fact or not. The Emcee—a character not found in the Isherwood stories—served as the ever more repellant guide into a morally declining world.

Rosenthal built a bank of lights close to the edge of the stage apron, which could be set at any height and aimed at any angle. Prince used it variously to create sharp shadows, disjunctive images, and "a curtain of dust" and even shined the lights directly in the audience's eyes on occasion.

The Taganka epiphany also meant that Prince was now speaking the native visual language of his set designer, who, in Prince's words, functioned like an "author": Boris Aronson.[47] As would become their process on all their collaborations to follow, Prince and Aronson talked for months, "rarely of things visual," as Prince recalled, but rather about philosophical, psychological, social, and political questions of human motivation and behavior. "When Boris talks," Prince said, "I hear and see things I neither heard nor saw before."[48]

In 1952 Aronson had designed van Druten's *I Am a Camera*. A realistic depiction of a shabby rented room, the set drew on Aronson's recollections of spaces he'd visited in Berlin when he lived there in the early 1920s. Sepia toned in his renderings, it featured heavy wooden furniture, a daybed center stage, a functional washstand, an antler hat rack hanging near the door. Aronson regarded the play as lightweight, barely concerned with the rise of the Nazis and of anti-Semitism.[49]

Cabaret gave him far more to work with. For the "real" places, he stuck to a naturalistic approach, wheeling in units from the wings for the train compartment where Cliff and Ernst meet in the first dramatic scene, for Herr Schultz's fruit stand, and so on. (Years later, Aronson said he would have done without all that furniture and all those wagons had he and Prince taken up the show at a later point, after they had grown more comfortable with the less conventional musicals they were helping to invent.)[50] The writing of those scenes matched their scenery: a troubled romance and a secondary troubled romance drove the plot, as in many a standard show. The only difference here was what caused, or resulted from, the troubles (anti-Semitism, an abortion). It was in the sordid cabaret and in the "limbo" area that Aronson and Prince could stretch themselves, their audiences, and the very form of the musical.

Typically, Aronson's designs for Prince included a "surprise"—an element they had never discussed but that was always visually, and especially thematically, useful to the director. For *Cabaret*, it was an iron staircase that wound its way upward stage left and helped to define the "limbo" area. This physical reality gave Prince one highly Piscatorian idea that came to define the production (and that he would repeat in their work on *Company* in 1970 and *Follies* in 1971): to place actors onstage as observers of the action. Here they were Kit Kat Club performers who lounged nonchalantly in the shadows, smoking and pointedly not paying attention to the events of the play. For Prince—and, he hoped, for the audience—they represented the dissociated German population generally.

Aronson came up with an even starker visual metaphor for Prince's intent to implicate the audience in the action. Prince wanted spectators sitting in the Broadhurst (and wherever the show would go on to play) to be addressed directly by Fräulein Schneider when she contemplates, in her act 2 song, whether to go ahead with her planned marriage to the Jewish fruit shop owner, Herr Schultz, in the face of rising Nazism: "What Would You Do?" Further, in the climate of American turmoil over racial inequality and the war in Vietnam—and, especially, of extreme measures to subdue the protest movements—Prince hoped to suggest an analogy: it *can* happen here. Aronson responded by placing a huge mirror upstage. "I wanted the audience to look at itself," he said.[51]

Situated upstage at the perspectival vanishing point and trapezoidal in shape like the floor below, the mirror tilted at different angles during the show. Sometimes, as the ceiling of the cabaret, it showed distorting reflections of the performers, making them seem misshapen, warped, perverse. When vertical—notably at the anti-Semitic turn at the close of the Emcee's song "If You Could See Her through My Eyes"[52]—it gave the audience a sharp, clear view of itself. It also greeted the arriving audience with its own reflection. Despite reigning convention, Aronson provided no show curtain. The show began, atypically, with no overture. Cymbals crashed, Joel Grey, playing the Emcee, came onstage, and a sign hanging over the stage, spelling out *Cabaret* in huge cursive letters, lit up its red bulbs. Audiences knew right away that they were in for a new experience. Though critics largely objected to what they regarded as a disconnect between the straight old plot and the disjunctive world of the cabaret, audiences didn't seem to mind. The show was huge at the box office, despite mixed reviews. It ran for almost three years.

Whether audiences thought about their own complacency in the face of social upheaval, as Prince had intended, is impossible to know, but given the show's popularity, it's fair to assume that they were not insulted by any implied accusation. (Accusation had become an acceptable if discomfiting mode downtown in quintessential 1960s works like Genet's *The Blacks* and the Living Theater's *The Brig*.) Certainly, though, whether or not reflectively, or even consciously, they had been drawn into one of America's newest and, it has turned out, enduring and often troubling ways of responding to the Holocaust: making an analogy of it. As the counterculture swelled and the antiwar movement escalated, the Holocaust became the rhetorical limit case for unaccountable evil, eventually appropriated for sloganeering against President Nixon or the European refugee masterminding the Asian war, Henry Kissinger.

Along with Prince and their other collaborators—not least among them, Stephen Sondheim—Aronson went on to bring more abstraction and innovation to the design of Broadway musicals. From the cold, steel urban jungle gym of *Company* (1970) to the dilapidated grandness of *Follies* (1971) to the ukiyo-e-inspired collages of *Pacific Overtures* (1976), the nonlinear, visually exciting alternative theater of Broadway that Aronson pioneered reflected his ingenious synthesis of the Russian avant-garde with America's exploratory energies of the sixties.

NOTES

1. Boris Aronson notes, Boris Aronson Papers and Designs, *T-VIM 1987–012, Billy Rose Theatre Division, New York Public Library for the Performing Arts (hereafter, BAPD), box 9, folder 12. I support here, too, the argument in Frank Rich and Lisa Aronson's indispensable and beautiful book *The Theatre Art of Boris Aronson* (New York: Alfred A. Knopf, 1987). While Boris Aronson's archived papers demonstrate the same points, Rich and Aronson's volume is an important source for this essay, and many of materials I found in those papers and quote here are also referred to in the book.

2. Aronson always maintained that he was born in 1900, but several sources correct the date to 1898.

3. For a discussion of many of these artists and their impact in the United States, see Joseph Horowitz, *Artists in Exile: How Refugees from Twentieth-Century War and Revolution Transformed the American Performing Arts* (New York: Harper, 2008). In this company, one should also mention the influential director Irwin Piscator. Though he and Aronson may have overlapped at the Group Theater, they do not appear ever to have worked together. One should note, too, designers of Aronson's generation who also did pioneering work—Mordecai Gorelik, Sam Leve, and Oliver Smith, to name only a few.

4. For discussion of Exter's work, see Nancy van Norman Baer and John E. Bowlt, *Theatre in Revolution: Russian Avant-Garde Stage Design, 1913–1935* (New York: Thames & Hudson, 1991).

5. Aronson notes, BAPD, box 9, folder 13.

6. Aronson, "Notes on Designing Musicals," manuscript, August 16, 1974, BAPD, box 9, folder 14.

7. John Mason Brown, *Theatre Arts Monthly*, n.d., clipping in BAPD, box 7, folder 2.

8. Lee Simonson "Russian Theory in the American Theater," *Nation*, June 12, 1929, 717–18.

9. "Interview with Hethmon," transcript, BAPD, box 9, folder 13.

10. Aronson notes, BAPD, box 9, folder 8.

11. Aronson notes, BAPD, box 9, folder 19.

12. Garson Kanin, "Boris Aronson (1900–1980): An Appreciation," BAPD, box 5, folder 1.

13. Aronson, interview by Kanin, transcript, BAPD, box 8, folder 22.

14. Kanin to Aronson, December 6, 1954, BAPD, box 35, folder 9.

15. Edna Nahshon, "From Page to Stage," in *Anne Frank Unbound: Media, Imagination, Memory*, ed. Barbara Kirshenblatt-Gimblett and Jeffrey Shandler (Bloomington: Indiana University Press, 2012), 61.

16. Aronson, interview by Kanin.

17. Ibid.

18. Ibid.

19. Kanin to Aronson, December 13, 1954, BAPD, box 35, folder 9.

20. Aronson, interview by Kanin.

21. Rich and Aronson, *Theatre Art*, 124.

22. Aronson, interview by Kanin.

23. Kanin to Aronson, December 13, 1954, BAPD, box 35, folder 9.

24. Among the most notorious redactions was the bowdlerization of Anne's adolescent musings about sex and the truncating of her statement of belief in the goodness of humanity. See Jeffrey Shandler, "Introduction: Anne Frank, the Phenomenon," in Kirshenblatt-Gimblett and Shandler, *Anne Frank Unbound*, 1–22; Sally Charnow, "Critical Thinking: Scholars Reread the Diary," in ibid., 291–308; and Anne Frank, *The Diary of a Young Girl: The Definitive Edition*, ed. Otto Frank and Mirjam Pressler (New York: Doubleday, 1995).

25. See Nahshon, "From Page to Stage."

26. Edward Shapiro, *A Time for Healing: American Jewry since World War II* (Baltimore: Johns Hopkins University Press, 1992), 15.

27. Will Herberg, *Catholic, Protestant, Jew: An Essay in American Religious Sociology* (1953; reprint, New York: Doubleday, 1983).

28. Shapiro, *Time for Healing*, 53.

29. Ibid., 37ff.

30. Ibid. See also Howard M. Sachar, *A History of the Jews in America* (New York: Vintage Books/Random House, 1993).

31. See the reviews by Walter Kerr, *New York Times*, November 21, 1966, 62; and by William Hawkins, *New York World Telegram*, November 21, 1966, n.p.

32. For the background of *Fiddler* and the making of the show, see Alisa Solomon, *Wonder of Wonders: A Cultural History of "Fiddler on the Roof"* (New York: Metropolitan Books, 2013).

33. Aronson qtd. in Rich and Aronson, *Theatre Art*, 22.

34. Aronson qtd. in ibid.

35. See Seth Wolitz, "The Americanization of Tevye, or, Boarding the Jewish Mayflower," *American Quarterly* 40.4 (1988): 514–36.

36. Matthew Frye Jacobson, *Roots Too: White Ethnic Revival in Post–Civil Rights America* (Cambridge, MA: Harvard University Press, 2006).

37. Aronson notes, BAPD, box 9, folder 14.

38. Ibid.

39. Barbara Kirshenblatt-Gimblett, "Imagining Europe: The Popular Arts of American Jewish Ethnography," in *Divergent Centers: Shaping Jewish Cultures in Israel and America*, ed. Deborah Dash Moore and Ilan Troen (New Haven, CT: Yale University Press, 2001), 155–91.

40. Betty Friedan, *The Feminine Mystique* (New York: Dell, 1963).

41. *American Jewish Yearbook* (New York: American Jewish Committee and Jewish Publication Society, 1899–2008).

42. Thomas B. Morgan, "The Vanishing American Jew," *Look*, May 1964, 43–46.

43. Prince recounts this experience in *Contradictions: Notes on Twenty-Six Years in the Theatre* (New York: Dodd, Mead, 1974). For a full consideration of the development and impact of *Cabaret*, see Keith Garebian, *The Making of Cabaret* (New York: Oxford University Press, 2011).

44. Prince, *Contradictions*, 144.

45. Ibid.

46. Ibid., 131.

47. Prince notes, BAPD, box 33, folder 1.

48. Prince, *Contradictions*, 131–32.

49. Aronson, interview by Kanin.

50. Aronson, draft for grant application, n.d., BAPD, box 8, folder 17.

51. Aronson, "Complete taped interview," transcript, n.d., interviewer not identified, BAPD, box 8, folder 24.

52. For discussion of changes to the ending of the song, see Garebian, *Making of Cabaret*, esp. 85–86.

David A. Crespy

Paradigm for New Play Development

The Albee-Barr-Wilder Playwrights Unit

Albarwild Theatre Arts, Inc.'s (ABW) Playwrights Unit would have never existed without the unique partnership of its off- and on-Broadway producers Richard Barr and Clinton Wilder and the playwright Edward Albee. The Unit was initially financially dependent on income from Albee's *Who's Afraid of Virginia Woolf?*, and its fortunes were directly tied to Albee's success as a new American playwright and his own explorations of dramaturgical form and content. It provided a meeting place in the 1960s between the professional but somewhat moribund off-Broadway theater of this period and the freewheeling noncommercial experimentation of the off-off-Broadway scene. For a period of nearly ten years, the Unit gave off-off-Broadway playwrights crossover opportunities to the commercial theater, blurring the boundaries between the two. It grew out of Albee's enormous influence on theater at the time and made it possible for the experimentation of noncommercial radical theater to organically influence and, ultimately, to transform the commercial mainstream theater.

From 1962 through 1971, Albee had the rare opportunity to serve as a co-producer of his works on Broadway. This fact, coupled with Albee's remarkable early success as a new young playwright on Broadway, supported and justified to Richard Barr his own central notion regarding the theater—that the playwright and the play are the unifying element of any theatrical production.[1]

Because of the initiatory nature of much of Albee's work, and because Albee did this experimentation in full public view on Broadway with no apology, the idea that American playwrights deserved a forum in which to learn and take risks in full public view was central to the ABW producing philosophy. Add to that Barr's interest in the new absurdist work of European authors, including Beckett, Genet, Ionesco, and Arrabal, and it becomes apparent that the ABW producing partnership created a remarkably fertile environment for new playwrights and their experimentation in the 1960s. The ABW Playwrights Unit was the jewel in the crown of that producing organization because its work represented the ABW producing philosophy at its most elemental and most important stage—at the point of discovery of new voices for the theater.

Albee's commercial success, in particular with his plays *Zoo Story* and *Who's Afraid of Virginia Woolf?*, stimulated an atmosphere in which new plays and new playwrights were suddenly hot ticket items. The Playwrights Unit was a significant manifestation of Albee's influence, and the Unit's success contributed to the much larger nonprofit business of new play development, which grew out of the off-off-Broadway movement and became fully realized in the creation of the National Playwrights Conference at the Eugene O'Neill Theater Center (for which Barr and Albee were consulted). Ironically, the business of new play development has become something that Albee has forsworn, but his success as a young playwright and his enthusiasm for supporting new work himself were its springboard.[2] Albee's guiding instruction when it comes to the training of playwrights in the theater, now and during the tenure of the Playwrights Unit, is, "Every time you write a play, try to fail. . . . Do what you don't know you can do."[3] This mantra was the basis of the work at the Playwrights Unit, and Albee's words echoed those spoken by off-off-Broadway impresario Joe Cino to his playwrights at the Caffe Cino: "Do what you have to do."

The Playwrights Unit, a project of Albarwild Theatre Arts, Inc. (Albee, Barr, and Wilder's not-for-profit organization), provided a professional workshop situation for playwrights from whose ranks came Louis Auchincloss, Mart Crowley, Charles Dizenzo, Gene Feist, Paul Foster, Frank Gagliano, John Guare, A. R. Gurney, LeRoi Jones, Lee Kalcheim, Adrienne Kennedy, Terrence McNally, Leonard Melfi, Howard Moss, James Prideaux, Sam Shepard, Megan Terry, Jean-Claude van Itallie, Lanford Wilson, Doric Wilson, and Paul Zindel. The significance of this group extends far beyond its brief existence as a producing entity. The Playwrights Unit, as a playwrights' workshop, served as an early model for such organizations as Playwrights Horizons and the Center Theatre Group at the Mark Taper Forum (both organizations were founded by Playwrights Unit managers) and, to a certain extent, the playwrights' laboratories of organizations such as Circle Repertory Theatre and the New York Shakespeare Festival.

Albee's point of view regarding new play development was that the new play, if it is going to work, will work, and if it doesn't, it wasn't a very good play in the first place. This is a radical departure from the current model of new play development, which seeks to "fix" plays through incrementally more complex concert and staged readings, workshops, and minimal productions. Albee attacked this model of new play development in an interview in *American Theatre*:

> It is to de-ball the plays; to castrate them; to smooth down all the rough edges so they can't cut, can't hurt. It's to make them commercially tolerable to a smug audience. It's not to make plays any better. Most playwrights who write a good play write it from the beginning.[4]

With this in mind, Richard Barr, Edward Albee, and Clinton Wilder tested plays at the Playwrights Unit, at the Cherry Lane, and on Broadway by the fire of full production. They were able to do this because their production budgets were tightly managed.[5] If the play worked and the critics were receptive, they kept it open; if it did not and was losing money, they closed it as quickly as possible and went on to the next play. (Albee later complained that Barr was perhaps too eager to close a play because of poor audience numbers.)[6] The scripts were, in Albee's, Barr's, and Wilder's opinion, as finished as they needed to be for production. Barr insisted on this when interviewed for an article in *Theatre Arts* in 1961:

> That's the first thing we've learned, or relearned: We are not going into rehearsal until the script we plan to open with, on Broadway, is in our hands. There will be changes made in that script, of course, but they'll be minor changes, not the terrible, frightening business of trying to create a whole new second or third act between New Haven and New York. Which brings us right up to the second point. If you start out with a finished play, there is no need for the week in Wilmington or wherever, and the two weeks in Philadelphia or Boston, where you're bound to lose a substantial amount of money.[7]

Barr and Wilder were certainly interested in the experimentation of off-off-Broadway but, as consummate professionals, their focus was always on the development of scripts for the commercial theater. In that sense, they "invented" play development as it is practiced today, moving scripts from workshop to professional production. Their form of development, however, was focused on full (albeit inexpensive) productions rather than on a series of incrementally more sophisticated readings.

Their reasoning was simple; they were trying to avoid what was then the standard practice of bringing a new play to Broadway—"the out-of-town tryout." Plays were tested for critical reception in places like Hartford, Washington, or New Haven to determine what additional changes needed to be made to the script before the all-important New York production. According to Barr and Wilder, the out-of-town tryout was not terribly useful as a means of developing a finished script:

And so you go into production and suffer through the ridiculous agony of having the author—and the director and the actors and various friends, enemies and people you meet in hotel lobbies—rewrite a three-act play in New Haven or Boston or Philadelphia. It's absolutely insane—and it's not really necessary.[8]

For Barr, the place to test new plays was off-Broadway at his Cherry Lane Theatre and at the Playwrights Unit—he also initiated the preview performance process on Broadway, providing audiences with an opportunity to judge a play on its own merits before a review changed their minds. A successful off-Broadway production provided a far better indication of what New York audiences would accept and support. Barr was convinced that if he liked a script enough to produce it in New York, it was as finished as it needed to be.

On the opposite extreme from the out-of-town tryout is the current model of the play development process, with its endless cycle of play readings. The primary difference between how plays were developed in the past and how they are developed now is the difference between the closed professional readings of the past, which led to full production, and the current model of public readings of new work followed by endless discussions and criticism, leading to more readings. The open reading or workshop production is not terribly popular among playwrights, and David Kahn and Donna Breed, authors of *Scriptwork: A Director's Approach to New Play Development*, elaborate why:

Any playwright, director, actor, designer, or audience member will prefer a full production to a workshop. Workshops are a means to that end, or at least they should be. Too often, workshops or other development "processes" are excuses to avoid the difficult and risky business of producing new plays. Consequently, there is frequently cited backlash against play development workshops conducted without the prospect of future production, or workshopping a play unnecessarily so that it becomes "developed to death."[9]

Play readings often involve postreading discussions with the audience, a process that many playwrights abhor. Douglas Anderson, in his *TDR* article "The American Dream Machine: Thirty Years of New Play Development in America," argues that the new play development process of play readings leads to plays that are wordy, untheatrical, and designed primarily to appeal to dramaturgy by committee. Plays that enter into that process as challenging, nonrealistic, nonlinear works that experiment with form and content become realistic, linear works that work along traditional dramaturgical techniques.[10]

In contrast to this current model of play development, the Playwrights Unit was run as a miniature of Albarwild's other venue, the Cherry Lane Theatre, rather than as a workshop per se. While there were certainly readings at the Unit (they occurred primarily toward the end of its existence), the focus was on production. Each play received a full production on a minimal budget with professional directors and actors. While the production values were certainly not at the level of plays produced in Albee/Barr/Wilder's off-Broadway venue at the Cherry Lane, the plays received nearly full scenic values, including lighting, sound, properties, costume, and scenic elements. There was little interference from either the producers or the managers of the Unit. As many of the playwrights who were interviewed for this study could attest, the primary relationship was one between playwright and director. While there is evidence of the use of mimeographed handouts for discussion purposes, there were rarely the postproduction discussions that have since become a familiar part of the new play development process. This prejudice toward full production of new plays was tied deeply to the personal histories of Richard Barr, Clinton Wilder, and Edward Albee—thus it makes sense to pause a moment to look at each career individually prior to the creation of the Playwrights Unit.

The Unit was the brainchild of Richard Barr, and it was Barr's skill as a producer and his fundamental belief in the playwright that provided the impetus for the Unit's creation. Barr's idealism as a producer grew out of his initial theatrical experiences with Orson Welles's Mercury Theatre. Starting as a gofer in the Mercury's productions on Broadway, including *Danton's Death* and the ambitious (and disastrous) *Five Kings*, Barr became Welles's indispensable assistant, right down to bringing him his enormous "regular" lunches every day on a tray, "without spilling," from the local Longchamps, a popular 1930s restaurant chain, consisting of "a large rare steak, salad, and a double portion of pistachio ice cream."[11] Barr took part in Welles's radio broadcast "The War of the Worlds" and went to Hollywood with Welles, where he was associate producer on *Citizen Kane*.[12] Barr actually appeared in *Citizen Kane* and caused a continuity problem; in the film he played a reporter but was caught in separate frames with and without his hat (perhaps ending an important career in film).[13] Barr's quixotic quests to produce the absurdists on Broadway and develop risky new work off- and off-off-Broadway were definitely influenced by his initial mentorship by Welles.[14]

During World War II Barr served as a captain in the U.S. Air Force, 1941 to 1946, and as a producer for its Army Air Corps First Motion Picture Unit (AACFMPU) in California.[15] After the war, Barr served as dialogue director on several films. Thereafter he decided to give up an acting career and went into directing and producing. From 1946 to 1948 he staged various summer stock productions. On Broadway, he directed José Ferrer in *Volpone*, Richard Whorf in *Richard III*, and Francis Lederer in *Arms and the Man*. In the 1950s, under the producing aegis of Bowden, Barr, and Bullock (with his Broadway producing partners, Charles Bowden and H. Ridgely Bullock Jr.), he produced several Broadway productions, none particularly successful, including *Hotel Paradiso*, starring Bert Lahr; *Fallen Angels*, starring Nancy Walker; and a triple bill entitled *All in One* that consisted of Leonard Bernstein's *Trouble in Tahiti*, a Paul Draper dance program, and Tennessee Williams's *27 Wagons Full of Cotton*.

Barr left the Broadway theatrical firm of Bowden, Barr, and Bullock in 1959 to found Theatre 1960 off-Broadway with H. B. Lutz and Harry Joe Brown Jr.[16] Their first production was an evening of two one-act plays, Samuel Beckett's *Krapp's Last Tape* and Edward Albee's first play, *The Zoo Story*, at the Provincetown Playhouse on January 14, 1960. The choice of one-act plays, particularly those of new writers, was calculated. Barr elaborates:

> Take men like Williams and Inge . . . they wrote dozens of one-act plays. We want to capture the possibilities of such men while they are still in the one-act stage, to speed the gestation period to Broadway.[17]

The decision to premiere Albee's first play was Barr's most inspired. In it he confirmed to himself and the critics that it was indeed possible to use off-Broadway as a springboard for important new playwrights. Several times over the years he stated that his continued support of new plays was part of a search for another Edward Albee.

Clinton Wilder, Barr's partner for much of his producing career, was, according to Edward Albee, "a dilettante, in the very best sense of the word." While certainly the financial heavyweight in the ABW partnership, Wilder was also an experienced Broadway producer. He was born Clinton Eugene Wilder Jr. on July 7, 1920, the son of Clinton Eugene and Frances (Kornreich) Wilder. Wilder's father was a successful engineer and manufacturer. Wilder attended Lawrenceville School in New Jersey and spent three years at Princeton. Serving in the U.S. Army, he manned antiaircraft artillery from 1942 to 1943 and served in the USAAF from 1943 to 1945, appearing in the USAAF production of *Winged Victory* (1943–44) during World War II. Wilder served as a member of the Actors' Equity Association, the League of New York Theatres, the League of Off-Broadway Theatres, and the Theatre Development Fund (he was both a founder and director of the fund).[18]

Wilder began his career in the theater as the stage manager for the 1947 tour of *Heartsong*, as well as serving as the stage manager for *A Streetcar Named Desire* at the Ethel Barrymore Theatre on Broadway (December 3, 1947). He then became associated with Cheryl Crawford in the production of *Regina*, Marc Blitzstein's musical adaptation of Lillian Hellman's *Little Foxes*, produced at the 46th Street Theatre in 1949.[19] He then produced Max Shulman and Robert Paul Smith's *The Tender Trap* at the Longacre Theatre and (with George Axelrod as coproducer) Gore Vidal's *Visit to a Small Planet* at the Booth Theatre. He produced, with Norris Houghton and T. Edward Hambleton, the Phoenix Theatre production of Luigi Pirandello's *Six Characters in Search of an Author* in 1955. In 1957 Wilder, in concert with Donald Albery, presented *The World of Suzie Wong* at the Prince of Wales Theatre, London. In 1961 Wilder joined with Richard Barr to found Theatre 1961 and thereafter, until the founding of the Playwrights Unit, he coproduced with Barr until 1968.[20]

The third partner in the producing partnership of Albee/Barr/Wilder was, of course, Edward Albee. The inclusion of a playwright in a major producing team was and remains very rare. One of Albee's more famous predecessors in this regard was Eugene O'Neill, who contributed greatly to the producing decisions made at the Provincetown Playhouse in the 1920s.[21] His first play, *The Zoo Story*, was produced in Berlin at the Schiller Theatre Werkstatt on September 28, 1959. Shortly thereafter, Richard Barr produced *The Zoo Story* at the Provincetown Playhouse on January 14, 1960, and in London at the Arts Theatre on August 25, 1960. Albee's *The Death of Bessie Smith* also had its premiere in Berlin at the Schlosspark Theatre and was later produced by Barr at the York Playhouse. His play *The Sandbox* premiered with four one-act plays in a production entitled *4 in 1* at the Jazz Gallery. Albee's *Fam and Yam* was produced at the White Barn at Westport, Connecticut, that summer. His *The American Dream* was paired with William Flanagan's musical *Bartleby* at the York Playhouse in 1961. Albee's first full-length work was the three-act *Who's Afraid of Virginia Woolf?*, which was produced on Broadway at the Billy Rose Theatre on October 13, 1962, and subsequently went on tour in the United States and in London. Albee began his producing career with Richard Barr and Clinton Wilder with Ugo Betti's *Corruption in the Palace of Justice* at the Cherry Lane Theatre under the aegis of Barr and Wilder's Theatre 1964. Albee shortly thereafter participated in the organization of the Playwrights Unit.[22]

The Unit was founded on September 29, 1963, the year when the Ford Foundation established its funding program for playwrights. Albee, Barr, and Wilder had been producing new works at the Cherry Lane Theatre before this time, but in 1963 the Village South Theatre on Vandam Street became the home of the Playwrights Unit and was leased exclusively for the development of new plays. The initial funding did not come from a foundation but rather from the profits of Albee's Broadway production of *Who's Afraid of Virginia Woolf?*. Later Albee and Barr did seek and receive funding from the Rockefeller Foundation, but initially the Playwrights Unit was funded privately through Albee's generosity.[23] Free of the financial constraints that plague such workshops today, the Unit reflected the idealism and genuine support for writers at the outset of what could be considered a golden age of American drama, from the early 1960s through the late 1980s.

Of the dramatists mentioned above whose first plays were produced by the Unit, more than fifteen have sustained important careers writing in the theater and have garnered the highest accolades and critical acclaim the American theater has to offer. While not every play that came out of the Unit was significant, it certainly provided fertile ground for the stimulation of playwriting talent. If the measure of success for a play development group is the sustained and significant careers of the writers it develops, then the Playwrights Unit was an unmitigated success. If one adds to that achievement the production of two of America's seminal works of alternative theater, LeRoi Jones's *Dutchman* and Mart Crowley's *The Boys in the Band*, then the Playwrights Unit and the producing philosophy of Richard Barr, Edward Albee, and Clinton Wilder remain unparalleled in recent theatrical history. For not only was the Albarwild producing team providing a laboratory for new work, they were producing that work professionally at the Cherry Lane Theatre and other theater spaces—work, it must be added, that could only be termed explosively experimental for its time.

The Playwrights Unit actually had its beginnings well before the initial meeting of playwrights on Sunday, September 29, 1963. The producing organization, Theatre 1960–1971 (the name changed each year), began with Barr's production of Albee's *Zoo Story* in 1959, which he paired with Samuel Beckett's *Krapp's Last Tape* at the Provincetown Playhouse. Later, in addition to producing new plays by lesser-known playwrights, Barr, Wilder, and Albee underwrote a series of Monday evening productions. John Keating describes this enterprise in his 1963 *New York Times* article "Action Speaks Louder . . .":

Broadening their search for the avant-garde playwrights they felt the theatre was ignoring, Barr and Wilder also put on occasional, admission-free Monday night performances of works by unknowns whose talents they admired but felt were not yet ready for regular production before a paying audience. Over the last two seasons, they have underwritten four of these "Monday Nights." The Playwrights Unit is a direct outgrowth of this project. Last month, they issued invitations to 35 young playwrights. Twenty-three writers answered the call, bringing a total of 20 scripts with them.[24]

Plays produced in this early period predating the Playwrights Unit include *A Toy for the Clowns*, by Gene Feist (founder of the Roundabout Theatre in New York City); *Chit Chat on a Rat*, by C. Skrivanek Atherton; *Prometheus Rebound*, by Lawrence Wunderlich; *Ex-Miss Copper Queen on A Set of Pills*, by Megan Terry; *This Side of the Door*, by Terrence McNally; and *Like Other People*, by Jack Owen. However, as Theatre 1964, the triumvirate of Albee, Barr, and Wilder procured the Village South Theatre at 15 Vandam Street, a small, 199-seat off-off-Broadway house that still exists as a working off-Broadway theater space, and with the managerial skills of director–literary agent Edward Parone they began the first season of the Playwrights Unit. Young playwrights, culled from Barr's enormous script collection and from his visits to off-off-Broadway theaters and cafés, were invited to participate. Twenty-four plays were performed in the Unit's initial year. Its first significant production, LeRoi Jones's *Dutchman*, directed by Parone, transferred off Broadway to the Cherry Lane Theatre with phenomenal success. The Playwrights Unit produced Jean-Claude van Itallie's first play, *War*, also with great success, although the play did not move immediately to another production. Other plays from the Unit's 1963–64 season that were later produced by Albee, Barr, and Wilder included Lee Kalcheim's *A Party for Divorce* and *Match Play* (produced at the Provincetown Playhouse, October 11, 1966); *Pigeons*, by Lawrence Osgood; and *Conerico Was Here to Stay*, by Frank Gagliano (produced as part of a series of ten new American plays at the Cherry Lane Theatre on March 3, 1965). Kalcheim later became the lead writer for television's *All in the Family*, and Gagliano later headed the playwriting program at Carnegie-Mellon University.

Running underneath the producing decisions made by Barr, Albee, and Wilder was the conviction that the playwright was the most important single artist in the theater and the corollary that the production of plays ought to revolve around the playwright's vision. In her 1968 *New York Times Magazine* article "Triple Threat On, Off and Off-Off Broadway," Barbara La Fontaine quoted Richard Barr on this subject:

> Barr says crisply, "A play needs a firm hand. Sometimes it is in the wrong place."—i.e., when the playwright's is tentative, being new or perhaps spectacularly poor, the hand may be that of a famous director, a star or a backer's

wife. But isn't a production a cooperative effort? "Indeed it is," Barr says, "but so is war, and I would like to see the individual in a war speak up and say, 'I'm going to go *this* way.' There is a hierarchy of command, and it should stem from the playwright's intention."[25]

Given this statement, the guidance of the Playwrights Unit was, not surprisingly, hands-off, with the playwright in charge of her or his own production. The day-to-day management of the Unit was left to its managing directors, Edward Parone, Charles (Chuck) Gnys, Robert Moss, and Bruce Hoover. All four managers of the Unit were energetic theater practitioners, primarily directors, who shared with the Albee/Barr/Wilder producing team the conviction that the playwright provided the guiding vision in producing the play.

Edward Parone was the first manager of the Unit, guiding its first season from September 1963 to May 1964. An experienced theater professional, Parone had served as production supervisor of special projects at the Phoenix Theatre and as an assistant to the producers T. Edward Hambleton and Norris Houghton for their production of Strindberg's *Miss Julie* and *The Stronger*. Parone then joined the staff of William Liebling and Audrey Wood as a play reader and later became an agent at the William Morris Agency. While at William Morris, Parone brought Edward Albee's *Zoo Story* to the attention of Richard Barr, sending him off on his cycle of Albee productions.

Parone then moved to California, where he directed all of Albee's short plays. Following his West Coast productions of Albee's work, he was invited by Barr and Albee to serve as managing director for the Playwrights Unit. Parone was the original director of LeRoi Jones's *Dutchman* at the Playwrights Unit and at the Cherry Lane.[26] Parone also directed Lawrence Osgood's *Pigeons* at the Playwrights Unit. After Parone left the Unit, he founded the playwrights' workshop of Mark Taper Forum, initially producing an evening of plays from the Playwrights Unit entitled *Collision Course*, which he later published as an anthology of plays under that same title.

Chuck Gnys, the manager of the Playwrights Unit from September 1964 through May 1970, was its longest and most important influence outside of Albee, Barr, and Wilder. A native of Central Falls, Rhode Island, Gnys served as the company manager of the Broadway productions of *Camelot* and *Kwamina* and was a production assistant for three shows, *The Perfect Setup*, *Viva Madison Avenue*, and *The Poker Game*. He directed Ann Jellicoe's *The Knack* at Dinner Theatres of America and served as the administrative producer of Jerome Robbins's American Theatre Laboratory. Gnys directed more productions at the Playwrights Unit than any other director involved in its productions, including

Up to Thursday and *4-H Club*, by Sam Shepard; *Hunting the Jingo Bird*, by Kenneth Pressman; *The Rape of Bunny Stuntz*, by A. R. Gurney Jr.; *A Great Career*, by Charles Dizenzo; *The Club Bedroom*, by Louis Auchincloss; *The Palace at 4 A.M.*, by Howard Moss; and Philip Magdalany's *Watercolor* and *Criss-Crossing*. Gnys also staged both *Up to Thursday* and *Hunting the Jingo Bird* off-Broadway at the Cherry Lane Theatre for Theatre 1965's New Playwrights Series. He produced Emanuel Peluso's *Good Day* and *The Exhaustion of Our Son's Love* in a double bill off-Broadway at the Cherry Lane. In 1970 Gnys directed Philip Magdalany's *Watercolor* and *Criss-Crossing* on Broadway at the ANTA Theatre as a production of the Playwrights Unit.

Following Gnys in 1970 was Robert Moss, the indefatigable director and producer who ran the Unit until its end in 1971, along with Bruce Hoover, a director and professional stage manager. Moss spent four years as the production manager of APA Repertory Company. In 1966 he directed Cliff Arquette in a summer tour of *You Can't Take It with You*. In 1967 he staged *Two Gentlemen of Verona* for the Los Angeles Theatre in the Parks program. He directed Stephen Jacobsen's *Needs* and Kenneth Pressman's *For Breakfast, Mr. Sachs* at the Playwrights Unit. Moss directed Louis Auchincloss's *The Club Bedroom* for the ANTA Matinee Series, *Summertime* for the American Academy of Dramatic Art, *Room Service* for the Comedy Club, *The Marriage of Figaro* for the Mc-Carter Repertory company, *Tunnel of Love* for Dinner Theatres of America, and *As You Like It* for Equity Library Theatre.

With a mailing list borrowed from the Playwrights Unit, Moss then founded Playwrights Horizons at the Clark Center for the Performing Arts. In a very real sense, Playwrights Horizons sprang forth directly from that mailing list, which Moss took as his final payment as the Unit's last manager. According to Edward Cohen, the former associate artistic director of Jewish Repertory Theatre and a playwright at the Playwrights Unit, Moss carried with him from the Unit the conviction that "if a new play had a page of talent, he would produce it."[27] It was perhaps this guiding principle that later led one reporter to call the Unit "surely the most generous and effective theatre workshop in the country."[28]

Speaking of Gnys's management, Richard Lipsett, a production assistant and script reader at the Unit, reinforced the notion that Barr, Albee, and Wilder left Gnys and his playwrights to their own devices.[29] While the "carte blanche" attitude of the producers with regard to both the playwright's work and Gnys's management of the Unit provided a certain degree of freedom, the producers were not entirely absent from the Unit's activities. Barr directed several productions at the Unit, all three producers attended many of its performances, and Albee, noticing a lack of member playwrights at performances at the Unit, wrote a general letter to the Unit playwrights exhorting them to read each other's scripts and attend performances. In an interview, Albee offered the reasoning behind his letter:

> A very important thing was the fact that I wanted each of the playwrights to involve themselves in the work of the other playwrights. On the understanding that you learn not only from what happens to your work but from following through what happens to another playwright's work—you might learn something constructive and useful about revision or lack of revision or digging your heels in. I wanted them to be helpful to one another, not only to themselves.[30]

Despite Albee's best hopes that the writers at his Unit would grow into a genuine community of writers, this was not happening. And Albee had growing concerns about internal operations of the Unit, the quality of the work, and the decisions regarding which plays were being produced. This led to him to submit his own short play *Box* to the Unit under the assumed name of Rayne Endars. Chuck Gnys's subsequent rejection of this script, while later dismissed as unimportant in a *New York Times* article about the Unit's activities, was the primary reason for Albee's decision to remove Gnys from his position.[31] In 1970 Gnys left to direct a rock musical, *The Survival of Saint Joan*, which had its beginnings at the Playwrights Unit, and went on to a successful career managing actors, musicians, and other performers under the aegis of Curtis Brown Management.

Despite the decision to fire Gnys, over the course of the Unit's existence, interference from the ABW producing management was minimal. In fact, the decision of the producers to keep a low profile at the Unit was a conscious one. Albee stresses this in Keating's article for the *New York Times*:

> "We hope the playwrights themselves will dictate the operation," he [Albee] said. "What we're going to do is to provide a theatre to work in, a stage, actors, a director, whatever we can do to be helpful. We are not going to say anything about the kind of work that should be done. If a man wants to do something that seems completely incomprehensible to us, fine." . . . Mr. Albee stressed the fact that the unit will not be a course in playwriting—"You can't teach that," he said—but he will be on hand to discuss, analyze and advise any writer who wants his help. "It will be a workshop operation," he said.[32]

The absence of the Albee/Barr/Wilder presence was, of course, a double-edged sword, for on the one hand there were none of the pressures associated with producing under the aegis of a famous producing group, while on the other hand there was little of the hoped-for advice, good or otherwise, that was expected or desired from the playwrights.

Edward Albee was, perhaps, of the three producing partners, the least available for consultation. James Prideaux, playwright and screenwriter, offers this remembrance, caught at a moment after a successful production of his play, *Postcards*, at the Playwrights Unit, a moment when Prideaux was particularly hungry for a response from Albee himself:

> On the way home, walking through Greenwich Village, I glanced into the window of a dusty old bookstore and there he [Albee] was, sitting in the back, bent over a book. For a moment he looked up and our eyes met. I was dying to go in, to tell him how much I admired his work, but he gave no sign of recognition and looked right down again. I walked on, a little saddened. Surely he must have thought something of me and my play or I wouldn't be a part of his Playwrights Unit. Later Richard told me he hadn't read *Postcards*. It was unusual that he had stopped into the Cherry Lane at all. In the years to come, I was never to forget that it was through Edward's Playwrights Unit that my career as a playwright was made possible. How could I not be grateful to him for that?[33]

It must be added that while other writers at the Unit had similar stories of only seeing Albee in the back of darkened theaters or catching a rare glimpse of him as he entered or left with brief business, others, like Kenneth Pressman, remember Albee as a motivating force in playwriting at that time.[34] Playwright John Guare, whose *For Wally Pantoni We Leave a Credenza* was produced at the Unit, referred in an interview to Albee as a sort of playwright-hero who had battled the forces of Broadway and had won.[35] Guare noted that Albee figured even more importantly than Barr as the motivating force behind the Unit, for even though his was a presence that was fleeting, it was the one that gave the Unit its unique importance in the milieu of the off-off-Broadway movement.

In 1970, after Gnys's departure, the management of the Unit was handed to Robert Moss, who had previously directed several productions at the Unit, and to his partner, Bruce Hoover, a director and Broadway stage manager. Moss managed the Unit until May 1971, producing the plays of Michael Carton, Edward M. Cohen, David Trainer, Stephen Jacobsen, Doric Wilson, Michael Wilkes, and Kenneth Pressman. The Unit closed shortly after the critical and financial failure of Albee's *All Over*, which was directed by John Gielgud on Broadway. The critical failure of *All Over* was an immediate financial cause for the Unit's closure, but the very nature of producing in New York City had

changed since the heady days of the early sixties. By 1966 the three producers had already made a major outlay of over $120,000 to run the Unit in its
three years of existence. The budget of the Unit grew from its initial outlay
of $23,232.88 in 1964 to $29,045.33 in 1967, a 25 percent increase in the cost of
its operation in three years. In the summer of 1968 Albarwild Theatre Arts,
Inc., received $197,000 in funding from the Rockefeller Foundation, $65,000
of which was to be matched. Of those funds, $32,000 was used to maintain
the Playwrights Unit, while $165,000 was to be used to cover operations at the
Cherry Lane Theatre.[36] Thus by 1968 the cost of running the Unit had increased
by at least 38 percent. By 1971, the year the Unit closed, the costs of operation
had reached $1,000 a week, or $52,000 a year, by Albee's own estimates.[37]

In another sense, the very success the Unit achieved may have sowed the
seeds of its own demise. One of the frequent comments that the playwrights
made in the interviews conducted for this study was that there were no reviews written of the productions of the Unit—in general the critical eye of the
New York theater was not on off-off-Broadway. However, with the phenomenal
success of *The Boys in the Band* in 1968, off-off-Broadway was suddenly seen
in a different light. John Guare, in a discussion about the Playwrights Unit's
production of his play *To Wally Pantoni We Leave a Credenza*, suggested that
the success of *The Boys in the Band* somehow ended the experimentation of
off-off-Broadway:

> One of the great things about it was that they [the off-off-Broadway pro-
> ductions] weren't reviewed . . . and then bit by bit, they got to be reviewed.
> One of the other things that was great was that they were sort of just done, I
> mean you just felt very safe and free. . . . There wasn't anyone there to move
> it or buy it. And then they suddenly got to be reviewed, brutally or extrava-
> gantly. . . . Off-off-Broadway had become something that fed commercial
> theatre rather than being experimental.[38]

In addition to the burgeoning critical consideration of off-off-Broadway, another reason for the closing of the Playwrights Unit and the demise of the importance of the off-off-Broadway scene was the growth of other competing not-
for-profit theaters like Circle Repertory and the New York Shakespeare Festival,
which rendered the Playwrights Unit somewhat redundant in its mission to
develop new playwrights.

The milieu of the off-off-Broadway theater of the 1960s and its coffeehouse
theaters—Caffe Cino, Café La MaMa, the Judson Poets Theater—provided a
fertile ground for the sort of experimental theater that Barr, Wilder, and Al-

bee were trying to develop. There is a sense, however, that Barr, in particular, felt that these playwrights were not being served in the cafés, that their talents were being dissipated in less-than-professional surroundings.[39] In addition, the ABW Playwrights Unit was specifically geared toward the playwright's work, unlike the Playwrights Unit of the Actors Studio, which at that time was controlled by actors and directors. James Prideaux, one of the playwrights at the Unit, had this brief statement to offer about the work at the Actors Studio:

> We met on Mondays at 5:00 PM, about 200 of us, all budding playwrights. Generally we would see a one-act or a scene from a play one of us had written, followed by an open discussion. These were savage. They all hacked away at what they had seen with a kind of vengeance. It was as if were one to succeed, others must be made to fail. I had entered the group in the hope of presenting some of my work there, but I soon saw that my self-confidence, tough as it was, couldn't withstand the kind of attacks they made on each other's work. I could never show them anything of mine. And many times, at the end of these discussions, I would swear to leave and never return.[40]

To this memory of the Playwrights Unit of the Actors Studio, Edward Parone, manager of the ABW Playwrights Unit, in his preface to his collection of plays from the Unit, *New Theatre in America*, adds this description:

> The Actor's Studio formed its Playwrights Unit a few years ago. Plays or scenes from plays by the members are performed usually, though not always, by Studio actors. The unit is run by a committee; meetings are held. Discussions take place after the performances. The unit is supported by the Studio, with foundation money for a specific number of projects. But the Studio, it seems from my observation, is in theory and practice an *actor's* studio, not a playwrights' or even directors'. And perhaps the following true story may be pertinent, though it may not be typical. A young actress, a member of the Studio, came to read for the part of the girl in LeRoi Jones' *Dutchman*. She mounted the stage and riffling the script in her hands and looking somewhere between the playwright and the director, said, "Uh, you don't care if I don't bother to use the lines, do you?"[41]

Terrence McNally had a similar complaint about the Actors Studio: "The Actors Studio, for all the good work that was done there, was always Lee [Strasberg]'s building somehow. Even though there was a playwrights unit there, you felt that you were talking about acting as much as the play. It was so hard to escape

Lee's presence."[42] Given the growing fascination with the performer and director, the ABW Playwrights Unit seemed a safe haven for playwrights learning their craft.

The Playwrights Unit also offered a somewhat more upscale venue, staffed as it was by theater professionals. Experienced directors and well-known actors like Frank Langella, Viveca Lindfors, James Coco, Margaret Hamilton, and Nancy Marchand were available for performances at the Unit because of the short runs and because of the influence and connections of Edward Albee and Richard Barr. What the Playwrights Unit offered, then, was a professional production in a theater with talented actors, an experienced director, and a mailing list of patrons who could be expected to support the work and perhaps provide the connections to move the plays or the playwright on to another level of production.

The Playwrights Unit came to be a stepping-stone, in that sense, from the experimentation and freedom of the cafés and coffeehouse theaters to a new level of professionalism. If a play was successful in the Playwrights Unit, the eyes of Albarwild were certainly upon it, although the plays were produced without options or obligations.[43] In the spring of 1965 a New Playwrights Series was produced by Theatre 1965 at the Cherry Lane Theatre; it consisted of ten plays, including *Up to Thursday*, by Sam Shepard; *Home Free*, by Lanford Wilson; *Balls*, by Paul Foster; *Conerico Was Here to Stay*, by Frank Gagliano; *Pigeons*, by Lawrence Osgood; *Lovey*, by Joseph Morgenstern; *Hunting the Jingo Bird*, by Kenneth Pressman; *A Lesson in Dead Language*, by Adrienne Kennedy; and *Do Not Pass Go*, by Charles Nolte.

In addition, Lanford Wilson's full-length *The Rimers of Eldrich* was first professionally produced by Theatre 1968 at the Cherry Lane. Wilson speaks of the experience:

> *Home Free* [at the Cherry Lane] was the first professional thing I had ever had done. . . . [It] had been done at La MaMa earlier but [at the Cherry Lane] it was for money! I got a percentage of the house, it was fabulous! Who had ever heard of such a thing—what a concept! . . . It certainly made you feel professional. . . . It was your first professional recognition also. I mean, we were reviewed for crying out loud . . . at the Cherry Lane. Most of them had never been reviewed before. At the Cherry Lane it was for real—it was for a limited run—but it was for real.[44]

As Wilson explains it, the Playwrights Unit and the productions given at the Cherry Lane were a validation of the artistic experimentation these playwrights were attempting. It is hard to imagine any major Broadway producers today, let alone any single American playwright, who would invest, for example, in an off-Broadway production of Adrienne Kennedy's *Funnyhouse of a Negro*. There was a certain heroism tied to this kind of producing and sponsorship of playwrights.

The positive reaction from most of the playwrights interviewed in the course of my research was somewhat deflated by one note of discord. Lawrence Wunderlich, whose plays *Nine-to-Five-to-Zero*, parts one and two, and *Prometheus Rebound* were performed at the Unit in 1964 and 1965, respectively, wrote of this experience:

> I don't want to belabor the whole first year's operation of the Playwright's Unit. But if Albee's "guess" is "that the theatre in the United States will always hew more closely to the post-Ibsen/Chekhov tradition" because "it is our nature as a country, a society," he was quite right when it came to *this* group; a good majority of the playwrights were hewing very closely indeed, so closely, in fact, that a quaint, nostalgic air of the past hung over most of their work; so closely that I could see very little in their work that had much if anything to do with *us*, *here*, and *now*, in the final third of the twentieth century.[45]

Although his article is fairly sketchy and disorganized, Wunderlich's primary argument against the Unit is its lack of consistent support for work that was experimental. And from the above excerpt, it is clear that he did not feel the Unit was producing scripts that represented the most avant-garde or most challenging work available (with the exception of several plays, including his own).

What is fascinating about the article is the discussion of several details. Wunderlich was not only a play reader for the ABW workshop but the manager of the Village South Theatre, where the Unit was located in its first seven years. Wunderlich chronologizes the first four years of the Unit through September 1967, discussing the initial meetings, the correspondence between the producers and the Unit playwrights, the various management techniques that Edward Parone and Chuck Gnys used to organize and inform the playwrights, and the sources of funding for the unit, and ends his article with an excellent chronology of productions through the spring of 1967.

At several points Wunderlich seems to question the very nature of a playwrights' workshop, wondering if a workshop as such can actually produce fine playwrights:

> We find ourselves face to face with a hodgepodge of romantics, cynics, realists, stoics, naturalists, nihilists, absurdists, Philistines, and incompetents.

And while we dimly suspect that such a "group" may contain the raw materials for the making of a democracy, we know that it contains little of the select material for the makings of a playwrights' workshop. It is, and it remains, a pastiche. And to paraphrase a statement attributed to Voltaire, I disapprove of a pastiche but I will defend to the death the right of the individual parts of the pastiche to operate autonomously.[46]

What Wunderlich offers, then, is a contrarian's view of the achievements of the Unit, which, even if it is not terribly successful in its criticism, at least provides a fairly detailed and well-supported argument for the Unit's eclecticism.

Certainly Wunderlich's reaction is a minority opinion. Almost all the playwrights interviewed had quite positive responses to their productions at the Unit, with James Prideaux articulating what seemed to be the "prototypical" Playwrights Unit experience:

When finally Richard forced me into the theatre, there were no seats left and so we had to sit on the steps next to the exit. The lights came down. The curtain went up. And the audience began to laugh. And clap. And laugh. And clap some more. *Postcards* is hardly more than thirty minutes long, but they were the greatest thirty minutes of my life. My heart soared, literally soared as I listened to the audience. At the end they wouldn't stop applauding and Richard pushed me to my feet, saying, "Jimmy, you'd better go up." So I ran up on stage and took a bow with my beaming actors. I suppose I went someplace after that. I assume I got home. But I have no recollection of it. I was in another world.[47]

Prideaux, in his interview for this study, confessed that in his career as a playwright and screenwriter no other moment was quite as stupendous or as memorable as this successful evening at the Unit.[48]

Mart Crowley, author of *The Boys in the Band* (produced at the Playwrights Unit in January 1968), spoke of the Unit's audience, as many of the playwrights did, in quite dramatic terms. He remembered looking out at the huge line of people waiting to get into the theater on a rainy January evening and imagining it was "like the third act of Wilder's *Our Town*—there were all these umbrellas."[49] Crowley later discussed the experience in an article in San Francisco's *Bay Area Reporter*:

Boys might have ended in that five-day workshop, except for one small miracle—audiences were wild about the play. "The first night," Crowley says, "I don't think anybody was there. But the second night, there was a line around the block. The New York intelligentsia [began to] descend on the play. And suddenly it was famous."[50]

The audience at the Playwrights Unit was invited and attended the performances free of charge. They were the product of a very carefully prepared mailing list that had been nurtured over many years by Chuck Gnys and the other managers of the Unit. Jean Claude van Itallie spoke about the houses being "packed, simply packed to the rafters," and other playwrights also referred to the responsive audiences.[51] Edward Parone spoke of the way the audience talked directly to actors in LeRoi Jones's *Dutchman*, in particular having a remembrance of Leontyne Price, "who lived in the neighborhood, suddenly bursting out with 'Right on!' and 'Say it!' several times."[52]

The success of the Unit was directly tied to the Broadway professionals who sponsored its activities. Ironically, even though Barr and Wilder rejected the worst of the commercial tastes of the Great White Way, they retained all the rigorous demands of professional production standards in the off-Broadway and off-off-Broadway milieu at their Playwrights Unit. It was also the connection with Broadway theater professionals—actors, directors, designers, stage managers, and administrative staff—that allowed Barr and Wilder to provide an extraordinarily nurturing experience to each new play they chose to produce. However, the Playwrights Unit existed within the world of the off-off-Broadway theater of the 1960s, and the milieu of this theater community provided a fertile environment for the Unit's success. Most of the playwrights who came to the Unit, though not all, had been produced earlier at venues such as Café La MaMa or Caffe Cino, and most continued to produce work at other off-off-Broadway venues during and after their productions at the Playwrights Unit. The Unit, however, and the Cherry Lane Theatre, gave most of these playwrights their first experience of working within the world of New York's professional theater, an experience, for better or worse, that was very different from the cafés and storefront theaters of off-off-Broadway and one that brought them into the critical focus of the New York theater community.

NOTES

1. Stuart Little, *Off-Broadway: The Prophetic Theater* (New York: Coward, McCann & Geoghegan, 1972), 216.

2. For a discussion of play development and its discontents, see Michael Bloom, "The Post-Play Discussion Fallacy," *American Theatre* 5.9 (December 1988): 31; Edward Clinton, "The Literary Manager: Vanguard of a Frustrating System," *Dramatists Guild Quarterly* 25.11 (Spring 1988): 17–19; Amy Davis, "Development of New Play Often a Rocky Road," *Variety* 330.8 (March 16, 1988): 105; Shelly Frome, "Fault-Finding Can Be

Fun for All Except the Paranoid Playwright," *Dramatists Guild Quarterly* 24.33 (Autumn 1987): 27–28; Marsha Norman and Jeffrey Sweet, "The Plight of the Playwright in Regional Theater, 1986–87," *Dramatists Guild Quarterly* 23.44 (Winter 1987): 18–33; Louis Phillips, "Why Shakespeare Might Not Succeed in Today's Theater," *Dramatists Guild Quarterly* 29.44 (Winter 1993): 31–33; Dale Ramsey and Thomas G. Dunn, "Speaking of Dramaturgs and Literary Managers," *Dramatists Guild Quarterly* 24.11 (Spring 1987): 12–17; Peregrine Whittlessey, "Developed to Death? Here's a Possible Antidote," *Dramatists Guild Quarterly* 25.33 (Autumn 1988): 21–22; and Peregrine Whittlessey, "Is There Life after Literary Management?," *Dramatists Guild Quarterly* 25.33 (Autumn 1988): 18–19.

3. Edward Albee, interview by author, tape recording, New York, NY, June 19, 1996.

4. Stephen Samuels, "Yes Is Better Than No: An Interview with Edward Albee," *American Theatre*, September 1994, 38.

5. John Keating, "A Producer Should 'Produce,'" *Theatre Arts*, September 1961, 76.

6. Albee, interview.

7. Keating, "Producer Should 'Produce,'" 76.

8. Ibid., 75.

9. David Kahn and Donna Breed, *Scriptwork: A Director's Approach to New Play Development* (Carbondale: Southern Illinois University Press, 1995), 79.

10. Douglas Anderson, "The Dream Machine: Thirty Years of New Play Development in America," *Drama Review* 32.33 (Fall 1988): 55–84.

11. Richard Barr, "You Have to Hock Your House," unpublished manuscript, 76, Richard Barr–Clinton Wilder Papers, Billy Rose Theatre Archives, New York Public Library for the Performing Arts at Lincoln Center.

12. Mervyn Rothstein, "Richard Barr, 71, Stage Producer and Theater League Head, Dies," *New York Times*, January 10, 1989.

13. Barry Plaxen, interview by author, tape recording, Bloomingsburg, NY, May 4, 1996.

14. Barr, "You Have to Hock Your House," 69–111.

15. Walter Rigdon, ed., *Notable Names in the American Theatre* (Clifton, NJ: J. T. White, 1976), 542–43.

16. Stuart W. Little, *Off-Broadway: The Prophetic Theater* (New York: Coward, McCann & Geoghegan, 1972), 219.

17. Faye Hammel, "Three for the Play: Theatre '64 says the Writer Must Be King," *New York Times*, March 3,1966,10.

18. Rigdon, *Notable Names*, 1226.

19. Thomas Morgan, "Clinton Wilder Is Dead at 65; Helped Develop Playwrights," *New York Times*, February 15, 1986, 33.

20. Rigdon, *Notable Names*, 1226.

21. Barnard Hewitt, *Theatre U.S.A. 1665 to 1957* (New York: McGrawHill, 1959), 360–65.

22. Rigdon, *Notable Names*, 500.

23. Sam Zolotow, "Playwrights Unit Receives Subsidy for Staging," *New York Times*, June 6, 1966.

24. John Keating, "Action Speaks Louder . . . ," *New York Times*, October 20, 1963, X3.

25. Barbara La Fontaine, "Triple Threat On, Off and Off-Off Broadway," *New York Times Magazine*, February 25, 1968, 36–46.

26. Edward Parone, interview by author, New York, March 14, 1995; also contact sheet from Merle Debuskey, Edward Parone Clippings Folder, Billy Rose Theater Archives.

27. Edward M. Cohen, interview by author, New York, NY, May 3, 1995.

28. La Fontaine, "Triple Threat," 37.

29. Richard Lipsett, interview by author, Bloomfield, NJ, February 27, 1995.

30. Albee, interview.

31. Ibid.

32. Keating, "Action Speaks Louder," X3.

33. James Prideaux, "Memoirs," unpublished, May 1995, 212–13.

34. Kenneth Pressman, interview by author, tape recording, New York, NY, November 19, 1994.

35. John Guare, interview by author, tape recording, New York, NY, March 28, 1995.

36. Sam Zolotow, "Playwrights Unit Receives Subsidy for Staging," *New York Times*, June 1, 1968.

37. Patricia Bosworth, "Will They All Be Albees?," *New York Times*, July 18, 1971, D1, 3.

38. Guare, interview.

39. Barr, "You Have to Hock Your House," 263–70.

40. Prideaux, "Memoirs," 232–33.

41. Edward Parone, ed., *New Theatre in America* (New York: Dell, 1965), 11.

42. Terrence McNally, "In Conversation with Terrence McNally: Edward Albee," *Dramatists Guild Quarterly* 22.2 (Summer 1985): 17.

43. Albee, interview.

44. Lanford Wilson, interview by author, tape recording, New York, NY, March 27, 1995.

45. Laurence Wunderlich, "Playwrights at Cross Purposes," *Works* 1.22 (Winter 1968): 23.

46. Ibid., 35.

47. Prideaux, "Memoirs," 214.

48. James Prideaux, interview by author, tape recording, New York, NY, March 27, 1995.

49. Mart Crowley, interview by author, tape recording, New York, NY, February 19, 1995.

50. Wendell Ricketts, "Talking Truth: *Boys in the Band* author Mart Crowley on his 'Gorgeous Little Monster,'" *Bay Area Reporter*, February 8, 1990, 35.

51. Jean-Claude Van Itallie, interview by author, New York, NY, February 16, 1995.

52. Parone, interview.

Cindy Rosenthal

From Stanislavski to Grotowski

Rethinking 1960s Acting Training and Practice

Truth in theatre is always on the move.
  —Peter Brook, *The Empty Space*

COME TOGETHER, RIGHT NOW

This essay interrogates the notion that a sharp binary existed between commercial/mainstream and avant-garde/experimental performance in the 1960s by turning a spotlight on actors' experiences and the craft of acting during the long decade. The sixties are often defined by revolution, transformation, and radicalism—but did these descriptors fit for the actor and her or his work? Were there common denominators between the mainstream and the experimental from an actor's perspective? For actors in the 1960s—those performing "uptown" in mainstream venues or "downtown" in experimental spaces—an active and vital flow existed between the two realms. Strong crosscurrents fostered creative connections in the actors' craft, rehearsal practices, and performance methods. In the 1960s, no hard and fast dichotomy existed between the mainstream and the experimental for the actor, after all.

The path of this essay traverses the mainstream/experimental "divide" many times, and in analyzing actors' experiences uptown and down, this much seems clear: in the 1960s, as in other eras, actors sought to increase their confidence, flexibility, strength, and skills; their desire was to work in a variety of interesting and challenging performance contexts and to create alongside and with a cohort of inspiring, dedicated artists. The ultimate goal was to reach spectators who would respond positively and perhaps even powerfully to the work. Peter Brook writes, "The only thing all forms of theatre have in common is the need for an audience."[1] Of course, on the opening page of *The Empty Space* (1968), Brook sets out his most essential claim, which inserts the actor, along with the spectator, into the picture: "A man walks across this empty space whilst someone else is watching him, and this is all that is needed for an act of theatre to be engaged."[2] From the beginning of theater's long history, spectators have viewed actors as the transformative agents at the center of the performance. Spectators receive entertainment value in their connection with actors, but sometimes there is enlightenment and even a kind of transformation of the spectator.

Peter Brook's important volume cited here is but one of a constellation of texts that attracted vast attention in the 1960s and 1970s and were held in high esteem not just among actors but among theater artists and theater enthusiasts generally. In exploring the question of whether or not there was a divide between the mainstream and the experimental from the actors' perspectives in the 1960s and 1970s, it might be useful to travel back in time and have a look at their bookshelves. What books informed and enriched their craft? You'd find Brook on their bookshelves, but also reflecting the "experimental wing," there would be Joseph Chaikin's *The Presence of the Actor* (1972), Jerzy Grotowski's *Towards a Poor Theatre* (1968), Eugen Herrigel's *Zen in the Art of Archery* (1971), R. D. Laing's *The Politics of Experience* (1967), Richard Schechner's *Environmental Theater* (1973), and Viola Spolin's *Improvisation for the Theatre* (1963). Alongside these, another assortment of texts on craft continued to pull actors' attention, to claim a place and have value in the studio, in the rehearsal room, and in the discourse. These books would be situated in the "mainstream" section, associated with more traditional and realistic forms of performance: Toby Cole and Helen Krich Chinoy's *Actors on Acting* (1970), Robert Lewis's *Method or Madness* (1968), and Sonia Moore's *Training an Actor: The Stanislavski System in Class* (1968) are examples. All of these texts fell under the long shadow of Constantin Stanislavski's iconic *An Actor Prepares* (1936). It's worth noting that you'd find a goodly sampling of "old school" and "new school" books shoved in together—indeed, a colorful mix that doesn't respect the boundaries of experimental and mainstream—which is exactly the point.

By examining the methods, styles, and working practices of a wide array of actors in the 1960s and 1970s, this essay sheds light on important exchanges and cross-fertilizations that dissolved the divide between experimental and mainstream theater. Tracing the ways in which the Stanislavski System was transmuted (primarily via the American Method teachings of one-time Group Theater and Actors Studio director Lee Strasberg) and continued to hold sway for actors working in experimental theater "downtown" contributes to a deeper understanding of how mainstream theater techniques melded with the experimental. Other working practices that crossed the divide but originated in the experimental realm were based on the exercises of Jerzi Grotowski (with actor Ryszard Cieslak) in *Towards a Poor Theatre* and the improvisational techniques of Viola Spolin. Experimentation stemming from the teachings of these important artists was central to the body/language of theater practices in a number of mainstream and commercial contexts "uptown." From the 1960s onwards, the downtown/experimental sector continued to feel the impact of Stanislavski and Strasberg, and uptown/mainstream theater continued to feel the intensely physical tremors of Grotowski and the playful flexibility of Spolin.

Crucial to an understanding of the actor's experience in the 1960s is an assessment of how spectators' expectations changed and how the relationship between the spectator and the actor changed. Breaking the "fourth wall" and staging performances in nontraditional venues became the norm in commercial as well as in avant-garde contexts by the end of the decade. Although performances in cafés, lofts, black-box theaters, and studios downtown (off- and off-off-Broadway) more frequently involved actor-spectator exchanges marked by physical contact and spectators actively participating in the performance, these experiences did occur "uptown"—on Broadway and in other mainstream contexts and venues.

The growth and importance of the ensemble is another fundamental development in both mainstream and experimental theaters in the 1960s. Interest in the actor as a solo entity and a celebrity presence eroded, and in its place was the experience of the performer's vibrant, creative connection to and collaborations with other performers in a variety of frameworks. In the same *TDR* essay ("Intentions, Problems, Proposals," Summer 1963) in which Richard Schechner articulates a binary distinction and declares his choice for the experimental over Broadway, he extolls the value of the ensemble for the future of the theater. "We must encourage our young writers, actors, directors and designers to work together as ensembles. No project should be forbidden them. . . . Their goal must be to discover and invent."[3] In 1970, when editors Cole and Chinoy published a revised edition of their esteemed 1950s-era tome *Actors on Acting*, they noted this "striking change" in the opening paragraph of their introduction: "Replacing the old star system are groups of actors working together in studios, ensembles, institutes and institutional theatres—communities of artists who are turning their backs on Broadway, the West End, and the Boulevards."[4] In this essay I argue that there was more fluidity than rigidity of movement in communities of artists in the sixties—and the choice was not as stark as either/ or. In fact, the focus on the ensemble, on the actor's physical body, on theater games and exercises, and on performing in differently configured spaces did not exist solely in the experimental realms but stretched across a broad theatrical spectrum. Many actors in the 1960s through the mid-1970s experienced a substantial and well-traveled bridge between the mainstream/commercial and the experimental sectors, rather than a solid divide.

HOLY THEATER/ HOLY ACTOR?

Brook's experimental theater "manifesto," *The Empty Space*, breaks contemporary theater into four categories. In the first section he describes "The Deadly Theatre," which he says should be abandoned and shunned. Deadly Theatre can be found anywhere, he declares, but on Broadway "the most deadly element is certainly economic. . . . Every artist has to have an agent to protect them."[5] In the book's second section Brook describes theater artists' yearning and quest for "The Holy Theatre"; at the core of this section are Brook's discussions of the explosive visions of Grotowski and Antonin Artaud. The third section is devoted to "The Rough Theatre," which Brook describes as "down to earth" and "lively." Bertolt Brecht's work is a focal point here. The final section, "The Immediate Theatre," addresses the power potential of a celebratory melding of actors and spectators and stresses, among other things, the importance of improvisation and theater exercises: "The aim of improvisation in training actors in rehearsal, and the aim of exercises is always the same: it is to get away from Deadly Theatre."[6] Improvisation breaks down entrenched and inhibiting behaviors, movements, and patterns and builds toward the presence and experience of truth—for actors and for spectators.

Truth in acting was the central goal for performers long before Brook expounded on what happens or should happen in "the empty space." Prior to the 1960s—before the groundbreaking impact of Brook's, Julian Beck's, Judith Malina's, Joseph Chaikin's, Richard Schechner's, and Jerzy Grotowski's writings about theater and their directing work—actors had sought to attain a sense of truth and believability onstage. Denis Diderot's *The Paradox of Acting* (1883) describes a dual understanding of the actor's practice: although experiencing "real" feelings onstage may be the goal, most of the time that is not what actually occurs. As persuasively argued by Joseph Roach, Diderot's *Le paradoxes sur le comedien* (1773) originated many of the concepts that would be developed and explored a century and a half later, in practice and in print, by Stanislavski and ultimately by his American interpreters. These include "emotion memory, imagination . . . ensemble playing, concentration, public solitude, character body, the score of the role and spontaneity."[7] A fundamental precept of Stanislavski's system is performing truthfully "as if" the actor is someone else. Stanislavski and his American interpreters (including Lee Strasberg, Stella Adler, Sanford Meisner, and Robert Lewis) worked for much of the twentieth century on developing a clear, utilitarian, and universal method or set of techniques that would meet this goal. With fervor in *Environmental Theater*, Schechner asks, "*Where does human truth lie? On the surface, in the behavior men show every day, or in the depths, behind social masks?"* (italics his). Switching back to roman font, he explains,

> The naturalists strive for a replication of just those everyday details that represent the essential man. The theatricalists strive for means to penetrate or surpass the masks of daily life in order to reveal the essential man. Stanislavski and Brecht are naturalists. Artaud and Grotowski are theatricalists. As with all great arguments most people take a little bit of this side and a little bit of that side.[8]

Of course there were many cross-fertilizations and interesting pairings between and among acting theorists and practitioners in the twentieth century. As Brook in *The Empty Space* and Schechner above note, Grotowski's goals for the actor seem to echo Artaud's call for an organic, explosive body-fire that "signals through the flames" toward the spectator. But Brook, in his preface to Grotowski's *Towards a Poor Theatre*, declares that "no one else in the world" is on the level of Stanislavski and Grotowski in the depth and comprehensiveness of their investigations of acting—as a phenomenon, a process, and a practice.[9] In the second paragraph of *Towards a Poor Theatre* Grotowski speaks of his debt to Stanislavski: "his persistent study" and "his dialectical relationship to his earlier work" are reasons why Grotowski regards Stanislavski "as my personal ideal."[10]

Lisa Wolford, in her thorough and thoughtful examinations of these two director-teachers, makes clear that Grotowski regarded his research as being on a parallel track with Stanislavski's, especially in terms of Stanislavski's later investigations, which were "in the domain of physical actions."[11] Toward the end of Stanislavski's life his actor-training emphasis shifted from the psychological to a method of scoring physical actions, which was of great interest to Grotowski. Grotowski, like Stanislavski, sought living truthfully onstage, but for Grotowski an actor's work was meant to catapult him or her beyond the banal and the everyday. For Grotowski, being able to do "something that any average person can do" was not a measure of acting skill—rather, the actor must be "capable of performing a spiritual act."[12] This was Grotowski's "holy actor," ready to play in Brook's "holy theatre" where a "total act" is possible—in fact, is mandated. In Wolford's astute analysis, a paradox emerges in the nature of this communion between actor and spectator. Grotowski seeks a kind of catharsis for spectators in the truth the actor reveals. Rather than "shocking" us by breaking with tradition, in this case Grotowski "shocks" us by going back to the tradition of the ancient Greeks, the foundation of mainstream theater, and activating the phenomenon of catharsis in his actors' performances. Here, even Grotowski, the legendary 1960s avant-garde teacher and director, turns the table on "the divide" by exploring catharsis—a strategy associated with mainstream, more traditional theater.

STANISLAVSKI, SPOLIN AND THEIR INHERITORS

Although Schechner famously declared himself on the side of the experimental, under his leadership, *TDR* published two issues in 1964 investigating Stanislavski's teachings and how his legacy affected American theater. Schechner's opening comment in the first of these Stanislavski-rich journals forecasts an endgame for the masters of the Method in its title, "Twilight of the Gods." Yet Schechner goes on to state, "Let us value the achievement of these older men who seem now in the flush of second life. Without them there would be no American theatre. With them alone there will be none."[13] Schechner's emphasis on integrating the contributions of older, Stanislavski-based statesmen into an assessment of American theater is significant. He is clearly interested in a nuanced understanding of American theater that includes a consideration of its hybrid form(s) and acknowledges multilayered experiences and structures, rather than a binary. Schechner himself conducted a number of the interviews with the legendary American Method and Stanislavski teachers, directors, and actors in these issues—Lee Strasberg, Robert Lewis, Paul Mann, and Elia Kazan. These were artists who, by the 1960s, were firmly established in mainstream theater—associated with Broadway, with the growing commercial off-Broadway, and with Hollywood films. With this in mind, what do we make of Schechner's declaration in the summer of 1963 of a preference for the experimental over Broadway if less than a year later he refers to these mainstream artists as elder statesmen and publishes lengthy interviews with them in *TDR*? With the majority of the space in two issues devoted to these particular teachers and directors, Schechner throws the hard and fast dichotomy into question. Is there truly a "divide," if mainstream actors' and acting teachers' voices are center-staged on the pages of *TDR*? Returning to Peter Brook's image of the empty space in which the actor is an essential element, Schechner focuses our attention on the actor, but in these two journal issues mainstream and commercial performers and teachers dominate the landscape.

Stage and screen actress Geraldine Page was also interviewed by both Schechner and Charles Mee in the journal. Although she is not referenced in Schechner's salute to the "gods" at "twilight," who are all male (the renowned acting teachers Stella Adler and Uta Hagen are surprising omissions here), Schechner's selection of Page points to his interest in the perspectives and experiences of leading (female?) actors on mainstream American stages.[14]

Echoing Schechner's declaration of the importance of ensemble work, Page states that the great boon of her time at the Actors Studio was sharing a common language and a way of working with other actors and experiencing the freedom of improvisation: "When I was in *The Rainmaker* everybody was from the Studio. It was the first time I'd been in a play where everybody had the same training. I never had such a good time in my life. That's one of the reasons we've gone through all the trouble of starting a theatre [the Actors Studio Theatre]—so we can work together." When Schechner asked her "What do you share?" she replied, "The freedom to improvise together."[15] In other words, what Page relished and regarded as a cornerstone of her craft as an actor in the mainstream was in the same vein as the process and practice Schechner endorsed for theater students coming of age in his 1963 essay "Intentions, Problems, Proposals"—situations where they create together, as part of an ensemble, using improvisation as a tool.

In the *TDR* Documents section in the second of the issues on Stanislavski, Schechner and Mee also interviewed practitioner-theorists Joseph Chaikin and Paul Sills, who land on the experimental side of "the divide." What was true for Page in the mainstream was also true for Joseph Chaikin in the experimental realm, as Schechner's interview with him in the same issue of *TDR* substantiates. In response to Schechner's questions about his work with the Open Theatre, Chaikin is Page's counterpart, voicing a preference for a more hybrid notion of the craft of acting:

> All of the actors have had extensive training with Method teachers . . . and some of us are still going to class. I can't imagine working with actors who don't have a Method background—such training, even when it's bad, helps an actor know how to use himself. But neither can I imagine working with actors who are content to stop with the Method. . . . One of the wonderful things is that we're willing to fail; it helps us go beyond the safe limits and become adventurers. This quality comes to a group only when each person trusts the other. It is never possible among actors who are together only for a single show. When we lose this trust, the workshop will die.[16]

Here, Chaikin, whose primary goal as the director of the Open Theatre was to create workshops that remained outside mainstream/commercial realms, declares himself an advocate of the Method—the Stanislavski System as interpreted by Lee Strasberg. The creative power of the ensemble that he emphasizes—built on trust and ease among the participants—reflects Page's comments too. The freedom to fail (without money pressures) was also key to maintaining the feeling of "flow" and the collective creativity of the Open Theatre workshops.

Two important fundaments of an acting process—grounded first with Method training, then opened up, stretched, and liberated through improv-based exercises—meet and mingle in the middle. Page and Chaikin may have started with different perspectives and different agendas, but in the rehearsal room there was no clear divide.

If Page is known for her connection to the mainstream and commercial sector and Chaikin is associated with the experimental, Paul Sills's life in the theater began in the experimental realm and moved in the direction of the mainstream. Sills's claim to fame is creating "Story Theatre," a performance-building technique and ultimately a production, which sprang directly from exercises and improv work. Sills first developed this way of working with a small company of actors in Chicago in the late 1960s amid the tumult of political protests. But "Story Theatre" eventually morphed into a unique commercial enterprise.

Sills, in his interview with Charles Mee, was on a quest to find community in contemporary theater—to create a positive network of connections that begins actor-to-actor but must reach the audience. "The community theatre should be more interested in the community than in the theatre," he tells Mee.[17] Sills was a founding director of the renowned Second City improv troupe in Chicago, along with Elaine May and Mike Nichols (who left because they became successful, Sill says). In the interview with Mee, Sills explains the intrinsic value in theater games that set up a simple exchange or agreement with everyone in the room and by extension the understanding that anyone in the community can and should participate/perform. As a child growing up in 1950s Chicago, Sills's artistic life was profoundly shaped by working with his mother, Viola Spolin, who developed nonverbal improvs, exercises, and games that served the immigrant communities she taught exceedingly well. Spolin gained wide recognition with her publication *Improvisation for the Theatre* (1963), a foundational text that continues to be used in a wide array of educational settings and theater institutions around the world.

Spolin's improvs, exercises, and games had a powerful impact on Joseph Chaikin too, who also began as a performer with Second City before he came to New York. "Sound and Movement," a fundamental (if now ubiquitous) exercise of Spolin's, was central to evolving the actor-driven transformational work of the Open Theatre's plays, such as *Calm Down Mother* (1965, with playwright Megan Terry) and *America Hurrah* (1966, with playwright Jean-Claude van Itallie). Chaikin steadfastly maintained an adherence to noncommercial, nonmainstream endeavors with the Open Theatre, much in the spirit of Jerzy Grotowski's "poor theatre." His preference for experimentation with actors and playwrights in the rehearsal room or loft rather than performing for audiences in the theater ultimately led to his disbanding the Open Theatre altogether in

1973, rather than institutionalizing the group or moving toward the creation of a commercial production company.[18]

Sills, however, made a different choice. In 1970 his adaptation of Grimm's fairy tales based on improvisations, theater games, and exercises with actors— *Story Theatre*—made it to Broadway following a sold-out run in Los Angeles; the show ran for over two hundred performances in New York. *Story Theatre's* journey to Broadway followed an interesting route; during its wildly successful Los Angeles run in the summer of 1970, numerous producers wooed Sills for the chance to bring the show to Broadway. But Sills would do it only on his own—very specific—terms. Zev Bufman, the New York producer who finally convinced Sills to move the show to New York, quotes Sills as saying, "I have no objection to making money, but I want the money to go back into creating theatre. I don't want it to go to some investor to buy a fur coat for his wife."[19] Sills's declaration of purpose and his plans for the capital generated by his art are in direct opposition to Schechner's and Brook's assumptions about what happens to the money associated with mainstream endeavors. Sills's revolutionary idea was to put monies back into creative coffers—not into producers' pocketbooks. Sills's re-visioning of the financial backing for and repurposing of the profits from his Broadway production illuminates once again how the mainstream/ experimental divide in the 1960s breaks down.

The production was financed through a nonprofit organization, Story Theatre Inc., and the bulk of the money was raised by Bufman without "angels"; the rest was cobbled together with the support of the Shubert Organization, the Theatre Development Fund, New York City Center, Columbia Records, and an enthusiastic scene builder.[20] The story of Sills's control over the process and his continued insistence on feeding any profits (in fact, there were none—the show closed with a deficit) back into the nonprofit sector vividly illustrates how, in the 1960s and 1970s, financial structures previously considered to be solid and immovable became malleable. The decision making of Broadway "powers-that-be" was directly affected by mainstream spectators' desire to experience the work of innovative/ experimental artists, which reflected the 1960s cultural zeitgeist.

Although the Story Theatre company's "Blue Light" segment did not make it into the Broadway production, Sills regards this piece as integral to the birth of Story Theatre, which was first launched in Chicago in 1968. During the fraught, explosive days of the Democratic convention in Chicago, Sills and his actors determined to fight back against politicians in the Democratic Party, whom they blamed for getting the country into and escalating the Vietnam War. The "Blue Light" tale was created out of this impulse. It concerns a soldier who is destroyed by a war, but as Sills tells it, there is a motif in fairy tales: the power that's given from nowhere, just when nothing seems possible. In the depths of the despair, there lies the spark: the transformation of reality. The soldier gets his revenge on the King, replaces him, and marries the Princess and triumphs over soldiers, judges, over all authority and power. And when the paternal power was overthrown, in the highly charged political situation of '68, the young people cried, "Right on!" It was just in the air. After all, we were doing the story during the convention.[21]

Story Theatre actor Paul Sand, who, like Sills and Chaikin, had been mentored by Spolin and had worked extensively and successfully with Second City in Chicago (his collaborators there were the celebrated performers Alan Arkin and Barbara Harris), won a Tony Award and a Drama Desk Award for Featured Performer in *Story Theatre* in 1971; Sills won a Drama Desk Award for direction and adaptation. Each received significant recognition from the heads of theater's commercial/mainstream, yet each was still tethered in important ways to Chicago's experimental and community-based theater worlds. Again, their work lives and artistic choices reflect the blurring of lines between mainstream and experimental; the critical kudos each received in the commercial realm for their experimentally based work is evidence of the bridges performers built and traveled between the two sectors, as opposed to maintaining a divide.

LIQUID THEATRE IN SOLID CITY: ACTING AND NOT-ACTING

The James Joyce Memorial Liquid Theatre is another example of an experimental project that took the leap into the mainstream. *Liquid Theatre* is also one of many performance works documented in *TDR* over the long decade of the 1960s that is situated on the "not-acting" end of the spectrum. Michael Kirby first explicated the "acting and not-acting" spectrum in his treatise on the subject published in the Winter 1965 issue of *TDR*. Kirby revisited this idea numerous times, using this phrase as the title of a *TDR* essay in 1972, in an issue devoted to an exploration of "acting exercises and physical disciplines."[22] In both essays Kirby distinguishes between matrixed and nonmatrixed performances (nonmatrixed performances operate without consideration of time, plot, place, and character), and he states that "there has, within the last ten years, been a shift toward the not-acting end of the scale. This means not only that more nonmatrixed performing has been used but that, in a number of ways, acting has grown less complex."[23] Simple acting, according to Kirby, has been around for a long time; he cites Viola Spolin's improvisations and exercises, which gained favor in the 1950s, as a prime example. Kirby also constructs a definition of a "happening" as "a performance using a variety of materials (films, dance, readings, music, etc.) in a compartmental structure, and making use of essentially non-matrixed performance,"[24] a category in which he situates Living Theatre works such as *Mysteries and Smaller Pieces* (1964) and *Paradise Now* (1968) and in which we would also find the Company Theatre's production of *Liquid Theatre*. As Kirby explains, an understanding of non-matrixed performances and happenings is crucial to analyzing acting methods and practice in the 1960s. *Liquid Theatre* is a lesser-known but important example of nonmatrixed performance—it provides further evidence that "non-acting"/experimental performance was taking place across a broad spectrum of venues and contexts, downtown and uptown, on Broadway, and beyond.

A *TDR* issue edited by Kirby and published in the summer of 1971 includes an essay by Lance Larsen, a member of the Company Theatre in Los Angeles, in which Larsen pens a kind of good-bye letter to *Liquid Theatre*. Dated June 1, 1971, Larsen's essay states that he is "saying good bye to a life-style."[25] His description of the event/party/"happening" that was *Liquid Theatre* sounds remarkably similar in tone and spirit to the opening text of the "Preparation" section of the script for *Paradise Now*, the Living Theatre's controversial, landmark audience-participation work:

> Judith Malina and Julian Beck of the Living Theatre: The play is a voyage from the many to the one and from the one to the many. It is a spiritual voyage and a political voyage. It is an interior voyage and an exterior voyage. It is a voyage for the actors and the spectators.[26]

Lance Larsen of the Company Theatre:

> The secret of the labyrinth does not rest in its contents. The real contents of the event are subconsciously invisible, like the foundation of a house. The secret of the labyrinth is contained within the minds and bodies of the people who pass through it. It is personal. People receive from it exactly what they bring to it. It is non-linear. The maze is never what people think it is going to be. It is both more and less than their minds have conjured.[27]

Reports from the field—from actors and directors "signaling through the flames" of experimental theater—were standard fare in *TDR* from the mid- to late 1960s onward. What *TDR* does not report on with regard to *Liquid Theatre*, however, is the leap into the mainstream/commercial realm the production made five months after Larsen's article was published. In October 1971 *Liquid Theatre* was reborn, repackaged for mainstream audiences—and very successfully at that. The Living Theatre's *Paradise Now*, which had its U.S. premiere at the Brooklyn Academy of Music in September 1968, also received offers to move "uptown," to Broadway, in fact. But the Living Theatre's cofounders, Malina and Beck, would have none of that.[28]

Although the decision-making process that resulted in bringing the Southern California production to the East Coast and situating it in an uptown, mainstream venue is not entirely clear at this writing, *The James Joyce Memorial Liquid Theatre* (so named because of a remote connection between the concept of the piece and a character in Joyce's *Ulysses*) was reproduced for a six-month run (179 performances) beginning in October 1971 in the lower-level auditorium of the Guggenheim Museum on Fifth Avenue in New York City. An article about the production on the Guggenheim's website states,

> For $8.50, ticket holders became participants in the theater; they were asked to put their personal items in a colored silk bag to be retrieved at the end of the night and were encouraged to take off their shoes. First greeted in the rotunda with coffee and tea while poetry was read aloud, groups were then led downstairs to the auditorium and asked to close their eyes for the main act—described in a press release as a "sensual maze during which [the participant] is caressed, whispered to, touched and perhaps even kissed" by the theater company members. The maze was followed by trust exercises, childhood games, and a ballet performance.[29]

Peter Friedman, now a sixty-something actor who has worked on and off Broadway with forays in film and television, had early set his sights on a career in the mainstream but was cast in *Liquid Theatre* after he graduated from college in October 1971. He described his background as being "in text-based theatre" and added that "this was a real departure." He found the job listing in *Backstage* (an actors' trade publication that posts audition listings) alongside casting calls for musical theater and other mainstream, commercial auditions. Friedman described performing in *Liquid Theatre* as being a meld of acting and not acting, structure and nonstructure: "It was more like playing—but it had its own structure. . . . We were leading spectators through theatre games. But it was still putting something on. Wearing a costume—a costume of being a free spirit."[30]

Although a number of the original Company Theatre actors and directors from California were involved in the New York production, *Liquid Theatre* at the Guggenheim (totaling forty performers) was made up primarily of young actors who, like Friedman, regularly "pounded the pavement" for whatever nonunion acting jobs they could get. Friedman could put on "a costume of being a free spirit" as easily as the next guy. No avant-garde or experimental performance experience necessary. *Liquid Theatre* at the Guggenheim was an Upper East Side, upper-middle-class, cultural tourists' version of a California happening, situated in the carpeted, sheer-curtained, circular lower-level space of the Frank Lloyd Wright–designed museum. The piece was described as "gentle" by the *Life* magazine critic Tom Prideaux.[31] Participants were handed the same standard *Playbill* that theatergoers received at Broadway shows. None of the performers were naked, although a few of the male actors performed shirtless.

It is likely that *Liquid Theatre*'s producers hoped to ride the coattails of the Broadway production of *Hair*'s phenomenal success. *Liquid Theatre*'s spectators, three years after *Hair*'s opening, were offered a much softer, gentler incarnation of audience-participatory, nonmatrixed works. Spectators who were able to pay the *Liquid Theatre* ticket prices did not have to venture downtown to experience the breakdown of the imaginary fourth wall. Instead, *Liquid Theatre* was gracefully and safely packaged for consumption on Fifth Avenue in the cool, modernist sanctity of the Guggenheim Museum. When the fourth wall dissolved for spectators in mainstream venues uptown as it did downtown, the imaginary divide dissolved between mainstream and experimental performance.

LETTING DOWN *HAIR* AND TAKING OFF CLOTHES

Peter Friedman was not the only actor in the 1960s whose career goals and theater experiences originated in mainstream/commercial theater but who landed in projects on and off Broadway that were in the experimental realm—in some cases, nonmatrixed performances, in others, working as part of an ensemble where the focus was on exercises, games, and improvisations. For Friedman and many others, the process began with an audition acquired through traditional "commercial" sources—by responding to a casting call in an acting "trade" paper (*Variety, Backstage, Show Business*) or via an appointment arranged through an agent. The actor was asked to prepare a monologue and/or a song. This process brought many of the original company members into the cast of *Hair* on Broadway.

Hair, "the American tribal love-rock musical," was an immediate sensation when it opened on Broadway at the Biltmore Theatre on April 29, 1968; the show closed on July 1, 1972 (almost a year and a half after *Liquid Theatre* ended its run). Although some of the actors in the Broadway production had been brought in by the producers "off the street" because of their free-spirit-in-everyday-life aura (Sally Eaton and Shelly Plimpton in the original cast were two examples), the majority, as in Friedman's account above, had landed the job through the more standard mainstream/commercial audition process (for *Hair*, this involved singing a prepared song in a rehearsal studio for auditioners behind a table).[32] Stephen Bottoms notes in *Playing Underground* that *Hair*'s achievements on Broadway were due in part to its productive melding of edgy/experimental and mainstream/commercial styles and milieus: "It had successfully fused middle-brow entertainment values with the now-fashionable appeal of 'alternative lifestyles.'"[33]

The director of *Hair* on Broadway, Tom O'Horgan, certainly brought a unique combination of temperament, taste, and skills to the creative table, but the show's crossover ease can also be credited to the performers themselves. *Hair*'s creators, Gerome Ragni and James Rado, not only wrote the book and the lyrics but also were the principal actors in the original production off-Broadway and on (Ragni played Berger and Rado, Claude). Both actor-producers had wanted O'Horgan to direct the piece from the beginning, but O'Horgan was committed to a La MaMa tour in Europe and was not available to rehearse for the initial production at the Public Theater. Gerald Freedman, associate artistic director at the Public, was selected by the Public's artistic director, Joseph Papp, to direct the first *Hair* instead.

Ragni and Rado brought multilayered theater backgrounds to the creative worktable. Rado, whose background included Method training with Lee and Paula Strasberg, had performed on Broadway in the leading role in *The Lion in Winter* and in other realistic plays.[34] Ragni had appeared on Broadway as well, in the Richard Burton *Hamlet* (1964) directed by John Gielgud. However, as a cofounder of the Open Theatre with Chaikin, Ragni had also performed in renowned experimental works, including the Open Theatre's *Viet Rock* (1966), which ran off-off- and off-Broadway. In the last scene of *Viet Rock*, actors entered the audience space, interacting with and touching spectators. This breakdown of the fourth wall set the stage for the actor-spectator physical contact that would follow in avant-garde works such as the Living Theatre's *Paradise Now* and The Performance Group's *Dionysus in 69* (1968) and in works that played in mainstream uptown venues, like *Hair* and *Liquid Theatre*.

In *Hair*, another frontier was traversed on Broadway when actors presented their naked bodies for close-range viewing to mainstream spectators. Schechner devotes a lengthy chapter in his *Environmental Theater* to investigations of the choice and practice of performing naked onstage—a phenomenon that took hold with gusto in mainstream theaters after *Hair* broke down the barrier, just as nakedness on stage had become a fixture of experimental performance slightly earlier in the 1960s. Schechner, the director of the 1960s radical theater ensemble The Performance Group, includes journal excerpts in *Environmental Theater* that trace his own complex responses to actors' experimentation and discourse on whether to be or not to be naked in The Performance Group's groundbreaking performance *Dionysus in 69*: "6 December. Naked = shock. Holy because so stark."[35] The decision to be naked was not unanimous among members of The Performance Group, nor did individuals consistently perform naked throughout the run of *Dionysus in 69*; this kind of fluctuation in decision making and practice occurred among cast members of the original Broadway production of *Hair* as well.

The legendary nude scene at the end of *Hair*'s act 1 was, in *Hair* actress Lorrie Davis's account, a kind of actor-driven improv that was performed during the first preview of the show on Broadway. She reports that director O'Horgan had always planned a nude scene but that the idea was never pushed on the performers by the artistic team or the management in any way. Instead, on the night of the first preview, without prior warning or discussion, "Steve Gamut, Steve Curry and Gerry Ragni all stood up nude. Everyone was momentarily shocked."[36] O'Horgan had already incorporated nudity into the mise-en-scène of his off-off- and off-Broadway hit productions of Rochelle Owens's *Futz* (1967) a year earlier. In the final scene of the play, which is about a man's passionate and sexual love for a pig, O'Horgan staged a writhing mound of naked actors. O'Horgan also directed the film version of *Futz* in 1969.

Hair was the first Broadway show to "sell" nudity as part of its appeal, and although it was not compulsory for *Hair* performers to strip, most did. *Oh! Calcutta!*, which opened in 1969 and closed for the final time in 1989, fully capitalized on the nudity of its entire cast. In *Environmental Theater*, Schechner critiques Eric Bentley's diatribe about "the naked American of the new theatre," citing Bentley's comment that the U.S. performer is "the old whore writ large." Bentley notes with distaste that spectators in the front rows of *Oh! Calcutta!* paid "twenty-five dollars a seat" (three times the price of the average orchestra seat on Broadway in the late 1960s).[37]

As actress Lorrie Davis's account of the "spontaneous" actor nudity in *Hair* makes clear, improv, which is usually associated with experimental performance, was alive and well on the Broadway stage. Davis, who came up with the "hip-talk" Gettysburg Address riff in the script while rehearsing the "Abe" Lincoln role in *Hair*, claims that the text for the Broadway production was in large part collectively created by the actors in rehearsal. She and other *Hair* actors complained that they were never formally credited for their contributions to the script—not even "a thank you for our efforts" or "a group footnote on the credit page in *Playbill*."[38] Actor improvisations and script fluidity continued to be hallmarks of the work, even as the show "settled" into its long run. This kind of fluidity moved back and forth just as actors and their cocreators did, between uptown and downtown venues, between the mainstream and the experimental realms. Almost a year after *Hair* opened, the *New York Times* (April 12, 1969) reported that the two author-performers Ragni and Rado were barred from their own hit show by Michael Butler, the producer, because they had taken their onstage improvisations too far. "It's a bizarre trial," Ragni was quoted as saying, with a smile. When Rado and Ragni returned to play their leading roles on Broadway after a five-month stint in California with the Los Angeles cast, management claimed that they "had been improvising their performances and not adhering to the script." In Richard Shepard's account of this episode, he states that Butler railed against Ragni's and Rado's "objectionable behavior."[39]

Davis credited O'Horgan for the "love" aspect of the "tribal love-rock musical." "He never lectured about it, but all the rehearsals and exercises were geared to this," she said.[40] O'Horgan, like Sills and Chaikin, had worked with Second City in Chicago before he came to New York. At Second City he performed improv, played a variety of musical instruments, and served as a resident composer. In 1964 O'Horgan joined forces with Ellen Stewart, founding director of La MaMa Experimental Theatre Club in New York's East Village. Although Stewart, aka "La Mama," was renowned for discovering and nurturing avant-garde and experimental artists downtown and internationally, she was a proud mother hen who glowed when her experimental "babies" achieved "big-time" mainstream recognition—Blue Man Group, a longtime Off-Broadway and international touring success story is but one case in point; O'Horgan's rise to fame on Broadway is another.

Stewart was an enthusiastic supporter of O'Horgan's Spolin-infused style of working with actors. As part of the original La MaMa Troupe, O'Horgan and actors created multiple performances based on theater games, exercises, and improvisations. O'Horgan encouraged playfulness and the simple and strategic use of props, much in the mode of what Brook calls "immediate theatre." O'Horgan's rich and eclectic musical background and tastes continued to inform his distinct brand of theater artistry. Stephen Bottoms describes O'Horgan-style "total theatre" as multilayered, the opposite of Grotowski's minimalist "poor theatre." Actors participated in a collaborative "madhouse of creativity" on one hand, but on the other, O'Horgan insisted on strict attention to time and rhythm; fine-tuning the improvisational cacophony into a precisely delineated "beat" or "frame" was vitally important.[41]

For Marilyn Roberts, a longtime member of the La MaMa Troupe who performed in several European tours that O'Horgan directed as well as at La MaMa in the East Village, "there was always a flow between uptown and downtown, between the commercial and the experimental."[42] She, like Chaikin, counted Strasberg as an important influence and teacher. She is a proud member of Actors' Equity Association (the professional stage actors' union) and has been since she was a child. She recalls that Strasberg's "sense memory" exercises were similar to some of Grotowski's exercises, which she was taught by Eugenio Barba in Odin, Denmark, while on tour with the La MaMa Troupe. Ellen Stewart had arranged for these special workshops with Barba for actors Roberts, Victor Lipari, and Jacque Lynn Colton, so they could return to the United States and teach Grotowski's exercises to the rest of the La MaMa actors. (Lipari's twin sister Marjorie was also a La MaMa performer; O'Horgan cast her in the original company of *Hair* on Broadway.) For Roberts, "O'Horgan was a musician, first and foremost" and was "most interested in the ensemble."[43] Roberts's long, colorful life in the theater defies the notion of a binary opposition between downtown and uptown, mainstream and experimental. Her most valued teachers and cocreators in the theater were drawn from a very wide spectrum—and she casts no judgments nor constructs any hierarchies in the worlds of theater she has worked and played in when she looks back on her six decades as an actor.

WHERE HAVE ALL THE ENSEMBLES GONE? RE-VIEWING "ACTORS AND ACTING" AT THE END OF THE 1960S

In the introduction to this anthology, James Harding and I concur with Frederic Jameson's, Anders Stephenson's, and Cornel West's determination that 1976 is the appropriate year for an endpoint to the long decade of the 1960s. With this in mind, it seems fitting to turn to the September 1976 issue of *TDR*, which Michael Kirby, the editor, titled "Actors and Acting." This was the first time in *TDR*'s history that an entire issue was devoted exclusively and solely to the actors themselves. In his introduction to the issue Kirby announces that readers will finally have the opportunity to glean—through the words of celebrated actors of the 1960s—what these performers want, what their challenges are, what they are working on, what they look forward to.[44] In the first section of the issue, stalwart performers of the avant-garde—Joseph Chaikin, Priscilla Smith, Kate Manheim, JoAnne Akalaitis, Meredith Monk, and Joan MacIntosh—share their individual perspectives and experiences with a team of *TDR* contributing editors and authors. In an interesting juxtaposition with these accounts, the issue also includes an article composed of interviews with a diverse selection of five "professional actors" who performed in Richard Foreman's production of Bertolt Brecht's and Kurt Weill's *The Threepenny Opera* "on Broadway" (actually, at Lincoln Center's Vivian Beaumont Theatre). Foreman, a renowned "downtown" auteur, took a leap into the heart of the mainstream/commercial world in 1976, as director Tom O'Horgan had done eight years earlier.

What comes across loud and clear in the accounts of the actors who performed in Foreman's *The Threepenny Opera*, whether they were downtown/experimental based (like Robert Schlee, who had worked with Foreman before), or a Broadway and London West End "veteran" with thirty years of mainstream theater experience (C.K. Alexander), or a singer-actor who had worked predominately in cabaret and film (Ellen Greene), or an American Stanislavski and "Story Theater"–trained television performer (Elizabeth Wilson), is that actors unanimously struggled in working with Foreman on his first and only adventure "on Broadway." The mutual trust and ease among actors and between actors and director that grew out of exercises, improvisations, and other aspects of the ensemble-building process that were integral to Chaikin's work and to O'Horgan's—uptown as well as down—did not exist in Foreman's rehearsal room. Nor was any character exploration akin to "the Method" part of Foreman's rehearsal process.

As Kate Davy writes in her essay on Kate Manheim, Foreman's life partner and the leading performer in most of Foreman's previous productions,

> The processes, methods, or techniques most often associated with "creating" a character do not apply. . . . The most distinctive feature of the rehearsal process involves Foreman's rigorous attention to, and accumulation of, the most minute details of staging. He controls every aspect of the work—the performers neither improvise nor initiate activity. He does not explain "why" an action must be carried out in one way rather than another. . . . One of the reasons it is assumed that there is no acting in Foreman's theatre is the fact that he usually does not use people with acting or performing backgrounds. There is no audition for casting a Foreman production. Occasionally he will ask someone to be in a play but generally he simply accepts volunteers.[45]

With *The Threepenny Opera* at Lincoln Center, Foreman was locked into a new kind of structure and schedule and forced to accept immediate and drastic changes to his usual process and routines—beginning with enduring "an agonizing audition period of three to four weeks." But Foreman and his musical director, Stanley Silverman, had agreed that they absolutely had to cast "real singers" and performers with "the ability to project."[46] Schlee explained the difficulties "professional actors" had with Foreman: "Foreman demands unusual things like monochromatic delivery. . . . [Actors] aren't sure what the results will be. They have reputations to maintain."[47]

In comparison with "traditional actors," Schlee sees "the Foreman actor" as a musician—one who learns to appreciate and follow the "fixed score."[48] This notion of constructing a precise framework that supports the overall piece recalls actors' experiences with O'Horgan, who built the company's respect for a score into his brand of "total theatre." O'Horgan's productions were born out of collective cacophony and improvisation, but he too sought a final product that adhered to a clear tempo and stayed within the bounds of a specific compositional structure. Above all else, for Foreman, the "total composition" took precedence. As he explains,

> The actors' role is the same as the role of the words, scenery, lighting et al. . . . I suppose the difference between me and a normal Method director is that I do often ask for results. I know enough about the Method to know that you are not supposed to do that . . . but this is what I want. I tried to stop myself from doing it too much, but I do ask for results because I am interested in surfaces.[49]

Foreman was not interested in actors as cocreators, as were O'Horgan, Chaikin, Sills, and other ensemble-oriented directors. In the quote above, he seems almost apologetic for the approach he takes, which he recognizes is entirely different from that of Method directors. But whether working off-off- or on Broadway, Foreman is an auteur who precisely selects the notes and elements needed in composing and scoring his performances. The work is not collaborative; Foreman's actors are not ensemble performers.

For Richard Foreman, the intricate blocking of the play was "the essence of directing."[50] Each of *The Threepenny Opera* actors Nahshon interviewed for her essay "With Foreman on Broadway" evolved her or his own way of working within Foreman's composition and design scheme and devised a process that allowed him or her to achieve and finally accept Foreman's "results" and "surfaces"—it was a "look," a "sound," "the effect he wanted."[51] No integrated, synthesized process or way of working evolved among the actors in rehearsal for *The Threepenny Opera*. Foreman articulated what he wanted to receive from the actors and each worked—on her or his own—to achieve these results.

In the *TDR* essay on Joseph Chaikin and his acting career, Chaikin's description of Malina's and Beck's directing style in the early 1960s correlates with *The Threepenny Opera* actors' discussions of their difficulties working with Foreman. Given that a few years later the Living Theatre would be regarded as one of the most important 1960s radical theater ensembles, known for nonmatrixed and collectively created work (such as *Mysteries and Smaller Pieces*), Chaikin's critique is unexpected. Certainly, Chaikin's description of the Living Theatre directors' need to block actors in a traditional, mainstream performance way and their disregard for an actor's process may come as a surprise, based on the rhetoric and the reputation of the Living Theatre that emerged in the mid- to late 1960s. Chaikin's report on working with Beck and Malina refers to his experiences at the Living Theatre's Fourteenth Street Theatre and his performances in Jack Gelber's *The Connection* and William Carlos Williams's *Many Loves*, which opened in 1959. He describes these rehearsal processes as having a "lack of direction. . . . I wasn't interested in the way they worked with actors which was essentially no way—you were staged."[52]

The beginning of the Chaikin interview focuses on his launch back into his acting career after a long hiatus and his choice to take on the title role in *Woyzeck* at the Public Theater in 1976. From 1963 to 1973, as the director of the Open Theatre, Chaikin rarely acted. Performing as Woyzeck was a significant departure from his work with the Open Theatre, where he and the company engaged in ongoing explorations of the acting process, using exercises, research, and improvisations to build performances rather than produce "old plays" from the Western canon, such as *Woyzeck*.

Although Malina and Beck would soon be renowned for creating "happening-like" productions with their company, Malina in particular had great respect for composition and was also interested in the precise staging of segments of her company's work, especially when the Living Theatre produced its own versions of "old plays," as in her long-running translation/adaptation of Sophocles's *Antigone*.[53] Although the rhetoric of the Living Theatre espoused collective creation as the method for building performances from *Mysteries* onward, Malina's journals and directing notebooks from the 1960s through the 2000s are filled with her sharply penned, minute drawings that detail actors' movements and the staging of moments and sections of productions. In "Directing *The Brig*" (1965) Malina describes the beauty and the benefits of the Marine Corps drill choreography and its discomfiting allure for and impact on actors and spectators alike. She acknowledges her debt to Artaud's Theatre of Cruelty in taxing *Brig* actors to a level of intensely painful athleticism but also attributes the "powerful rhythmic discipline of the actor's body" to the training she gives her actors in Vsevolod Meyerhold's "bio-mechanics"

> The drill had an enlivening effect. The marching is a ritual of great beauty only grown hideous because it stands for the marches towards the fields of death . . . and because it has come to signify the loss of character. . . . Meanwhile the rhythm of mutuality entices the kinetic senses. The sense of moving in a mutual rhythm with one's fellow man. . . . The reverberating rigid sound takes over. How pleasant the steady drone is after the wild clangor. The drill sounds are regular, organized, orderly, controlled, disciplined.

They are regular and law abiding. The actors were troubled by how restful it was. They didn't want to be enfolded in its harmony, the reconciliation of its smooth, untroubled, monotonous comfort.[54]

Malina admired the choreographic symmetry, beauty, and harmony of the drill sequences in *The Brig* and worked rigorously with her actors to achieve this desired effect. She, like Foreman and O'Horgan, had a use and an intense appreciation for maintaining a strict rhythm and adhering to a tight composition and design when the need arose, abandoning the free-form flow of rehearsals and mandating a strict schedule, discipline, and set of rules and regulations, with herself, as director-auteur, in the role of commander in chief.

IN CONCLUSION, INVOKING ADDIE BUNDREN

Schechner begins a *TDR* Comment with a quote from Addie Bundren in William Faulkner's *As I Lay Dying*: "Words don't ever fit even what they are trying to say at." He goes on to explain why he cites "Mrs. Bundren":

> Words aren't enough anymore, not even for playwrights and critics. . . . The answers can be found only by doing the work. And I am as aware as anyone of the contradictions implicit in many of the things printed in *TDR* and elsewhere, seen in many performances, heard at many rallies. These contradictions don't annoy me or put me off. Experimentation is a word to be taken seriously.[55]

Schechner reminds us that with all of the words filling *TDR*'s pages throughout the long decade of the 1960s, there are bound to be plenty of contradictions.

Kirby, in his treatise "On Acting and Not-Acting" (1972), emphatically and refreshingly declares that in examining acting—a process and practice of wide-ranging methodologies and practitioners—judgments should be withheld:

> Everyone now seems to realize that "acting" does not mean just one thing—the attempt to imitate life in a realistic and detailed fashion. Thus eclecticism or diversity in the approaches to acting is one aspect of the recent change in American theatre. . . . It must be emphasized that the acting/not-acting scale is not intended to establish or suggest values of any kind. Objectively, all points on the scale are equally good. It is only personal taste that prefers complex acting to simple acting or non-matrixed performing to acting. The various degrees of representation and personification are "colors," so to

speak, in the spectrum of human performance; the artist may use whichever colors he prefers.[56]

This essay spotlights actors' perspectives and experiences, along with accounts of performances in the 1960s and acting theories articulated by directors and teachers. With regard to the craft of acting there never was a divide between experimental and mainstream performance. As we have seen from the reports of a panoply of theater artists, each made choices in her or his process from across the spectrum of "colors," from the experimental to the mainstream. "The new theatre" for actors in the 1960s was an experiment, an exploration, and a practice that took place in off-off-Broadway theaters, in studios, in cafés, and—yes—on Broadway.

NOTES

1. Peter Brook, *The Empty Space* (1968; repr., New York: Atheneum, 1987), 140.

2. Ibid., 9.

3. Richard Schechner, "Intentions, Problems, Proposals," *Tulane Drama Review* 7.4 (1963): 20.

4. Toby Cole and Helen Krich Chinoy, eds., *Actors on Acting* (1949; repr., New York: Crown, 1970), xiii.

5. Brook, *Empty Space*, 15, 17.

6. Ibid., 112.

7. Joseph R. Roach, *The Player's Passion* (Ann Arbor: University of Michigan Press, 1993), 117.

8. Richard Schechner, *Environmental Theater*, (1973; repr., New York: Applause, 1994), 126; italics in original.

9. Peter Brook in Jerzy Grotowski, *Towards a Poor Theatre* (New York: Simon and Schuster, 1968), 13.

10. Ibid., 16.

11. Lisa Wolford, "Grotowski's Vision of the Actor," in *Twentieth Century Actor Training*, ed. Alison Hodge (London: Routledge, 2000), 193.

12. Ibid., 197, quoting Grotowski, *Towards a Poor Theatre* (London: Methuen, 1975), 33.

13. Richard Schechner, "Twilight of the Gods," *Tulane Drama Review* 9.2 (1964): 17.

14. "I consider this woman the greatest actress in the English language" was actor F. Murray Abraham's statement when he presented Page with her first Oscar in 1985 for her performance in *The Trip to Bountiful* (after seven nominations for Best Actress over twenty years). Her performance in Tennessee Williams's *Summer and Smoke* in 1952 established her as a rising star; some regard this production, at Circle in the Square downtown, as the beginning of off-Broadway. She went on to perform in dozens of Hollywood films and Broadway shows, worked closely with Lee Strasberg and José Quintero, and studied acting with Uta Hagen. See "Geraldine Page," IMDb.com, http://www.imdb.

com/name/nm0656183/; and "Geraldine Page," in Cole and Chinoy, *Actors on Acting*, 635.

15. Geraldine Page, interviewed by Richard Schechner, edited by Charles L. Mee, Jr. "The Bottomless Cup," *The Tulane Drama Review*, 9.2 (1964): 25.

16. Joseph Chaikin, interview by Richard Schechner, "The Open Theatre," *Tulane Drama Review* 9.2 (1964): 193, 196.

17. Paul Sills, interview by Charles L. Mee Jr., "The Celebratory Occasion," *Tulane Drama Review* 9.2 (1964): 180.

18. Eileen Blumenthal, *Joseph Chaikin: Exploring the Boundaries of Theatre* (New York: Cambridge University Press, 1984), 25.

19. Sills qtd. in Lewis Funke, "Broadway 'Story'" and "Operation Rescue," printed in the *Playbill* for *Story Theatre*; selections reprinted from *New York Times*, October 10, 25, 1970.

20. Ibid.

21. "Interview: Paul Sills Reflects on Story Theatre," by Laurie Ann Gruhn, Paul Sills' Wisconsin Theater Game Center, http://www.sillsspolintheaterworks.com/biography/interview-paul-sills-reflects/, reprinted from *Drama Theater Teacher* 5.2 (n.d.).

22. Michael Kirby, "An Introduction," *Drama Review* 20.3 (1976): 2.

23. Michael Kirby, "On Acting and Not-Acting," *Drama Review* 16.1 (1972): 11.

24. Michael Kirby, "The New Theatre," *Drama Review* 10. 2 (1965): 29.

25. Lance Larsen, "Liquid Theatre," *Drama Review* 15.2 (1971): 90.

26. "Preparation," in *Paradise Now*, collective creation written down by Julian Beck and Judith Malina (New York: Vintage, 1971) 5–13.

27. Larsen, "Liquid Theatre," 93.

28. See my unpublished PhD dissertation, "Living the Contradiction: The Living Theatre's Revision of Sophocles' *Antigone* through Brecht and Artaud" (New York University, 1997), 147–48, for a discussion of the conflicts within the Living Theatre about whether or not to perform *Paradise Now* on Broadway. According to Mark Amitin, who had worked with the company as general manager during their 1968–69 U.S. tour, Beck was in favor of it, as was a third of the company. But the final decision was a no. (My interview with Amitin was on October 7, 1996.)

29. Sarah Haug, "The James Joyce Memorial Liquid Theater," Guggenheim blog, September 4, 2013, http://blogs.guggenheim.org/findings/the-james-joyce-memorial-liquid-theater/.

30. Peter Friedman, interview with the author, February 28, 2014.

31. Tom Prideaux, *Life*, December 10, 1971.

32. See Lorrie Davis, *Letting Down My Hair* (New York: Arthur Fields Books, 1973), 17–22, 80; and Eric Grode, *"Hair": The Story of the Show That Defined a Generation* (London: Carlton, 2010), 57.

33. Stephen Bottoms, *Playing Underground: A Critical History of the 1960s Off-Off-Broadway Movement* (Ann Arbor: University of Michigan Press, 2004), 211.

34. Richard Ouzounian, "*Hair* Gets Tangled," *Variety*, March 27, 2006, 64.

35. Schechner, *Environmental Theater*, 116.

36. Davis, *Letting Down My Hair*, 59–60, 75.

37. Schechner, *Environmental Theater*, 115, quoting Eric Bentley, *Theatre of War* (New York: Viking Press, 1972), 377.

38. Davis, *Letting Down My Hair*, 107–10.

39. Richard Shepard qtd. in Ragni's *New York Times* obituary, July 13, 1991.

40. Davis, *Letting Down My Hair*, 40.

41. Bottoms, *Playing Underground*, 199.

42. Marilyn Roberts, interview with the author, March 10, 2014.

43. Ibid.

44. Kirby, "An Introduction," 2.

45. Kate Davy, "Kate Manheim," *Drama Review* 20.3 (1976): 40, 39.

46. Edna Nahshon, "With Foreman on Broadway," *Drama Review* 20.3 (1976): 84.

47. Ibid., 88.

48. Ibid.

49. Ibid., 89.

50. Ibid.

51. Ibid., 92.

52. Alice J. Kellman, "Joseph Chaikin," *Drama Review* 20.3 (1976): 18–19.

53. See my essay *"Antigone*'s Example: A View of the Living Theatre's Production, Process and Praxis," *Theatre Survey* 41:1 (May 2000), 84, where I discuss Malina's directing notebooks and the intricate staging drawings found in them.

54. Judith Malina, "Directing *The Brig*," in *The Brig*, by Kenneth H. Brown (New York: Hill and Wang, 1965), 85–86, 97, 106.

55. Richard Schechner, "The Journal of Environmental Theater," *TDR* Comment, *Tulane Drama Review* 11.3 (1967): 19, 22.

56. Kirby, "On Acting and Not-Acting," 15.

Marvin Carlson

Theater of the Sixties

The German Connection

The American theater in the mid- to late twentieth century was not notably welcoming to plays from other countries, with the notable exception of England. The 1960s saw a distinct increase in such work, however. Older American theatergoers will doubtless remember that the 1960s saw the arrival on American stages of the French theater of the absurd, led by Beckett and Ionesco, both first presented off-Broadway in 1958 and shortly followed by Genet, who in fact enjoyed the greatest success with a two-year run of *The Balcony* at the Circle in the Square and a three-year run of *The Blacks* at St Mark's Playhouse. Ionesco's breakthrough came with a much-praised production of *Rhinoceros* starring Zero Mostel on Broadway in 1961, which was presented again on Broadway in 1968 by Ellis Rabb's Phoenix Theatre, a venue that also offered *Exit the King*. With these two exceptions, however, the absurdists were represented entirely off-Broadway and essentially only in the first half of the sixties. In fact, much less remembered today is that the contemporary German theater was far better represented during this decade on both Broadway and off-Broadway, and moreover it was strongly represented from the beginning to the end of the decade.

The country most on the American mind during the 1960s was the Soviet Union, the global adversary whose political, military, economic, and scientific threat permeated most aspects of American life. After the Soviet Union, the foreign country most in the American consciousness in the first half of this decade was West Germany, and in the second half, Vietnam, both because of the perception that these places represented the front line of the ongoing struggle against the Communist menace. In 1945, after its defeat in the Second World War, Germany was divided into four zones, occupied by the United States,

France, England, and Russia. In 1949 the first three zones were united into the Federal Republic of Germany (West Germany) and the Russian-occupied zone became the German Democratic Republic (East Germany). This placed Germany at the center of the Cold War during the 1950s, its division solidified by the erection of the first Berlin Wall in 1961. Against this backdrop John F. Kennedy gave his "Ich bin ein Berliner" speech in 1963. Germany lost its position as the Cold War focus in the latter half of the decade, after the Tonkin Gulf Resolution began the long and costly involvement of the United States in Vietnam. By 1968 there were 540,000 American soldiers in that country and the Vietnam War had moved to the center of American consciousness, bitterly dividing the country.

It is probably not coincidental that during the early 1960s, when Germany was a center of American attention, German drama was unusually well represented on American stages. Nor is it surprising that the central figure in this German vogue was Bertolt Brecht. Brecht's popularity was not without its contradictions, however. At the height of the Cold War he remained a dedicated, if unconventional, Marxist and he spent his final years in the enemy capital of East Berlin, making his theater there, the Berliner Ensemble, into one of the most distinguished in the world. Brecht spent the mid-1940s in America, an exile from Nazi Germany; in the United States he was politically viewed first in a positive way as a German dissident but increasingly as sympathetic to Communism, eventually being examined by the House Un-American Activities Committee in a tragicomic hearing that convinced him he could not remain in America.

For almost a decade after his departure from America Brecht received little attention there, but toward the end of the 1950s the situation distinctly changed. Probably the most striking indication of this was the enormous continuing success of *The Threepenny Opera* at the Theatre de Lys in Greenwich Village. It was first presented for ninety-six performances in 1955 but was forced to close to make way for an incoming production. When both critics and the public demanded its return, it reopened and then ran for six years, until 1961, making it the longest-running musical in the history of New York theater. It was the first great hit of the off-Broadway movement and contributed significantly to establishing that movement.

Quite likely contributing to a new interest in Brecht in this period was the enormous success of the 1956 tour of the Berliner Ensemble to London. Such a tour would have been unthinkable in the United States during the Cold War, or indeed for many years after (the company in fact first appeared in New York more than fifty years later, in 2011, with, as it happened, *The Threepenny Opera*, directed by America's own Robert Wilson). In England, however, the company was not only welcomed but enormously influential both on playwrights (Brecht was probably the single most important influence on the emerging generation known as the "angry young men") and in scenic design.[1]

Whatever the reasons, the late 1950s and early 1960s saw a wave of Brecht studies and translations appearing in America. Eric Bentley, who had befriended Brecht in the 1940s, was a major champion of his work, translating not only *The Threepenny Opera* used at the Theatre de Lys but most of the other major Brecht works between 1948 and 1956. His collection *Seven Plays* in 1961 was standard reading, and early in 1962 Cheryl Crawford announced a plan (never realized) to stage all seven on Broadway, beginning with *Mother Courage*.[2] No less than four major works on Brecht's plays and theories were published in the United States between 1959 and 1962. The first of these was *Brecht: A Choice of Evils*, by Martin Esslin, who two years later published his most famous work, *The Theatre of the Absurd*, thus calling attention, at the beginning of the decade, to the two styles of playwriting that would frame the period's experimental work.

Although the absurdist dramatists surely attracted at least as much attention as Brecht and his German contemporaries, they were in fact much less produced in the major commercial theaters of New York during the 1960s. In the smaller experimental theaters, German and French experimental work was about evenly balanced, but on Broadway only two plays from the so-called French absurdists were presented during this decade, both by Eugène Ionesco. The first was *Rhinoceros* in 1961, which achieved major success thanks to the performance of Zero Mostel in the leading role, and the much less successful *Exit the King*, presented by Ellis Robb's APA-Phoenix in 1968. In contrast, Brecht was represented on Broadway in almost every season of the decade. Eric Bentley wrote in 1981 that "until the sixties, Brecht never caught on in America. It was Vietnam that made the difference."[3] The first of these statements is indisputably true, but in the second Bentley's memory apparently played him false. Doubtless the Vietnam War helped to encourage interest in Brecht, especially as a politically engaged playwright, but by the time the first American troops were sent to Vietnam in 1965 the surge of interest in Brecht was already well established. What in fact apparently made the difference was the unprecedented success of *The Threepenny Opera* at the Theatre de Lys, immediately followed by the highly popular *Brecht on Brecht* at the same theater, starring Kurt Weill's wife, Lotte Lenya. This evening of Brecht songs, poems, and short dramatic pieces was originally scheduled for a six-week run and eventually ran for two hundred performances.

Already by early in 1962 Weis Funke announced in the *New York Times'* News of the Rialto column that "everyone and his uncle suddenly wishes to produce

Brecht." To support this conclusion, Funke cited an impressive range of current Brecht projects, ranging from New York's most visible commercial producers, like Kermit Bloomgarden and Cheryl Crawford, to such clearly nonestablishment ventures as the Living Theatre.[4] In the event, the proposed Bloomgarden production of *Mahagonny* never took place, despite the success of the Brecht-Weill *Threepenny Opera*, but Crawford and Jerome Robbins produced *Mother Courage* on Broadway in 1963 with Anne Bancroft in the title role. Play and producing organization were not a good match, especially since Eric Bentley, whose translation was used, seemingly insisted on as close an approximation as possible of the original, now almost legendary, Berlin production. Anne Bancroft, trained in the Method approach, almost as far as possible from Brecht's epic style (the previous year she had won an Academy Award for her nuanced realistic performance in the film *The Miracle Worker*), clearly struggled with the role and the production was condemned by some as under-rehearsed and by many as flat and uninteresting. It ran for six weeks, not an outright failure, but hardly distinguished, and was nominated for a Tony, doubtless based on Brecht's reputation, since Bancroft herself received no nomination.

Funke's implication that the Living Theatre productions were part of the new surge of interest in Brecht is not quite accurate. In fact the Living Theatre was one of the few experimental companies in America that had been presenting Brecht for more than a decade. Judith Malina, cofounder of the theater, had enrolled in the New School in 1945 to study theater with Erwin Piscator, with whom Brecht had collaborated in the late 1920s and who much influenced Brecht's development of epic theater. Piscator introduced Malina to Brecht's works, and Brecht was among those authors featured in the early years of the Living Theatre, founded by Malina and Julian Beck in 1947. Brecht's *He Who Says Yes* and *He Who Says No* were two of the five short plays presented in the first official program of this new group, staged in the Becks' apartment in August 1951. For the next several years Beck and Malina concentrated on the poetic drama of experimental authors like Gertrude Stein, Paul Goodman, and William Carlos Williams, but at the beginning of the next decade, in 1960, they returned to Brecht with one of their most successful productions to date, his early, rather expressionistic *In the Jungle of Cities*. On their first and second tours of Europe, in 1961 and 1962, they presented this production along with their other most successful work at the time, Jack Gelber's *The Connection*. Their first new production upon returning to New York in the fall of 1962 was Brecht's *Man Is Man*, with Joe Chaikin in the leading role.

It is an indication of the strength of the Brechtian vogue in New York at the beginning of the 1960s that at one time in 1962 there were simultaneous productions of the same Brecht work playing both on Broadway and off, and this not even one of his major works. Such a situation would have been almost unthinkable in New York at any period before or since.[5] The Broadway version of *Man Is Man*, starring John Heffernan and Olympia Dukakis, opened in September of that year and ran for 175 performances.

The very next year, 1963, saw two more Brecht productions on Broadway, the Bancroft *Mother Courage* in March and in November George Tabori's translation of *Arturo Ui*, Brecht's comic allegory of the rise of Hitler. The latter production avoided what many considered a mistake in *Mother Courage* of trying to fit an American Method actor to a Brechtian role. Director Tony Richardson chose another, but equally unsuccessful, alternative, selecting the classically trained Canadian actor Christopher Plummer to play Brecht's grotesque gangster hero. Nor did Richardson try to copy a Berliner Ensemble approach, instead utilizing a hodgepodge of styles in a production that was an outright failure, lasting a mere six performances. *Times* reviewer Howard Taubman concluded dryly, "It is a happy sign that Broadway at last acknowledges the significance of Brecht. Now it must master the art of presenting him with the coherence and eloquence that are his right."[6]

After the embarrassingly rapid demise of *Arturo Ui*, Taubman was besieged with letters berating him for not giving Brecht more support. He responded in a "postmortem" on the production that Brecht, like most major dramatists, needed a kind of audience and company unknown to the New York commercial stage. "New York," he argued, "should have a theater with subscribers indifferent to critics and the hit-or-flop psychosis where plays like 'The Caucasian Chalk Circle,' 'Mother Courage,' 'The Good Woman of Setzuan' and 'Galileo' could be mounted on a healthier basis than the one-shot Broadway system."[7]

Taubman suggested the Lincoln Center Repertory for a beginning of this approach.[8] And hardly surprisingly, since this institution, essentially a creation of the 1960s, was formed precisely to fill the need he articulated. A general plan for a major new multiarts center began to form among city planners in 1955, but not until 1960 was the inclusion of a European-style repertory theater added to the plans, a nonprofit theater with a permanent company offering seasons of classic and new plays. In 1962 Robert Whitehead and Elia Kazan were appointed its directors. Since the permanent home of the company, the Vivian Beaumont, was not complete, the company was launched in a temporary theater erected in Washington Square. The first season consisted of three plays, all American, headed by the premiere of Arthur Miller's *After the Fall*. Neither this nor the next season gained much praise from either audiences or critics, and in 1964 both directors departed. They were replaced in 1965 by Herbert Blau and Jules Irving, who had made the San Francisco Actors' Workshop one of the most highly regarded of America's regional theaters. It was Blau and Irving who opened the long-delayed Vivian Beaumont in 1965, and significantly not, as the previous administration had done, with an American play, but with a classic of the German theater, Georg Büchner's *Danton's Death*, produced only once before in New York, by Orson Welles at the Mercury Theatre in 1938.

Danton's Death was indifferently received. The demands of this complicated and challenging work revealed stresses in both the new company and the new theater. Director Blau chose to make up his Robespierre to resemble Barry Goldwater, just defeated in the 1964 presidential race by Lyndon Johnson and portrayed by his liberal opponents as a revolutionary radical, a concept that suggested a contemporary political reading that the production as a whole did not really support. After the second production, Wycherly's *Country Wife*, Taubman was calling for a radical rethinking of the project, and when after several additional productions failed to attain a single clear success, Blau announced his resignation in January 1967. After several further years of mixed successes, Irving followed him in 1972.

Interestingly enough, the two productions most generally considered successes during the Blau and Irving years at Lincoln Center were, as Taubman predicted, stagings of major Brecht works, *The Caucasian Chalk Circle*, directed by Irving, in 1966 and *Galileo*, directed by Canadian John Hirsch and starring Anthony Quayle, in 1967. Stanley Kauffmann reported in the *Times* that *The Caucasian Chalk Circle* was the theater's "best production to date, and a good production by any standards."[9] Apparently *Galileo* was even better, if one may believe Walter Kerr, Taubman's successor as lead theater critic for the *New York Times*, who (probably unconsciously) echoed Kauffmann in calling *Galileo* "easily the Vivian Beaumont's best production to date."[10] In any case the two productions were an important breakthrough for Brecht. *Chalk Circle* had never been presented before by any New York theater, and *Galileo* only once, twenty years before, by Charles Laughton. The Lincoln Center productions also dominated the Brecht offerings in the latter half of the decade, which offered in all only six Brecht shows, as opposed to thirteen between 1960 and 1965. Aside from Lincoln Center, only one of these was at a Broadway house, a poorly received adaptation by Swedish puppets that ran only nine evenings in 1966.

Of the six Brecht productions off-Broadway from 1965 to 1970, the most successful was the short *Exception and the Rule*, presented in 1965 at the Greenwich Mews Theater, an early encourager of black theater, in a double bill with Langston Hughes's *The Prodigal Son*. Joseph Chaikin, who had left the Living Theatre in 1963 to found his own company, the Open Theatre, was still also performing as an independent actor and won an Obie in 1965 for his portrayal of the Coolie in Brecht's play. Another off-Broadway Brecht production of 1965 was involved in an equally odd pairing. The previous summer James Earl Jones, then just at the beginning of a career that would make him one of America's leading actors, had enjoyed great success in *Othello*, presented the summer of 1964 during the Public Theater's free Shakespeare at the Delacorte Theatre in Central Park, a program established only two years earlier. The *Othello* was so successful that it was revived in the fall season by the Martinique Theatre, which had the idea of offering it in repertory, with the odd but fascinating selection of Brecht's rarely produced first play *Baal*, to be presented on alternate nights with the same cast. So James Earle Jones appeared as Baal's friend Ekart while Mitchell Ryan, Iago in Shakespeare's play, performed the title role.

The Martinique project was the inspiration of two of the pioneers of the off-Broadway movement, Theodore Mann and José Quintero, who during the 1950s had made their Circle in the Square into one of the country's most admired experimental theaters. Although the theater was particularly associated with the work of Eugene O'Neill, Mann in particular became interested in Brecht and in fact planned a Broadway production of *Mother Courage*, which eventually was pushed aside by the rival Anne Bancroft production.[11] This new Brecht undertaking was developed the season after the disappointing run of the Bancroft *Courage*. *Baal* in fact had an almost identical run, only forty-seven performances. The next season Mann tried again with Brecht's second play, *Drums in the Night*, which was also presented in repertory with an incongruous piece, this time Henry Livings's short absurdist farce *Eh?*, starring the then almost unknown Dustin Hoffman. The selection of these two works, never before seen in America, suggests that Mann may have had an idea of working his way chronologically through the canon, but *Drums* proved only slightly more successful than *Baal*, and the Circle in the Square returned to its emphasis on American works.

So far as German dramatists are concerned, Brecht quite dominated the American stage of the 1960s, although critics constantly complain of his apparent incompatibility with this stage. Certainly of the many professional Brecht productions of this decade, only two achieved a clear success, the Theatre de Lys *Threepenny Opera*, actually a product of the previous decade, and the subsequent review *Brecht on Brecht*, not actually a Brecht work but a collection of selections from his writings.

Other German dramatists, represented by far fewer works and productions, made a more significant mark on the actual production history of the decade. One might argue that the predominant figure among these was Peter Weiss, whose *Marat/Sade* (the universally used short form of its actual title: *The Persecution and Assassination of Jean-Paul Marat as Performed by the Inmates of the Asylum of Charenton under the Direction of the Marquis de Sade*), staged by the Royal Shakespeare Company and directed by Peter Brook, was unquestionably one of the major offerings of the 1960s. For most Americans, however, the German connection was scarcely noticed, such was the reputation of the Royal Shakespeare Company, now at the height of its powers, and such was the powerful stamp put upon this staging by Peter Brook, who was now widely regarded as the most imaginative and innovative director in the English-speaking world. Weiss's work was in many way perfectly suited to the times, a complex intellectual exploration of the dynamics of revolution, in one of the most revolutionary decades of the century, carried out by these two historical figures in arguments and dramatic strategies that clearly suggested the approaches of Brecht and Artaud, two of the truly iconic figures of 1960s theater. The play's construction, though not its central debate, owed a great deal to Brecht, but Brook's brilliant staging gave it a success in America totally eclipsing anything ever achieved there by any Brecht work.

Without disputing Brook's achievement, however, one must note that the play was a major international success, interpreted with great acclaim by other directors in Germany, Sweden, Poland, Australia, and elsewhere. Its international success was all the more impressive in that its author was before this work almost unknown as a dramatist, even in Germany or in his adopted Sweden, where he fled when the Nazis came to power. Before *Marat/Sade* he had a modest reputation as an experimental novelist, painter, and filmmaker and had written only one play (in Swedish), a short, nightmarish radio play about the weight of memory, premiered in 1950 and translated into German only in 1963.

The success of *Marat/Sade* established him on the world stage, however, and during the next five years he followed this with five other major works that were widely produced, though with nothing approaching the acclaim that surrounded his best-known work. The next, *The Investigation*, opened simultaneously in seventeen German cities in October 1965, with the keynote production in West Berlin, staged by Erwin Piscator. Ingmar Bergman staged it at the Royal National Theatre in Stockholm and Peter Brook organized a reading of it in London. Not only was it presented on Broadway for a two-month run in the fall of 1966, but it was televised early the following year on NBC-TV, the first production of a Broadway play ever signed for television before the work had even gone into rehearsal.[12] Much of this interest, of course, was due to the success of *Marat/Sade*, but much also came from the subject and approach of the new play. In the mid-1960s a profound shift was taking place in the West German theater, of which Weiss's new play was an important and highly representative example. In the postwar years the West German theater was primarily concerned with reestablishing Germany's reputation as a country of high culture, after the horrors of the Nazi era. Thus the theaters emphasized elegant and respectful productions of figures like

Shakespeare, Goethe, and Schiller and avoided all political themes, especially anything recalling the recent German past. Brecht, both political and working in East Germany, was particularly avoided.

After 1965 a new theater generation appeared in West Germany, sharing the radical, antiestablishment orientation of their colleagues in contemporary France and the United States. Suddenly political theater, including, of course, Brecht and focusing on the hitherto avoided recent German past, became a central concern of young theater directors like Peter Stein and Claus Peymann and of a few engaged directors of the previous generation like Piscator. Central to this project were a number of plays like *The Investigation*, built out of the raw material of historical documents, in this case the court records of the trials of camp directors from Auschwitz held in Frankfurt from 1963 to 1965. This type of theater, called "documentary theatre" in Germany and "docudrama" in England and America, became an important international form in the late 1960s. Thomas Irmer, in a recent general survey of the form, suggests that there have been three distinct phases of such drama in Germany (and, one might add, in the United States).[13] The first came to Germany in the 1920s with the documentary political performances of Piscator (followed by the similar Living Newspapers in the United States). The second came with the political turn of the West German theater in the mid-1960s. The third, in the late 1990s, returned to auteur-directors like Piscator gathering material representing significant recent sociopolitical events or general social concerns.

Weiss's *The Investigation* was one of the most contemporary as well as one of the most powerful of the 1960s docudramas. The Auschwitz trials ended only two months before the German premieres of the Weiss play and were composed in significant part of trial transcripts made by the author during the proceedings, which were open to the public. For the first time detailed information was made available to German and international audiences on the operations of the Holocaust, which made a tremendous impact. In the United States, reviewers in Chicago and Los Angeles provided their readers with comments on the New York production. Moreover, the interest in *The Investigation* encouraged further attention to *Marat/Sade*, even without the attraction of the Peter Brook–Royal Shakespeare Company production. It was presented later, in 1966, from coast to coast, at the Goodman Theatre in Chicago, the Carousel Theatre in Los Angeles, and by the National Players Company at the Barrymore Theatre on Broadway, a company formed in 1949 and pledged to present major foreign works utilizing American actors. Despite inevitable and not very favorable comparison with the outstanding Royal Shakespeare Company version, this new production ran for seven weeks, somewhat longer than Anne Bancroft's disappointing *Mother Courage*.

One more Weiss play was presented professionally in the United States during this decade, and it united the German stage significantly with one of the major movements of the decade, the rise of an autonomous black theater. One of the first major manifestations of this movement, designed to challenge the almost total white domination of the American stage, was the Negro Ensemble Company (NEC), founded in the summer of 1967 by actor and playwright Douglas Turner Ward, actor Robert Hooks, and producer-director Gerald Krone. Although black controlled and dedicated to drama involving the black experience, the NEC was criticized for its integrationist orientation by more radical black artists like LeRoi Jones (Amiri Baraka), whose founding of the Black Arts Repertory School in Harlem in 1965 is generally considered the beginning of the Black Arts Movement. The NEC was criticized for its integrated administration (Krone was white), its reliance upon funding from the Ford Foundation, its location in Greenwich Village, traditionally the location of white avant-garde theater, and its opening season, which indeed expressed the theater's commitment to integration by including two plays each by black and white authors and opening with Weiss's *Song of the Lusitanian Bogey*, his first drama since *The Investigation*.[14] The play was a theatrical satire on colonialism, closer in spirit to *Marat/Sade* than to *The Investigation* and dealing with the Portuguese colonization of Angola. Although its remoteness from the African American experience and its white authorship gained it the condemnation of the rising Black Arts Movement, the spirited theatricality of the production was highly praised by the critical establishment.

Documentary theater dominated the German stage of the 1960s and the three plays universally recognized as the outstanding works in this genre were among the first: Rolf Hochhuth's *The Deputy* (1964), Heinar Kipphardt's *In the Matter of J. Robert Oppenheimer* (1964), and Peter Weiss's *The Investigation* (1965). Although in fact only two of these are composed largely of material from specific documents, all deal searchingly with recent highly charged political material, all created major political scandals, and all three were originally directed by Piscator, giving them a particular resonance in this politically conscious decade. All three were given American productions soon after their premieres in Germany. The first and most successful was *The Deputy*, which had an eight-month Broadway run in 1964.

Although it was later often characterized as a documentary drama, that term was not yet familiar to the theater public, and the play was designed by its author's term, "A Christian tragedy." Although the play contains many historical figures and characters, including its Protestant hero, the Holocaust witness Kurt Gersten, it is much more a polemic history play than a documentary, charging Pope Pius for his refusal to speak out against the Holocaust. The play, not surprisingly, created one of the major theatrical controversies of the decade and came to New York in February 1964 after more than a year of newspaper reports on the protests and even riots it had stimulated across Europe. The *New York Times* article announcing its long-anticipated arrival in that city began: "It is now more than a year since Rolf Hochhuth's 'The Deputy' had its premiere on a West Berlin stage. In the interim, it has become one of the most explosively controversial plays in modern theatrical history."[15] The press avidly pursued major Jewish and Catholic groups for official statements, only to discover that while the play was attracting great interest, most groups were strongly divided on the matter. On the eve of the premiere, which the author attended, coming from Germany, a press conference was called at the Waldorf Astoria by a group of prominent Catholic, Protestant, and Jewish religious leaders, who issued a statement neither defending nor attacking the play but calling for the defense of free speech for all opinions.[16] So many attacks, defenses, and manifestos were in fact produced, however, that Grove Press published a collection of them in 1964, edited by Eric Bentley.[17]

Approximately 150 demonstrators gathered to picket the production's opening, and almost one hundred city police were present to prevent trouble. According to the *Chicago Tribune*, however, a "stunned audience," after a three-hour production (uncut, the play would run to around eight), a harrowing conclusion, and no curtain calls, "staggered to the exits" to find a large waiting crowd containing more policemen and photographers than picketers or protesters.[18] Reviews of the production, which starred Emlyn Williams made up to resemble Pius XII, generally considered that as drama the work was flawed but as a polemic it was compelling and powerful, a view apparently shared by most of the public. The production ran for eight months, but clearly on its reputation as the most controversial play of the decade rather than, like *Marat/Sade* the following year, on its success as a piece of theater. Continued attacks by the Vatican and prominent Catholic figures probably did the production more good than harm, but they did help to spread the reputation of *The Deputy* as a work of questionable morality. As it neared the end of its run, coproducer Herman Shumlin attempted to organize a national tour but found so many major cities (among them Cleveland, Baltimore, and Minneapolis) concerned by Catholic reactions that the tour never occurred. In the summer of 1965, however, Gordon Davidson of the Mark Taper Forum created a *Deputy* at the UCLA Summer Theatre that toured with success in the fall and winter of that year to Boston and Chicago.

Hochhuth's next play, *Soldiers*, premiered in Germany in 1967 and, like *The*

Investigation, was preceded in the United States by a storm of publicity about the controversy it had aroused in Europe. Although the intended theme of the play was the wholesale bombing of civilian populations during the Second World War, this concern was totally overshadowed by Hochhuth's negative portrayal of Winston Churchill, here depicted as ordering the death of the Polish prime minister in an airplane crash in 1943 that had been officially labeled an accident. In England a proposed production at the National Theatre starring Richard Burton was not permitted by the theater board, despite the vehement protests of director Laurence Olivier and dramaturg Kenneth Tynan. Their plan to move to another theater was then thwarted by the Lord Chamberlain's Office, which banned any public performance of the play in England (this was one of the last such decisions, as this two-hundred-year-old censoring function was abolished in 1968). As a result, the English-language premiere of the play took place in Toronto in March 1968, and its director, Clifford Williams, and three of his leading actors, including John Colicos as Churchill, opened the play on Broadway in April. Colicos was warmly praised by all reviewers, but otherwise critical reception was mixed, and there was little of the scandal in America that had surrounded *The Deputy*. *Soldiers* received only twenty-one performances.

The third major German docudrama of the 1960s was Heinar Kipphardt's *In the Matter of J. Robert Oppenheimer*. Such was the European interest in this play that even before its opening, in October 1964, it was scheduled for productions in Milan, in Paris, and in twenty-two German cities. Oppenheimer's career touched on many of the most troubling social and political concerns of the time. A key figure in the development of the atomic bomb, Oppenheimer later campaigned against the arms race with the Soviet Union, drawing upon him the wrath of anti-Communist political figures like Joseph McCarthy. His security clearance was revoked at a hearing in 1964, which stripped him of political influence. The three-thousand-page transcript of this hearing served as the raw material for the Kipphardt drama. Oppenheimer wrote a letter of protest to several theaters objecting to the representation of himself and the dynamics of the trial, and these threats apparently caused producer David Merrick to drop plans for a Broadway production. In any case, this play alone of the major German works presented on professional American stages during the 1960s did not premiere in New York, but at the Mark Taper Forum in Los Angeles in 1968, a year after Oppenheimer's death. Its producer and director was Gordon Davidson, who had achieved a major success in Los Angeles with *The Deputy* in 1965. Jules Irving, now alone at Lincoln Center, invited Davidson to present the play there in the spring of 1969, his first New York assignment. The production received warm reviews, Eric Bentley remarking that no contemporary American dramatist could do justice to such a subject,[19] and it was extended four times, running well into the fall of 1969.

Brecht, Weiss, Hochhuth, and Kipphardt were by far the most important German representatives on the professional American stage of the 1960s. There were, of course, a few others, but comparatively their contributions were fairly minor. Strikingly, almost all the German authors presented were from the twentieth century, the most important exception being the distinctly challenging choice of Büchner to open the Irving-Blau administration at Lincoln Center. The only other German classic authors were Schiller, represented by a twenty-six-night run of *Don Carlos* at the Masque Theatre in 1962, and Wedekind, whose *Awakening of Spring* was presented for only eight nights at the Pocket Theatre in 1964.

Rather better represented were two other twentieth-century German dramatists, Max Frisch and Friedrich Dürrenmatt, both of whom built their reputations working in Switzerland during the Nazi years. Dürrenmatt entered the decade much better known, since the recently retired Alfred Lunt and Lynne Fontanne, a couple who had dominated the American stage for three decades, had achieved their last major success in 1958 in Dürrenmatt's best-known play, *The Visit*. That success was often mentioned by critics reviewing Dürrenmatt's distinctly lesser *Romulus*, adapted by Gore Vidal and starring Cyril Ritchard, which opened on Broadway in January 1962 and lasted for only sixty-nine performances. One might have expected a warmer reception for Dürrenmatt's *The Physicists*, which opened at the same Broadway house (after a preview in Washington) two years later. This was directed by Peter Brook (who had just presented the play in London with the Royal Shakespeare Company) and starred Hume Cronyn and Jessica Tandy, the acting couple widely regarded as the successors to the much-loved Lunts. Nevertheless the production had even a shorter run than *Romulus* (fifty-five nights), and Peter Brook had to wait two more years before his production with his own company of another German play, *Marat/Sade*, gave him a major Broadway success. In 1967 Henry Popkin, a leading editor of and commenter upon the contemporary stage, assumed the challenge of selecting the greatest living dramatist (the deaths of Shaw in 1950, O'Neill in 1953, and Brecht in 1956 having "cleared the field"). After considering and rejecting Sartre, Beckett, Genet, and Williams, Popkin argued that the clear choice was Dürrenmatt, for his sustained excellence and depth.[20] Many in Europe might have agreed with this assessment in the late 1960s, but arguably, aside from *The Visit*, America found Dürrenmatt, like Brecht, not really compatible with its theatrical taste.

Dürrenmatt's countryman, Max Frisch, did even less well. The omens were not good for his *Andorra*, scheduled to open on Broadway in February 1963 after a series of out-of-town previews. The previews were cancelled and the opening delayed three days. Nevertheless, for a brief period it appeared that Frisch might be headed for success in America. His absurdist allegory, *The Firebugs*, opened at the Maidman Theatre the same week as *Andorra*, so that Frisch had the distinction of simultaneous productions running on and off Broadway. Moreover, Howard Taubman in the *New York Times* gave *Andorra* a very positive review, beginning with the note that in 1962 *Andorra* had been performed more times in West Germany than any other play except one by Goethe.[21] Nothing positive came from these omens, however. Both the Broadway and off-Broadway productions lasted slightly more than a week, and an attempted off-Broadway revival of *The Firebugs* in 1968 did no better.

Even these modest contributions, however, added their bits to the international flavoring of the American theater in the 1960s, and if even such major contributors as Brecht and the docudrama playwrights enjoyed a lesser success in America than had been their fortune in Germany, and indeed in Western Europe in general, it still remains indisputably true that the modern German theater made a truly significant contribution to the American stage during that turbulent and pivotal decade.

NOTES

1. Janelle Reinelt significantly calls her excellent study of the "angry young men" generation *After Brecht* (Ann Arbor: University of Michigan Press, 1994).

2. Sam Zolotow, "'Mother Courage' to Be Staged Here," *New York Times*, January 8, 1962, 24.

3. Eric Bentley, introductory remarks to the reprint of a 1964 essay written by Bentley as a preface to Brecht's "A Man's a Man," in *The Brecht Commentaries* (New York: Grove Press, 1981), 108.

4. Weis Funke, "Brecht on the Rise," *New York Times*, February 11, 1962, 109.

5. Although in fact at the very beginning of the decade New York was facing the prospect of two productions of *Mother Courage* opening on Broadway the same *night*, October 15, 1959. One, translated by Marc Blitzstein and organized by Theodore Mann and José Quintero of the Circle in the Square, was to star Siobhan McKenna. The other, translated by Eric Bentley and produced by Lee Paton and Robert Welber, would star Katina Paxinou and feature designs by Ted Otto, who created the scenery for the original production. Both claimed the approval of the Brecht estate. See Arthur Gelb, "Brecht Play Set by 2 Producers," *New York Times*, June 2, 1959, 40. By fall, Mann and Quintero had shelved their project, but the rival producers continued, signing up Darius Milhaud to compose the score. See Sam Zolotow, "Milhaud Writes Music for Show," *New York Times*, September 23, 1959, 44.

The Brechts' son, Stefan, brought legal action against the Paton project, claiming that the Blitzstein translation was the only one approved by the estate. Eventually a settlement was reached in favor of the Bentley project, which opened on Broadway in 1963 with Anne Bancroft instead of Paxinou, Ming Cho Lee instead of Ted Otto, the original music of Paul Dessau, and Jerome Robbins as director.

6. Howard Taubman, "Bertolt Brecht's 'Arturo Ui,'" *New York Times*, November 12, 1963, 47.

7. Howard Taubman, "On Brecht, 'Ui': Style and Our Theater," *New York Times*, November 24, 1963, 27.

8. Ibid.

9. Stanley Kauffmann, "At Last, 'The Caucasian Chalk Circle,'" *New York Times*, March 25, 1966, 35.

10. Walter Kerr, "'Galileo' a New Hope?," *New York Times*, April 23, 1967, 97.

11. See note 5 for details.

12. George Gent, "Weiss Play on Auschwitz Trial Listed by N.B.C.-T.V. for 1967," *New York Times*, August 10, 1966, 61.

13. Thomas Irmer, "A Search for New Realities: Documentary Theatre in Germany," *TDR* 50.3 (Fall 2006): 16–28.

14. The four plays in the opening season were Peter Weiss's *The Song of the Lusitanian Bogey*, Ray Lawler's *The Summer of the Seventeenth Doll* (previously produced on Broadway), Wole Soyinka's *Kongi's Harvest*, and Richard Wright's *Daddy Goodness*. The casts were all black.

15. Robert C. Doty, "'The Deputy' Is Here," *New York Times*, February 23, 1964, X1.

16. Richard F. Shepard, "'Deputy' Author Hopes His Play Will Be 'Factually' Received," *New York Times*, February 25, 1964, 23.

17. Eric Bentley, ed., *The Storm over "The Deputy"* (New York: Grove Press, 1964).

18. John Chapman, "Audience Stunned by 'The Deputy,'" *Chicago Tribune*, February 27, 1964, C1.

19. Eric Bentley, "Oppenheimer Mon Amour," *New York Times*, March 16, 1969, D1.

20. Henry Popkin, "Switzerland's Duerrenmatt—No. 1 among World's Dramatists?," *Los Angeles Times*, October 15, 1967, D20.

21. Howard Taubman, "Theater: 'Andorra,'" *New York Times*, February 11, 1963, 5.

Neil Blackadder

"The Best Contemporary Theatre Is International"

Plays in Translation on and off Broadway in the 1960s

As late as 1966, Robert Brustein characterized the American theater scene as "void of any excitement or vitality" in contrast to new European work.[1] And in a 1963 *TDR* Comment in which Richard Schechner and Theodore Hoffman outlined a "framework of commitment" that would help promote "a real theatre on this continent," they advocated "a recognition that the best contemporary theatre is international."[2] But to what extent did the division between international and U.S. work parallel that between the experimental and for-profit (in Schechner's favored term, "commodity theatre") realms? Where did foreign plays fit into the landscape of production and reception on Broadway/off-Broadway/off-off-Broadway in the 1960s?

I have pursued those questions by investigating productions of new plays in translation—that is, scripts written and first staged since the mid-1950s and primarily in productions originating in the United States. (These criteria exclude the plays of Bertolt Brecht [d. 1956], though certainly the gradually increasing openness to and interest in his work was an important part of the theater scene—in the regional theaters as well as in New York—during the 1960s.) The most prominent and significant of such productions can be categorized thus:

- Later work by two French-language playwrights associated with the theater of the absurd, Eugène Ionesco and Jean Genet—including two by Ionesco staged on Broadway (*Rhinoceros* and *Exit the King*), otherwise produced off-Broadway
- Later work by established Swiss writers Friedrich Dürrenmatt and Max Frisch—two by Dürrenmatt produced on Broadway; one by Frisch produced on Broadway, one off

- Documentary theater, translated from German, by Rolf Hochhuth, Peter Weiss, and Heinar Kipphardt, mostly produced on Broadway
- Weiss's *Marat/Sade*; while the Peter Brook production that became a 1966 Broadway hit originated in England, it was unquestionably a landmark event, and Weiss's play was revived on Broadway as soon as the next year
- Plays from Communist countries—Aleksei Arbuzov produced on Broadway, Vaclav Havel and Slawomir Mrozek off-Broadway

I shall begin with the first category, and with a book that cast a remarkably long shadow. Martin Esslin's 1961 study *The Theatre of the Absurd* influenced conceptions of and attitudes toward drama of its era as perhaps no other critical work has done before or since. Esslin doesn't appear to have set out to change the course of theater history; in his original preface, he even suggested that the title was an already established phrase rather than his own invention: "This book is an attempt to define the convention that has come to be called the Theatre of the Absurd."[3] And by the time the book appeared, over a decade had passed since the work Esslin focuses on reached the stage—the first productions in Paris of Ionesco's earliest plays. Esslin's study certainly helped people to understand the perplexing Nouveau Théâtre that had emerged from France in the 1950s, but its gratefully received elucidation also jeopardized other interpretations; as Schechner wrote in 1965, "When Martin Esslin wrote *The Theatre of the Absurd* he probably had no idea how difficult it would be to discuss Genet, Ionesco, and Beckett in the aftermath of his book."[4] More significantly still, Esslin's hit study threatened to overshadow any other approaches to current and future new writing for the stage. For instance, regarding LeRoi Jones's *Dutchman*, Stephen Bottoms writes that for its 1964 off-Broadway production "it was billed alongside Samuel Beckett's *Play* and Fernando Arrabal's *The Two Executioners*, apparently in an attempt to contextualize it not as a drama about race, but as 'theater of the absurd'—a category that, thanks to Martin Esslin's book of that title, could now be sold to discerning theatergoers."[5] Similarly, Henry Hewes, then the editor of the *Best Plays* volumes, wrote that "overnight the phrase became a hot conversation topic and one convenient for those who wished to merchandise plays that might be rejected by the public unless they were made to seem something new that the theatregoer could not afford to miss."[6]

As will become clear from my frequent references to Esslin's book and to the notion of "absurdism," there's no question that the prominence of the "theater of the absurd" label affected the reception of plays produced in New York during the sixties—on and off Broadway, and in translation or not. One thing the publication of *The Theatre of the Absurd* did not lead to was a significant increase in productions of the plays Esslin himself analyzed. The Broadway production of Ionesco's *Rhinoceros* preceded the publication of Esslin's book, as did the off-Broadway stagings of Genet's *The Balcony* and *The Blacks*; Ionesco's *Exit the King* premiered in France in 1962 but wasn't staged in New York until 1968; Beckett appears surprisingly little in the seasons even of off-Broadway theaters after a 1962 production of *Happy Days*. Instead of prompting New York theaters to stage the plays Esslin examined, his book seems above all to have provided companies, critics, and audiences with a handy lens through which to evaluate other new drama. Some 1960s scholars did believe that, quite apart from Esslin's book, the Paris-based playwrights of the previous decade had beneficially influenced their American counterparts; thus Alan S. Downer wrote in 1967, regarding Pinter along with Beckett, Ionesco, and Genet, "Such plays and playwrights, however, are important not merely for broadening or internationalizing the American repertory but because they have been absorbed into the experience of American playwrights."[7] But in the same volume, Bernard Dukore referred directly to Esslin's book in representing emerging American playwrights as characterized precisely by their not following the same path as Ionesco and others: "European playwrights are creating various dramatic visions which constitute what Martin Esslin has called 'the theater of the absurd.' The major experimental playwrights of the United States are pursuing their own visions and do not, in the main, appear to be tormented by 'the absurdity of the human condition.' This may be a blessing, for the concept has become a cliché."[8] In principle, the success of *The Theatre of the Absurd* signaled an opening up of American theater to ground-breaking dramatic writing from overseas. As Esslin wrote in his introduction, "Most of the incomprehension with which plays of this type are still being received by critics and theatrical reviewers, most of the bewilderment they have caused and to which they still give rise, come from the fact that they are part of a new, and still developing stage convention that has not yet been generally understood and has hardly ever been defined."[9] Such was the currency of Esslin's idea of "theatre of the absurd" that it seems unlikely any playwright would not at least have been aware of the phenomenon. Yet in practice the book's success led to two other consequences. On the one hand, it promoted an insufficiently nuanced conception of new foreign drama, much of which did not reflect the new convention Esslin had set out to define. And on the other hand, it interfered with the response to—if not the creation of— contemporary American work.

Schechner wrote at some length about another key aspect of the interpretation of new foreign drama in the United States at this time: how the plays were staged. Was the American theater equipped to do justice, in production, to the foreign work he considered superior to anything currently generated in the United States? In his third issue as editor of the *Tulane Drama Review* in 1963, Schechner emphatically answers in the negative, introducing an issue devoted to Genet and Ionesco by regretfully remarking, "Yet their work, well known and often performed, remains but barely understood in this country. We need only cite the New York productions of Genet's *The Balcony* and Ionesco's *Rhinoceros* as examples of this misunderstanding."[10] But it was not until the next issue of *TDR* that Schechner explained his position more fully. Schechner argues that "it is becoming more and more difficult to distinguish between the intentions of Broadway and off-Broadway," then lays out why he believes that blurring of distinctions has happened, and why he considers it "destructive."[11] The plays he then discusses at most length are Genet's *The Balcony*, Dürrenmatt's *The Visit*, and Ionesco's *Rhinoceros*.

For Schechner, a "smearing of lines" has been taking place in both directions—off-Broadway borrowing from Broadway, and vice versa—but he spends most time on instances in which "off-Broadway taught Broadway that 'good theatre' can be profitable." He declares that "more often than not Broadway's bows to culture are crippled gestures," and the examples he then gives consist of two "director-rewrites" by Elia Kazan of plays by Williams and MacLeish, two plays by Dürrenmatt, and Ionesco's *Rhinoceros*.[12] Maurice Valency's adaptation of Dürrenmatt's 1956 play *Der Besuch der alten Dame*, which premiered on Broadway in 1958, certainly does demonstrate the surprising liberties translators are sometimes permitted to take. It is simple for Schechner to argue his point: with just a few quotations, he quickly demonstrates how Valency made Claire Zachanassian younger and more glamorous, elided the fact that Koby and Loby haven't merely been blinded, but also castrated, and omitted the townsfolk's final speech so that the play could end with the exit of the (no longer quite so) old lady. In Schechner's view, Valency tamed Dürrenmatt's hard-edged parable, and if he hadn't, the play would not have become a Broadway hit. Judging from a 1961 interview, Valency would probably have pleaded guilty as charged: as he saw it, "The special problem confronting the adaptor in handling *The Visit* was to transform the grotesque into the beautiful, the poignant into art, and a somewhat cynical, bitter comedy into a modern tragedy."[13] Valency's adaptation (quite often inaccurately labeled simply a translation) is an outstanding example of Schechner's point that the "commodity theatre" can make rich and challenging work profitable by taming it; the interview reveals that one of Claire's husbands was cut to save on actors' salaries and that various parts, including the ending, were repeatedly changed in response to the reactions of out-of-town audiences. However, *The Visit* represents more an exceptional case than an emblematic one: surveying the 1960s, I found that while there were attempts to create a Broadway hit through a watered-down version of a foreign play—including one of the others Schechner cites among the "crippled gestures," Gore Vidal's adaptation of Dürrenmatt's *Romulus*—none was anywhere near as successful.

But, as Schechner goes on to quite rightly point out, "our theatre's bowdlerizations do not end with the script; the director as well as the adapter is only too happy to 'interpret' the material."[14] In discussing Ionesco's *Rhinoceros*, Schechner quotes at length from the playwright's own published reflections on Joseph Anthony's production of his play, the success of which "delights me, surprises me, and makes me a little sad, all at the same time." Ionesco felt Anthony had distorted the two main characters, making Berenger harder than he wrote him—"a sort of lucid intellectual" instead of "an indecisive character"—and Jean softer, weaker. He also takes issue with certain things he saw in Anthony's production that were not indicated in his stage directions, which, he says, "are to be respected as much as the text"; for instance, "If I have not indicated that Berenger and Jean must fight each other on stage and twist each other's noses that means that I don't want this to be done."[15] It is, of course, problematic for a playwright to insist that directors should never have actors do anything not spelled out in the stage directions, but in this case Ionesco's displeasure is warranted and borne out by the reviews. The critics enthused about how humorous *Rhinoceros* was, calling it a "cleverly crazy comedy."[16] And many of the reviewers praised Anthony's production, several underlining how much more imaginative it was than the—in Howard Taubman's words—"rather stuffy, subdued version" presented in London the previous year. For Taubman, the New York *Rhinoceros* "has been staged and performed with a mad, inventive gusto that never loses sight of the important things behind the parody, horseplay, and calculated illogicality."[17] Ionesco did not agree that Anthony had got that balance right, lamenting that he had instead "made something funny out of it."[18] In Schechner's view, it was only by having his play "crippled" that Ionesco, still regarded as "a vastly contentious writer," had his first Broadway hit.[19]

Had Schechner been writing even a few months later he might have also considered a striking example of a translated play that failed miserably on Broadway in spite of a certain amount of adaptation: Max Frisch's *Andorra*, which ran for all of nine performances in February 1963. As German journalist Sabina Lietzmann wrote shortly after the production closed, "The critical reception of *Andorra* embodies the American conception of the nature and function of theatre. Seldom has an event so glaringly and unmistakably demonstrated the fundamental difference between the US and Europe."[20] Almost all of those who wrote about this case—in Europe or in the United States—held George

Tabori's translation partially responsible; but while Tabori does seem to have carried out a good deal of adaptation (his version has never been published), he did not distort the thrust of Frisch's play as Valency did with Dürrenmatt's. Most critics who believed the production failed to do justice to *Andorra* also held the director, designer, and actors responsible, such as Hans Sahl, writing in another German newspaper, in a piece entitled "The Mistreatment of Max Frisch," who felt Michael Langham's staging "tried to adjust the harsh, rough, woodcut-like style of Frisch's poetic vision to suit Broadway taste." European observers tended to believe that most of the New York reviewers simply failed to understand Frisch's play, and for Sahl that failure was typical: "European playwrights be warned: in America, people only half-understand your work and therefore don't perform it in the right way. Ionesco has almost always been staged incorrectly, to say nothing of Dürrenmatt."[21]

While Sahl's comments are perhaps too sweeping, there is plenty of evidence that plays like those by Frisch and Dürrenmatt did require an altered stance from directors as well as audiences and that such a shift needed some time. And it was not simply a matter of Broadway being the wrong venue for such work: Frisch's *The Firebugs* opened off-Broadway around the same time yet also closed after only eight performances—and lasted only for an equally short run when revived, again off-Broadway, in 1968. Hewes attributed the play's lack of success in 1963 to "an overly self-conscious production."[22] One American director who had proven he could effectively stage the work of European authors was Alan Schneider, who wrote a short article on the flops of Frisch's two plays in 1963. He called that piece "The Failure of Seriousness," arguing, as did many other commentators, that plays like Frisch's were offering audiences something more demanding than many of them wished to engage with. Schneider characterized the Broadway audience as "attuned to sensation, speed and sentimentality" and "generally disinclined to allegory (sweet or sardonic), irony (bitter or otherwise), moral fervor, or poetry (whether subtle or overblown)."[23] The technique of allegory or parable comes up repeatedly as something American audiences were uncomfortable with (which of course also, earlier and continuing into the 1960s, contributed to the delayed receptivity to Brecht in the United States). Lietzmann conceded that a few New York critics did understand *Andorra*, "But even those positive voices took exception to the way the theme was built into a parable, and in so doing touched on a fundamental characteristic of the American theatre."[24] And 1964 brought another effort to find success on Broadway with a Dürrenmatt play, this time *The Physicists*; but, rather than repeating the success of *The Visit*, it ran for even fewer performances than *Romulus*. As Peter Bauland summarizes it, "The general response to *The Physicists* was that it was too grotesque to be serious, too serious to be funny, too analytical to be entertaining, too distant to be moving, and too didactic to be stimulating. This reception has greeted the play nowhere but in the US."[25]

Although Schechner wrote his essay before the productions of *Andorra* and *The Physicists*, some of the conclusions he draws regarding Broadway's treatment of *The Visit* and *Rhinoceros* relate to this issue of American audiences' expectations, the kind of engagement they expect drama to ask of them. Schechner contends that in both cases "our commodity theatre was unwilling to confront us in their pure form with plays which said that we are responsible for our communal fate." For Schechner, the "crippling" of both those plays reflects a fundamental feature of American drama: "Our theatrical literature has never surpassed psychological naturalism . . . because psycho-pathology is *always* an individual matter." Regarding the plays by Dürrenmatt and Ionesco, he writes, "We were asked to accept history as *our own* fact, brutal and uncomfortable as that fact may be. But our theatre 'saved' us from the indictment of these plays by making us feel that we were Berenger and Ill, the oppressed and not the oppressors."[26] A similar issue arose with *Andorra*: Lietzmann wrote that most of the critics misunderstood the play, believing its action took place in an anti-Semitic country when in fact the opposite is true, and is crucial to Frisch's parable.[27] Even though many of those who saw *Andorra* seem to have assumed its indictment aimed at others rather than themselves, the production failed, apparently due to other shortcomings. Perhaps a different team could have made *Andorra* succeed commercially by doing more thoroughly and effectively what Schechner charged the productions of *The Visit* and *Rhinoceros* with—adjusting the play so that American spectators could feel entertained but not implicated.

A later Ionesco play provides a quite different case study for the reception of new plays in translation on Broadway. *Exit the King*, which premiered in Paris in 1962, was produced on Broadway by the APA-Phoenix Repertory Company in 1968, playing for nearly fifty performances. By that time Ionesco was well known, described by one reviewer as "one of the most glittering stars in the avant-garde galaxy," yet this play bears few of the characteristic features of the so-called theater of the absurd.[28] Written almost fifteen years after Ionesco first made his mark with the "antiplay" *The Bald Soprano*, *Exit the King* is generally regarded within the French context as surprisingly classical, with its linear structure and inexorable movement toward a quite logical ending. If *Exit the King* departed at all from New York audiences' expectations of what a play should entail, it did so both quite gently and entertainingly. Not that death does not constitute weighty subject matter, but Ionesco's treatment of his themes here is much less jarring than in his earlier work; as Clive Barnes put it, "In meditating on death, somehow Ionesco confirms the joy of life."[29] *Exit the King* is one of the best examples in the whole decade of a new play in translation that reflected crucial developments in playwriting without truly challenging its audience and was therefore able to find moderate, unsensational success.

Schechner's main example for the blurring of distinctions in the other direction—in other words, the fact that "the commodity theatre taught off-Broadway to be 'popular,' [and] to go for the long run"—is Circle in the Square's production of Genet's *The Balcony*, which opened in March 1960. In Schechner's view, the U.S. premiere production of Genet's best-known play was unduly influenced by director José Quintero's recent work on Broadway: "He brought the impure intentions of the commodity theatre back with him." Schechner briefly describes omissions and additions to Genet's play designed, in his view, to make it more "manageable" and more "theatrical."[30] Genet himself strongly criticized Quintero's approach to the script, writing that he "quite simply cut everything to do with the revolution."[31] The fact that *The Balcony* ran for two years in New York can no doubt be attributed in part to that depoliticization, and the success only reinforces Schechner's point: "Its very popularity was bought at the expense of its purity."[32]

Impure or not, and even staged off-Broadway, it is striking that such a stylized, non-naturalistic play as *The Balcony* should have done so well in a theater scene that, at the beginning of the decade at least, was still largely reluctant to take on Brecht or Beckett. Somehow Genet seems to be a special case, since his *The Blacks*, produced at St. Mark's Playhouse beginning in May 1961, also became a surprise hit, running for over fourteen hundred performances. Even Louis Kronenberger, then editor of the far from experimentally oriented *Best Plays*, wrote that *The Balcony* "emerged as the most profound and poetic play of the season," while in the following season "it was Jean Genet's *The Blacks* which became the most discussed play."[33] Similarly, Stuart Little describes those two productions as "two of the most significant productions in the twenty years of off-Broadway. Both were immensely complex plays, poetic in language, filled with imagery, ritualistic in construction."[34] And Genet won Obies for both plays—for Best Foreign Play for *The Balcony* and for Best New Play for *The Blacks*.

Little also points to the long-running production of Genet's *The Blacks* as "the real beginning of the black theater";[35] it's a remarkable feature of 1960s New York theater history that a translated play by a white Frenchman, and moreover a difficult, controversial play, became a landmark in the history of African American theater. *The Blacks* also presents an unusual case because its importance lay perhaps as much in the advances it brought about for black theater artists as it did in the resonance of Genet's script. As one of the standard accounts of African American theater history puts it, "Although many African Americans objected to the play's thesis—if Blacks came to power, they would be as oppressive as Whites—for three years the production provided dozens of black actors with regular paychecks, and the play's absurdist style, combined with its confrontational stance, awakened and aroused American playwrights."[36] The astounding success of *The Blacks* calls into question Schechner's argument about the other Genet production: if *The Balcony* fared quite well off-Broadway only because it was presented in a Broadway-influenced, impure manner, how come *The Blacks* ran longer still? Part of the answer lies in the differences among off-Broadway theaters—Circle in the Square, where Quintero's *The Balcony* was produced, was in effect at the more Broadway-like end of the off-Broadway spectrum; St. Mark's Playhouse was closer to the off-off-Broadway end and thus had an audience more receptive to confrontational work. But *The Blacks* also seems to be an instance where controversy made for a show people wished to see for themselves. According to John Warrick's essay on the play's reception and impact, the "overwhelming majority of the audience were Whites."[37] As one African American writer put it, Genet's play was "an absolute insult to the white audience [and] yet still the hordes keep coming to be insulted," though not everyone agreed with that analysis.[38] The public debate surrounding *The Blacks* also involved such figures as Langston Hughes, Lorraine Hansberry, Norman Mailer, and Harold Clurman. As Clurman wrote, "*The Blacks* is not the kind of play of 'social significance' that we are accustomed to: it is not melioristic or benign. It is dangerously explosive. . . . Most plays dealing with the race 'problem' (or prejudice) are pathetic, constructive, patient."[39] This does seem to capture why Genet's play succeeded: the situation regarding race in the theater and beyond needed a jolt, in some ways the more divisive the better. As John Warrick summarizes, "Despite the reservations of black intellectuals and artists, no one could deny that *The Blacks* marked an important turning point for African American theatre: it put black theatre firmly on the public map and provided a physical (if not aesthetic or mental) space where Blacks and Whites could meet."[40]

One wonders what role Esslin's book played in the reception of the two Genet plays that did so well in the early 1960s. It appears his notion of the "theatre of the absurd" (often simplified into "absurdism") quickly gained currency even among people who hadn't read and would be unlikely to read a long study of the French Nouveau Théâtre—but did it therefore make such people feel they understood work they would previously have stayed away from? One can only speculate, but it does seem likely that some people who went to see *The Blacks* when it had already been running for some time did so having gathered that it was an example of that "absurdism" they'd been hearing about, as well as a provocative play about race. Another thing that stands out here as with other translated plays is how little was made of the fact that Genet wrote in another language and from the perspective of another culture. The African Americans who responded to *The Blacks* did, naturally, focus on his whiteness—Hansberry "categorized him as a paternalistic white writer," Hughes referred to him as a "neurotic white writer"[41]—but his being French as well as white rarely came up. This in part reflects the nature of Genet's work and some of the opposition to it: as Warrick writes, Hansberry and Hughes felt that black theater "had to be specific, positive, and grounded in the reality of black experience," which *The Blacks* certainly was not.[42] But perhaps Genet's nationality as well as his dramaturgy contributed to the play's impact: if *The Blacks* had been written by a white or black American with a particular regional, historical, and cultural background, knowledge of all that would have influenced the reception and prevented the play from becoming such a focal point for the discussion of racial issues in the abstract.

Essays lamenting the blurring of distinctions in the New York theater scene tend to predate the advent of a quite new kind of play: translations of German "documentary theatre" produced on Broadway. On the face of it, these plays were not well suited to the "commodity theatre," yet they found a good deal of success. The first such play to reach Broadway, Hochhuth's *The Deputy* (1964), is less "documentary" than much of the other work in the same vein but does constitute an instance of what the authors themselves preferred to call *realistisches Zeittheater* (realistic theater of the times). That was followed by Peter Weiss's *The Investigation* (1966)—his edit of transcriptions of the 1964–65 Auschwitz trials in Frankfurt—Hochhuth's *Soldiers* (1968), and Kipphardt's *In the Matter of J. Robert Oppenheimer* (1969). *The Deputy* ran for nearly a year, and Weiss's and Kipphardt's plays had respectable runs of several months. Hochhuth's first play, a fierce indictment of Pope Pius XII's attitude toward the persecution of Jews during World War II, prompted a huge amount of debate, what Eric Bentley in his 1964 collection of material dubbed *The Storm over "The Deputy,"* and much of that storm preceded the actual opening.[43] Once the production did open, no doubt—as with *The Blacks*—its ticket sales benefited from the theatergoing public's interest in seeing for themselves a work that they knew to have been so contested. As Bauland emphatically puts it, "The sheer controversy that had already been generated by the play kept it running for 316 performances despite the abysmally bad production." For Bauland, Hochhuth's play as adapted by Jerome Rothenberg was "presented without any integrity, a shameless exploitation of its sensational reputation."[44] Few if any of the critics at the time evaluated the production so negatively, and all recognized that the unwieldiness of Hochhuth's full script—which would take about eight hours to perform—made cuts unavoidable. The reviews tended to declare the work seriously flawed as drama but nonetheless interesting and worthy due to the important historical and moral issues raised.

That was largely the attitude taken to all the productions of German documentary theater on Broadway during the 1960s. The text of Weiss's *The Investigation* consists entirely of words spoken as testimony during the Frankfurt trials, which led reviewers to remark that he "offers us non-theater, for his own good reasons" and that "criticism is, in a way, irrelevant."[45] While Kipphardt's *J. Robert Oppenheimer* was a less extreme case—much more document based than *The Deputy* yet involving more authorial intervention than *The Investigation*—that too had critics describing it as a "play, or dramatization."[46] Hochhuth's second play, *Soldiers,* is an indictment of Winston Churchill's conduct during the war and a plea for the application of the Geneva Convention to aerial bombing. When it ran for three weeks (in a production that originated in Canada), the critics largely agreed that the script was better written than *The Deputy*'s, though with some of the same shortcomings, but also that the play "is important and involving because its subject is important and involving."[47] None of them seemed to even think it worth reflecting on what impact Hochhuth's two successes might have, as if he was sui generis and that went without saying. In general, there was surprisingly little consideration among the established critics and other commentators of the implications for the present and future of theater that four such plays, all in various ways departing from standard dramatic fare and all translated from German, had found a home on Broadway. Even Otis Guernsey of the *Best Plays* series describes *The Investigation* as "remarkable as the only no-doubt-about-it-serious theater success of the Broadway season" of 1966–67;[48] if one didn't know, one might think this referred to a hit comedy or even a musical, rather than to a work whose reviews had titles like "'Investigation': More History Than Play."[49] Perhaps the support given to and relative success of translations of German documentary theater reflected weariness with the tropes of "absurdist" playwriting—as if, after so much drama, and so much discussion of drama, reflecting existential meaninglessness, the theatergoing public and the critics were more than ready to engage with work that so clearly related to recent historical events. Documentary theater also did not aim to elicit a particular response in its audience beyond enhanced understanding and—especially in the case of *The Deputy*—retrospective indignation. Schechner was convinced that the Broadway productions of *The Visit* and *Rhinoceros* had succeeded only because the plays had been modified so that the spectators didn't feel collectively implicated; in a different way, documentary theater's treatment of history also allowed those theatergoers to maintain a certain distance, did not compel them to consider how they and their own society might have behaved.

Something else that probably fostered receptivity to Weiss's *The Investigation* in 1966 was the resounding success a year earlier of his *The Persecution and Assassination of Jean-Paul Marat as Performed by the Inmates of Charenton under the Direction of the Marquis de Sade*. The Royal Shakespeare Company (RSC) production directed by Peter Brook undoubtedly stands out as one of the key productions of the 1960s, though it significantly departs from rather than typifies the route to Broadway success. As Bauland points out, "Several analysts of the Broadway business scene have said that had the *Marat/Sade* company not been subsidized as an international cultural enterprise, it could not have made expenses despite completely soldout houses. Left to its own devices, Broadway might never even have attempted the play."[50] Brook's company of actors had carried out meticulous research on madness, on the basis of which they created an unprecedentedly vivid depiction of an asylum, described by one New York review's headline as a "horrifying drama brilliantly staged and played."[51]

With a different directorial approach, one more true to Weiss's own position, *Marat/Sade* might have fared no better on Broadway than did *Andorra*—or than *The Visit* and *Rhinoceros* would have, had they not been, to follow Schechner, "bowdlerized." Brook's production presented the Broadway audience with something utterly new yet whose spectacular intensity appealed to them. In considering this, Alan Downer remarks that two earlier European dramatists who found less success in America than one might have expected, Brecht and Anouilh, "share a characteristic which the American audience seems unready to accept. They repeatedly draw back from their work, they interrupt the dramatic experience." For Americans, theater is "experience," "a surrender of your own life for several hours to the life of the play." And that is what Brook's production provided: "It was a performance they chose freely to attend, an experience they chose to subject themselves to."[52] In fact, Weiss's script systematically incorporates interruption of the dramatic experience, yet in Brook's staging, the experience was allowed to overwhelm the interruption. Some observers did recognize this: as Bauland writes, Harold Clurman "noted that the audience was not ultimately engaged by the play but only by the display"; and Bauland himself makes the point that "almost all reviewers approached the production as if it were by Peter Brook instead of Peter Weiss."[53] In a 1966 forum about the RSC *Marat/Sade* (an edited transcript of which was published in *TDR*), Norman Podhoretz disagrees with one of the other participants, saying, "I don't see, as Leslie Fiedler does, a dialogue between sanity and madness. I don't take the madness of the play that seriously. The play is largely about politics."[54] Weiss himself would probably have appreciated that viewpoint; he had mixed feelings about Brook's production, admiring the rigorously researched portrayal of the asylum inmates but finding that its vividness overshadowed the debate between

Marat and Sade and that Brook allowed Sade too clearly to triumph over Marat at the end.

Regardless of how one might judge Brook's interpretation of Weiss's play, there is little question that his production—like Esslin's book and, within a more circumscribed realm, the St. Mark's Playhouse production of *The Blacks*—changed the landscape regarding the kind of plays that could reach the stage. That was probably more true off than on Broadway; for instance, in his history of the off-off-Broadway movement, Bottoms mentions that the Open Theatre's *America Hurrah* "was an unlikely candidate for commercial success, but it benefited considerably from fortunate timing," namely, the recent run of Brook's production of Weiss's play, which "played to great acclaim in New York, acclimatizing critics and public to the arrival of 'new theater techniques' (a label increasingly applied by the press to anything nonnaturalistic)."[55] *The Theatre of the Absurd* had made "absurdism" more marketable, and now *Marat/Sade* did the same thing for non-naturalistic approaches to performance and production. But it is significant just what kind of nontraditional techniques were now more readily accepted. The introduction to the 1966 forum described Brook's production as "achieved through its fusion of Artaudian and Brechtian techniques," but if the RSC *Marat/Sade* did usher in new openness to such techniques, it did so more with the Artaudian than the Brechtian.[56] In a 1977 collection of statements looking back at the 1960s, Carl Weber takes the strongest position regarding foreign work and directly addresses this issue, arguing that in the early sixties,

> For a short while there was an intensive interest in the work of Brecht and in his example of a politically committed, but very "theatrical" theatre. However, this interest was very superficial. What made the greatest impact on American professionals and students of the theatre was the less socially oriented or totally anti-social developments in the European theatre: Artaud, the absurdists, Grotowski and others. They became the true "gurus" for most of the American experiments in theatre.[57]

Weber argues that it wasn't until the late 1970s that the development of more politically engaged theater made itself felt in the United States.

For the most part, then, translated plays succeeded on Broadway only when their political implications for an American audience were tempered by adaptation and production or when the material treated was as specific as World War II–era history. Off-Broadway, the plays in translation whose productions proved most significant both dealt with race; Genet's *The Blacks* was not the only translated new work to play a meaningful role in the development of African American theater. In 1968 the first-ever production by the Negro Ensemble Company was of Peter Weiss's *The Song of the Lusitanian Bogey*, aptly described by one reviewer as "a fierce denunciation of colonialism, specifically that of Portugal."[58] The script is more a series of vignettes than a conventionally composed play, and Weiss had given the new company's artistic director, Douglas Turner Ward, permission to freely adapt the piece. The resulting show, which made extensive use of dance as well as music, was lauded as an impressive debut for the company and as an extremely powerful experience—as Clive Barnes wrote, "It is not a pretty song, but even if you try to block up your ears, its pervasive agony will corrode your heart."[59] This production by an important new company has been relegated to the status of at best a footnote in theater history, yet at the time the established reviewers expressed great admiration for both the performance and its resonance. Martin Gottfried praised the cast's teamwork and went on: "That it is being done to project a matter of great importance not merely to world decency, but, obviously, to an America with a Negro population at the boiling point, makes it all the more powerful."[60] The so-called theater of the absurd arguably had some lasting influence on Broadway during and after the 1960s, while translated documentary theater was important at the time but with less clearly discernible consequences; surprisingly, it is in the history of black theater that plays in translation, produced off-Broadway, played the most significant role in the 1960s.

Another factor that influenced attitudes toward plays in translation, especially away from Broadway, was the shifting relationship between playwright and director. Brustein, for instance, felt that "what we are witnessing is the effort of the avant-garde to translate 'participatory democracy' into artistic terms, demanding a new egalitarianism that gives equal rank to everyone except the author."[61] That was especially true in the off-off-Broadway environment. Very little foreign work in translation was produced by those theaters because, as Bottoms puts it, the movement was "in large part defined by the collaborative, interactive relationships that developed among playwrights, directors, and performers."[62] One way to quickly capture how insignificant foreign plays in translation were to off-off-Broadway is to note that the chronology included in Bottoms's book lists no such works at all. (That inventory neglects, however, to do justice to the work being presented at La MaMa E.T.C., which during the 1960s included work by such writers as Arrabal, Klima, and Mrozek, as well as Ionesco and Genet.) And the emphasis on one-act plays in the off-off-Broadway environment probably also made the production of works in translation less likely: "Freed by circumstances from the commercial expectation that they write so-called full-length works prioritizing linear narrative or psychological characterization, off-off-Broadway playwrights specialized in creating one-act pieces cohering around distilled, emblematic images or confrontations, which often had as much in common with performance poetry or visual art as with conventional drama."[63] In Bottoms's analysis, Edward Albee's *Zoo Story* "revived, almost single-handedly, the American little theater tradition of the self-contained one-act drama, and did it by fusing a distinctly American urban realism with new ideas derived from the European 'theater of the absurd.'"[64] Thus drama in translation did have an impact on off-off-Broadway but in an indirect way, through its influence on American writers rather than through actual productions of foreign work.

Joseph Papp's prominence in the 1960s to some extent compensates for off-off-Broadway's relative neglect of the playwright, particularly in the final part of the decade, once the Public Theater opened in 1967. As one of Papp's former students at Yale, where he began teaching in 1966, recalled, "We directors weren't getting to work on original plays. For Joe, theater was about the word. Playwrights were the name of the game and we directors were their servitors."[65] Papp's taste for "plays that are hard to explain, that leave you with more questions than answers" along with his preference for "plays he had come upon through personal encounters" with playwrights led to the 1968 Public Theater production of novelist Jakov Lind's dramatization of his own work, *Ergo*.[66] And a similar but ultimately much more productive relationship developed between Papp and Vaclav Havel, whose *The Memorandum* he directed in 1968, and which won that year's Obie for Best Foreign Play.

Havel's work, from Czechoslovakia, along with that of the Russian Aleksei Arbuzov (*The Promise*, produced on Broadway in 1967) and the Pole Slawomir Mrozek (*Tango*, off-Broadway, 1969), raised more complex issues of interpretation even than the theater of the absurd plays that reached New York a decade or so earlier. Walter Kerr argued at some length that such plays, which would not have made it past the censor in the playwrights' own countries if they made their satire of the totalitarian regimes clear, are inevitably "blind" to us: "When we go to see a play like *Tango* . . . and when we attempt to see in its Off Broadway gestures the assault on Communist behavior we would like to see, we simply don't know what we are doing." Later he adds, using a different example,

> It's not possible to enjoy a piece like Vaclav Havel's *The Memorandum* as the Czechs must have enjoyed it; if its satire on totalitarian bureaucracy seemed tepid and repetitive here, it is no doubt because all of the slightly lifted eyebrows that conveyed to its home audiences the nuances they wished to overhear had vanished into thin air, had proved untranslatable and unexportable.[67]

Most critics did not agree that these plays are unexportable, agreeing rather with the sentiment expressed by Clive Barnes regarding *The Memorandum*: the work "has a message for us as well as for Eastern Europe, because the concept that the human being is more valuable than any bureaucratic organization controlling him is not irrelevant to our own paternalistic corporation-structured society."[68] Kerr does, however, have a point, and at least some of the other reviewers of *Tango* bear him out as they try less than convincingly to interpret what they are pretty sure is a parable. As with the productions of, broadly speaking, allegorical work translated from German, it is apparent that American critics do not feel altogether comfortable with drama whose action alludes indirectly to rather than straightforwardly depicting social and historical situations.

Kerr deserves some credit for even spending some time considering such issues of intercultural reception. It is surprising how seldom the New York critics of the 1960s wrote at any length about the simple but significant fact that a particular play had been translated from another language; often, while they may dutifully have named the translator, they in effect responded to the play as if Frisch or Ionesco or whoever had written in English. And when the established reviewers did reflect on the significance of particular plays having originated in particular countries and cultures, they tended to do so in very general terms—the Germans were grappling with the trauma and shame of the Third Reich, the Russians were trying to get beyond Socialist Realism, and so on. And this attitude was not restricted to the critics. The 1966 forum on *Marat/Sade*, whose panelists included Peter Brook, did address questions relating to Peter Weiss's intentions and ideas but overall devoted more time to Brook's production than to Weiss's play—and never even mentioned the fact that the play Brook directed had been not merely translated but significantly adapted from Weiss's German text.

In considering how much—or how little—translated drama was produced on New York stages in the 1960s, one must keep in mind the interests of the American playwrights struggling to be produced. It's perfectly reasonable that some critics at the time advocated more opportunities for new homegrown drama. Guernsey, for instance, responding to the 1967–68 Public Theater season that included the plays by Havel and Lind, wrote, "My only quarrel with Papp, Freedman and their interesting troupe would be in the choice of two foreign scripts while our own authors are clamoring to be produced";[69] he also repeatedly urged the Lincoln Center Repertory Company to produce more contemporary American work. In applauding Lincoln Center's greater emphasis on American plays in the 1969–70 season, Guernsey reiterated his fundamental position regarding the balance of U.S. and foreign work—a position we can reasonably assume was shared by many others observing and involved in the New York theater—"The first business of a New York-based and New York-supported permanent repertory company, surely, should be to acquire proficiency in the production of American plays, just as the comparable British and French companies are first of all adept at interpreting their home-grown works, with foreign material sometimes staged as a special event."[70] During the 1969–70 season, Lincoln Center Repertory actually combined the production of American work in its larger house with the introduction of foreign work in the smaller Forum Theater, including the second play by Havel to reach New York, *The Increased Difficulty of Concentration*, and Peter Hacks's *Amphitryon*. Guernsey also had a point when he wrote—of the 1965–66 season, when he felt the plays from Europe had largely proven "interesting failures" whereas the American plays were "sad disappointments"—that, "of course, American scripts on Broadway are usually raw and new, while European scripts were tested before being imported—somebody loved them enough to bring them over here."[71] As we have seen, in some cases the success in Europe of foreign drama did not yield similar popularity in the United States, while in others the pretested work succeeded only after significant modification.

In Schechner and Hoffman's 1963 comment aimed at promoting a new vitality in American theater, they wrote, "If it seems distressing that the people we rightly admire most are Europeans, we may soon encounter, without chauvinistic compulsion, American figures to admire." They believed that American theater artists needed to acknowledge the international, cross-fertilizing nature of the form—"There is no major theatre artist alive today who has not been influenced by colleagues in other countries"—and allow themselves to absorb and respond to that influence.[72] It is, of course, difficult to measure just how much that did happen during the remainder of the decade—to what extent new directions pursued, in playwriting especially, can be associated with productions of plays in translation. Some would argue that the impact was negligible. In a 1977 collection of statements reassessing the 1960s, Michael Feingold writes about changes he characterizes as "secondary and peripheral," including some that can justifiably be attributed to the influence of foreign playwrights, especially "ideas of playwriting that break out of the degenerated 'well-made play' model that for many years was the only one acceptable in this country." But he goes on to observe both that such changes "have been assimilated easily and with gratitude" and that "they haven't changed the overall face of the theatre very much."[73] For me, Feingold represents the evolution of playwriting during the 1960s as a smoother, less troubled process than it was; plays in translation—especially from French and German—did figure prominently in that development. While Schechner was right to object to the dilution of some plays in order to bring about success on Broadway, it is also true that plays such as *The Deputy* and *The Investigation* stretched previously established notions of what would and would not make it on the Great White Way. Certainly the reception of different productions revealed limitations as to what Broadway audiences would readily embrace: in particular, they tended to resist work whose implications were too directly political and work that demanded to be read allegorically. Off-Broadway would seem the more obvious venue for more innovative, challenging drama and did indeed prove to be the site of Genet's main successes—but was also the context in which plays in translation contributed significantly to the advancement of black theater. Considered in relation to previous and subsequent decades, New York in the 1960s, on and off-Broadway, presented quite an impressive range of translated drama.

NOTES

1. Robert Brustein, *The Third Theatre* (New York: Alfred A. Knopf, 1969), 4.

2. Richard Schechner and Theodore Hoffman, "TDR: 1963–?," *Tulane Drama Review* 8.2 (1963): 10–11.

3. Martin Esslin, *The Theatre of the Absurd*, rev., updated ed. (New York: Anchor, 1969), xiv.

4. Richard Schechner, "Theatre Criticism," *Tulane Drama Review* 9.3 (1965): 14–15.

5. Stephen J. Bottoms, *Playing Underground: A Critical History of the 1960s Off-Off-Broadway Movement* (Ann Arbor: University of Michigan Press, 2004), 86.

6. Henry Hewes, ed., *The Best Plays of 1961–1962* (New York: Dodd, Mead, 1962), 7.

7. Alan S. Downer, "The Future of the American Theater," in *The American Theater Today*, ed. Alan S. Downer (New York: Basic, 1967), 198.

8. Bernard F. Dukore, "The Noncommercial Theater in New York," in ibid., 166.

9. Esslin, *Theatre of the Absurd*, 3.

10. Richard Schechner, "Contributors," *Tulane Drama Review* 7.3 (1963): 4.

11. Schechner, "Intentions, Problems, Proposals," *Tulane Drama Review* 7.4 (1963): 8.

12. Ibid., 8, 10.

13. Randolph Goodman, "*The Visit* Undergoes a Sea Change: An Interview with Maurice Valency," in *Drama on Stage* (New York: Holt, Rinehart and Winston, 1961), 395.

14. Schechner, "Intentions, Problems, Proposals," 12.

15. Ibid.

16. John Chapman, review of *Rhinoceros*, by Eugène Ionesco, *Daily News*, January 10, 1961, repr. in *New York Theatre Critics' Reviews*, 1962, 400.

17. Howard Taubman, review of *Rhinoceros*, by Eugène Ionesco, *New York Times*, January 10, 1961,repr. in *New York Theatre Critics' Reviews*, 1962, 398.

18. Schechner, "Intentions, Problems, Proposals," 13.

19. John McClain, review of *Rhinoceros*, by Eugène Ionesco, *Journal American*, January 10, 1961, repr. in *New York Theatre Critics' Reviews*, 1962, 397.

20. Sabina Lietzmann, "Warum Frischs *Andorra* in New York unterging," *Frankfurter*

Allgemeine Zeitung, February 26, 1963, repr. in *Frischs Andorra*, ed. Walter Schmitz and Ernst Wendt (Frankfurt am Main: Suhrkamp, 1984), 245.

21. Hans Sahl, "Der schlechtbehandelte Max Frisch," *Die Welt*, February 26, 1963, repr. in schmitz and Wendt, *Frischs Andorra*, 249.

22. Henry Hewes, ed., *The Best Plays of 1962–1963* (New York: Dodd, Mead, 1962), 13.

23. Alan Schneider, "The Failure of Seriousness," *New Leader*, March 1963, 29.

24. Lietzmann, "Warum Frischs *Andorra* in New York unterging," 245.

25. Peter Bauland, *The Hooded Eagle: Modern German Drama on the New York Stage* (Syracuse, NY: Syracuse University Press, 1968), 206.

26. Schechner, "Intentions, Problems, Proposals," 13–14.

27. Lietzmann, "Warum Frischs *Andorra* in New York unterging," 245.

28. Martin Gottfried, review of *Exit the King*, by Eugène Ionesco, *Women's Wear Daily*, January 10, 1968, repr. in *New York Theatre Critics' Reviews*, 1969, 394.

29. Clive Barnes, review of *Exit the King*, by Eugène Ionesco, *New York Times*, January 10, 1968, repr. in *New York Theatre Critics' Reviews*, 1969, 395.

30. Schechner, "Intentions, Problems, Proposals," 8.

31. Jean Genet qtd. in David Bradby and Clare Finburgh, *Jean Genet* (New York: Routledge, 2012), 140.

32. Schechner, "Intentions, Problems, Proposals," 8–9.

33. Louis Kronenberger, ed., *The Best Plays of 1959–1960* (New York: Dodd, Mead, 1960), 44; Louis Kronenberger, ed., *The Best Plays of 1960–1961* (New York: Dodd, Mead, 1961), 42.

34. Stuart W. Little, *Off-Broadway: The Prophetic Theater* (New York: Coward, McCann & Geoghegan, 1972), 118.

35. Ibid., 127.

36. Errol G. Hill and James V. Hatch, *History of African American Theatre* (Cambridge: Cambridge University Press, 2003), 388.

37. John Warrick, "*The Blacks* and Its Impact on African American Theatre in the United States," in *Jean Genet: Performance and Politics* (Basingstoke, UK: Palgrave Macmillan, 2006), 132.

38. Qtd. in ibid., 137.

39. Qtd. in ibid., 135.

40. Ibid., 138.

41. Ibid., 136, 139.

42. Ibid., 132.

43. Eric Bentley, ed., *The Storm over "The Deputy"* (New York: Grove, 1964).

44. Bauland, *Hooded Eagle*, 219.

45. Norman Nadel, review of *The Investigation*, by Peter Weiss, *World Journal Tribune*, October 5, 1966,repr. in *New York Theatre Critics' Reviews*, 1967, 281; Walter Kerr, review of *The Investigation*, by Peter Weiss, *New York Times*, October 5, 1966, repr. in *New York Theatre Critics' Reviews*, 1967, 284.

46. James Davis, review of *In the Matter of J. Robert Oppenheimer*, by Heinar Kipphardt, *Daily News*, March 7, 1969, repr. in *New York Theatre Critics' Reviews*, 1970, 339.

47. Martin Gottfried, review of *Soldiers*, by Rolf Hochhuth, *Women's Wear Daily*, May 2, 1968, repr. in *New York Theatre Critics' Reviews*, 1969, 286.

48. Otis L. Guernsey, *Curtain Times: The New York Theater 1965–1987* (New York: Applause, 1987), 66.

49. Nadel, review of *The Investigation*, 281.

50. Bauland, *Hooded Eagle*, 223.

51. John Chapman, review of *Marat/Sade*, by Peter Weiss, *Daily News*, December 28, 1965, repr. in *New York Theatre Critics' Reviews*, 1966, 213.

52. Downer, "Future of the American Theater," 201, 203.

53. Bauland, *Hooded Eagle*, 223.

54. Peter Brook, Leslie Fiedler, Geraldine Lust, Norman Podhoretz, Ian Richardson, and Gordon Rogoff, "Marat/Sade Forum," *Tulane Drama Review* 10.4 (1966): 222.

55. Bottoms, *Playing Underground*, 183–84.

56. Brook et al., "Marat/Sade Forum," 214.

57. "American Experimental Theatre, Then and Now," *Performing Arts Journal* 2.2 (1977): 19.

58. James Davis, review of *The Song of the Lusitanian Bogey*, by Peter Weiss, *Daily News*, January 3, 1968, repr. in *New York Theatre Critics' Reviews*, 1969, 267.

59. Clive Barnes, review of *The Song of the Lusitanian Bogey*, by Peter Weiss, *New York Times*, January 3, 1968, repr. in *New York Theatre Critics' Reviews*, 1969, 266.

60. Martin Gottfried, review of *The Song of the Lusitanian Bogey*, by Peter Weiss, *Women's Wear Daily*, January 3, 1968, repr. in *New York Theatre Critics' Reviews*, 1969, 267.

61. Brustein, *Third Theatre*, 39.

62. Bottoms, *Playing Underground*, 5.

63. Ibid.

64. Ibid., 21.

65. Qtd. in Helen Epstein, *Joe Papp: An American Life* (Boston: Little, Brown, 1994), 199.

66. Ibid., 202.

67. Walter Kerr, "There's No One to Tell Us Its Secret," *New York Times*, February 9, 1969, repr. in *New York Theatre Critics' Reviews*, 1970, 279–80.

68. Quoted in Carol Rocamora, *Acts of Courage: Vaclav Havel's Life in the Theater* (Hanover, NH: Smith & Kraus, 2005), 92.

69. Guernsey, *Curtain Times*, 109.

70. Ibid., 162–63.

71. Ibid., 41.

72. Schechner and Hoffman, "TDR: 1963–?," 10, 11.

73. "American Experimental Theatre," 23.

Kate Bredeson

How France Canonized the
American Avant-Garde

In April 1968 New York's Bread and Puppet Theater arrived in France for the first time. Founder and director Peter Schumann and his company traveled to the World Theatre Festival of Nancy to present *Fire* and *A Man Says Goodbye to His Mother*. Following the French premieres, journalists and audiences swooned; the esteemed critic Émile Copfermann christened the festival "The Discovery of New York's 'Bread and Puppet.'"[1] A flurry of rave reviews from France and beyond emerged from Nancy, where critics called Bread and Puppet "the first big shock,"[2] the "revelation" of the festival, which "shook up" audiences[3] and whose debut was a "shock" of "exceptional quality."[4] Journalists described in great detail Schumann's formidable puppets, the street as performance venue, and production values of silence and simplicity; glowing interviews with Schumann emerged alongside dramatic photos of the giant, solemn, moon-faced puppets. Audiences too swooned; enthusiastic crowds attended the revelation of the Bread and Puppet Theater. In Nancy the company enjoyed housing and pay for their work, status alongside other international artists in a highly publicized festival, and wide attendance by public audiences and France's cultural and intellectual elite. After five years[5] of struggle in New York—for space, subsistence, audiences, and critical attention—Schumann's group instantly became a sought-after commodity in France and beyond.

Bread and Puppet's experience exemplifies the emergence of the 1960s as a defining decade for Americans in France, where a particular kind of American theater theretofore considered "alternative" in the United States found great critical attention, wide press coverage, large audiences, and the fulfillment of basic needs of the company members: housing, performance space, and pay. In this essay, these are the criteria I use when I discuss the "success" of these companies. Bread and Puppet and the Living Theatre, today two icons of the American theater that scholars consistently define as "experimental," "alternative," and/or "avant-garde," both visited France on the cusp of the turbulent May 1968 student and worker events. Each presented at one of France's international festivals to audiences made up of students, workers, intellectuals, and France's lead culture makers. Embraced in France by both the elites and broad, diverse public audiences, the fringe of America played in the same cultural houses as Racine and Molière, as well as on streets and in public squares. Both companies returned stateside with the French stamp of approval, went on to perform in larger venues to greater numbers of audiences, and received wider critical and scholarly attention and more support for their work. While their French successes did not return them home as mainstream fare, their time in France propelled both companies to a new echelon of the avant-garde, that of the revered alternative theater: the avant-garde canon. Today when we talk about the quintessential American avant-garde, it is Bread and Puppet and the Living Theatre that best embody the term; it was in France in 1968 where the reputations of both of these companies were sealed, commoditized, and brought to a new level of reverence and visibility within the American avant-garde.

In France the lines separating experimental and commercial theaters often intersected, and the categories were not so neatly divided. Americans coming to this system found themselves in a different theater culture, without a Broadway/off-Broadway landscape, with a very different funding structure, and where student theater companies played professionally. The posited divide between experimental and commercial theaters, seemingly upheld in the United States in the 1960s, or at least in the way theater scholars and critics talk about 1960s theater in the United States, did not pertain in the same way to France. This allowed American noncommercial, "experimental" theaters like the Living Theatre and Bread and Puppet to achieve a level of visibility and acclaim in France that theretofore had been impossible to achieve at home. When they returned to the United States after their time in France in 1968, Bread and Puppet and the Living Theatre were more desirable, marketable, and chic. Whereas U.S. critics and historians tend to recognize straightforward divisions among university, commodity, and off-Broadway theater, a chief question is the role of these terms and the related terms *avant-garde*, *commercial*, and *mainstream*. In this essay *mainstream* indicates work embraced by critics and popular audiences, as seen through attendance numbers, funding, and critical attention in widely circulated newspapers and other publications. I use the term *avant-garde* to describe the Living Theatre and Bread and Puppet, drawing on James Harding's discussion of the avant-garde as defined by the unifying factor of having a "sense of rebellion" and existing in a mode of opposition.[6] I equally draw on Arnold Aronson's definition of avant-garde performance as that which "strives toward a radical restructuring of the way in which an audience views and experiences the very act of theatre, which in turn must transform the way in which the spectators view themselves and the world."[7] What marks both the Living Theatre and the Bread and Puppet Theater during their French experiences in 1968 is a tremendous sense of restructuring and rebellion: against prevailing dramaturgical structures and themes on both sides of the Atlantic, against capitalism, against conventional methodologies of making and staging theater, against lifestyle conventions, and against political and social stances of their home country. And yet in this context these terms are called into question. What does *alternative* or *mainstream* mean when considered in another national context? Can something be avant-garde in one country and commercial in another—or even in the same—country? How do these concepts translate across borders and when placed in very different cultures of audience, support, and success? These questions become part of the story of Bread and Puppet and the Living Theatre in France in 1968.

In part, these two companies landed in France at the ripe time of a particularly receptive and energetic moment. Political, social, and cultural opposition defined the 1960s in France—from the Algerian War to the French feminist movement to the occupied streets, schools, factories, and theaters of May '68. This sense of opposition was pronounced in French theater. The work of the so-called absurdists[8] that dominated the 1950s and early 1960s began to wane in terms of new plays and new productions; young playwrights emerged, crafting radical, visionary plays about possible new ways of life and politics, collectives formed that challenged male director-centered hierarchies of theater production, theater makers experimented with productions performed outside of traditional spaces, and agit-prop and protest theater accompanied the political events of Algeria and May '68. A proliferation of student theater troupes exploded onto the scene—from the Sorbonne, the Ecole Normale Supérieure, and even aviation and dental schools; companies organized that went on to mark contemporary French theater: the Théâtre de l'Aquarium, the Nouvelle Compagnie d'Avignon, and the Théâtre du Soleil. The French also began to look toward international performance to study and to extend invitations for performance collaborations. This perspective shift marked part of a general overhaul in the methods and means of making theater in the 1960s, as well as a leap beyond subject matters and places of performance. It took further the impulse in the 1950s and 1960s to decentralize French theater—to expand theater outside of Paris and into the provinces. As theaters sprouted up in regional centers, some French theater makers looked beyond "L'Hexagone" and across borders and oceans. Further, this move echoed the internationalism of the French absurdist writers, among whom were an Irishman (Samuel Beckett), a Romanian (Eugène Ionesco), and a Russian (Arthur Adamov).

During the 1960s the increasing presence of theater festivals, the growing openness to international theater, and augmented state support for theater all contributed to provide infrastructure for artists from around the world to travel to France, as well as an openness to experimentation. The UNESCO-supported Théâtre des Nations organization, founded in 1957[9] and located first at the Théâtre Sarah Bernhardt and then at the Odéon until 1968, became one of the first to feature a program devoted to international work and collaboration; its offshoot, the Université du Théâtre des Nations, started in 1961. Other significant examples of this extended gaze include the smashing debut of the Berliner Ensemble in Paris in 1954, with their production of *Mother Courage*, which inspired a veritable Brecht mania in France and repeat visits from the company in subsequent years. In the mid- to late 1950s and the 1960s France hosted theater companies from Turkey, Japan, Germany, Chile, Poland, Algeria, and England, among many other countries. As the 1960s progressed, France increasingly welcomed American theater companies too, most notably the Living Theatre, which performed *The Connection* at the Théâtre du Vieux-Colombier in 1961 and visited France multiple times throughout the decade.[10] Americans produced in France during the 1960s included William Carlos Williams, El Teatro Campesino, Firehouse Theater, Jack Gelber, Bread and Puppet, and the Living Theatre—all considered to be in opposition to the Broadway/off-Broadway model, or "experimental," in their home country. These companies arrived in France thanks to a new cohort of visionary directors, including Jean Vilar, Jean-Louis Barrault, and Jack Lang, all of whom shared an attention to international politics and art and a devotion to the expansion of theater programming and possibilities in France. At the end of this period, in 1971, Robert Wilson's *Deafman Glance* premiered in Nancy, the beginning of an ongoing rhapsody that the French have for Wilson.[11]

As the French theater community grappled with its identity and purpose during the political and social movements of the late 1960s and the previously prevailing absurdist theater waned, theater directors, producers, and playwrights drew inspiration from other countries that they encountered at theaters and festivals in Paris and the provinces. By the late 1960s the United States drew a particular focus. Critic and scholar Françoise Kourilsky, in particular, emerged as a prominent voice writing about American theater in France; in 1967 her book *Le théâtre aux États-Unis* came out, which covers the development of American theater from the 1920s through the mid-1960s. She discusses Broadway (*Annie Get Your Gun*, *South Pacific*), off-Broadway (the Living Theatre, Jack Gelber), and what she calls "un théâtre en marge de la société"

(Judson Poets' Theater, Happenings).[12] Three years later Kourilsky adapted her Sorbonne thesis and published *Le Bread and Puppet Theatre*, the first French book about the company. Kourilsky helped draw French attention to American theater, as did the multiple visits of the Living Theatre to France during the sixties. In the Living Theatre, and in images and stories of Bread and Puppet and other American alternative companies, French cultural elites and popular audiences alike found intriguing lifestyles, political engagement on and off stage, new dramatic forms, and a spectacular yet technically streamlined production style. The latter indicated the new French fascination with the *théâtre d'image*, a theater that explored the value of spectacle over words—a big shift away from the long-standing French reverence for *le texte* and, in theater, a dominance of literary and philosophical dramas in the period of the second World War and its aftermath, and the subsequent orgy of wordplay of absurdist theatre. In Bread and Puppet and the Living Theatre, French directors, critics, and audiences found theater that nearly jettisoned the text in favor of bold images, pulsing bodies, and, in the case of Bread and Puppet, figures and props largely composed of cardboard, paste, and papier-mâché.

France is known for its ability to support and showcase the best international work at theaters like Théâtre de la Ville and the Odéon and especially at its many prestigious festivals, like those in Limoges (International des Francophones), Bobigny (MC93 Standard Idéal), Créteil (Exit), Paris (Automne, International d'Art Dramatique de la Ville de Paris) as well as several street theater festivals. Additionally, performance festivals exist in many of France's major metropolitan areas, including Aix-en-Provence, Montpellier, Dijon, Marseille, and, most famously, Avignon. The Festival d'Avignon, founded in 1947 by theater director and visionary Jean Vilar, remains France's oldest and most acclaimed theater festival, and its trajectory serves as a model for understanding the development and role of the festival in France. Founded one year after the glittering Cannes film festival, Avignon started in the wake of World War Two, part of a postwar momentum for arts programming and decentralization. This movement sought to bring theater to regional cities and to middle- and working-class audiences, and it did so mainly by establishing permanent, regional cultural houses throughout the nation. Festivals, usually located far from Paris, soon began to provide alternatives in terms of programming—increasingly throughout the sixties they produced the work of grassroots locals (like André Benedetto and Gérard Gelas in Avignon) or rising international artists (Bertolt Brecht, Jerzy Grotowski, Peter Brook). Journalists and critics flocked to the festivals, writing up special journal issues full of interviews, feature articles, photos, and criticism. The result was that the French festivals ascended in terms of critical attention and audience attendance, while the boulevard theaters (perhaps the closest equivalent to Broadway, but with a far less varied repertoire) began to decline.[13] These festivals earned critical and popular praise, had steadily increasing attendance records and media attention, and welcomed broad and diverse, and increasingly international, audiences, as well as programming from throughout France and around the world.

The Nancy festival in particular emerged as a crucial performance site for American theater artists in Europe and as the first French venue where many American artists performed. Americans performed at Nancy even before they did at Avignon. Founded by Jack Lang in 1963 as the World Theatre Festival of Nancy, the festival, Lang proposed, would serve

(1) To be a "meeting place for noncommercial, creative, and original theatrical productions . . ." where groups "can meet and exchange ideas and have an exceptional opportunity to perform their creations in front of audiences from all over the world." And (2), to "offer a panorama, as accurate as possible, of new tendencies of theatrical creation and research work" from as many countries as possible.[14]

The first season featured eight university student theater troupes from Europe and two from Turkey. The Purdue University Theater of Lafayette, Indiana, the first American group to present at the festival, brought their production of *The Fantasticks* to Nancy in 1965.[15] By 1968 the Bread and Puppet Theater became the fifth American troupe to present;[16] four years later the festival had expanded to host fifty-two companies from twenty-nine nations.[17] Nancy's audience was similar to Avignon's—broad, popular, and diverse in terms of class and vocation—and the city was also situated far from Paris: Nancy is located over two hundred miles to the capital's east. It quickly became a prominent site for showcasing what would become some of the most revered and critically lauded theater work in France. And, like Avignon, it also soon sprouted its own "off" festival, where fringe productions not associated with the festival were showcased.

In 1968 the Nancy festival devoted its program to theater by young companies and an international lineup. El Teatro Campesino and Minneapolis's Firehouse Theater had their French debuts, and the Bread and Puppet Theater smashed onto the scene as the exciting "revelation" of the year. Bread and Puppet came to Nancy at the request of the critic Christian Dupavillon. Jack Lang had hired Dupavillon to scout companies for Nancy, and Dupavillon heard of Schumann from someone in London. When he was in New York during the winter of 1967, he went to see the company perform *Fire* in Washington Square Church. He was "completely shaken up. I had never seen theatre like that. I went to see Peter Schumann and invited [the company] to Nancy. Peter said no.' So I went to his home and invited them again. He said he's come if they could come to Berlin afterwards."[18] Company member Margo Lee Sherman writes,

> How was B & P invited to Nancy 1968? Funny story: It was after one of those Monday night performances of FIRE in the basement of Wash. Sq. Methodist Ch. A French guy with the most ridiculous accent came up to us and invited us to perform at a festival in Nancy. I had never heard of Nancy. We thought it was a joke. The guy was ridiculous. But he visited the Schumanns in their Lower East Side apartment and somehow convinced them. And the rest is history. The guy's name is Christian Dupavillon [*sic*]. He was Jack Lang's talent scout I guess. Christian is the funniest storyteller I've ever met. Naturally he also worked with B & P and has funny stories to match.[19]

Sherman also recalls, "It's like someone coming up to you and saying, would you like to make a movie in Hollywood. The Puppet Theater? It wasn't part of our frame of reference. It was a joke. The theatre world, the *Village Voice* despised us, except for Arthur Sainer. We didn't think people noticed us much."[20] For Bread and Puppet's first European performance, Peter Schumann brought to France an abbreviated version of the company. Sherman recalls, "Our company from NYC consisted of Peter, me, Bob Ernstthal, Maurice Blanc, plus Irving and Pearl Oyle, who could afford to buy their own airplane tickets, joined us. Our friend Bruno Eckardt, who lived in Germany, joined us in Nancy."[21] Transporting the puppets, however, proved a problem.

> The festival didn't allot enough pounds for the international travel of puppets. . . . So, Peter went to a refrigerator store on the Lower East Side, picked up some left-over empty cardboard boxes and brought them back to our place of work, the Old Courthouse on Second Ave. and 2nd St. He put duct tape along the edges of the boxes, gessoed them white and painted 'Bread & Puppet Theater, 2nd Avenue & 2nd Street, New York.' We packed the puppets in the boxes, and we each had whatever weight was left over was for our personal belongings. It came to 11 pounds for each person.[22]

They landed in Paris in April 1968 and traveled east to Nancy to participate in the April 19–28 festival. A dazzling who's who of the French performance and cultural criticism scenes made up the guest list for the special festival program: Robert Abirached, Pierre Bourdieu, Peter Brook, Bernard Dort, Armand Gatti, Jean-Luc Godard, Françoise Kourilsky, Roger Planchon, and Jean Vilar. Other theater companies presenting at the festival included Teatro Oficina (Sao

Paulo), Les Saltimbanques de Montréal, Université Internationale du Théâtre de Paris, Firehouse Theater (Minneapolis), La Nouvelle Compagnie d'Avignon, and the Council of Youth of India (Madras), among others. Young professional theater companies performed alongside university student performance troupes; no boundaries existed to distinguish students from professionals, experimental theater from anything else. Lang designated this incarnation of the Nancy festival the first edition of the World Festival of Youth Theatre.

Bread and Puppet's contributions were two productions they had already performed in New York: *A Man Says Goodbye to His Mother* and *Fire*. The first is a compact and elegant antiwar ode that lasts under twenty minutes, the latter concerns the destruction of a Vietnamese village by fire; the two pieces are united by their unambiguous opposition to American involvement in Vietnam. Crafted in 1966 as a response to a group of East Harlem mothers with children in Vietnam, *A Man Says Goodbye to His Mother* is a straightforward lament for war and death. It features a death-masked narrator and a pair of puppeteers who play in the street, with accompanying musicians. War accouterments populate the world of the play: an airplane, a trumpet, a drum, fire, a body covered in a white sheet, a letter that reads "We regret to inform you." It is a short play with few words, except for the solemn, rhythmic, and dispassionate dispatches from the narrator, referred to as "Voice." The play begins with an embrace between mother and son, where she "gives an army bag to the man. He puts it on and they embrace." The narrator says, "A man says goodbye to his mother," followed by a "melody on drum and trumpet." Voice, action, and music cycle throughout the short piece. The mother becomes a villager, and her children die in war. When she becomes the mother from the beginning again, she learns through a letter that her son has died. Photos from the Nancy production show three performers in simple costumes.[23] Two wear black robes, one of which carries a death mark. The other black-robed performer, in a peaceful mother mask, holds a soup pot. The third performer is in an army shirt, army bag slung across his body and gas mask around his neck; in one hand he holds a puppet airplane. The regal Palais de Gouverneur is the backdrop; one palace guard can be seen upstage of the performers. Kourilsky notes how this molded the space: "When it is played in front of a palace guarded by sentinels (the Governor's Palace, Place de la Carrière in Nancy), it's naturally towards them that the body is posed, because the palace is thus the real 'set' of the play: it plays an integral part of the scenery, as also do the soldiers."[24] A focused audience stands around the intimate performance scene, with Nancy's cathedral looming behind them.

Fire, dedicated to several Americans who self-immolated in protest of the Vietnam War, in particular caught the attention of critics and spectators in Nancy. Bob Ernstthal recalls that it was created in an era of terrible emotional upheaval. . . . The climate was very heavy. We felt isolated, torn, oppressed. We felt that this war in Vietnam asked for something more interior, more human that these big stories that we'd made till then—all these Crucifixions. We'd had enough of banging on drums, of blowing in trumpets, of making noise and agitating. What we wanted was to get inside the bodies of others, completely.[25]

Elegant in its simplicity, *Fire* lasts about one hour and is spare in text and movement. Five actors cloaked in black swathes of cloth play the Vietnamese peasants, and an ensemble of about ten unmoving puppet figures looms behind the moving puppet actors. All wear matching black cloaks and arresting papier-mâché mask moon faces, surrounded by black hoods. Kourilsky writes that this was one of the "big 'ideas' of the performance: this inextricable mixing of actors and the puppets."[26] Their puppet and mask eyes turn down and their mouths are short dashes, their faces blank and yet soulful in their starkness. During the performance, the only sounds are percussive, a gong, a violin, and a rattle, and the main action is the unfurling of scarlet tape—the fire that slowly consumes the villagers. There is almost no text at all, except for the announcements of the days of the week, followed by "fire." The women move throughout the piece, from talking and eating to burning after an air attack. As the women burn, a Buddhist nun self-immolates in protest. Schumann explains, "It's not about a Vietnamese village. . . . It's the form that the piece takes as it tells something to the audience."[27] The piece is structured as a sequence of days, starting with a prelude that announces its dedication to the Americans who self-immolated; the performers and spectators share bread. *Fire* then proceeds day by day: Monday through Wednesday presents "life," Thursday and Friday "death," and Saturday and Sunday "war," with an eighth day added for "fire." *Fire* is one of what Schumann calls "chamber pieces,"[28] adapted for performance in smaller, intimate spaces. He specifies that the ideal audience number is around fifty. In New York, *Fire* was most often performed in churches. In Nancy, Dupavillon recalls, Schumann presented it in the basement of city hall, and it was performed up to four times per day. Margo Lee Sherman recalls that the New York audiences were small, fewer than twenty people, and that "they were silent after the show"; in Nancy they were large, and "the audience gave a huge applause after every performance," which the company found jarring.[29]

The French marveled at the efficacy of the company's skeletal production techniques and the brashly political content of their plays; multiple essays and articles used the word *revelation* to describe the company and their work. Nicole Zand wrote in *Le Monde*, "Peter Schumann succeeds, truly, and without words, without terrorist aggression of the conscience or the senses, to define the war and to convey in an illuminating way a vision of Vietnam; and, better than the ideological apologies, the goodwill films, the images of napalmed children, he gives us the unexpected 'reality' even of this war."[30] Christian Dupavillon remarks that Schumann presented

> a very well organized, very technical spectacle. It's true that they taught us another way to be on the stage, to make theatre. I learned a lot from this theatre. What I love with [Schumann] is his manner to pass along a message. It's always surprising. It's formidable. It's not just the masks. It's the story itself. It's the way he tells it. And that, it's all him. You can't learn it in a book. He's a real artist. I know very few artists like him. [He's] capable with three words, a few pieces of paper, to tell something so big. And I think that there he is a genius.

He adds that it was remarkable "to see a theatre from the US speaking with such energy about the war."[31] Émile Copfermann saw Schumann and his company's presence as indicative of a larger change in both theater and society: "That New York's Bread and Puppet Theater chooses the street as their place of performance and that, in doing so, with rudimentary means, they equal and surpass ten big subsidized, institutionalized theatres, is not only damning for the dominant and prosperous forces here and there: it's a call to order."[32] Of the Nancy revelation, Kourilsky writes, "It was a revelation not only of a new theatrical language that mixes masked actors and giant puppets, but also of a new 'politics' of theatre."[33]

Bread and Puppet's success at Nancy exposed on a very public stage many of the techniques of company organization, production methodologies, and aesthetics that young French theater troupes like the Aquarium (present at the 1968 Nancy festival under the auspices of the Université Internationale du Théâtre de Paris) and the Théâtre du Soleil were experimenting with on smaller stages in the mid-1960s. It also echoed an approach to storytelling that André Benedetto's *Napalm* and Armand Gatti's *V comme Vietnam*, both written in 1967, had employed: both plays took a leftist stance and critiqued American involvement in Vietnam, as in *Napalm*, where Lyndon B. Johnson and Robert McNamara are portrayed as hammy, cartoon-like buffoons as they discuss America's foreign policy. In *Fire* and *A Man Says Goodbye to His Mother*, French audiences saw an American company, directed by a German, grapple with its own country's involvement in Vietnam and flat out condemn their country's policy. Bread and Puppet presented an image of America in "unexpected" dialogue with its own war, in front of a foreign audience with a particular vested and complicated interest in Vietnam. Bread and Puppet also provided an example of very different production methodologies and production values—a stripped theater of relevance and political topicality. The company distilled the essence of theater by eliminating nearly all text, instead relying on striking and simple visual cues to tell the call-to-action stories at the heart of the plays. This was a theater of pure images, of immediacy, and of social change via intense spectacle. In the middle of a cultural debate, led by Roland Barthes, that questioned the stability of "the text,"[34] as well as one that prominently raised Guy Debord's "society of the spectacle," Bread and Puppet's nearly wordless, highly visual theater proved revelatory in Nancy one month before the May '68 events erupted in the streets of Paris.

While Bread and Puppet jolted Nancy, the festival also provided a defining moment for the Bread and Puppet Theater. Margo Lee Sherman asserts, "Nancy was an extraordinary experience and definitely a turning point in B & P's history. . . . In New York City, we had audiences of no more than 20 people."[35] Bob Ernstthal remembers, "Also Nancy was a time when I got a taste of people trying to interview us. It was really exciting. Peter also got some relieved [*sic*], although he would never show it. It was exciting. We were in demand. People were coming—please play at our place. Please come to Paris. Please come to London."[36] After their time in Nancy, they were invited to London. Sherman recounts,

> Since FIRE was such a huge success in Nancy, we were immediately invited to perform at a snooty place in London, the ICA. We hated it. A wonderful couple, Peter and Joan Oliver, who ran the Oval House, which was a great settlement house with radical theater in SW London, saw our show. They invited us to move to the Oval House and perform there. HOORAY! We quit the ICA for the Oval House.[37]

Also at Nancy, they were invited to Amsterdam, The Hague, and Paris. And, though not invited, they went to Berlin, where they played in university halls and at the Forum Theatre at 11:00 p.m., following a Heiner Müller performance.[38] In Paris, they arrived in the middle of the May '68 events and stayed in Stefan Brecht's apartment.[39] They played their production *Speech* at the Théâtre de la Commune d'Aubervilliers in early May and *A Man Says Goodbye to His Mother* in front of the Hispano-Suiza automobile factory in Bois-Columbes.

The turning point from marginalized struggle to quick fame both excited and disturbed the company. Margo Lee Sherman explains, "It could be quite yucky. Because we never had a chichi audience in New York, and suddenly we became a theatrical success in Europe, and it was the thing to do to come and see the Bread and Puppet Theater."[40] As in the London example, even when offered space and support at prestigious performance venues, the company felt most comfortable in schools, streets, and radical venues with friends. After Paris in May, they returned to New York, where they began work on a new show. At the same time, the company began to expand, and their sights were already set on the next Nancy festival. Sherman narrates,

> We came home in May 68. Soon after Peter said to me, "I want to build *Beasts*." He built many beasts, we began trying them out to "see what they can do." This was the beginning of the Big Show, *The Cry of the People for Meat*. We worked on it summer, fall, winter 1968–9. Why? To bring it to the Nancy Festival in 1969, and the 8-month Big Tour of Europe, April through November 1969. We departed NYC around April 18 with 20 or 21 adults and 5 children. Upon our arrival in Nancy the next day, B & P grew by 3 more adults and 2 more kids. During the tour the company grew to 40 adults.[41]

They grew in numbers, in scope, in national and international exposure. Bread and Puppet became a staple of radical theater gatherings like the Radical Theater Festival in San Francisco in September 1968, where they performed alongside El Teatro Campesino and the San Francisco Mime Troupe. After working in a variety of temporary spaces in New York churches, courthouses, lofts, and streets, the company found two long-term homes, first a four-year residency at Goddard College, where they produced their first Domestic Resurrection Circus, and then on their own land in northern Vermont, where the company settled and still resides. This new trajectory in the United States was in part due to expanded success provided by their time in Europe; at the same time, it was in part due to losing their space in Manhattan in 1969 and company members' own desires to settle outside of the city. Nancy left a lingering imprint, though, and Schumann kept his sights on returning, which the company did in 1969, 1972, 1976, 1977, and 1979.

The 1968 Nancy festival was the last festival that played as scheduled during the spring of 1968; subsequent art and theater festivals in May and June folded due to the countrywide rupture of the May events. Copfermann's "call to order" of producing theater through pared-down means, outside of traditional theater spaces, via different collaboration models, and with engaged and political themes would come to a peak during the events of May '68 and with full ecstatic force during the spectacular premiere of *Paradise Now* by the Living Theatre in July 1968 at the Festival d'Avignon.

Avignon reigned as the king of French festivals during the latter half of the twentieth century, and it continues to do so today. Founded by Jean Vilar as part of his project to bring the Théâtre National Populaire, where he was also artistic director, to the provinces in the summer, by the 1960s it was established, increasingly international in scope, and widely popular in terms of attendance and press coverage. Given the debate in France at the time about decentralizing theater to make it more available to a larger spectrum of society, Vilar worked hard to make his theater accessible to wide audiences. Edward Baron Turk writes, "Vilar, however, was proud of what he thought of as the distinctly popular quality of his audiences. Avignon festivalgoers tended to be unpretentious, uninhibited, and open-minded, and they were alert to and comfortable with their diversity of social standing and educational background. . . . Vilar kept ticket prices low and surrounded performances with free concerts and informal talks with artists."[42] Indeed, as Philippa Wehle reports,

> As the Festival drew larger and larger audiences (they would reach over 100,000 in 1971, the year of Vilar's death), sociological studies made in 1967 showed it to be a young group (over half under 30) of diverse backgrounds—students, high school teachers, lower civil servants, office workers, small shopkeepers and tradespeople—80% representing the French provinces. . . . [The audience] had a distinctly popular spirit."[43]

While the audiences grew greatly between 1947 and 1968, the festival programming also changed. The early years featured three stage productions per summer, and the festival ran for about a week.[44] The first instance of what would become the festival was called "a week of art in Avignon." The early repertoire was composed of Théâtre National Populaire offshoots: French-directed productions of Shakespeare, Büchner, and Kleist and French plays by Claudel, Corneille, de Montherlant, and Molière. In 1963 Vilar left his position as director of the Théâtre National Populaire in order to lead Avignon full time. At this point, starting in 1964, Vilar gave the festival a makeover in terms of seating and venues, and the festival's gaze extended beyond directors associated with the Théâtre National Populaire as Vilar worked to make the programming contemporary. Dance officially became a part of the festival in 1966, when Vilar invited Maurice Béjart and his company from Belgium. In the same year the festival expanded from two weeks to four, and from two main productions to three. That year Vilar took a step back from stage directing, with Roger Planchon and Georges Wilson directing several feature productions. Georges Jean led a conference on Popular Culture and the Culture of the Avant-Garde, and Orson Welles's film *The Lady from Shanghai* was screened. In 1967 film would officially become part of the festival and the second performance space, in the Carmes Cloister, opened. Amiri Baraka (LeRoi Jones) became the first American produced at the Festival d'Avignon, when Antoine Bourseiller directed *Dutchman* and *The Slave* (*Le métro fantôme/L'esclave*). Additionally, the 1967 festival produced Philippe Adrien's *La baye*, dance productions by Maurice Béjart, and a screening of Jean-Luc Godard's film about student revolutionaries, *La chinoise*. Twenty years after the inaugural "week of art," Vilar reorganized the 1967 festival, shaking up its outlook and aims. In the following year the festival would experience a seismic rupture with the arrival of the Living Theatre. When the Living Theatre left New York in 1963 they were seen as tax-evading hippies who played to small houses. When they returned in 1968, they were fresh from playing full stadiums across Europe.

By the time cofounders Julian Beck and Judith Malina and their company landed in Avignon in spring 1968, the group already enjoyed status as a critical and popular darling of France and had been performing at France's festivals and national theaters since their work at the Vieux-Colombier in 1961. In 1962 the company performed at the Théâtre de Lutèce and the year after that at the American Students and Artists Center. In 1966 they mounted *The Brig* at the Odéon and in the same year performed *Mysteries and Smaller Pieces* at the Festival de Cassis. In 1967 they performed *Antigone* at the Théâtre Alpha 347 and revived *Mysteries and Smaller Pieces* at the University of Nanterre, just outside of Paris, where the redheaded sociology student Daniel Cohn-Bendit—who would become the symbolic figurehead of May '68—was allegedly among the audience members.[45] Also in the audience at Alpha 347 was Festival d'Avignon assistant director Paul Puaux and his wife, Melly Puaux, a festival employee. Impressed, they met with Beck and invited the troupe to the summer festival. Puaux asked that the company create a new spectacle for Avignon. Melly Puaux remembers the meeting as very pleasant and describes Beck as "very nice." Everyone left with an agreement that the Living Theatre would perform *Antigone, Mysteries and Smaller Pieces*, and the new piece that Beck called *Paradise Now*—described by Beck at this point as a creation devoted to "happiness."[46] After that meeting, Beck and Paul Puaux corresponded by mail. Beck wrote (in French) that the Living Theatre was "ripe to create a new spectacle in which we hope to develop even further the ideas of theatre we began to explore in our work here in Europe."[47] The company negotiated in its contract an unprecedented three months of housing in Avignon and planned a mid-May arrival. Following their time in the south of France, the Living Theatre anticipated a return to the United States after their four-year exile and hoped for a tour with their new piece.

The love affair between France and "le Living" was long-standing and mutual. The company saw fame in France unaffected by their contentious and difficult reception at home in the United States. In France they had funding, space, and housing. While the troupe spent much time in Italy, Germany, and Belgium, among other European destinations, Julian Beck felt a particular affinity for France due to the country's superior, he felt, treatment of artists, and especially because of his devotion to Antonin Artaud. As Kimberly Jannarone notes in *Artaud and His Doubles*, Artaud was a great source of personal, artistic, and political inspiration for Beck and Malina. She cites the famous quip by Beck: "The ghost of Artaud became our mentor."[48] The company also found European audiences more open to their work. French audiences in particular responded to their repertoire of the midsixties: *The Brig, Mysteries and Smaller Pieces*, and *Antigone*. David Bradby and Maria M. Delgado call the troupe's French appeal "irresistible" in terms of lifestyle and form:

> The Living Theatre arrived in France with an irresistible combination of utopian communal lifestyle and anarchic "happenings" and performances promoting freedom from all restraints. Their practice affirmed, on the one hand, the interconnectedness of everything, while, on the other, it challenged every conventional or social restriction, especially the division of human beings into nation states. It was a theatre dedicated entirely to internationalism. Its approach was very simplistic . . . but it seemed immensely attractive to those who felt that nothing short of a revolution could change the power of repressive institutions in France.[49]

The attraction was mutual. In the work of the Living Theatre "French theatre workers felt they had discovered a revelation of a theatre of immediacy and gut reaction, which possessed an emotional force that had sometimes been lost by excessive attention to Brecht and to the theatre of reason."[50] Like Bread and Puppet, the French saw in the Living Theatre American artists engaged in serious critiques of American values and politics. French critics and students found themselves especially interested in the group's link to Artaud. In the program for the 1966 Cassis festival, Beck wrote, "If our work should succeed, at any moment, it is because we on the stage will reflect every man in the street; that is, we will have achieved Artaud's vision of the actor 'being like victims at the stake, signaling through the flames.'"[51] The French lauded the Living Theatre for their innovations in acting style, their belief in the Artaudian connection to the body. This was especially significant in a country that had pioneered many schools of physical performance (by Jacques Copeau, Emile-Jaques Dalcroze, and Jacques LeCoq, among others) in the twentieth century. Following the introduction to Brechtian staging and theory during the late 1950s and 1960s, the French rediscovered interest in the relation of their fellow Frenchman to Brecht. Copfermann wrote,

As for the Living Theatre of Judith Malina and Julian Beck, who performed many times in France, it wants to affirm a path that reconciles Brecht and Artaud, the theater of reflection and the consumption of the actor overtaken by his role. This is manifest at Caen, in 1967, with *Frankenstein*, and then *Antigone* in Paris, which opened the way to a controversy. Are the two theories of theater reconcilable? Can the aggression of the audience transform them into an active partner?[52]

The theater of *le Living*'s lifestyle equally fascinated critics and audiences. As Copfermann noted, for the Living Theatre "quotidian life become performance. . . . The theatrical event, in that case, is no longer the theatre, but the street."[53] Beck himself said, "The community of the Living is, I think, in a certain way, the most important aspect of our work."[54] So revered was the Living Theatre in France that in April 1968 an endorsement from Julian Beck appeared under the announcement of Bread and Puppet's inclusion in the program at the Nancy festival: "We salute our friends the 'Bread and Puppet Theater': you have our admiration for having given them the opportunity to perform at your artistic home. Their work is truly superb, and Peter Schuman [*sic*] is a creator of a very high level. Signed, Julian Beck of the Living Theatre."[55] After seven years of attraction, the Living Theatre's invitation to the prestigious Avignon festival signaled to France and beyond their official embrace by French culture at its highest level.

Fresh from Italy, the company members arrived in Avignon at the end of April 1968, ahead of their scheduled arrival. From that moment on, the members of the Living Theatre sparked a French frenzy with their nontraditional lifestyles, unusual habits, unconventional (and minimal) dress, and long hair. Their arrival was noisy for a relatively small, walled city like Avignon. Stories began to circulate. Melly Puaux recalls that the company arrived unannounced and with no money. She remembered it as an instantly stressful situation, because the festival housing was not yet ready.[56] So Vilar and Puaux installed the approximately fifty company members in a local hotel. They were kicked out, however, after some were allegedly found roaming the halls in states of undress. Paul Puaux arranged for them to move into the Lycée Mistral, a former high school, where he had water and electricity reinstalled in the school and arranged for mattresses and sheets to be borrowed from a local psychiatric hospital (where the artist Camille Claudel spent her later years). Melly Puaux remembers that soon after the company moved in, Beck appeared at the festival office and said that they needed more beds. When Paul Puaux expressed confusion, as he had specifically acquired one for every member of the group, Beck informed Puaux that several people could sleep only when two or three mattresses were stacked on one another. According to Melly Puaux, some troupe members dyed their sheets black, saying they couldn't sleep on white sheets and that they wanted their bedding to look like anarchy flags. When others in the group weren't happy with the school environment, Paul Puaux arranged for them to visit a local farm; when some were ill, he negotiated free medical care. The company was paid up front in full for their contracted twenty-one performances. Avignon playwright Gérard Gelas recalls helping paint the walls of the *lycée* and decorating the rooms with brightly colored paper as well as chalk slogans such as "révolution," "amour," "indiens," "guérilla," and "rite." He reminisced, "It became clear that at last we were in the presence of something other than just a theatre troupe, it was a matter of a lifestyle and that was the innovation."[57]

The intrigue continued throughout the spring and summer. Newspapers from Provence to Paris disseminated snapshots of the Americans as they navigated the former papal city. A May 7 story in *Le Provençal* reported, "The presence of the troupe the Living Theatre at the 22nd [*sic*] Festival (Carmes Cloister) likely worries poorly prepared and little informed spectators."[58] Also in May, scholar and critic Françoise Kourilsky gave a public talk to discuss the company history and context, in an effort to prepare the public. More attention was sparked on May 12, when Beck and Malina rushed to Paris after the protests were underway. They participated in discussions that led to the month-and-a-half-long occupation of the Odéon Théâtre de France, and Odéon artistic director Jean-Louis Barrault reported seeing them in the audience at the occupied theater.[59] Beck made a speech at the Odéon, in French:

> What is happening here is the most beautiful thing I've seen in the theatre. For twenty-five years, we've been calling the revolution. . . . And it seems to me that, these past few days, we have seen the beginning of the revolution. But it's important to remember: it's a matter of a beginning. The revolution must continue, that's the most important thing.[60]

He ended his speech with, "We have to seek to change the world without using the forms and the ends of the civilization we seek to destroy."[61] But Beck and Malina were back in Avignon on May 17, according to logs kept by Paul and Melly Puaux.[62] Given that Beck and Malina found in Paris the beginning of the revolution they so craved, it remains a question why they left so quickly. The French press dissected this, too:

> The situation became dubious since the only troupe called to play [at Avignon], the Living Theatre, was rehearsing their show at the same moment

as all the others were voluntarily unemployed. This bordered on the absurd: Julian Beck was part of a group who occupied the Odeon, thus closed to the theater community Barrault's theater, and then left to go put the finishing touches on *Paradise Now* that his company would play as part of Vilar's festival.[63]

Rehearsals and preparations continued throughout the rest of May and June and into the middle of July. News articles and stories continued to emerge. On June 12 Gilbert Girard of *Le Meridional* published a poll of six Avignonnais about what they thought of the company; his lead to the article explains, "For several weeks, the Living Theatre 'actors' have been inside our walls and the Avignonnais have been able to get to 'know' them, notably, on the Rue de la République, where they wander, bearded men, hairy . . . the women in multicolored tunics, threadbare pants; the children—because they have them—barely clothed."[64] Reporting picked up in the days leading up to the festival opening, especially given that all of the other scheduled performers and companies, except for the Belgian dancer Maurice Béjart and his troupe, had dropped out due to May '68–related travel and production problems. This left the Living Theatre as the only theater company in the Avignon Festival, and one that bore much focus, as the media was looking for ongoing spectacle in the wake of the May events. In July the mainstream weekly news magazine *Le Nouvel Observateur* published a rehearsal photo of company members with long hair in slight dress: leotard-clad Jenny Hecht and Henry Howard, shirtless in blue jeans, leaning over another company member in a bikini bottom. Alongside these photos is the headline "Satan in Avignon."[65] In the accompanying article, Guy Dumur writes, "In Paris, it was revolution. The presence of The Living [Theatre] in Avignon was signaled on the day of the Odéon occupation. The people of Avignon thought they'd seen the arrival of Satan worshippers." The twelve large photos published in *L'Accent* on July 17 depict, among other things, the naked children of company members, a still from *Mysteries and Smaller Pieces*, and performers practicing meditation, as well as a trio of headshots that feature three of the actors, Birgit Knabe, Echnaton, and Petra Vogt, with especially garish, freakish expressions. "The Living [Theatre] in the Papal City," published in the July 28 edition of *Le Provençal*, showcased four photos: one of lank Beck, eyes half closed and spindly arms outstretched; one of Beck and Malina in rehearsal; another of an emaciated cast member doing yoga; and the fourth of Echnaton dressed in an embroidered poncho smoking outside a Monoprix shop. After May '68 lingered into late June and few political changes had ensued in France, the Living Theatre's particular message of paradise, revolution, and alternative lifestyle (they were called by more than one journal "les hippies") was greeted by some with skepticism; others continued to look to the Living Theatre in particular as torchbearers of the lingering May drive for utopia. Beck and Malina saw May–July 1968 in Paris and Avignon as a definitive moment; Malina recalls that during the period of late spring and summer of 1968 she and Beck came the closest they ever had to feeling that the revolution they hoped for seemed both possible and imminent, saying, "The feeling in Avignon was that we were on the brink of a volcanic revolution."[66]

While the press focused on the Living Theatre, the company also looked to craft coverage of themselves. They had been in Europe for months, on self-imposed exile in response to the political and social troubles they experienced in New York: poverty, arrests, and charges of tax evasion. With the Avignon premiere of *Paradise Now*, the company prepared for what they hoped to be a glorious return to New York after the festival. They created their own press buzz to assist with this, in the guise of a boisterous film crew who followed them. Saul Gottlieb, who identified himself to Paul Puaux as a reporter for the *New York Times*, helmed the crew. Shortly after Gottlieb spoke with Puaux, a reporter named Howard Taubman arrived in Avignon. Taubman identified himself as the cultural editor for the *New York Times*. Puaux recounted, "On July 27 I received, preceded by a letter of accreditation, Mr. Taubman, editor of the cultural section of the *New York Times*, who burst into laughter at the idea of some 'Gottlieb' sent by his paper. Cover blown, Gottlieb's objective was to provoke events as he saw fit to best catch them on film in order to prepare for the media return of the Living Theatre to the USA."[67]

The festival opened on July 17 against the unusual backdrop of Avignon that summer, where groups of youths who had been involved in the May '68 activities, called *enragés* (enraged ones), arrived throughout July, looking to stir up further opposition. During the opening ceremony, the *enragés* staged the first of what would be many manifestations at the Place de l'Horloge in the middle of Avignon. The students who drifted from Paris's Boulevard St. Michel to Avignon's Rue de la République turned the Place de l'Horloge into a drop-in center for constant conversation and provocation. Each night of the festival, they gathered at the place and spoke out against the festival as a symbol of bourgeois complacency and commercialism, distributed manifestos, and held dialogue sessions called *les forums permanents* between five and seven each evening. The city, relatively untouched by May '68, had never seen anything like it. Raymond Dumerliat remarked,

> What struck me was a very particular ambiance that was never again replicated afterwards. At the Place de l'Horloge, everything was discussed, it was funny, there would be two people who would begin a discussion, a circle would

form, and then all of a sudden when one got tired, another would replace him, and the discussion would last until three or four in the morning. About theater, about democracy, about society, I even heard discussions at the Place de l'Horloge about philosophy, about mathematics. . . . All the discussions started as discussions about theater, and after became about society.[68]

The Place de l'Horloge became the occupied Odéon of the south, ruled by some who had been expelled from the Parisian theater only weeks before. As the barricades were being dismantled in the north and the Odéon forcibly emptied, the *enragés* looked to Avignon as a new site for discussion and demonstration. Vilar's *discussion libre* transpired in the streets before his officially scheduled festival debates even began. This atmosphere divided Avignon. On the second day of the festival, July 18, the *enragés* gathered again, distributing a tract calling Avignon a "supermarket of culture" and calling for the closing of the festival.[69] As a collective composed of self-proclaimed anarchist-pacificist vegetarians who lived and made art together, slept together, and raised children together, the Living Theatre itself reflected many of the cultural and political debates that were being discussed at the Place de l'Horloge.

Judith Malina's adaptation of *Antigone* was supposed to open on July 18, but instead that night the company led a public dialogue about the censorship of local playwright Gérard Gelas's nonfestival play *La paillasse aux seins nus*, which had been banned by Avignon mayor Henri Duffaut. This act inflamed the *enragés* and much of the local theater community. On July 20 the Living Theatre performed *Antigone* with the entire company of Gelas's Théâtre du Chêne Noir seated upstage, wearing French tricolour tape over their mouths in protest.[70] Even with the attendant scandal, *Antigone* received wide critical and popular praise, and this only heightened the anticipation for the company's upcoming debut. And then, on July 24, the Living Theatre performed the world premiere of *Paradise Now*, the production that would become the calling card for the company in its quest for an unabashedly utopian, anarcho-pacifist revolution. Not just a depiction of the revolution but, in the eyes of the Living Theatre, a tool with which to achieve it, *Paradise Now* had an express political and social goal in which engagement with spectators was key. *Paradise Now* opened in Avignon to a full-to-capacity audience. More than five hundred people waited near the Cloître des Carmes gates, trying to get in. Judith Malina remembers hundreds of *enragés*—many of whom had spent time with the troupe at the Lycée Mistral—assembled at the theater entrance, trying to attend the performance for free. The production started at ten o'clock at night and lasted over four hours, culminating in an early morning procession through the Carmes neighborhood.

Paradise Now was novel even for the Living Theatre; though it shares some thematic similarities to *Mysteries and Smaller Pieces* and *Antigone*, it goes much farther than any of the troupe's previous works and functions explicitly as a personal instruction manual for "the beautiful, nonviolent, anarchist revolution. The purpose of the play is to lead to a state of being in which nonviolent revolutionary action is possible."[71] Beck explained, "Our task is to show people the greatest number of points to which they can direct themselves; not the way to ameliorate life conditions according to the bourgeois criteria, but to say that the revolution permits a greater freedom."[72] The company wanted something that would evolve and change, depending on where it was performed and for whom. The performers shifted languages depending on where they performed; in Avignon they performed in French. What wouldn't change was the ultimate radical goal of the work: "The act would project a revolutionary situation and lay the groundwork for anarchist action cells which would begin the work of revolution."[73] The desired revolution was not purely physical, but spiritual as well; the company described *Paradise Now* as

> a voyage from the many to one and from the one to the many. It's a spiritual voyage and a political voyage. It is an interior voyage and an exterior voyage. It is a voyage for the actors and the spectators. It begins in the present and moves into the future and returns to the present. The plot is The Revolution. The voyage is a vertical ascent toward the Permanent Revolution.[74]

The structure of *Paradise Now* resembles that of an initiation rite and an enlightenment. It portrays a journey from darkness to lightness, from the base of the body to the head, from repression to liberation. It is a traditional structure—it follows a chronological, linear progression. But within that progression, the framework of the audience/actor relationship is put into question, as is the basic concept of character. The "script" that the troupe developed was a hand-drawn chart that resembles a ladder with eight rungs.[75] Each rung contains a "rite," a "vision," and an "action." The rung of "the sexual revolution: the exorcism of violence" includes "the rite of universal intercourse," "the vision of apokatastasis," and the action "Jerusalem: the victims become executioners. What do the pacifists do?" The company performs the rites and visions; the goal is that the spectators will perform the actions, led by the company members. In *Paradise Now*, members of the Living Theatre disrobe, burn money, shake, quake, and pulsate. They participate in the "rite of universal intercourse" and invite the audience members onstage, with the event culminating in a street procession with group chanting. This kind of theater event was unprecedented for audiences in either France or the United States, and at the Festival d'Avignon.

On the second night, a huge conflict erupted among Vilar, Beck, and the masses waiting at the venue entrance. Vilar stood at the door, refusing to let in the extra people. Beck appeared from behind metal bars, picking out like a caged animal,[76] and asked Vilar to be less rigid. Vilar refused to budge. Beck spoke to those assembled, telling them that even if they couldn't get into *Paradise Now*, "paradise" could come to them. The waiting people hurled vicious insults at Vilar. Television crews filmed the entire episode; they recorded Beck asking Vilar, "How can one love Racine and Shakespeare and have that attitude?"[77] During that night's performance, Vilar remained at the door, blocking the entrance as he was pelted with insults. After 2:00 a.m., when the troupe emerged from the theater, the waiting *enragés* followed them to the Place de l'Horloge for a night of discussion led by the artist, critic, and activist Jean-Jacques Lebel.

Reactions to *Paradise Now* varied widely. Many spectators walked out; the masses waiting at the door rallied to take over the abandoned seats but were refused. Some just expressed confusion. Several of the technicians who set up the lighting equipment for the performance later asked Paul Puaux and Vilar why the actors weren't allowed to eat chickpeas (they misheard "haschisch" as "pois chiches" [chickpeas] in the line "Je veux du haschisch" [I want hashish]).[78] Police in civilian clothes lurked among the audience members. The *enragés* who saw the spectacle loved it; many of them joined the troupe onstage for the disrobing and other moments of audience participation. But not all of them were able to get into the theater, and many protested the admission charge, creating their own versions of *Paradise Now*'s lines: "I can't see the Living without money!" The neighbors in the Carmes quarter hated the animalistic screaming that dominated the early morning street parade; they complained to Vilar and Duffaut. The critics' reactions varied. René Sirvin called *Paradise Now* "a nightmarish vision of hell, a delirious happening executed by thirty dirty, drugged-out hippies, totally naked except for suggestive, carefully designed mini-bikinis."[79] Claude Baignères simply stated, "The Festival d'Avignon is dead."[80] Edith Rappoport compared the company favorably to Artaud and the Greeks.[81] Michèle Grandjean's mused, "As a revolutionary act—but that word's been so debased lately that it's hard to use it—*Paradise Now* is without a doubt the most accomplished, the most just one that we've seen in a long time."[82] Réjane Tronel exclaimed, "The Living Theatre is crazy, but what theatre! And what a document of our society."[83] Tronel also discussed the production's timing in relation to the May events and the group's status as leaders of the era's youth movement: "The subject—the revolution in all its forms—evoked in a series of twenty scenes, is naturally the reflection of a larger movement that's shaking up youth all over the world, of which the Living Theatre has been, for the past few years, the precursor. It's not by accident that *Paradise Now* was created in Avignon. France, since the month of May, is at the forefront of this movement."[84]

Paradise Now played in Avignon for only three nights. There were five additional scheduled performances, and Beck announced a free performance in a public square for Saturday the twenty-eighth. But on the afternoon of July 27, Mayor Duffaut met with Beck and Malina and forbade the company from engaging in any further performances of the work. Duffaut asked the troupe to replace the remaining representations of *Paradise Now* with *Mysteries and Smaller Pieces* or *Antigone*; he left it up to the company to decide which one. On Saturday afternoon Beck met with Duffaut to hear the city's reasons for the ban. According to Duffaut, the reasons were simple and had nothing to do with revolution or politics. Duffaut considered Beck, Malina, and company to have breached their contract, which specified that they would play only within the walls of the Cloître de Carmes. He also refused to allow a public performance because "forcing" a spectacle on an unwitting audience would be a "violation of conscience."[85] Things unraveled from that moment on, with the Living Theatre noisily withdrawing from the festival and leaving Avignon in a flurry. The *enragés* coined the slogan "Vilar, Béjart, Salazar," equating Vilar and Béjart with the Portuguese dictator, and hurled it at Vilar during the melée and ensuing days. The company's recognition soared. International invitations to stage the banned play flourished, as did even more news coverage, self-generated and otherwise. City officials and some of the media condemned the Living Theatre, but audiences throughout France and Europe lauded them. In many ways, Duffaut's ban forever sealed the Living's reputation in France as mythic revolutionaries who said no to authority and still triumphed. The 1968 festival, too, garnered a reputation as the site where all of the unfinished business of May '68 was unleashed: fights between students and police, art and government, free expression and state control. Gérard Gelas summed up the Avignon summer: "The goal, the function: to exorcise May '68 from right to left."[86] The ongoing legacy of the *Paradise Now* affair remains infamous in Avignon lore. Edward Baron Turk reports that at the commemoration of the sixtieth anniversary of the festival, during Olivier Py's homage to Jean Vilar,

> Actors dressed as student radicals raced up and down the Honor Court aisles, noisily chanting the now infamous slogan equating *Vilar* and the regularly invited choreographer Maurice *Béjart* (1927–2007) with Portugal's longtime dictator Antonio de Oliveira *Salazar* (d. 1970); a few moments later an ersatz reassembling of Judith Malina and Julian Beck's Living Theatre company, notorious for having smashed bourgeois prudery, engaged in an awkward onstage orgy.[87]

By 2006, the legend of *Paradise Now* had become so entrenched in the lore of the Festival d'Avignon, as well as in popular French culture, to be a recognized in a main stage spoof during the anniversary celebration.

Fresh from their time in Avignon, the Living Theatre went on an unprecedented European tour. Whereas before Avignon they performed in theaters and festivals, with this tour of *Paradise Now* they performed in stadiums in Switzerland and Germany, among other venues. Then they returned, amid a giant hubbub, to New York, where they performed *Paradise Now* at the Brooklyn Academy of Music and the Yale School of Drama—far from the Cherry Lane and other pocket theaters in downtown New York, these were the bastions of the canonized avant-garde. In New Haven, the Living Theatre and trailing audience participants were arrested during the street parade. They toured across the United States, particularly to universities, all the way to Portland, Oregon, where they performed at Reed College. They appeared in major issues of *TDR* and *Yale/Theater* and became the darlings of the New York intelligentsia critical scene. In reviews of them and their work, the company's time in France in 1968 consistently emerged as a turning point in their artistic style and trajectory.

The American theater companies were not the only ones to leave the 1968 encounter marked. The performances at Nancy and Avignon in the sixties generated a terrific enthusiasm for American theater in France, and even some spinoff companies: "Guillaume Lagnel's Théâtre Arche de Noé began in southern France in 1968, inspired by American avant-garde companies such as the Open Theater and the Living Theatre, but particularly by Schumann and Bread and Puppet, who were instantly celebrated in French cultural circles when they arrived in Paris in the midst of the student uprisings of 1968."[88] Street theater, puppetry, collective creation, theater taking place outside of traditional theater spaces, and a blurring of life and art all were the subjects of renewed and invested exploration and enthusiasm for the rest of 1968 and its immediate aftermath. In 1971 Françoise Kourilsky noted, "The Bread and Puppet Theater became a model for young troupes increasingly looking to step outside of theatre institutions and become involved directly in life."[89] Susan Haedicke notes that American companies particularly marked the domain of street theatre and that the form was propelled to the French "mainstream in [the] 1980s and 1990s."[90] This revelation not only inspired some French companies but set the scene for a long-standing romance on the part of the French for American theater. After the Living Theatre and Bread and Puppet came, among others, Robert Wilson, Richard Foreman, and Peter Sellars—all still more embraced, lauded, and recognized in France than in the United States.

For both Bread and Puppet and the Living Theatre, France was a turning point. Nancy and Avignon were big successes in terms of getting both of them onto international stages and enjoying momentary steady support for their work and tremendous desired critical and popular attention. In the street parades in Avignon, as well as the lifestyle groupies of the Lycée Mistral, the Living Theatre found another level of success beyond the artistic one of the show; they found participants who praised and joined them. When Bread and Puppet returned to France in 1969, they were bigger in numbers, and people they met on tour joined the company. Both companies moved more strongly and consistently into the streets at the French festivals. In France, both companies filled out their own mythmaking and storytelling. The responses to *Fire, A Man Says Goodbye to His Mother*, and especially *Paradise Now* have become part of the spectacles, and the shows and responses have become inextricable in the cases of these productions in Nancy and Avignon. These expanded narratives propelled both companies to a new level of the avant-garde canon: after their time in France in 1968, the Living Theatre and the Bread and Puppet Theater emerged in America as the very definition of avant-garde performance, and they ascended to a new level of institutionalized alternative theater. Upon their return stateside, institutions of higher learning embraced them, offering them funding, space, and tour invitations, and in some cases residencies, part of what Sally Banes calls "the academic mainstreaming of avant-garde performance."[91]

Neither company returned home to financial security, and both today continue to struggle for funding, yet their time in France left both companies marked as commodified, legitimate, and serious names in the theater world. In theater history, they are the defining examples of the American avant-garde, and it was in France in 1968, when both companies presented work critical of their home country, that they were propelled to this new level of the avant-garde canon.

France has long been a crossroads and a home to internationalism in politics and performance, a "Paris jigsaw" in the words of David Bradby and Maria Delgado. In France in the 1960s, lines dividing politics and performance sometimes blurred, particularly in the cases of May '68 and the 1968 Avignon Festival. In that decade, too, and beyond, the boundaries between commercial theater, experimental theater, and university theater were not always maintained or embraced. This was true at the highest level; Jack Lang, founder of the Nancy Festival with its noncommercial agenda and success as a showcase of the avant-garde, went on to become France's minister of culture in 1981 and then minister of education in 1992. To contemporary scholars and historians, the 1960s emerges as a defining decade for Americans in France, particularly in terms of the festival culture and influence and the space that these blurred lines provided. The massive political, cultural, and social changes happening in France throughout the sixties inspired a great self-reflection and a concurrent look outward toward other models. The French festivals, and notably Nancy and Avignon in 1968, became sites where these reflections and projections were embodied and enacted, where new cultural methods and makers were revealed and transformed en route back to their homes, forever leaving marks on French theater and culture—and theater histories—on both sides of the Atlantic.

NOTES

All translations from French to English are the author's, unless otherwise noted.
The author thanks Kris Cohen, Hannah Kosstrin, Natalie Joy, and Michele Matteini. Special thanks to Margo Lee Sherman.

1. Émile Copfermann, "Au festival de Nancy: La découverte du 'Bread and Puppet' de New York," *Les Lettres Françaises*, May 8, 1968.

2. Nicole Zand, "Révelation du 'Bread and Puppet' de New York au festival de Nancy," *Le Monde*, April 25, 1968.

3. Franck Jotterand, "Une révélaton au festival de Nancy," *La Gazette de Lausanne*, April 27, 1968.

4. Raymonde Temkine, "Au Festival du Jeune Théâtre de Nancy: Le choc de deux spectacles de qualité exceptionnelle," *L'Humanité*, April 27, 1968.

5. For a discussion of the various interpretations of the beginning moment of the Bread and Puppet Theater, see James M. Harding, "The Bread and Puppet Theater: Historical Overview," in *Restaging the Sixties: Radical Theaters and Their Legacies*, ed. James M. Harding and Cindy Rosenthal (Ann Arbor: University of Michigan Press, 2006), 355–57.

6. James M. Harding, introduction to *Contours of the Theatrical Avant-Garde: Performance and Textuality*, edited by James M. Harding (Ann Arbor: University of Michigan Press, 2000), 6.

7. Arnold Aronson, *American Avant-Garde Theatre: A History* (New York: Routledge, 2000), 7.

8. Martin Esslin coined the term *absurd* in 1961 to describe Beckett, Adamov, Genet, and Ionesco, among others. In France this group was known as *le nouveau théâtre*, a term created by Geneviève Serreau in her book of the same title.

9. An early incarnation of this organization started in 1954, but it wasn't until 1957 that the organization officially took form.

10. For a larger discussion of these, and of Paris and internationalism, see David Bradby and Maria M. Delgado, *The Paris Jigsaw: Internationalism and the City's Stages* (Manchester: Manchester University Press, 2002).

11. Frédéric Maurin, "Did Paris Steal the Show for American Postmodern Directors?," in ibid., features a discussion about post-1970 American influence in France.

12. Françoise Kourilsky, "Theatre on the Margin of Society," in *Le théâtre aux États-Unis* (Bruxelles: La Renaissance du Livre, 1967), 55.

13. Christopher Campos discusses boulevard theater in his essay in *The Cambridge Companion to Modern French Culture*, ed. Nicholas Hewlitt (Cambridge: Cambridge University Press, 2003), and notes that while this genre remains steadfast in its existence, the number of boulevard playhouses has "gradually shrunk (some sixty playhouses in 1900, forty-five in 1945, and fifteen in 2000)" (250).

14. Victoria Nes Kirby, "Festival Mondial du Theatre," in "International Festival Issue," *Drama Review* 17.4 (December 1973): 7.

15. M. Rémy and J. M. Bonnet, "La presence américaine au Festival Mondial de Théâtre de Nancy," in "Les théâtres de l'Amerique," special issue, *Revue Française D'études Américaines* 10 (October 1980): 245.

16. Other American companies to present at Nancy were the Eastern Little Theater of Richmond, Kentucky (1966), the Mime Group from the University of Adelphi in New York (1967), and the Southwestern Players of Lafayette, Louisiana (1967).

17. Nes Kirby, "Festival Mondial du Theatre," 7.

18. Christian Dupavillon, interview with the author, Paris, October 1, 2012.

19. Margo Lee Sherman, e-mail to the author, September 5, 2012.

20. Sherman qtd. in Stefan Brecht, *The Bread and Puppet Theatre* (New York: Routledge, 1988), 1:710.

21. Margo Lee Sherman, e-mail to the author, September 4, 2012.

22. Ibid.

23. Françoise Kourilsky, *Le Bread and Puppet Theatre* (Lausanne: Editions L'Age d'Homme, 1971).

24. Ibid., 160.

25. Ibid., 83.

26. Ibid., 84.

27. Ibid., 180.

28. Ibid., 82.

29. Margo Lee Sherman, e-mail to the author, September 4, 2012.

30. Zand "Révelation du 'Bread and Puppet.'"

31. Dupavillon, interview.

32. Copfermann, "Au festival de Nancy."

33. Kourilsky, *Le Bread and Puppet Theatre*, 9.

34. David Bradby and Maria Delgado, introduction to *Paris Jigsaw*, 7–8.

35. Margo Lee Sherman, e-mail to the author, September 2, 2012.

36. Ernstthal qtd. in Brecht, *Bread and Puppet Theatre*, 1:711.

37. Margo Lee Sherman, e-mail to the author, September 4, 2012.

38. Ibid.

39. Sherman recalls, "I remember where we slept in Paris: Another funny story: Stefan had given us the keys to his apt in the Latin Quarter. As far as we could tell, the apt contained only a kitchen. We slept on the tile floor. When we came home, Stefan told us the key opened another apt. across the hall, which contained bedroom (s?)" Ibid.

40. Sherman qtd. in Brecht, *Bread and Puppet Theatre*, 1:711.

41. Margo Lee Sherman, e-mail to the author, September 4, 2012.

42. Edward Baron Turk, *French Theatre Today: The View from New York, Paris, and Avignon* (Iowa City: University of Iowa Press, 2011), 260–61.

43. Philippa Wehle, "A History of the Avignon Festival," *TDR* 28.1 (Spring 1984): 56.

44. For example, the 1947 festival, called a "week of art," ran September 4–11, and the theater offerings were Shakespeare's *La tragédie du roi Richard II*, Paul Claudel's *Histoire du Tobie et Sara*, and Maurice Clavel's *La terrasse de midi*. In 1948 the week of art became a "festival" and was produced in July for one week.

45. John Tytell, *The Living Theatre: Art, Exile, and Outrage* (New York: Grove, 1995), 224.

46. Melly Puaux, quoting Julian Beck, interview by the author, tape recording, Paris, November 13, 2004.

47. Beck qtd. in Jean-Claude Bardot, *Jean Vilar* (Paris: Armand Colin, 1991), 499.

48. Kimberly Jannarone, *Artaud and His Doubles* (Ann Arbor: University of Michigan Press, 2012), 13.

49. Bradby and Delgado, Paris Jigsaw, 6.

50. David Bradby, *Modern French Drama, 1940–1980* (Cambridge: Cambridge University Press, 1984), 141–42.

51. Antonin Artaud, *The Theater and Its Double*, New York: Grove Press, 1994, 13.

52. Émile Copfermann in *La décentralisation théâtrale 3: 1968, le tournant*, 2nd ed., ed. Robert Abirached (Arles: Actes-Sud, 2005), 19.

53. Émile Copfermann, *La mise en crise théâtrale* (Paris: François Maspero, 1972), 75.

54. Beck qtd. in ibid., 105.

55. "Vie Festival Mondial," special issue, *Théâtre et Universitaire no. 14* (April, 19–28, 1968), 100.

56. Puaux, interview.

57. Gérard Gelas, *Théâtre du Chêne Noir: Essais et documents* (Paris: Éditions Stock, 1972), 30.

58. "Avant le XXIe Festival . . . Connaissance du 'Living Theatre,'" *Le Provençal*, May 7, 1968.

59. Jean-Louis Barrault, *Souvenirs pour demain* (Paris: Seuil, 1972), 355.

60. Julian Beck, *Le Théâtre 1969–1*, ed. Fernando Arrabal (Paris: Christian Bourgois, 1969), 161.

61. Ibid., 163.

62. Rauch, "La prise de l'Odéon," in Abirached, *La décentralisation théâtrale 3*, 72.

63. "Et si ce n'était pas Vilar? . . . ," *Les Lettres Françaises*, August 28, 1968.

64. Gilbert Girard, "Enquête sondage dans les rues d'Avignon: Le 'Living Theater' condamné sans appel?," *Le Meridional*, June 12, 1968.

65. Guy Dumur, "Satan à Avignon," *Le Nouvel Observateur*, July 22–28, 1968.

66. Judith Malina, interview by the author, tape recording, New York, May 22, 2004.

67. Paul Puaux qtd. in Abirached, *La décentralisation théâtrale 3*, 98.

68. Raymond Dumerliat, "Avignon 68: Quelques témoinages/A few statements," *UBU: Scénes d'Europe/European Stages* 10 (July 1998): 20–27.

69. Quoted in Bardot, *Jean Vilar*, 504.

70. For a more complete account of the Chêne Noir controversy, as well as a larger discussion of Avignon in 1968, see Kate Bredeson, "In the Jungle of Cities: May '68 Arrives in Avignon," *Theatre Symposium* 14 (2006).

71. Aldo Rostagno with Julian Beck and Judith Malina, *We, the Living Theatre* (New York: Ballantine, 1970), 172–73.

72. Beck, *Le Théâtre 1969–1*, 224.

73. Tytell, *Living Theatre*, 226.

74. Living Theatre, *Paradise Now*, written down by Judith Malina and Julian Beck (New York: Vintage Books, 1971), 5.

75. *Paradise Now: Collective Creation of the Living Theatre* was published three years *after* the debut performances. The published script remains mostly faithful to what was presented in Avignon and even includes some text specific to the Avignon performances in "Rung Three, Action Three."

76. Some of these images are shown in Sheldon Rochlin's documentary *Signals through the Flames*, which features footage from throughout the Avignon festival experience.

77. Beck qtd. in Maurice Sardou, "Les incidents d'Avignon," *Le Méridional*, July 19, 1968.

78. This popular story was recounted by both Melly Puaux and Judith Malina and can also be found in Bardot, *Jean Vilar*.

79. René Sirvin, "Nouvelle agitation en Avignon où Vilar invite Sauvageot," *L'Aurore*, July 26, 1968.

80. Claude Baignères, "Le 'Living' seul foyer d'agitation," *Le Figaro*, July 25, 1968.

81. Edith Rappoport, "Paradise Now: Un cataclysme théâtral," *France Nouvelle*, July 31, 1968.

82. Michèle Grandjean, "Création mondiale du Living Theater: 'Paradise Now,'" *Le Provençal*, July 26, 1968.

83. Réjane Tronel, "Aux Carmes d'Avignon 'Paradise Now' par le Living Theatre,'" *Le Dauphine Libéré*, July 23, 1968.

84. Ibid.

85 Jean-Jacques Viton, "La municipalité au 'Living Theater': Remplacez 'Paradise Now' par 'Antigone,'" *La Marseillaise*, July 28, 1968.

86. Gelas, *Théâtre du Chêne Noir*, 38–39.

87. Turk, *French Theatre Today*, 271.

88. John Bell, "Bread and Puppet and the Possibilities of Puppet Theater," in Harding and Rosenthal, *Restaging the Sixties*, 363.

89. Kourilsky, *Le Bread and Puppet Theatre*, 9.

90. Susan Haedicke, "Breaking Down the Walls: Interventionist Performance Strategies in French Street Theatre," in *Contemporary French Theatre and Performance*, ed. Claire Finburgh and Carl Lavery (Hampshire, UK: Palgrave Macmillan, 2011), 163.

91. Sally Banes, "Institutionalizing Avant-Garde Performance," in Harding, *Contours of the Theatrical Avant-Garde*, 231.

PART IV
THE RISE OF
REGIONAL THEATERS

Dorothy Chansky

Alphabet Soup

The Acronymization of the American Theater

ALPHABET SOUP

A play in one scene

Time: the early twenty-first century
Setting: an apartment in Brooklyn

Characters:

Tyler, a recent college graduate with a major in theater, early to mid-twenties
Tracy, a recent college graduate with a major in theater, early to mid-twenties

TYLER
How was your URTA[1]?

TRACY
I was pretty nervous. I've *got* to get into a decent MFA[2] program!

TYLER
C'mon. It was the same piece that got you to the finals at ACTF,[3] right? I'll bet
  you rocked.

TRACY
I hope. Hey, guess who was there? On the other side of the table?
  Dana Spelvin!

TYLER

As what? A go-fer? Dana's got what, a BFA[4] in technical theater from some school that's not even NAST[5] accredited? All Dana ever wanted in life was airfare to USITT[6] and maybe to ASM[7] something going to ACTF.

TRACY

Dana's now the AD[8] at a LORT B+.[9]

TYLER

B *plus*? What's that? Grade inflation?

TRACY

You're so harsh. We talked really briefly. TCG[10] directing fellowship, day job for a while at TDF,[11] a NYSCA[12] internship.

TYLER

I guess when your mother read all those FEDAPT[13] publications and your dad was Mr. OOBA[14] you've got connections even if you don't have talent. Probably gets NEA[15] money, too.

TRACY

Whatever. I just hope I get a callback. Hey! Are there any good TDF offers for tomorrow?

TYLER

Not really. Wanna try TKTS?[16]

TRACY

Sure. Maybe it'll take my mind off things.

   THE END.

A dramaturg from another planet, another century, or another country would have her work cut out for her with the above playlet. Identifying the acronyms is, of course, largely just a matter of a few mouse clicks, as is learning what the various entities shorthanded above currently do and provide. But understanding their centrality as an interrelated web on which much American theater depends—note that the two aspiring professionals in the above scenario never mention Broadway—is perhaps best approached as a historical question. With the exception of the bachelor's and master's of fine arts degrees (BFA and MFA) and the assistant stage manager (ASM) and AD (artistic director) job titles, ten of the remaining twelve acronyms so glibly tossed out by the fictional dramatis personae came into existence in the 1960s. (The eleventh, OOBA, was founded in 1972 as a resource for nonprofit theater companies in New York, and the twelfth, TKTS—the pavilion in Times Squares that sells discounted theater tickets on the day of performance and a project of the born-in-the-sixties TDF—debuted in 1973.) Indeed, one of the forerunners, the MFA, arrived a generation before the 1960s, but this decade injected it with growth hormones and gave it a pedigree that linked it at the hip with the professional, mainstream theater. That these acronyms are now taken for granted—indeed, that they define the landscape of American theater—points to the decade of their emergence as an institutional tipping point. Put bluntly, American theater prior to the 1960s meant almost exclusively two things: for-profit (Broadway, summer stock, and some touring shows) or local/community/amateur theater. Beginning in the Kennedy years and ramping up under Johnson, the fabulous invalid was repurposed as a not-for-profit creature with direct ties to universities and government funding.

Readers not inside academic or professional theater most likely would recognize the National Endowment for the Arts (NEA) and perhaps imagine it as the model or inspiration for the other acronymed entities. Founded in 1965, the NEA was preceded by a few of the above-cited organizations; it directly created others; and it was a means of support for later arrivals. The goals of the NEA were and are to make the arts more widely available to more Americans; to preserve cultural heritage; to strengthen cultural organizations; and to foster creative development of artists.[17] The fictional Dana's fictional theater would today be eligible for NEA funds for various kinds of endeavors, ranging from a residency for a playwright to educational outreach to puppetry to the invitingly capacious (perhaps because vague) category of "experimental work."[18]

The NEA is a good place to begin untangling the acronym tapestry, and some might see it as the DNA or the matrix for this tapestry. All of its strands emerged in a post–World War II climate that saw greater prosperity for more Americans and a political investment in using "culture" as a Cold War weapon. The former meant an interest in "serious" theater available locally (i.e., not requiring a trip to New York); the latter meant a willingness to support such theater for cachet abroad and for clout at home.[19] All of the arts benefited in this climate, but theater was especially fortunate that the first chair of the NEA, Roger Stevens, was a longtime Broadway producer who brought both his sympathies and his contacts to the job. Indeed, in the first five years of NEA grants, more money went to theater than to any other branch of the arts.[20] Stevens was by no means a last-minute appointee, however. In 1961 he had been tapped by John Kennedy to chair an advisory commission on a national cultural center, an entity that would be realized and named for the late president after his assassination. Stevens served as a full-time arts advisor to both Kennedy and Lyndon Johnson before starting at the NEA.

Alice Goldfarb Marquis makes clear in her history of public arts funding that Kennedy, "an instinctively political animal," was less an arts lover than he was a strategist. He endorsed a State Department document on cultural policy that asserted that improving the arts "would be a boost to national morale [and] would do no less than transform the national character and open, for the whole world to see, an exhilarating new chapter in the American Revolution for the 1960s." Kennedy himself told the new advisory commission that "every stone" placed in the new cultural center "would strike a blow against the Soviet Union's 'major effort in this field. . . . [The Soviets] recognize, even though they manipulate this desire, the tremendous interest people have in the arts.'"[21] To tweak a title previously used in a study of the left-wing political stage, theater was a weapon.[22] But the Soviets, in Goldfarb's history, were not the only rivals against whom Kennedy envisioned using the arts as a necessary weapon.

Anticipating Nelson Rockefeller as his likeliest opponent in the 1964 election, Kennedy knew he needed to shore up his arts bona fides. Rockefeller's place in the acronymization of the American theater world had already been staked out, and its genesis was both proactive and possibly reactive. In 1960, in Rockefeller's second year as governor of New York, the state legislature created the New York State Council on the Arts (NYSCA), a project directly attributable to the man who had proposed such an entity as early as his 1957 gubernatorial campaign position paper.[23] NYSCA's mission includes the words *preserving, expanding, artistic excellence, sustaining, celebrating, encouraging,* and *broadening public access.*[24] (Dana's NYSCA internship would have provided training in an environment all about balancing excellence and access—good skills for grant endeavors at a LORT B+ in any state.)

Rockefeller's model program was embraced by the NEA, as the Endowment's enabling legislation mandated a federal-state partnership, precisely "to appease those who feared the creation of a dominating, European-style 'Ministry of Culture.'"[25] In 1967 the NEA began offering block grants to state arts councils, and in short order every state had one.[26] But Rockefeller's motivations may have been competitive as well as sui generis. His family and their foundation were instrumental in the founding of Lincoln Center for the Performing Arts, an entity that would change the face of the performing arts in the arts heart of the United States. The financial and real estate challenges of creating Lincoln Center were being tackled at the same time that the Ford Foundation was starting to give grants to the performing arts: the late 1950s. Rockefeller perspectives were not always identical to Ford Foundation perspectives,[27] so the governor's ability to put his own stamp on support for the arts cannot be regarded as emerging in a vacuum.

The Ford Foundation is a key player in the acronymization of the American theater because it was the original source of major grants to regional theaters starting in the late 1950s. The influence of W. McNeil Lowry, Ford's arts guru, has been rehearsed elsewhere, but a thumbnail is apropos here.[28] Lowry's initial belief that grants to arts organizations should lead to the organizations becoming self-sustaining was not precisely the route that the NEA would take, as the federal Endowment recognized that demonstrating "need" sometimes involves showing strategic loss; the NEA also sought to serve a broad swath of audiences by including populism and "outreach," as well as "serious art," contra Ford's initial interests largely in the latter. Too, the NEA from the start was interested in new programs and not merely sustenance. Once the NEA was up and running, Ford branched into more experimental funding that was not only about institutional stabilization.[29] In its fledgling years of favoring institutional self-maintenance *über alles*, Ford funded one of the earliest of the emergent and tenacious theater acronyms—one that was neither a theater company nor an artist but that would come to influence management, casting, the careers of emerging directors, and communication among theaters across the country into the next century. This was the Theatre Communications Group (TCG).

TCG, generally described as a service organization, was conceived at a 1959 Ford meeting and was formally launched in 1961. Its mission was to foster communication among professional, regional, and community theaters; the goal of this mission was to "improve standards."[30] In 1967 TCG limited its services to thirteen theaters, favoring them because they manifested the Ford Foundation organizational desiderata linked to stability. In its first decade, TCG was best known for running auditions that enabled "out-of-town" theaters to see talent in New York and for promulgating the formula, championed by publicist Danny Newman, that subscription is the key to a theater's institutional health.[31] Both endeavors fostered similarity among regional theaters, which were encouraged to see the same actors and embrace the same organizational, fundraising, and marketing strategies. TCG was no Ford house organ, however. Its focus in the 1960s was regional theater, but in 1972 it was restructured to serve experimental and ethnic theaters as well.[32] By 1990, the NEA's

> Theater Program turned directly toward its service organizations to sustain
> the infrastructure of the field, with the Theatre Communications Group
> (TCG) being the most prominent. Since then, the NEA has collaborated with

TCG in a number of ways. For instance, the NEA/TCG Theater Residency Program for Playwrights was created in 1996 at the initiation of Chairman Jane Alexander and Theater Director Gigi Bolt, and support for early career directors and designers was reshaped into the NEA/TCG Career Development Programs for Directors and Designers.[33]

(The latter program would have been the source of Dana's plum directing fellowship.) TCG's publication *ARTsearch* and its magazine *American Theatre* might have been sources of information, scripts, apprenticeship opportunities, or jobs for all three characters in *Alphabet Soup*. TCG today boasts seven hundred member theaters and affiliate organizations, publishes plays and books, and administers $2 million in grants annually to artists and theaters. A Ford Foundation endeavor now partners with the NEA to support a huge network of regional and other theaters, helping launch careers and keeping students and professors in the professional loop.

My use of the word *professional* in the previous paragraph and, indeed, throughout this essay, points to a problem ghosting any assessment of changes in American theater in the 1960s. What, exactly, did the term mean? Were all regional theaters that putatively eschewed amateurism by definition professional? If theaters issuing union contracts to actors were officially professional but needed help from TCG, for example, to "professionalize" their operations, who was writing the guidelines? If a theater was non-Equity but sought to be fiscally responsible and artistically exciting, surely the adjective to which it aspired was "professional."[34]

Two acronyms in particular stand out for their role in solidifying definitions of professional status for theaters starting in the 1960s. The League of Resident Theatres (LORT) was formed when twenty-six already existing regional theater companies banded together in the interest of creating a regular, shared category of contracts for hiring actors who were members of the professional actors' union, Actors' Equity Association. Prior to the existence of the League, each theater negotiated individually for professional actors—often based in New York—when it wanted to employ them locally—almost always outside of New York.[35] (Dana, therefore, would know precisely the cost of hiring actors for an upcoming season at a LORT B+, or at least a minimum cost, and would not have to negotiate show by show and actor by actor.) LORT's concerns were that Broadway and stock contracts—those used by Equity on a case-by-case basis in the early years of the regional theaters—failed to recognize the different scheduling needs in a repertory situation, where, for instance, multiple costume fittings would be required for an actor opening in multiple shows on a contract that recognized only the time required for fittings for a single production. Also, actors hired in the early years of regional theater could not necessarily count on accrued vacation time as a contractual right, despite union membership and a union contract. The LORT contract also created a new category of "journeyman actor," which made it possible for LORT theaters to hire student actors on a formal, contractual, professional(izing) basis. Here, clearly, "professional" was driven by the status of the actor the theaters wanted to employ.[36]

Two years after LORT was born in 1966, another service organization with professionalization built right into its name arrived on the scene. The Foundation for the Extension and Development of the Professional Theatre (FEDAPT) also emerged from the halls of Actors' Equity and was briefly called Actors' Equity Foundation to Extend the Professional Theatre. Almost immediately, however, it severed its institutional ties with the union and sought foundation support.[37] A press release issued on its tenth anniversary called FEDAPT "the singular service organization devoted to the nuts and bolts of theater management and administration," quoting its executive director, Fred Vogel, as being concerned with "effective offstage success" and thereby "providing the atmosphere for theatre to 'fail or succeed on its own terms.'"[38]

FEDAPT finessed, or perhaps sidestepped, the definition of "professional" by publicizing, five years into its existence, its mission of providing "consultation and guidance for any *professionally oriented* [emphasis mine] theatre project in the United States."[39] A project might be a one-off such as a festival or fundraiser. It certainly did not need to be affiliated with any theater unions. But the FEDAPT mind-set was clearly one of systematization. It offered, in short order, seminars and publications, the latter with no-nonsense titles such as "Subscription Guidelines," "Box Office Guidelines," "The Business of Dinner Theatre Business," and "Investigation Guidelines for Setting Up a Theatre," subtitled "Look Before You Leap."[40] In theory, FEDAPT was willing to divorce ideas of artistic excellence or visionary purpose (the "terms" on which the theater would "fail or succeed") in the interest of organizational regularity and professionalism (arguably being sold as the terms on which the theater would fail or succeed, or at least being touted as the surefire means of blaming any failures solely on the art and not on the management). FEDAPT, within four years of its founding, began receiving NYSCA funds on a regular basis. By 1976 its supporters included the NEA, several private foundations, and the Actors' Equity Association (again).[41] FEDAPT demonstrated its own efficiency not by making a profit but by supporting itself via healthy grants (as well as, of course, conference fees and the sale of its publications). FEDAPT is the only acronymed entity in Tracy and Tyler's world that is no longer in existence. It closed its doors in 1991. But then its executive director, Nello McDaniel, announced that the work would continue in the context of an entity called Arts Action Research, an organization still in existence and dedicated to providing individualized services to theatres and other arts organizations to meet present-day challenges of sustaining meaningful artmaking in changing communities and cultural climates.[42] The union of professional, regional, nonprofit, and educational theater (a blended family, as it were) was thriving.

Dana's mother's affiliation with FEDAPT may be how she met her husband, who was affiliated with OOBA, the Off-Off-Broadway Alliance. OOBA became A.R.T./New York, ironically adopting the word *resident* in its name, although its mission is, as was OOBA's, to provide services in the form of information concerning all the sorts of managerial and contractual and publicity topics that were and are the concerns of LORT and TCG. The difference is that OOBA members were (and A.R.T./New York members are) nonprofit companies based in New York, none of which is properly a "resident" company and many of which use Equity actors only on waiver contracts. If Dana's mother knew her FEDAPT-ese and Dana's father was OOBA-literate, they could well have inculcated their offspring with the importance of knowing the ins and outs of theater administration part and parcel with knowing how to paint scenery or run a casting call. If this mind-set is not in the blood, it can be acquired at the dining room table or on mom and dad's coattails, although, as Tyler notes, the contacts one might have made at a FEDAPT seminar or via an OOBA colleague could also lead to contacts down the road.

Two concepts have been lurking in all the preceding paragraphs, but perhaps especially in the last two. These are decentralization and alliance with universities. The *R* in LORT stands for *resident*, and resident companies were a goal for many of the earliest theaters setting up shop in the 1960s in cities not New York. But, following the lead of a major chronicler of the phenomenon, Joseph Wesley Zeigler, I have called them regional theaters, foregrounding their goal of doing good work all around the country. This common goal of decentralization, however, was ever a problem (although the dream of resident companies proved more so; decentralized theater has survived, while the resident idea is infrequent at best). In his 1972 introduction to *Regional Theatre*, Alan Schneider tartly notes that the regional theater

> rarely, if ever belonged to its region. Whenever a regional theatre sought deliberately to become regional, either in its choice of play material or in its personnel, it was too provincial or too folksy. When it wasn't doing new plays, we blamed it for timidity and conventionality. When for varying reasons and under varying pressures it started to do that and when the new plays increased in both quality and quantity, we said it was just interested in doing tryouts for New York.[43]

Non-New York theaters were founded, learned the management ropes, and held on in the 1960s. The Ford Foundation and the NEA were leaders in locating and supporting these theaters. TCG and FEDAPT helped them operate on sound business bases, but these—as well as NEA guidelines—helped make them more like each other than was to everyone's liking. In other words, decentralization of the geographic sort quickly morphed into centralization of the conceptual sort. Zeigler complained in 1973 that in the hope of Ford Foundation support and with Ford's underwriting of TCG, theaters "homogenized themselves."[44] As early as 1968, in his study of the economics of American theater, Jack Poggi also noted the danger of "mammoth subsidy . . . turn[ing] theaters into Institutions."[45] In Poggi's study, the network of new, outside–New York (regional) nonprofits appears in a chapter that calls them "The Resident Theatre," but his point matches Schneider's regarding an absence of focus on developing unique regional profiles: "It seems somewhat paradoxical that a movement that set out to decentralize the theater is now spending so much of its energy trying to recentralize it."[46] TCG is a culprit on Poggi's list, as the TCG list of worthy theaters (in 1967, when it decided to focus on just thirteen) had three marks of strength: "administrative and economic structure capable of gaining support, continuity of artistic and managerial leadership, and cooperation with other theatres and with TCG programs."[47] Noticeably, art qua art was absent. Paul DiMaggio calls networks such as the regional theater "organizational fields," identifying "institutional isomorphism" as a product of 1960s government and corporate funding, as the big donors created a system in which "organizational isomorphism" emerged in response to the requirements for providing data and rhetoric in grant proposals.[48]

Decentralization may have created its own kind of homogenization, but in so doing it succeeded in both expanding opportunities and providing places for more artists, managers, and helpers (not to mention the obvious: making more "serious" theater available to more spectators in more places). Where better to turn for eager participants willing to start for little pay and keen to learn from established professionals than colleges and universities? Between 1965 and 1969 theater studies in American colleges and universities went from being a sparsely populated major to one with a national accrediting board (the National Association of Schools of Theatre, or NAST); a festival culminating in publicized performances in the nation's capital (American College Theatre Festival, or ACTF); a nonprofit that enabled graduate programs and regional theaters to audition students in central locations rather than one by one (University Resident Theatre Association, or URTA); and an affiliation with the world of professional design and theater technology (United States Institute of Theatre Technology, or USITT). These are the entities by which the fictional

Tyler and Tracy assess and seek to place themselves (and the hero/loser Dana) in professional theater.

USITT began in 1960 as a resource-sharing network of professional theater designers, architects, engineers, and technicians linked to an international theater technicians' organization. But when its journal, *Theatre Design and Technology*, made its appearance in 1965 courtesy of the Department of Theatre at the University of Pittsburgh, the academic connection was front and center for all to see.[49] With thirty-seven hundred members as of 2012, USITT "connects performing arts design and technology communities to ensure a vibrant dialog among practitioners, educators, and students."[50] Because the organization deals with technical production and safety regulations as well as with the newest bells, whistles, software, and gadgets that are the lifeblood of those who design for theater and/or execute designs, Tracy and Tyler may have missed some of the aesthetic depth or ideological sophistication in Dana's interest in following the means to think about and render a rich mise-en-scène and its aural analogue. Dana may indeed have started out in love with sound effects and rigging, but USITT was ever about wedding vision and means. The organization quickly realized the value of spreading its wealth (and assuring excellence in its ranks) by including students and using the words "educators and students" in the mission statement. Indeed, Dana as AD may be better at budgeting and hiring designers precisely because of an undergraduate career in the thrall of cool toys and software and doing technical theater into the wee hours. Tracy and Tyler, as actors, may never have attended USITT's annual conference and may have little idea that the organization's reach exceeds the grasp and purview of an emerging undergraduate largely interested in working backstage, even as it may sow the seeds of a later, expanded awareness.

Still, Dana's school was not accredited by NAST, a criterion by which an increasing number of theater programs (178 in 2012) measure and advertise their credibility. NAST was a latecomer to academic arts acronyms, being constituted in 1965. It was preceded in the Council of Arts Accrediting Associations (CAAA) by the National Association of Schools of Music, founded in 1924, and the National Association of Schools of Art and Design, founded in 1944. NAST accreditation cannot guarantee excellence any more than TCG affiliation can be a promise of galvanizing art. But NAST guidelines stipulate a certain number of course offerings, sufficient areas of faculty expertise, generous library resources, and adequate facilities and resources for teaching and executing design in order for a school's program to merit the NAST imprimatur. Tracy and Tyler scorn Dana's school's lack of NAST accreditation, although, to be fair, this may be more important in some areas than in others. A liberal arts college focused on experimentation, original writing, performance as research, theater for social change, or a host of other laudable theater pedagogies outside preprofessional training may see no need to invest in the resources to satisfy NAST. Dana's BFA in technical theater, as a preprofessional rather than a liberal arts degree, would, admittedly, likely have more clout on paper coming from a NAST-accredited program. Historically, the creation of NAST meant that theater, however late it was coming to the arts accrediting party, had at last arrived, and those focused on professional degrees pay attention to that.

All three of our fictional characters respect the American College Theatre Festival, founded in 1968 by the redoubtable Roger Stevens, then nearing the end of his term as first head of the NEA and after having served as arts consultant to two presidents. Stevens had been approached by actress Peggy Wood, who was a veteran of several guest artist roles in campus productions and who believed that student talent should be showcased beyond the one or two weekends it might get in its local setting.[51] The first festival, in 1969, featured Los Angeles City College performing William Congreve's *The Way of the World* and Hofstra University presenting Fay and Michael Kanin's *Rashomon*, both in Washington, D.C. Over the ensuing decades, the festival has ballooned into a multipronged endeavor with annual regional competitions throughout the nation that lead to finalists competing at the Kennedy Center each spring. Since 1972 ACTF has been giving acting awards named after vaudevillian Irene Ryan, who left money to ACTF to provide scholarships for promising young actors. Indeed, the prizes are disbursed to the schools the winners choose to attend, and not to the winners themselves, so the link to education is secure. If Tracy was a winner and not just a finalist at ACTF, some money would already be available to go to toward an MFA program, pending acceptance. Of course, another perspective, articulated as ACTF was starting its second decade, is that "the festival dangles the twin carrots of success and attention before college students, encouraging them but also giving them erroneous notions of a profession which does not willingly grant either success or attention."[52] Dana aspired simply to work on a production that made it to D.C., although, again, the value of just getting there and managing the speed and precision with which one's one show must be set up and broken down, not to mention getting to see the creative nature of the designs of the finalist productions, could have served the fledgling artistic director better than fledgling actor Tracy may realize.

Nowhere is the marriage of the professional and the university in the American theater rendered in higher relief than in URTA, the University Resident Theatre Association, the newest acronym on the block in 1969.[53] URTA emerged at a conference sponsored by the Johnson Wax Foundation in Wisconsin; the meeting was organized by Keith Engar, executive director of the Department of Theatre at the University of Utah. The assemblage brought together forty "leaders of university professional drama programs" to form a special division within the American Educational Theatre Association.[54] From the outset, the idea that professional theater already existed within American universities was asserted without being precisely defined. Likewise, the assumption that government and foundation support would be the organization's lifeblood was taken for granted.

In 1970 the first issue of the URTA newsletter laid out its mission. "The premise of URTA," stated on the opening page, "is that the University is the ideal patron for professional theatre . . . and that, like other professions, together we can achieve the strength and support from state and federal sources to become the backbone of the American professional theatre."[55] University=patron of the professional; being professional requires state and federal funding; patron will seek that funding while claiming to be both artist (professional) and outside supporter (patron). This canny Möbius strip of logic depends on the privilege of using *"professional"* very flexibly. The unified auditions, which allow students and some early professionals to audition for graduate programs and other university-sponsored theaters, were (and remain) at the heart of URTA's mission. (This is the audition about which Tracy is stressing.) Within a year, URTA had garnered grants from Rockefeller and NEA, both to help support regional auditions in New York, Chicago, Memphis, and San Francisco.[56]

What students were auditioning for was a tangled web of possibilities, not all resembling each other. In the early years, for example, the University of Northern Colorado auditioned students for a summer season in a nonunion company that had "featured guest stars Katharine Haughton [*sic*] and Jeremiah Sullivan on actor-teacher contracts." At Florida State, affiliated with the unquestionably professional Asolo State Theatre Company, the setup included eleven Equity actors, thirteen administrative staff, and sixteen technical staff, plus fifty Florida State students during the year. What the students got to do is not specified. The University of Minnesota Theatre Company operated the Peppermint Tent for Children during the summer and the University Theatre during the entire year. The "resident company" of the University of Utah Pioneer Theatre Company comprised primarily graduate students on stipends, "but guest artists are brought in."[57]

Students make up the cast in "professional" companies; "guest artists" are somehow more or better or different professionals, and sometimes they are teaching the other "professionals." This use of quotation marks is not only mine. When *Variety* reported on URTA's work, its headline was "U.R.T.A. Subsidizes 'Professional' Training."[58] The URTA informational brochure for the 1971–72 auditions announces auditions for "engagements in university professional theatres." Nearly all the positions were for students who would be getting scholarships for coursework or credit leading to graduate degrees in theater. (The sole exception was the Annenberg Center at the University of Pennsylvania, whose description reads, "The Center is an experimental laboratory in theatre for professionals and highly committed non-professionals. It is not a school with students or admission requirements."[59]) Musicals, summer theater, European classics, American realism. In this protean profile, the new (university-affiliated) professional theater resembled the old one (Broadway and stock), albeit in dispersed (and young) form. The idea of being a laboratory—one of the university's traditional roles—was the exception, not the rule.

University theater programs, whether they supported fully professional theaters on their own campuses or not, did come into their own in the 1960s, with the MFA achieving unprecedented status in this decade as the gateway to professionalism. Between 1960 and 1967 the number of undergraduate theater majors tripled, growing from about fifty-five hundred to eighteen thousand, and twenty schools added graduate programs, so that in 1967 there were 168 institutions offering master's degrees and thirty-eight offering the doctorate.[60] The advent of theater studies fits with the long history of American education moving toward secularization, specialization, democratization, and the practical.[61] A shift among university scholars to reconnect with the public realm characterized much of the progressive academy after World War II, and in the 1960s, theater programs were a part of this trend.[62] As early as 1962, none other than the Ford Foundation's W. McNeil Lowry observed that universities had taken over the training of theater artists but had (ironically?) sacrificed professional standards in so doing. His strong recommendation—noting that the trend was irreversible—was that graduate programs forge ties with professional theaters, indeed, that their "responsibility is to support new forms of cooperation between the university and truly professional institutions in the arts, however small or financially pressed such institutions may be."[63] For Lowry, professionalism had to do with a combination of talent and burning with the proverbial hard, gem-like flame, but he was quick to add that schools unwilling to forge professional ties would do better to toss their students out into the fray and have them learn on the job.

Universities, needless to say, did not do this. Instead, they formed (among other things) URTA. They also retooled their own faculties and standards. In 1966, when the University of Minnesota sponsored a conference whose findings were published with the title "Relationships between Educational Theatre and Professional Theatre," the forty-three participants, drawn from both the academy and industry, had but four MFAs among them.[64] Many, but not all, of the academics held PhDs. Others had cut their teeth in the commercial field. In Jack Morrison's 1973 study of arts on American campuses, only six of seventeen schools profiled in depth required an arts professor to hold an advanced degree in order to have a regular faculty appointment. Two of the six (Harvard and Duke) would allow "equivalent" status in standing or recognition. In the 1960s, in other words, professors of theater had either earned doctorates or had worked in the industry. That changed. As early URTA brochures indicate, many of the financial rewards offered to students for work in "professional" companies came in the form of MFA tuition. Earning the MFA meant achieving professional status. The new training ground for mainstream theater professionals would rapidly become the academy. The academy also absorbed many of its trainees, for all of whom there was not at the outset of these programs, and is not now, sufficient room or demand in the paying theater. The MFA emerged rapidly as the gateway into a career as an artist (actor, director, designer, playwright, dramaturg) or an administrator (although the MBA holds equal sway in the upper echelons of arts administration job titles) or in the academy, where few schools, with the exception of some community colleges, will hire regular faculty without a terminal degree.[65]

As Tracy and Tyler mark time waiting to hear about Tracy's acceptance into an MFA program, they turn to the single 1960s acronym that was always linked to Broadway and the profit-making theater: TDF. The Theatre Development Fund was formed right from the outset as a nonprofit with gifts from the Rockefeller Brothers Fund, the Twentieth Century Fund, and the NEA. Its goal was to support serious plays on Broadway that might, without special help, fail to thrive quickly enough to stay open. The impetus for the organization was a 1966 research report issued by the Twentieth Century Fund that pointed out, "The commercial theater is subject to all the cost pressures which beset noncommercial live professional performance but does not benefit from the growth in giving to the arts."[66] This might be the first historical indication that not-for-profit had replaced for-profit as the most viable business model for most American theater.

TDF's simple function was to purchase tickets at a reduced rate and resell them to schools, teachers, union members, and other groups.[67] By 1972, TDF hit on the idea of creating one-price, all-purpose vouchers that could be used at seventy participating off-off-Broadway theaters, most of them members of OOBA. TDF sold vouchers to its twenty thousand members for $2.50 apiece. Any theater at which a voucher was used received $2.00. TDF used the remaining fifty cents toward its operations and projects. In 1973 it opened a discounted ticket sales booth in Duffy Square, and its sales were no longer linked to particular plays it deemed "worthy." It was a middleman for any show willing to sell discounted tickets on the day of performance. Vouchers and mailings eventually went the way of the rotary-dial telephone; Tracy and Tyler buy their

TDF tickets online. Still, last-minute Broadway offerings don't always show up online, where many of the offerings are off-Broadway or off-off, and the need for something big and special—here a possible last-minute Broadway ticket— may be looming large during the post-audition, nail-biting period.

Every acronym in this chapter stands for an organization that changed the face of the American theater, either right in the 1960s, directly emerging from a 1960s project, or as the result of a growth spurt in that decade. Nonprofit theaters are now among the most visible, sizeable, and posh in the United States. (Indeed, other than addresses outside of Times Square, nonprofit theaters are no more legible as "different" from earlier for-profit models than are nonprofit hospitals from their profit-sharing siblings.) Many nonprofit theaters aspire to and succeed in sending plays to Broadway. Of the forty-five Pulitzer Prizes awarded in drama since 1965, more than thirty have gone to works that originated in an NEA-supported nonprofit theater, including *August: Osage County*, by Tracy Letts, developed at Steppenwolf Theatre in Chicago; *Anna in the Tropics*, by Nilo Cruz, developed by Florida's New Theater and New Jersey's McCarter Theatre; Suzan-Lori Parks's *Top Dog/Underdog*, developed at the Public Theater in New York; and Doug Wright's *I Am My Own Wife*, developed through workshops at Chicago's About Face Theatre and California's La Jolla Playhouse.[68] The alphabet soup that was nouvelle cuisine in the 1960s is now comfort food.

NOTES

1. University Resident Theatre Association, pronounced ER-ta, and sometimes written U/RTA.

2. Master of fine arts. Pronounced EM-EFF-AY. This is regarded in the United States as a terminal, professional degree, analogous for a practitioner to the PhD for a scholar. Yale conferred its first MFA in drama in 1931. See http://drama.yale.edu/history. The first MFA was given in painting by the University of Iowa in 1940. See http://www.lib.uiowa.edu/spec-coll/archives/faq/faqfirsts.htm.

3. American College Theatre Festival. Pronounced AY-SEE-TEE-EFF.

4. Bachelor of fine arts. Pronounced BEE-EFF-AY.

5. National Association of Schools of Theatre. Pronounced "nast."

6. United States Institute of Theatre Technology. Pronounced YOU-ESS-EYE-TEE-TEE.

7. Assistant stage manager, but in this context used as a verb: assistant stage manage. Pronounced AY-ESS-EM.

8. Artistic director. Pronounced AY-DEE. This abbreviation can also mean assistant director. Either one would work for this scene, although as the dialogue progresses the former makes more sense, as it denotes institutional power and oversight.

9. League of Resident Theatres. Pronounced "lort." The designation B+ was added

in 2010 to indicate a theater with a larger budget than theaters in what had previously been a large-B category. (LORT B still exists.) Other categories include D, C, and A+. See www.lort.org.

10. Theatre Communications Group. Pronounced TEE-SEE-GEE.

11. Theatre Development Fund. Pronounced TEE-DEE-EFF.

12. New York State Council on the Arts. Pronounced NISS-Kuh.

13. Foundation for the Extension and Development of the American Professional Theatre. Pronounced FED-apt.

14. Off-Off-Broadway Alliance. Pronounced OO-buh. Changed its name in 1982 to Alliance of Resident Theatres/New York (A.R.T New York; pronounced Art New York).

15. National Endowment for the Arts. Pronounced EN-EE-AY.

16. After more than thirty years of using this entity, I realized I don't know what its letters stand for. Ticket Kiosk Times Square? In fact, while TKTS recognizably says "tickets," the facility was identified in the original TDF memorandum of 1973 as the Times Square Theatre Centre. It's pronounced TEE-KAY-TEE-ESS. See "Times Square Theatre Centre," Memorandum for the League of New York Theatres, TDF, May 3, 1973, clippings file, TDF, New York Public Library, Lincoln Center for the Performing Arts; and Louis Calta, "Discount Ticket: New Role Downtown," *New York Times*, October 3, 1974, 52.

17. Dick Netzer, *The Subsidized Muse: Public Support for the Arts in the United States* (London: Cambridge University Press, 1978), 62.

18. http://www.arts.gov/artistic-fields/theater-musical-theater.html.

19. The National Endowment for the Arts and its twin, the National Endowment for the Humanities, fall under the overall rubric of the National Foundation on the Arts and Humanities. Each of the two endowments has its own individual advisory council, a group that makes final recommendations on individual grants, the first assessments for which are made by discipline-specific panels. See Mark Bauerlein, *National Endowment for the Arts: A History, 1965–2008*, with Ellen Grantham (Washington, D.C.: National Endowment for the Arts, 2009), http://purl.access.gpo.gov/GPO/LPS113863; Alice Goldfarb Marquis, *Art Lessons: Learning from the Rise and Fall of Public Arts Funding* (New York: Harper Collins, 1995); Charles Christopher Mark, *Reluctant Bureaucrats: The Struggle to Establish the National Endowment for the Arts* (Dubuque, IA: Kendall/Hunt, 1991); Livingston Biddle, *Our Government and the Arts: A Perspective from the Inside* (New York: American Council for the Arts, 1988); Netzer, *Subsidized Muse*; and Jack Poggi, *Theater in America: The Impact of Economic Forces 1870–1967* (Ithaca, NY: Cornell University Press, 1968). Clear information about the present-day structure and operations of the NEA are available at www.nea.gov.

20. Theater grants totaled $7,177,000 between 1966 and 1970. The next-highest recipient category in the arts was music, garnering a total of $5,379,000 in the same period. The only program receiving more money than theater in this period was the Federal/State Partnership—the program guaranteeing grants to the state arts councils. This program received $7,405,000. Since some of the state monies likely went to theater, it is clear that theater was the biggest winner in the realm of government funding in the latter half of the 1960s. Compiled from NEA annual reports and reported in Netzer, *Subsidized Muse*, 65. A full list of recipients reveals a stunning array of applicants, including thirty-four grantees under the Professional Experimental Theatre Development rubric, thirty-three Resident Professional Theatres, and an array of other kinds of projects and

nonprofits, including an American Educational Theatre Association-supported survey of secondary school theater (the American Educational Theatre Association was the forerunner to today's Association for Theatre in Higher Education), and professional projects based at Boston University and Brooklyn College. As well, grants were made to children's theater projects and endeavors aimed a school tours. For a full list, see Mark, *Reluctant Bureaucrats*, 221–26.

21. Marquis, *Art Lessons*, 55.

22. I am referring to Morgan Y. Himelstein, *Drama Was a Weapon: The Left-Wing Theatre in New York, 1929–1941* (New Brunswick, NJ: Rutgers University Press, 1963).

23. Netzer, *Subsidized Muse*, 80.

24. New York State Council on the Arts, Mission and Values, http://www.nysca.org/public/about/mission_values.htm.

25. Julia Lowell, *State Arts Agencies 1965–2003: Whose Interests to Serve?* (Santa Monica, CA: RAND, 2004), xi.

26. Prior to 1967, only twenty-two states appropriated any funds to a state arts agency. Netzer, *Subsidized Muse*, 89–90.

27. Marquis notes differences of opinion between W. McNeil Lowry of the Ford Foundation and John D. Rockefeller III concerning many facets of funding and configuring Lincoln Center and, while the Ford Foundation did contribute generously to Lincoln Center, Henry Ford was skeptical about involvement in what he called "a Rockefeller town," even as Lowry, the Ford Foundation's arts expert, thought the Rockefellers to be primarily knowledgeable about real estate and not the arts. Marquis, *Art Lessons*, 20, 30, 37–38.

28. See Marquis, *Art Lessons*; Poggi, *Theater in America*; and Joseph Wesley Zeigler, *Regional Theatre: The Revolutionary Stage* (New York: Da Capo Press, 1973). Broadway acknowledged Lowry's role in the health of the American theater by awarding him a special Tony (Antoinette Perry) Award—Broadway's highest prize—in 1963. Jack Anderson, "W. McNeil Lowry Is Dead; Patron of the Arts was 80," *New York Times*, June 7, 1993.

29. Zeigler, *Regional Theatre*, 183. See also Poggi, *Theater in America*, 231, regarding a shift in Lowry's thinking after the mid-1960s and an acceptance of the idea that deficits were a reality in not-for-profit arts. Lowry was not alone in coming to embrace this idea, which historians of the arts and of financial thinking of the era attribute to the huge influence of *Performing Arts: The Economic Dilemma*, by William J. Baumol and William G. Bowen (New York: Twentieth Century Fund, 1966), whose thesis is that the performing arts are hands-on, labor-intensive endeavors that cannot be mechanized or otherwise made more "efficient." Their costs rise but their ability to streamline or morph into other than what they are is inelastic. Dick Netzer, an economist, calls "the success of this idea . . . mainly a tribute to its internal logic [and the fact that it is] attractive to some arts advocates because it makes a case for open-ended public support for *all* forms of the performing arts, whereas most other arguments call for more limited and, in some cases, diminishing public support" (*Subsidized Muse*, n. 237). Marquis bluntly calls this "advocacy clothed as serious scholarship," pointing to the possibilities of recordings, larger venues, traveling, and other means of maximizing performance endeavors in the interest of *not* remaining in a constant state of deficit (*Art Lessons*, 66–67).

30. Zeigler, *Regional Theatre*, 184.

31. Newman's book *Subscribe Now! Building Arts Audiences through Dynamic Sub-

scription Promotion (New York: TCG, 1977) was considered a nonprofit theater marketing bible for at least a decade.

32. Zeigler, *Regional Theatre*, 236.

33. Bauerlein, *National Endowment for the Arts*, 250.

34. Historians of institutional theater in the 1960s struggle with defining professionalism. Jack Poggi (see especially *Theater in America*, 214–18) tries to use Equity contracts as the division between the professional and the amateur, a benchmark also legible to the Ford Foundation. Yet he acknowledges that some artistically and fiscally successful theaters hit roadblocks when trying to convert to Equity contracts. For Richard A. Peterson, following the pathbreaking work of Paul DiMaggio, the professionalization of arts administration has been the make-or-break criterion for all nonprofit theaters in the wake of the hegemony of the NEA and its model for detailed, record- and report-driven applications. See Peterson, "From Impresario to Arts Administrator: Formal Accountability in Nonprofit Cultural Organizations," in *Nonprofit Enterprise in the Arts: Studies in Mission and Constraint*, ed. Paul J. DiMaggio (New York: Oxford University Press, 1986), 161–83.

35. See Louis Calta, "26 Stage Troupes Form League to Bargain with Actors Equity," *New York Times*, April 1, 1966, 36; and Calta, "New Pact Covers Resident Actors," *New York Times*, September 16, 1966, 33.

36. LORT also has contracts with the directors' and choreographers' union and standard contracts for designers. All contracts, of course, can be amended to offer artists greater than the minimum salary and/or other favorable terms.

37. *Variety*, unsourced clipping dated October 2, 1968, FEDAPT clippings file, New York Public Library, Lincoln Center for the Performing Arts.

38. Susan Bloch, letter dated October 30, 1978, FEDAPT Clippings file, New York Public Library, Lincoln Center for the Performing Arts.

39. "General Information," November 1973, FEDAPT clippings file, New York Public Library, Lincoln Center for the Performing Arts.

40. Ibid.

41. FEDAPT, "Transition in the Not-for-Profit Theatre, 1976," FEDAPT clippings file, New York Public Library, Lincoln Center for the Performing Arts.

42. http://www.artsaction.com.

43. Schneider qtd. in Zeigler, *Regional Theatre*, ix.

44. Zeigler, *Regional Theatre*, 184.

45. Poggi, *Theater in America*, 234. Marquis quotes a 1966 letter from Michael Murray, the artistic director of the Charles Playhouse in Boston, to Jules Irving, then director of Lincoln Center's Vivian Beaumont Theatre: "Murray was dismayed that the musty 'living library' of classical plays, 'tossed out years ago' by progressive directors, was 'now being solidified, institutionalized, and enshrined by business managers and boards . . . the creative possibilities are diminishing . . . something drastic must be done to locate new plays and new audiences—whether that be street theater, black theater, guerilla theater, cinematic theater or what have you.'" Marquis, *Art Lessons*, 84.

46. Poggi, *Theater in America*, 235.

47. Ibid., 236.

48. DiMaggio qtd. in Peterson, "From Impresario to Arts Administrator," 171.

49. Joel E. Rubin, "The First Decade," *Theatre Design and Technology* (Spring 1990): 9, 46–47.

50. "About USITT," http://www.usitt.org/about.

51. Richard L. Coe, "American College Theatre Festival," *Washington Post*, April 10, 1983.

52. David Richards qtd. in Ernest Weatherall, "College Legit Fest—Exposure but No Guarantee of Pro Jobs; Gibson: 'It's a Terrible Life,'" *Variety*, May, 2, 1979, 140.

53. For information on the organization today, visit www.urta.com.

54. University of Michigan, "University Professional Theaters Organize Nationally; Appoint Hatcher and Schnitzer to Executive Posts," news release, December 8, 1969, University Resident Theatre Association clippings file, New York Public Library, Lincoln Center for the Performing Arts.

55. URTA Newsletter, number 1, August 1970, University Resident Theatre Association clippings file, New York Public Library, Lincoln Center for the Performing Arts.

56. URTA, "University Resident Theatre Association Receives Rockefeller Foundation Grant for National Auditions," press release, n.d., University Resident Theatre Association clippings file, New York Public Library, Lincoln Center for the Performing Arts. The press release lists URTA as based at the Mendelssohn Theatre at the University of Michigan and as a division of the American Educational Theatre Association; the document is stamped as received by the New York Public Library on February 24, 1971.

57. URTA Newsletter, number 1, August 1970, pp. 4, 6, 7, University Resident Theatre Association clippings file, New York Public Library, Lincoln Center for the Performing Arts.

58. "U.R.T.A. Subsidizes 'Professional' Training," *Variety*, July 5, 1973, 3.

59. "University Resident Theatre Association Information on Unified Auditions for Engagements in University Professional Theatres for the Season 1971–72," University Resident Theatre Association clippings file, New York Public Library, Lincoln Center for the Performing Arts.

60. Jack Morrison, *The Rise of the Arts on the American Campus* (New York: McGraw-Hill, 1973), 10–11.

61. See William V. Mayville, "Institutional Contexts for Curricular Change," in *Federal Influence on Higher Education Curricula* (Washington, D.C.: American Association for Higher Education, 1980), 27–31.

62. See Ira Katznelson, "From the Street to the Lecture Hall: The 1960s," in *American Academic Culture in Transformation: Fifty Years, Four Disciplines*, ed. Thomas Bender and Carl E. Schorske (Princeton, NJ: Princeton University Press, 1997), 331–52.

63. W. McNeil Lowry, "The University and the Creative Arts," *Educational Theatre Journal* 14.2 (May 1962): 106, 112.

64. "Relationships between Educational Theatre and Professional Theatre: Actor Training in the United States," special issue, *Educational Theatre Journal* 18.3 (November 1966): 309–80.

65. Both Marvin Carlson and Joseph Roach, senior scholars in theater studies who have also worked as designers and directors, see the MFA, following its apotheosization in the 1960s and its entrenchment thereafter, as detrimental to theater departments, which increasingly split their intellectual from their production endeavors, turning their backs on a model in which the two had been wed. Carlson bemoans the "widespread corrupt neo-Romantic assumption (and alas not only in theatre) that all art must come directly from the heart and from inspiration and that thinking or dealing in any way discursively about your art corrupts it." He also points out that many of the MFA pro-

grams started after the 1970s never had any illusion that their graduates would go into professional theater but gave "professional" degrees anyway. Roach derides the "would-be teachers [with MFAs] whose theory was that their practice was self-justifying." See Carlson, "Inheriting the Wind: A Personal View of the Current Crisis in Theatre Higher Education in New York," *Theatre Survey* 52.1 (May 2011): 117–23 (quote on 120); and Joseph Roach, "Reconstructing Theatre/History," *Theatre Topics* 9.1 (1999): 3–10 (quote on 7).

66. William Glover, AP Drama Writer, "Theatrical Angel," August 4, 1968, TDF materials, mwez + n.c. 23, 397, New York Library for the Performing Arts, Lincoln Center Branch.

67. As if proving that acronyms and the nonprofit world were news to Broadway, *Playbill* ran a lighthearted but earnest piece on the organization's benefit to students. The article had the subheading "TDF (Theatre Development Fund) is not a new psychedelic drug but rather a financial shot-in-the-arm for good plays and young audiences." Joan Alleman Rubin, "TDF and 'Mr. Lee's Trip,'" *Playbill* 6 (January 1969): 59–61.

68. Bauerlein, *National Endowment for the Arts*, 251–52.

Susannah Engstrom

Twin Cities Theater in the 1960s

Negotiating the Commercial/Experimental Divide

INTRODUCTION: A NEW THEATER

On May 7, 1963, a trio of trumpeters announced that members of the Twin Cities elite, along with critics and special guests from across the country, all elegantly attired for the opening of the Guthrie Theater's production of *Hamlet*, should take their seats. The evening held much of the glamour of a Broadway premiere, its grandeur signaled by ladies in "satin and mink" and chauffeured cars pulling up to the main doors.[1] Yet despite echoes of openings in New York and Los Angeles, the launching of the Minneapolis theater's four-hour *Hamlet* marked the emergence of something quite different: the professional, nonprofit regional theater. While not the first such institution in the United States, the Guthrie was the original "oak tree," in the words of chronicler Joseph Zeigler, established from the top down, complete upon its founding with substantial financial support from a major foundation and members of the local population.[2] Its opening signaled the beginning of an era in which well-funded, high-profile theater institutions would dot the landscapes of metropolitan centers around the country.

Subsidized professional theaters with a mission to produce drama as high art had existed previously, but the Guthrie represented a new mode of artistic organization, bolstered by powerful foundations, corporations, and eventually government sources, professional in administration and production, adamantly distinguishing itself from both commercial and amateur operations in structure and artistry.[3] Early subsidization followed by the development of a loyal and educated subscription audience was meant to enable risk taking and the production of serious, sometimes unpopular work, impossible for an

251

entity reliant solely on the whims of single-ticket buyers. And the theater's claims to professionalism suggested that those productions would be meticulously conceived and executed, providing the audience with a worthwhile experience and theater artists with artistic opportunity and economic stability. Subsidized and subscription-based professionalism made possible ambitious, time- and resource-intensive endeavors that could not be attempted elsewhere. On the other hand, at times the demands of nonprofit professionalism seemed to stymie the theater's overall goals, minimizing risk taking and depth of artistic production.

The prominence of nonprofit regional theater in the 1960s disturbs the commercial/experimental dichotomy through which most theater of the era has been discussed. Epitomized by the Guthrie, these institutions steered a third path, promising challenging, intellectually ambitious, not necessarily risky but also less than popular work, in locales often far from the artistic center of New York. Yet they were hardly of a different world than the groups more often discussed: the regional theaters incorporated (and helped legitimize) elements of the experimental theater as they became more socially acceptable. And the theaters could not avoid aspects of commercialism; although subsidization promised freedom from the whims of the single-ticket buyer, most supporters required evidence of community support, and theaters relied on box office for a significant share of their income, even after the premise that the theaters would become self-supporting proved unachievable. Furthermore, claims to professionalism seemed to guarantee a certain level of audience experience, a requirement that made risk taking very difficult, as in the commercial theater. And although audiences to a certain degree expected rigorous dramatic material from a theater company that purported to be a civic entity akin to the public library, many also desired the sleek production values of commercial theater and were unwilling to wade into territory they found unpleasant or confusing.

The regional theaters were a distinct breed, but their influence—and particularly their emphasis on professionalism—radiated beyond their own borders. Indeed, the nonprofit professional formula became for many artists in the 1960s the ideal institutional structure. Thus the organizational, social, and aesthetic effects of professionalism were insidious, altering even the work of groups dedicated first and foremost to experimental, antiestablishment theater as they faced new pressures to appeal to funders as well as meet the expectation of audience members increasingly conditioned to expect professional "excellence." Examining the regional theater is therefore important not only to complicate the commercial/experimental binary that dominates discussion of theater in the 1960s but because ultimately this new form left a deep imprint on cultural production more generally. To explore some aspects of this development in detail, this chapter will focus on the Twin Cities, a burgeoning cultural center in the mid-twentieth century, and the endeavors of two groups: the Guthrie, local exemplar of the new professionalism, and the experimental Firehouse Theater.

THE RISE OF NONPROFIT PROFESSIONALISM IN THE TWIN CITIES

Conditions were ripe for the rise of the nonprofit arts sector in Minneapolis and St. Paul in the early 1960s. The region was anchored by the University of Minnesota and a network of surrounding colleges and universities, and a knowledge-based white-collar economy had overrun the cities' earlier industrial base, anchored in flour and sawmills.[4] The cities and surrounding suburbs, the latter expanding at accelerating rates, contained an educated and wealthy potential audience as well as a robust tradition of philanthropy and an active network of foundations and community-minded corporations. At the same time, the growth of suburbia and the deteriorating economic vitality of the central city, problems shared by most midcentury American cities, worried local leaders and politicians, who began searching for ways to reinvigorate their urban cores. The arts, it seemed, might be one way to do so.

The increased attention urban leaders paid to culture converged with what appeared to be a "developing consensus" on the national level among cultural commentators, foundation directors, and numerous politicians and businessmen that Americans, especially those outside of the traditional cultural capitals of New York and California, deserved and in fact required exposure to high-quality, professional art.[5] These sentiments were the product of a Cold War environment that stacked American cultural achievements against those of the Soviet Union, alongside increasing anxieties about declining cultural standards due to mass media and the perceived materialism of America's consumer economy.[6]

This was not the first time Americans hoped to use the arts as a salve. In the late nineteenth and early twentieth centuries urban elites built cultural institutions as a way, scholars have argued, of strengthening their hold over rapidly changing cities; in the Twin Cities this movement gave rise to the Minneapolis Symphony Orchestra and the Minneapolis Institute of Arts.[7] By the early 1960s the Twin Cities could boast a vibrant musical and visual arts tradition, but the region lacked world-class theater, a realm of the arts just beginning to gain legitimacy in the eyes of civic and national leaders. Instead, residents of the Twin Cities region participated in amateur theater organizations, attended the commercial Old Log Theater for a range of plays and musicals, and took in challenging fare through student productions at the University of Minnesota.[8]

Thus when Twin Cities leaders led by University of Minnesota professor Frank Whiting and John Cowles Jr. of the *Minneapolis Tribune* stumbled upon the opportunity to attract one of the great theater directors of their time to the region to found a full-fledged theater institution, they leapt at the chance. A sophisticated theatrical enterprise would be irrefutable evidence that the Twin Cities had arrived on the national cultural scene.

The project that became the Guthrie Theater was born out of an announcement in the *New York Times* in 1959 that famed director Tyrone Guthrie and Broadway veterans Oliver Rea and Peter Zeisler were searching for an American city outside of New York, preferably far from the Eastern Seaboard, where they could establish a professional venue for the production of the great classics of Western dramatic literature. Rejecting the commercialism of Broadway, and perhaps underestimating the rich regional culture of the American Midwest, Guthrie and his colleagues hoped to deliver what they considered high-quality theater to a "grossly under-supplied" city, preferably in the middle of the country, with a major university nearby to provide audiences and financial support.[9] Twin Cities leaders responded enthusiastically to the solicitation and began to court Guthrie, Rea, and Zeisler, rallying the region's philanthropic class. Ultimately, the enthusiasm of these "heirs apparent," as Guthrie called the young leaders, the education level of the area, and most importantly a large gift from the local T. B. Walker Foundation convinced Guthrie, Rea, and Zeisler to choose Minneapolis and St. Paul over contenders including Ann Arbor, Cleveland, and Milwaukee.[10]

Guthrie's proposed theater was to be first and foremost highly professional, employing seasoned actors from New York and perhaps Canada, where his Stratford Festival was located, and producing classic and potentially classic plays. The first season would consist of *Hamlet*, Chekhov's *The Three Sisters*, Moliere's *The Miser*, and Arthur Miller's *Death of a Salesman*. As a repertory company, the theater would provide actors with a full season of work and the opportunity to take on a variety of roles and develop a tightly knit working ensemble, a setup that would result, Guthrie and others believed, in more accomplished performances. Students from the University of Minnesota would join the Guthrie as fellows, injecting some local flavor into the company, but the ensemble would consist mostly of out-of-town professionals.[11] Guthrie believed a nonprofit theater company of this sort, situated in an accepting environment and offering carefully rehearsed productions of great plays, might develop a tradition of professional American theater unlike anything yet achieved.

The Guthrie's emphasis on professionalism matched the priorities of those calling for support for culture on the national level. Only art of the highest quality, according to key establishments like the Ford and Rockefeller Foundations, would prove to the world that America was capable of great cultural accomplishments. This largely unquestioning embrace of professionalism indicated that any major surge in the arts at this time would manifest as the establishment of institutions controlled by board members and funders, rather than development of grassroots, participatory creative involvement. This approach was encapsulated in *The Performing Arts: Problems and Prospects*, an influential 1965 report by the Rockefeller Brothers Fund, which, along with William J. Baumol and William G. Bowen's famous 1966 text *Performing Arts: The Economic Dilemma*, laid out a blueprint for nonprofit professionalism. Prepared by a geographically diverse panel of economic and intellectual leaders, including the Guthrie's Oliver Rea, the Rockefeller report urged a vigorous commitment to support of arts institutions on the part of corporations, foundations, individuals, and the government. With such help, the report claimed, a democracy could produce art just as impressive as that produced under any other form of government, but it added that only *professional* artistic excellence could bolster the nation's prestige.[12] Heralding a national explosion in culture, the panel concluded that "next to this glowing picture must be placed another, more sobering one: *Almost all this expansion is amateur.*"[13]

But what exactly did these figures mean in pressing for professionalism? Of course, in one sense they meant that theater artists would be paid a living wage and therefore able to spend the bulk of their days practicing their craft. Yet even representatives of Actors' Equity, themselves paragons of professionalism, acknowledged this definition to be incomplete, as articulated in a paper prepared for the Rockefeller report: "The concept of the professional as a performer who is paid, as opposed to the amateur who is not paid, is generally put forward as the primary basis for a definition. But . . . quite early in our research we found that such descriptions are meaningless repetitions of a dogma that offers almost no insight into what is meant by those who use the terms 'amateur' and 'professional' in the theatre."[14] Beyond the exchange of money—crucial, to be sure, for artists who found themselves with increasing opportunities to make a living—how were the arts to be identified as professional? And why was such a seemingly vague concept so fervently embraced at this time?

For one, professionalism implied a high level of control over organizational operation and artistic product: the theater would be run by administrative and artistic experts, its productions peopled by trained, skilled performers, designers, and stagehands. Administrative staff would qualify for their positions through experience or education (newly available in emerging arts administration programs); actors would have marked control over their physical and emotional persons, as well as the proper behavioral discipline to work in a professional setting, dutifully realizing the director's conception.[15] Such a process would ensure the carefully managed development of a polished and conceptually unified production as well as reinforce the gap between artists, who were actively immersed in the work, and audience members, watching from a distance.[16]

On an organizational level, professionalism indicated the development of long-standing institutions. The new regional theaters would create the conditions for organizational longevity through careful financial management and, ideally, broad support in the community and beyond. To build and maintain a stable institution, the theaters developed significant staffs of administrative workers and directed increased institutional energy toward administrative rather than solely artistic goals, focusing on marketing, public relations, development, and other areas. While institutionalization had obvious advantages for stability, its tendency toward bureaucratization also presented problems, as presaged by Max Weber and other theorists.[17] Administrative buildup could not help but affect artistic choices, as we shall see, and the kind of predictability and order that institutionalism promised was sometimes at odds with the unpredictable nature of live theatrical performance.

Ultimately, adopting the mantle of professionalism allowed practitioners to claim legitimacy for the kind of theater they promoted. Although scholars like Lawrence Levine trace the sacralization of certain artistic forms to the late nineteenth century, prior to the 1960s powerful societal interests outside of New York City had not yet embraced theater as a high art form akin to music or the visual arts.[18] Thus those who believed theater to be worthy of esteem equal to that afforded orchestras across the country sensed an opportunity to claim jurisdiction, as sociologist Andrew Abbott puts it, over the field of legitimate theater and determine the parameters of the profession.[19] For its most strident supporters, serious theater would not mean participatory amateur work nor popular commercial fare or the untested experiments of the avant-garde. Rather, legitimate theater would be defined as serious productions of meaningful plays, produced by experts and appreciated by respectful audiences. The administration of such professional theaters would align with widely held (although increasingly challenged) values of the day: the utilization of specialized knowledge and expertise within a rational and efficiently run operation.

Determining professional jurisdiction in such a way may have been particularly valuable to those in the early 1960s who were hoping to revive the reputation of urban centers outside of New York. Despite the efforts of artists in the earlier little theater movement, many Americans still considered theater volatile, with the potential to cause social or political disruption. Theater was live and unpredictable, ephemeral, capable of introducing unsavory or dangerous ideas with little warning. Commercial theater, on the other hand, was subject to the crass impulses of the masses, and some still associated it with showgirls and hedonism.[20] The professionalization and institutionalization of theater would help rein in these impulses and align the work of the theater with mainstream values. Supported by upright members of the community, professional theaters would rise above commercial displays and could incorporate edgier elements of the art form while controlling and containing their expression.

THE GUTHRIE THEATER SETS THE STANDARD

At the new Guthrie Theater, these many aspects of professionalism—the opportunity to develop high-quality and elaborate productions and the possibilities and demands of institutionalism, as well as the embrace of values such as control, expertise, and efficiency of administration—were evident at the opening of *Hamlet*. As both the premiere of Guthrie's production and a social event of immense importance for the Upper Midwest and the larger theater world, opening night demonstrated many of the challenges the resident professional theater would face.

The Guthrie's professionalism was manifest in part through the effort to ensure that not only the play but the theater event—the "occasion" of the play—be slickly controlled and composed, capable in this case of attracting not the best actors but the most prominent members of Upper Midwest society. A choreographed opening was important on the one hand for proclaiming the Guthrie's entrance to the cultured world but also because it would signify that dramatic art was worthy of lavish celebration; it would be a "social signal," in Raymond Williams's words, that theater was Art.[21] "In addition to what goes on on our stage, it is equally important that we knock everybody's eyes out in and around the theatre for that period of time," Oliver Rea instructed board chair Roger Kennedy. "People should not feel that they are <u>just</u> seeing a show. They should be made to feel the magnitude of the occasion."[22] As much as Guthrie insisted on the nonpretentious quality of his work, as much as the theater's founders proclaimed their art to be for all the community, the opening night of *Hamlet* was a spectacle of midwestern wealth and extravagance. Attendees dressed to see and be seen: "Mrs. Roger G. Kennedy plans to wear chiffon and lace in shades of pink," the *Twin Citian* attested in a preview article, and Mrs. Robert van Fossen chose "shocking pink slippers, a twilight blue stole, and twilight blue gloves."[23] In the audience was "almost everybody who is anybody in state and local government, the music and art worlds, and society."[24]

These were not everyday attendees for the Guthrie, but they were an audience to which the theater had to cater in order to exist financially as a major institution. Such elite patrons were crucial for their connections to funders, for the press exposure they promised, and because they would become the base of a loyal subscription audience. While foundation and corporate support did in some ways free the theater from the ups and downs of individual ticket sales, it did not provide total insulation from the market. Large entities like Ford and Rockefeller did not want to be the sole, continual funders of any artistic organization, but saw themselves as funding catalysts, inspiring others to donate. Thus any funded entity had to prove itself more widely desirable by showing that it could maintain significant box office sales.[25]

As the wealthy, educated population of the Twin Cities region was most likely to attend the theater, the Guthrie could not afford to ignore it. The challenge was to balance solicitation of elites with claims that the theater existed for everyone, demonstrating that theater could be simultaneously glamorous and democratic, classy and unpretentious. This endeavor entailed convincing potential audiences "that the Guthrie Theatre is *not* so highbrow, cultural, classic, intellectual and socially oriented that they cannot enjoy it, *without* destroying the highbrow, cultural, classic, intellectual and social appeal that is necessary to keep the Yeses [the assured high-art audience] in the fold."[26] Yet scenes of women in ball gowns were not easily forgotten, and like most regional theaters, through its early years the Guthrie's audience consisted predominantly of the upper-middle-class, well-educated sector. The Guthrie staff later tried to reverse the image these opening nights displayed, but the pattern was largely set.[27]

In any case, one wonders how the august attendees at the opening night of *Hamlet* felt about their carefully chosen ensembles when they spent the bulk of the evening sitting in the dark, looking primarily not at each other but at the stage. Indeed, the awkward fit between audience expectations for an exciting and celebratory night and the production of a contemplative work of dramatic literature was painfully clear to Guthrie himself: "What this audience at this moment wanted was a bullfight, or a belly dancer going far too far, or two heavyweights bashing the daylights out of each other. . . . What they were going to be asked to give was four hours of solid, concentrated attention."[28] Much of the audience, Guthrie recalled, began to fidget.

Yet Guthrie's *Hamlet* was not a sleepy production. In many ways unorthodox, it employed modern dress (still a relatively new idea), tennis rackets, umbrellas, and flashlights—sometimes pointed through the audience—"touches of wild anachronism," which according to one critic included an African American actor in the role of Horatio.[29] The production took advantage of the thrust stage, which Guthrie had insisted on in the construction of the theater, incorporating movement even into soliloquies and letting audience members see one another out of the corners of their eyes and take an active part in imagining the play's settings, a constant reminder that theater was illusion, as Guthrie, who despised naturalism, insisted.[30] The thrust stage also allowed audiences to easily take in what some critics disparagingly referred to as stage "business," such as Claudius sneaking bullets out of Laertes's gun or characters grabbing drinks from cocktail carts. Some critics found the production brilliant and refreshing, a dusting off of a tired classic; others thought it obfuscating and gimmicky, in the words of one disgusted critic, "absurdly and arrogantly over-directed."[31]

Through his directorial choices Guthrie hoped to deromanticize Shakespeare and present *Hamlet* as fresh and relatable, a goal he believed achievable only through "constant experiment" in production.[32] Although he could not ignore the audience's interests, the theater's organization as a subsidized entity may have afforded Guthrie a measure of freedom to experiment in such a way. More importantly, such a setup allowed him to use an almost entirely uncut version of Shakespeare's text, something that would be nearly impossible to support in the commercial theater. Yet such seriousness of artistic purpose, which the nonprofit resident theater enabled, was incongruous with the theater's function as a social realm, as illustrated by the misalignment between audience expectations and the theater's delivery. Although the Guthrie hoped its audience would become educated to better appreciate its artistry, this discrepancy would prove a constant problem for the professional regional theater.

The production of opening night as a social event also revealed the centrality of administrative functions for the new theater. A highly developed and complex operation from the get-go, the Guthrie immediately directed significant energy toward nonartistic goals. Along with administrators in areas such as audience development, marketing, and publicity, contributions from foundations, corporations, and government sources required staff members dedicated to relationships with supporters. The need for such administrators was underscored by funders' expectations for what they considered professional behavior from theaters: timely production of budgets and reports, systematized management of staff, and a polished, digestible presentation of organizational identity. "Quite frankly," stated David Rockefeller, "it has been my observation that some cultural organizations don't always make the most intelligent and forceful case for themselves when they seek corporate support. . . . Even the most public-spirited corporation has, I think, a right to expect the organization seeking its help to prove that it has competent management."[33] Such apparently reasonable demands placed new pressures on arts organizations to maintain careful control over their administrative management.

The organizational changes demanded by professionalism influenced the Guthrie's artistic work, despite efforts to keep the arenas separate. Guthrie artistic leaders were continually involved in grant proposals and meetings with donors and foundation representatives, and watched over the audience development measures administrators were using. At the forefront of public relations and marketing, staffers employed surveys and other measures to break audiences down by education level, income, age, and other factors, determining to whom they ought to advertise and in what ways. While attractive to board members and funders, this approach sometimes disturbed artistic personnel such as Douglas Campbell, who insisted that "asking people who come to the theater to fill out some kind of bloody form," as they did for the theater's surveys, was "outrageous."[34] Yet ultimately no one would block tactics that might bring in audiences, and the more successful the techniques used, the more staff was needed to conduct them; increased staff time necessitated further financial support, which necessitated further staff to apply for such support, and on and on in a snowballing fashion.[35]

Some also saw the diversion of energy toward administrative concerns as affecting the aesthetic qualities of productions, resulting in satisfaction with polish, even perhaps superficiality of production, rather than the expected messiness of creative exploration. Playwrights in particular noted a lack of commitment to what they thought should be a deeper artistic process. James Lineberger, playwright in residence with the Guthrie in 1966, thought the theater's work anemic due to its backward prioritization, which asked actors to capitulate wordlessly to the whims of the director and the institution, "to whom the highest values would appear to be health, happiness, family, good speech, and a fair income, in that approximate order."[36] In other words, the Guthrie prioritized survival rather than art. Fellow playwright Fred Gaines agreed: "The Guthrie is turning out to be about what I expected: a packaging house of enormous proportions. We turn out highly polished and very expensive products but that doesn't change the basic nature of our production line. This must be the most expensive theater in America and the least ambitious."[37] Critics noticed similar effects: in 1964 Don Morrison thought the actors in *The Glass Menagerie* "seemed to be reciting lines" and noted "the absence of spark and a sense of life" in the play as a whole, and the *Times* of London called the Guthrie's 1966 season "businesslike."[38] The bureaucratic, rationalized approach of the institutional theater seemed, in these cases, incompatible with an art form widely understood as an exploration of human experience and connection.

Such challenges did not mean that the Guthrie prized only security in its artistic endeavors. The theater found ways to dabble in riskier work, for instance through collaboration, as early as 1964, with the Office for Advanced Drama Research (OADR), a Rockefeller-funded program run through the University of Minnesota that matched new plays with area theaters to develop workshops or full productions. In its collaborations with the OADR, the Guthrie worked with such writers as Megan Terry and Rochelle Owens, with whom it helped craft the famously controversial *Futz*. Commitment to workshops was relatively harmless, as the Guthrie neither promised nor delivered full productions.[39] In 1968, however, the Guthrie took a bolder step in its work with experimentalism by opening a second stage, the Other Place, to develop and produce work like *The Hostage*, by Brendan Behan, and Beckett's *Krapp's Last Tape*. Yet even this move betrayed ambiguity about experimentalism, cordoning it off in a small, less prestigious space. Through the Other Place and work with the OADR the Guthrie contributed to the development of experimental work and remained in touch with new theatrical currents without hazarding too much financially or challenging too seriously the tastes of its audiences or funders.

Rather than ideal venues for the exploration of experimental work, nonprofit professional institutions were perhaps best suited to large-scale productions of ambitious classical works, equally difficult to produce in the commercial theater or through a smaller entity with limited funding. In the Guthrie's early years, this kind of project was epitomized by the theater's three-hour production of Aeschylus's massive *Oresteia*, complete with accompanying symposia, lectures, and demonstrations to help audiences appreciate the work. The production took years of planning, which included the commissioning of a more accessible translation and intricate costume and scenic design. Initially imagined in 1963 and planned for 1965, the three-play cycle, renamed *The House of Atreus* and consolidated into one long evening, did not open until 1967.

The House of Atreus, it was noted with pride, presented an enormous challenge for the theater and the community, one that seemed best undertaken by professionals with skill, training, and expertise: "It will make great demands upon the energies of all concerned, whether as performers or audience," Guthrie claimed, heralding the regional theater's responsibility to present serious, even difficult work.[40] Made possible by an influx of resources from major funders, the investment on the part of artists in both conceptual development and rehearsal would take considerable time, time most likely impossible to accommodate in a commercial or even an academic production. In the new situation of the non-profit institution, however, "a professional production under experienced auspices in uniquely favorable economic conditions" was possible.[41] The Guthrie's ambitious endeavor—grandiose and expensive but hardly controversial—was very attractive to funders and gained support from the Ford Foundation, the National Foundation on the Arts and the Humanities, and many smaller entities.[42] Acclaimed by audiences and critics, the production toured to New York and was revived in Minneapolis the next year. "In the production of *The House of Atreus*," wrote critic Don Morrison, "everything that the Guthrie troupe can do and be comes together in shining splendor. All the manifold resources of the company are mobilized for a stunning and powerful experience."[43]

PROFESSIONALISM AND EXPERIMENTALISM: THE CASE OF THE FIREHOUSE THEATER

While the Guthrie revealed the opportunities and obstacles a professional non-profit entity might encounter, theaters fully devoted to experimental work also faced challenges in confronting the new professionalism. In Minneapolis, the Firehouse Theater, an avant-garde group directed by Open Theatre alumnus Sydney Walter, found itself in a tricky position by the mid-1960s. Established as an amateur organization in 1963 and devoted to the production of bold, defiant, even radical theater—from absurdist playwrights to collaboratively created, non-text-based works—the group's leaders quickly determined that in order to produce such work in a way that would meet rising audience expectations and satisfy their own desire for higher-quality performance, they needed to spend increased time in rehearsal, hire more skilled artists, and expand their season.[44] As the Guthrie Theater demonstrated, nonprofit professionalism seemed the path to follow. Yet for members of the Firehouse, the problems of American society, which they pledged to resist through their work, were in many ways epitomized by the institutional Guthrie and the managerial class that financed it. To build an organization capable of paying its actors and devoting full days to rehearsal but committed to producing work that questioned the status quo, would the Firehouse have to compromise its principles? As Jack Poggi put it in his analysis of theater economics, in trying to achieve professional standards, "the danger is that the rebels will become like their enemies."[45]

The problem of appealing to mainstream sources of revenue was reinforced by the Firehouse's oft-articulated aim to break down the barriers between theater and daily experience, to fulfill Artaud's plea to "protest against the idea of culture as distinct from life."[46] "The Firehouse has no intention of making a convenient separation between the problems of art and the problems of society," wrote Sydney Walter in 1966.[47] This conviction would discount any differentiation between criticism of mainstream society within productions and collusion with that society outside of them, a potentially debilitating stance in a milieu in which foundation, corporate, and government financing was becoming de rigueur. Although the theater faced such a contradiction from the very beginning in that it received early support from the family money of cofounder Marlow Hotchkiss, the son of a wealthy businessman, this unsolicited financing was probably easier to justify than direct pleas to powerful funders.

To make matters more difficult, the Firehouse emphasized the permeation of borders in ways that were sometimes hard to reconcile with professional ideals. One method of integration was through audience participation, erasing the boundaries between performers and audience members and creating an immersive artistic experience. Doing so, company members hoped, would ensure that audiences carried the plays' ideas with them into the rest of their lives, informing their political, social, and economic choices. The atmosphere of collective exploration created in the theater, the "sacrifice of . . . individual egos" involved in collaborative work, would remain with attendees when they left.[48] The Firehouse thus not only embraced participation but also tried to eliminate any visible transition between the performance and the rest of the day. In *Rags*, for instance, the actors faded off stage, with no house lights to indicate the end: "no one claps—there must be more . . . then someone reaches for his coat; another claps embarrassedly."[49]

Such performance techniques fit well with the Firehouse's use of "transformation theater," a newly popular style, pronounced in the work of Megan Terry and Jean-Claude van Itallie, in which actors moved fluidly between characters, illuminating the unsolidified, inconsistent nature of human existence. As Walter noted, "The character is approached entirely through his drives, rather than his characteristics. No attempt is made to achieve consistency. . . . The result is more like a collection of characters springing from one human being," or a number of beings inhabiting one character.[50] In the company's interpretation of *Antigone*, for instance, various actors assumed the title role at different times, offering multiple perspectives on the character.[51] This technique underscored not only the mutability of human experience but the possibilities for change in all realms of society.

The Firehouse's controversial 1969 interpretation of *Faust* presented a culmination of the theater's creative method, demonstrating its devotion to fluidity, spontaneity, and the entangling of performers and audience. For a theater struggling to retain its rebellious soul while requesting money from establishment sources, *Faust* was an apt choice. But the Firehouse did not tell the tale in a straightforward way; instead, participants slipped in and out of roles and the audience was called on to shape its own experience. Asking entering audience members if they wanted to "see Faust or to be Faust," the ensemble continued throughout the production to draw them, willingly or unwillingly, into their creation. The production was not necessarily meant to be enjoyable, as the company poured forth words and images, immersing participants in an intense sensory experience: "The audience is assaulted, embarrassed and backed against the wall," wrote critic Mike Steele, "to the point where only the masochistic remain."[52] Audience members sat on the floor, "in a theater devoid of circulation and permeated by body smells."[53] After two hours, performers asked audience members if they would like to stay to experience it all again; some did, others happily left.

Such blending of audience and performers challenged the professional precept that performers were skilled experts distinct from the lay audience. More so, aggressive audience participation and non-narrative work made many observers uncomfortable, and while the Twin Cities had a substantial countercultural and student community on which to draw, the Firehouse could not possibly attract wide enough support to fund such work through the box office. In theory if not financially, Twin Cities leaders supported the Firehouse—Oliver Rea and Mayor Arthur Naftalin penned notes of support for the theater to use in its appeals to donors—and it was generally appreciated by local critics, who showed patience in the face of less-successful productions: "Experiments are risky," critic Mike Steele explained. "Sometimes you conquer nuclear power while modestly seeking a dandruff remover, and sometimes you blow up the whole laboratory."[54] Despite this support, however, it remained impossible to raise large enough amounts through ticket sales to produce professional-level work, let alone pay adequate salaries.

Thus, while appealing to foundation and government funders caused internal struggles—former Firehouse member Martha Boesing recalled heated discussions over whether to accept "dirty money" from the National Endowment for the Arts—the company ultimately determined that such support was necessary.[55] Over the years it received minor gifts from local foundations, but the theater's limited box office remained problematic in an era of matching grants, when, for instance, a $10,000 gift from the National Endowment for the Arts, which the theater received in 1967, demanded equal funds from the community. And for a company that needed basic operating support, foundation missions were sometimes unhelpful, as Nancy Walter of the Firehouse expressed to Norman Lloyd at the Rockefeller Foundation: "You said that you had to finance an expanded activity of the theater or make possible a project that was not otherwise possible for the theater. . . . I am puzzled about how the Firehouse Theater can present such a proposal to you." But, she added, "we desperately need outside support."[56]

Beyond the difficulties caused by restricted audience appeal, the ideals of transformation theater—movement, mutability, change—were difficult to square with professionalism on another level. While it was able to demonstrate the principles of transformation within its performances, the need to present a coherent, legible identity for public consumption and grant applications curtailed the theater's potential to embody this philosophy on an organizational level. Unlike the Open Theatre, which Joseph Chaikin described as "in process" and which refused to pigeonhole itself organizationally, members of the Firehouse worked to present a cohesive identity.[57] In part the theater did this by accepting its role as part of a long historical tradition. A 1965 Firehouse artistic statement claimed, "Every society that has not thoroughly stagnated spawns an artistic avant garde. It is this avant garde, with its new voice, that expresses the development of the society. Orthodox art affirms the continuing values; avant garde [art] celebrates or criticizes the new values."[58] The Firehouse had a clear role to play in the Twin Cities as the critical sister to the Guthrie's orthodoxy. Its relationship with the Guthrie was therefore more complementary than confrontational. Promising not to "concern itself primarily with direct criticisms of social institutions," the Firehouse would not upend the social order but instead would feed ideas into circulation.[59] "Of all the experimental theaters working in America today," Firehouse artist Nancy Walker assured the Rockefeller Foundation, "ours has one of the strongest possibilities of revitalizing the theater, of influencing through the back door the work of the Guthrie Theater."[60]

By the end of the 1960s, however, the Firehouse was beginning to fill a rather dependable role within Twin Cities society. "The past few Firehouse performances have become what I never thought they would, predictable," wrote Mike Steele in 1969. "There's the opening music, usually chanting . . . there's the clash of chords as the play starts, the racing about screaming words, the group grope, the confrontation of audiences, the quiet talk, then the self-conscious nudity."[61] By the end of the decade the Firehouse was becoming a venue through which audiences could get their fill of the now faddish radicalism, rather than take the theater's ideas seriously. "It seems to me there is a rising percentage of obviously wealthy, slick, heavily made up establishment types," noted one critic of the changing Firehouse audiences. "They come in dressed for slumming, flouncing their Edwardian shirts and $100 Dayton's mod apparel. You can see they think themselves ever so 'in' as they wait with obvious glee for the real live hippies to take off their pants."[62] The Firehouse artists desired a diverse audience that would reflect on their shows, not those who came for a predictably audacious spectacle.[63] But as a semiprofessional theater, attracting an audience of any kind was necessary. Like its board member Gordon Morris, who described himself as wracked by "schizo twins pulling on me," one in the direction of stable family life and one toward exploration and experimentation, the Firehouse found itself teetering between two poles, and not particularly satisfied with the balance.[64]

In the end, the difficulties of staying true to a vision of uniting "art and the problems of society" in an increasingly professionalized artistic world may have lessened the Firehouse's enthusiasm for continuing in the Twin Cities.[65] At the close of 1969 the Firehouse was evicted from the building it had occupied since the early sixties and replaced by a furniture store, an indication of the fickle relationship between Twin Citians and their primary avant-garde theater. The Firehouse leaders, claiming they had been dissatisfied with Minneapolitan audiences for some time, took the eviction as an opportunity to leave the Midwest. They headed to San Francisco, where the theater promised a new approach, living communally—"a social experiment to complete the artistic experiment"—and trying to more directly engage audiences in a search for a new way of life.[66] Without much funding or community support, however, and facing internal divisions, the Firehouse soon folded. It was not alone in its frustrations. Across the country, avant-garde theater groups struggled to reconcile their missions with the necessities of professionalization. The Open Theatre closed rather than appeal obsequiously to the mainstream. And Judith Malina, faced with the possible loss of foundation support, claimed the Living Theatre would become "a theatre not so dependent on fund-raising campaigns. I don't know how yet, or where," demonstrating what a struggle it was to imagine a theater existing without such support.[67]

CONCLUSION: THE CONTRIBUTION OF NONPROFIT PROFESSIONALISM

In cities across America, from Minneapolis to Milwaukee to Dallas to Louisville, nonprofit professional theaters presented new possibilities for those interested in producing or participating in the many varieties of theatrical art. The new framework was meant to solve the perceived problems of the existing theater, gather prestige locally and nationally, fulfill the needs of ostensibly culture-deprived Americans, and provide a space for the development of serious artistic productions. Nonprofit professionalism was a boon to artists hoping for a professional career to gain support and security for their work, and it enabled the production of theater that otherwise might not have been attempted, including ambitious productions of important theatrical works like *Oresteia*. But professional institutions were not the solution to all the problems they were meant to address. Rather than lessen pressure on theaters to cater to audiences, they resulted in organizations with marketing and development departments that concentrated all of their energy on finding audiences and pleasing donors. Although they provided a safer platform to develop challenging work, many regional theaters relied for their box office on safer classical work or already-proven Broadway or off-Broadway hits, while groups devoted to experimentalism were both attracted to professionalism and unable to fully achieve it. And while advocates often claimed that professional arts organizations would benefit their entire community, due to various pressures and motivations they in fact catered largely to a very specific segment of the population.

In later years artists would begin to develop new approaches to professionalism, building hybrid semiprofessional structures and finding niche audiences to which they could offer unconventional fare. By the 1970s many major funders, in turn, began to widen their focus and to support work developed from or aimed at minority audiences. Yet the framework of nonprofit professionalism established in the mid-1960s, and the kind of work it yielded, set the initial pattern that much of the cultural production of the rest of the century would follow.

NOTES

1. Margaret Morris, "Guthrie Theater Has Glittering First Nighters," *Minneapolis Star*, May 8, 1963; and Margaret Morris, "An Evening to Remember," *Sunday Suburban Life*, May 12, 1963. For the first few years of its existence, the repertory company founded by Tyrone Guthrie was called the Minnesota Theatre Company, a name chosen in part to emphasize that the theater belonged to all Minnesotans, not just Minneapolitans or even Twin Citians. For purposes of clarity, I will refer to the Minnesota Theatre Company as the Guthrie Theater throughout this paper.

2. Joseph Zeigler, *Regional Theatre: The Revolutionary Stage* (Minneapolis: University of Minnesota Press, 1973), 62.

3. The regional professional theaters fit the mold of the "high culture model," as defined by Paul DiMaggio, which segmented "serious" art from commercial culture through entities subsidized by trustees and exempt from taxation and was employed by certain theaters in a limited way during the first half of the twentieth century. I believe, however, that the regional professional theaters that emerged in the 1950s and 1960s were a new and much more influential model with much more powerful societal support. Paul DiMaggio, "Cultural Boundaries and Structural Change: The Extension of the High Culture Model to Theater, Opera, and Dance, 1900–1940," in *Cultivating Differences: Symbolic Boundaries and the Making of Inequality*, ed. Michele Lamont (Chicago: University of Chicago Press, 1992), 22.

4. For the political and economic history of the Twin Cities, see, for instance, Elizabeth Faue, *Community of Suffering and Struggle: Women, Men, and the Labor Movement in Minneapolis, 1915–1945* (Chapel Hill: University of North Carolina Press, 1991); William Millikan, *A Union against Unions: The Minneapolis Citizens Alliance and Its Fights against Organized Labor* (St. Paul: Minnesota Historical Society Press, 2001); John Earl Haynes, *Dubious Alliance: The Making of Minnesota's DFL Party* (Minneapolis: University of Minnesota Press, 1984); Charles Rumford Walker, *American City: A Rank and File History of Minneapolis* (Minneapolis: University of Minnesota Press, 2005).

5. "Developing consensus" is from Rockefeller Brothers Fund, *The Performing Arts: Problems and Prospects, Rockefeller Panel Report on the Future of Theatre, Dance, Music in America.* (New York: McGraw-Hill, 1965), 4.

6. Writers and intellectuals like Paul Goodman and Dwight MacDonald were at the center of such anxiety, fearful that Americans were filling up their increased leisure time with meaningless, wasteful activities. On competition with the Soviet Union and the importance of culture domestically, see articles like Frank Thompson, "Are the Communists Right in Calling Us Cultural Barbarians?," *Music Journal* 13.6 (July–August 1955): 5; "The New Role for Culture," *Life Magazine*, December 26, 1960; "New World Prepares to Show Its Cultural Achievements to Old World," *New York Times*, March 11, 1958. On American cultural programs abroad, see, for instance, Frances Stone Saunders, *The Cultural Cold War: The CIA and the World of Arts and Letters* (New York: New Press,

2000); Penny von Eschen, *Satchmo Blows Up the World: Jazz Ambassadors Play the Cold War* (Cambridge, MA: Harvard University Press, 2004); Laura A. Belmonte, "Exporting America: The U.S. Propaganda Offensive, 1945–1959," in *The Arts of Democracy, Art, Public Culture, and the State*, ed. Casey Nelson Blake (Philadelphia: University of Pennsylvania Press, 2007) 123–50.

7. For the earlier phase of institutionalization see for instance Paul DiMaggio, "Cultural Entrepreneurship in Nineteenth-Century Boston," in *Nonprofit Enterprise in the Arts: Studies in Mission and Constraint*, ed. Paul DiMaggio (New York: Oxford University Press, 1986) 41–62; Helen Lefkowiz Horowitz, *Culture and the City: Cultural Philanthropy in Chicago from the 1880s to 1917* (Lexington: University Press of Kentucky, 1976); Steven Conn, *Museums and American Intellectual Life: 1876 to 1926* (Chicago: University of Chicago Press, 1998); Kathleen McCarthy, *Noblesse Oblige: Charity and Cultural Patronage in Chicago, 1849–1929* (Chicago: University of Chicago Press, 1982). Neil Harris traces a shift in the nineteenth century similar to the one I am interested in from "participation to . . . certification," with a "new interest in achievement and cosmopolitan excellence." *Cultural Excursions: Marketing Appetites and Cultural Tastes in Modern America* (Chicago: University of Chicago Press, 1990), 19–21.

8. For an overview of theater in the Twin Cities, see Frank M. Whiting, *Minnesota Theatre: From Old Fort Snelling to the Guthrie* (St. Paul: Pogo Press, 1988).

9. Tryone Guthrie, *A New Theatre* (New York: McGraw-Hill, 1964), 36.

10. Ibid., 58.

11. According to an early Guthrie publicity pamphlet, "the cast will be all-professional, coming from Broadway, London, and Canada," thereby discounting any local hopefuls beyond the University of Minnesota fellows who, after years of training, might have had a chance at joining the ensemble. "Facts about the Tyrone Guthrie Theatre Project," Administrative Files, 1961, Guthrie Theater Archives (PA3), Performing Arts Archive, University of Minnesota Libraries, Minneapolis (hereafter PAA).

12. Rockefeller Brothers Fund, *Performing Arts*, 12.

13. Ibid., 14.

14. Dick Moore and Jack Golodner, "The Amateur and the Professional in the American Theatre," prepared for the Special Studies Project, Box 573, Unprocessed Material, RG3, Rockefeller Brothers Fund Archives, Rockefeller Archive Center, Sleepy Hollow, New York (hereafter RAC).

15. Or as Theodore Hoffman dryly put it, "Don't criticize anyone, be a pollyana, and treat the producer as an invaluable avuncular sage." Theodore Hoffman, "Report on the Training of Actors," submitted to the University of Minnesota for the Conference on the Education and Training of Actors, May 1965, Administrative Files, 1965, Guthrie Theater Archives (PA3), PAA. Nick Salvato has discussed the ways in which professionalism connotes mastery over one's body and emotions, whereas excessive effusion is associated with both amateurism and effeminacy, themselves inextricable in his definition. Salvato, "Out of Hand: YouTube Amateurs and Professionals," *TDR* 53.3 (Fall 2009): 67–83.

16. Raymond Williams points out the connection between the rise of managerial power in the labor market and the ascent of the director in the theater: "The 'producer,' 'director' or 'manager' emerged when wholly coordinated production not only of the acting but of new staging techniques, including new kinds of design and lighting, was seen as necessary and desirable. . . . The new role rapidly increased in importance until by the mid-twentieth century the director could see himself, and was often seen by oth-

ers, as the central productive figure." *The Sociology of Culture* (Chicago: University of Chicago, 1981), 114. By the late 1960s, however, the role of the director was also widely challenged, as collaboratively-produced theater grew in popularity.

17. Weber's contention that bureaucracy essentially means "without regard for persons," in that offices are not contingent on the people who inhabit them, may have particularly important implications for the arts, where the expressive acts of performance would have little to do with the administrative structures that control them. *From Max Weber: Essays in Sociology* (New York: Oxford University Press, 1958), 215.

18. Lawrence Levine, *Highbrow/Lowbrow: The Emergence of Cultural Hierarchy in America* (Boston: Harvard University Press, 1990).

19. Andrew Abbott, *The System of Professions: An Essay on the Division of Expert Labor* (Chicago: University of Chicago Press, 1988).

20. Susan Harris Smith attributes the lag in accreditation given theater to a convergence of related factors, including "a fear of populist, leftist, and experimental art . . . a disdain of alternative, oppositional, and vulgar performances." *American Drama: The Bastard Art* (Cambridge: Cambridge University Press, 1997), 3.

21. Williams, *Sociology of Culture*, 130–31: "The most common kinds of signal are those of *occasion* and *place*."

22. Oliver Rea to Roger Kennedy, December 14, 1962, Administrative Files, 1962, Guthrie Theater Archives (PA3), PAA.

23. Marjorie Ellis McCrady, "A Premiere and Its Pageantry," *Twin Citian*, May 1963.

24. Margaret Morris, "Guthrie Theater Has Glittering First Nighters," *Minneapolis Star*, May 8, 1963.

25. "It would . . . be unwise for the Foundation merely to underwrite artistic deficits or to subsidize a level of activity which could not be maintained when at some future date it becomes necessary for the Foundation to withdraw support." Report prepared for the Rockefeller Brothers Fund's *Performing Arts: Problems and Prospects*, box 1, folder 7, series 911, RG 3.1, Rockefeller Brothers Fund, RAC. In 1965 Richard Schechner was among the first to point out this problematic situation: the Ford Foundation, he wrote, "makes of theatre (and the other arts) an *industry*, which, in times of 'depression,' needs only 'pump-priming' until the usual 'laws' of supply and demand can healthily assert themselves." Thus theaters had to continually appeal to those "*currently* most likely to pay for tickets," those already interested in and able to afford theatergoing. Richard Schechner, "Ford, Rockefeller and Theater," *Tulane Drama Review* 10.1 (Autumn 1965): 26–27.

26. Bradley G. Morison and Kay Fliehr, *In Search of an Audience: How an Audience Was Found for the Tyrone Guthrie Theater* (New York: Pitman, 1968), 54.

27. Ibid., chapter 14.

28. Guthrie, *New Theatre*, 109.

29. The *London (Ontario) Free Press*, reprinted in "What Other Critics Said," *Minneapolis Tribune*, May 8, 1963.

30. The theater, Guthrie claimed, was "interesting and exciting not the nearer it approached 'reality' but the farther it retreated into its own kind of artifice." Qtd. in "If You Like Theater, Listen to Guthrie," *Minneapolis Sunday Tribune*, March 26, 1961.

31. Sydney J. Harris, *Chicago Daily News*, reprinted in "What Other Critics Said," *Minneapolis Tribune*, May 8, 1963.

32. Guthrie, *New Theatre*, 104.

33. "Culture and the Corporation," address by David Rockefeller, box 304, folder 2832, series 200R, RG 1.2, Rockefeller Foundation Archives, RAC.

34. Morison and Fliehr, *In Search of an Audience*, 26. "There were many strenuous but sincere objections during our tenure to efforts to run even one phase of the theatre's operations like a business," Morison and Fliehr wrote at another point. *In Search of an Audience*, 15.

35. "The larger and more complex the operation," explains Jack Poggi, "the more likely a theater is to shift its major emphasis from putting on plays to insuring its growth and survival as an institution." *Theater in America: The Impact of Economic Forces, 1870–1967* (Ithaca, NY: Cornell University Press, 1968), 235. Others have noted the blending of artistic and administrative functions in professional theater companies. See, for instance, Richard Peterson, "From Impresario to Arts Administrator: Formal Accountability in Nonprofit Cultural Organizations," in DiMaggio, *Nonprofit Enterprise in the Arts*, 161–83.

36. James Lineberger, "Sir Tony and the American Dream," *Tulane Drama Review* 10.3 (1966): 182.

37. Fred Gaines to Pat Drake, April 9, 1967, box 3, Correspondence, Frederick Gaines Papers (PA22), PAA.

38. Don Morrison, "*Menagerie* at the Guthrie Just Isn't Moving," *Minneapolis Star*, June 2, 1964. Dan Sullivan also wondered whether the theater's production of *The Glass Menagerie* "isn't a bit too entertaining for its own good," with characters sometimes becoming caricatures. "Guthrie Gives *Menagerie* in Entertaining Version," *Minneapolis Tribune*, June 2, 1964; "London Critic Views Season, Finds Guthrie Still the Best," review from *London Times* reprinted in the *Minneapolis Star*, November 1, 1966. By 1965 commentators were noting a trend of emptiness among regional theaters nationally: "The resident theatre is now facing stultification," as Theodore Hoffman put it in a conference, organized by the *Tulane Drama Review* to discuss the "New Establishment" theater. Richard Schechner, comp., "'The New Establishment?' Fragments of the TDR Theatre Conference," *Tulane Drama Review* 10.4 (Summer 1966): 110.

39. This policy sometimes ran them into trouble with playwrights. Terrence McNally, Arthur Kopit, and Rochelle Owens all ended their collaboration with OADR on sour notes having to do with lack of production or commitment to their work. See, for instance, "U Censorship Is Charged in Play Tryouts," *Minneapolis Tribune*, January 13, 1964; and Rochelle Owens, "An Open Letter to the Minnesota Theatre Company," *Tulane Drama Review* 10.3 (Spring 1966): 209–15.

40. "Dr. Guthrie's Announcement to Board for Future Plans, Oresteia," September 18, 1963, Administrative Files, 1963, Guthrie Theater Archives (PA3), PAA.

41. Ibid.

42. In an announcement of the foundation's matching grant of $45,000, the *Minneapolis Tribune* claimed, "It is estimated that the expense of presenting the trilogy will be about $90,000 in excess of the average cost of production of a play by the company." "Guthrie Players Get $45,000 Grant," *Minneapolis Tribune*, August 30, 1966.

43. Don Morrison, "Guthrie Troupe Mobilizes All Its Resources," *Minneapolis Star*, July 22, 1967.

44. The Firehouse's decision to professionalize is described in a grant proposal from 1965. Box 1, Firehouse Theater Archives (PA70), PAA.

45. Poggi, *Theater in America*, 194.

46. Antonin Artaud, *The Theatre and Its Double* (New York: Grove Press, 1958), 10.

47. "Appendix B: Notes on the Artistic Policy," in September 1966 proposal written by Sydney Walter, box 1, Firehouse Theater Archives (PA70), PAA.

48. Sydney Walter, "Theater Today Must Stage Protest," *Minneapolis Tribune*, March 26, 1967.

49. Judy Galt, "'Rags'—Gripping Chaos," *Minnesota, an Independent Student Publication*, November 27, 1968, Firehouse Theatre Company Archives, D-064, box 2, folder 33, Department of Special Collections, General Library, University of California, Davis (hereafter UC-Davis)

50. "Appendix B: Notes on the Artistic Policy," in September1965 proposal written by Sydney Walter, box 1, Firehouse Theater Archives (PA70), PAA. On transformation theater, see Kerstin Schmidt, *The Theater of Transformation: Postmodernism in American Drama* (New York: Rodopi, 2005); Robert Pasolli, *A Book on the Open Theatre* (New York: Bobbs-Merrill, 1970), in which Pasolli describes the use of the transformation idea in improvisation exercises (20–22). An emphasis on movement vs. stasis, or change vs. rootedness, has been noted as an aspect of postwar theater by other scholars, for instance in the chapter "Changing Decorum" in Marc Robinson, *The American Play: 1787–2000* (New Haven, CT: Yale University Press, 2009).

51. Judy Galt, "'Antigone': Biting, Insightful & Innovative," *Minnesota Daily*, January 17, 1969.

52. Saul Gottlieb, "Awkwardness Is Not a Bad Thing: An Interview with Sydney Walter and Marlow Hotchkiss of the Firehouse Theater, Minneapolis," *The Drama Review: TDR* 14.1 (Autumn 1969): 122; Mike Steele, "Firehouse Gives Its View of Faust," *Minneapolis Tribune*, March 8, 1969.

53. Mike Steele, "Firehouse Gives Its View of Faust," *Minneapolis Tribune*, March 8, 1969.

54. Letters of support from Oliver Rea and Arthur Naftalin to Marlow Hotchkiss, box 1, Firehouse Theater Archives (PA70), PAA; Mike Steele, "Firehouse Theater Introduces Its Own Version of 'Antigone,'" *Minneapolis Tribune*, January 11, 1969.

55. Martha Boesing, interview by author, May 10, 2011.

56. Nancy Walter, Firehouse Theater, to Norman Lloyd, Rockefeller Foundation, June 19, 1968, box 3, folder 3, Firehouse Theater Company Archives, UC-Davis.

57. Chaikin quoted in Kermit Dunkelberg, "Grotowski and North American Theatre: Translation, Transmission, Dissemination" (PhD diss., NYU, 2008), 218.

58. "Notes on the Artistic Policy," appendix to grant proposal, 1965, box 1, Firehouse Theater Archives (PA70), PAA.

59. Ibid.

60. Nancy Walter to Norman Lloyd, Rockefeller Foundation, June 19, 1968, box 3, folder 3, Firehouse Theater Company Archives, UC-Davis. The theatrical techniques the Firehouse introduced to the region were indeed adopted by other companies, as Peter Altman explained in the *Minneapolis Star*: "Almost everybody else in drama has been using the Firehouse's techniques of audience-involvement, mixed-media, and transformational theater." "Time Accentuates Creative Pace of Firehouse Troupe," undated, but most likely October 1968, box 1, folder 83, Firehouse Theater Company Archives, UC-Davis.

61. "Firehouse Introduces Its Own Version of *Antigone*," *Minneapolis Tribune*, January 11, 1969.

62. John Fenn, "Faustus at the Firehouse," *Twin Citian Magazine*, May 1969.

63. In "Playwright Appeals for Varied Audience," Elizabeth Doolittle Johnson, working with the Firehouse, complained of the lack of diversity in the theater's audience: "I write as much for people who attend Doris Day-Rock Hudson movies as for those who attend theater regularly,' she said. 'The only problem is that a general audience doesn't come, for some reason.'" Untitled and undated newspaper clipping, box 6, folder 1, Firehouse Theater Scrapbook: 1963–1968, Firehouse Theater Company Archives, UC-Davis.

64. Mike Steele, "'Gemini' Plays Two Roles," *Minneapolis Tribune*, February 2, 1969.

65. "Notes on the Artistic Policy," appendix to grant proposal, 1965, Box 1, Firehouse Theater Archives, PAA.

66. From *Firehouse Theater: A Spiritual History*, box 3, folder 36, Firehouse Theater Company Archives, UC-Davis.

67. The Open Theatre dissolved when it could no longer retain organizational flexibility: "As the structure called the Open Theatre we can no longer be transitional and in process without ourselves becoming an institution fixed in a single direction, so we are announcing a deliberate end to our work in this particular formation." Dunkelberg, "Grotowski and North American Theatre," 218. Richard Schechner, "Interviews with Judith Malina and Kenneth Brown," *Tulane Drama Review* 8.3 (Spring 1964) 207–19.

Donatella Galella

Making Art and Making Money

Arena Stage in the 1960s

There are other signs that money will not right, but which cannot be
righted without money since money is the exchange commodity of
our life.
    —Zelda Fichandler, "Theatres or Institutions?"[1]

Arena Stage was one of the first companies to navigate the waters of U.S. regional theater. Founded as a for-profit corporation in 1950, Arena filled a niche
in the Washington, D.C., professional theater scene when the National Theatre
went dark rather than admit an integrated cast and audience. Offering popular
fare performed by Equity actors, Arena Stage became the city's first professional
resident theater company. Producing director and cofounder Zelda Fichandler
envisioned a large, in-the-round, public theater that staged entertaining comedies, challenging contemporary works, and classics that spoke to present issues.
She wanted to model European theaters that boasted resident acting companies
and rotating repertories. Most importantly, she needed a permanent home.

To raise funds for these ambitious projects, Arena Stage reorganized as a
nonprofit, a relatively new idea for a theater in 1959 but now a model that has
become dominant for regional theaters. Nonprofit status allowed for more innovation and expansion: larger, stable homes, resident acting ensembles, and
new programming. It did not, however, fix all fiscal problems and permit total artistic license. In the midsixties, Arena Stage and other rising nonprofit
theaters struggled for the first time with rising deficits. With nonprofit status,
Fichandler was able to push the company's physical, aesthetic, and financial
boundaries further than before, yet she had to consider how far she could go
when leveraging the deficit. At times she risked and even disavowed monetary
gains in order to obtain prestige and to experiment, yet a level of financial sustainability provided a foundation for the company. Arena's success in the sixties largely flowed from Fichandler's accumulation and negotiation of different
kinds of capital, particularly with the help of her economically savvy husband
Thomas Fichandler and W. McNeil Lowry of the Ford Foundation.

Critics such as Richard Schechner and Martin Gottfried had initially welcomed regional theaters as alternatives to Broadway in the early sixties. But a mere few years later, they accused artistic directors of selling out by selecting the repertory based on what might thrive on Broadway or receive foundation and government grants. They viewed, in Bourdieuian terms, economic and symbolic capital as antithetical.

In "The Mythologizing of American Regional Theatre," Vincent Landro astutely critiques the critics for romanticizing the origins of regional theater and reifying the idea that a theater can have either artistic or commercial success, "a simplistic bipolar model of theatre history typical of the polarized thinking in the 1960s."[2] Many theaters had set out not to reject Broadway altogether but to develop institutions for professional theater outside of New York City. Moreover, institutionalizing, professionalizing, and maintaining a balanced budget did not necessarily mean reducing artistic standards and experiments.

As this chapter shows by examining the history of Arena Stage through the 1960s and focusing on the intersections of commerce and aesthetics that shaped the extent to which Zelda Fichandler's ideas materialized, money and art cannot be conceived of as mutually exclusive. Arena was initially a for-profit corporation that behaved much like a not-for-profit, thereby troubling these economic terms. Its programming cannot be simplified and categorized into classic moneymakers and avant-garde prestige plays. Political works, for example those by or indebted to Brecht, were often economic and artistic hits with audiences in the sixties. Furthermore, the maintenance of Arena's adventurous endeavors, including the rotating repertory, integrated ensemble, and world premieres, though funded by grants and seemingly free from market forces, were ultimately contingent on the kinds and amounts of capital they produced. In "Theatres or Institutions?," published in 1970, Fichandler articulated the fundamental need for funding, repeating *money* three times because it is the "exchange commodity of our life" in theater. Her wording, in its awkwardness, reflects the complex relationship between art and money, and her theater institution provides a productive site for interrogating that apparent binary and reconsidering regional theater.

FOR-PROFIT IN THE 1950S

In 1950, director and theater professor Edward Mangum and his graduate student Zelda Fichandler cofounded Arena Enterprises, Inc. Representing the generally skeptical attitude toward nonprofit theater in the 1950s, Mangum remarked, "I knew of no one who wanted to contribute his hard-earned cash to a non-profit enterprise as shaky as a legitimate theatre can be. I did know some friends who were willing to gamble on my making a success of a new kind of theatre."[3] They raised $15,000 from forty stockholders, whose occupations ranged from ambassador to carpenter, a point that Arena Stage's own narrative often emphasized to underscore its populist beginnings. The stockholders donated their time to transform an old movie theater, the Hippodrome, into a 247-seat theater-in-the-round.

The company opened with *She Stoops to Conquer* and produced a repertory largely of classics. The first season boasted seventeen productions, including *The Importance of Being Earnest*, *She Stoops to Conquer*, and *Twelfth Night*, which were so popular that they were brought back the next season. Arena gained Equity status after its first year, and Mangum left for other ventures in Hawaii. After four more years with Zelda Fichandler at the helm, the company's corporate worth nearly doubled.[4]

In 1955 Fichandler persuaded the stockholders to move Arena Stage to a larger space, arguing that more seats would generate more income. But she did not intend for the profits to go to the stockholders; rather, the money would go back into the theater because it "has entailed too many hardships, including that of low salaries, the pressures of constant bargain hunting in all departments, and the necessity to make too many artistic judgments on the basis of the dollar sign alone."[5] This was not a typical corporation calculating every decision to increase the value of its holdings and distribute those dividends regularly. Even sold-out runs, such as the Washington premiere of *The Crucible*, lost money, indicating that Fischandler was willing to keep ticket prices low and to produce work for artistic and political reasons at an immediate financial loss. She wanted to make theater affordable for students and the average D.C. resident, and for producing one of her favorite plays, she and her husband were investigated by the FBI. In her five-year report to the stockholders, she also imagined Arena Stage at age ten with a permanent acting ensemble, a playwright in residence, and educational initiatives—programs that later became the purview of nonprofit theaters.

Fichandler appeared to be following the model of another regional theater pioneer: Margo Jones of Theatre '47. In her influential tract *Theatre-in-the-Round*, Jones recognized that a theater set up as a for-profit company could work as long as the investors did not compromise artistic standards for big dividends. Jones, meanwhile, had famously opened her theater as a nonprofit, though theater in general had not yet joined the solidly nonprofit ranks of the symphony and opera house. Jones nevertheless insisted, "Unlike many nonprofit organizations, a theatre should and can make enough money to pay for itself, provided an initial sum is raised to start it."[6] That theaters should raise money principally through capital campaigns, not on an ongoing basis, was a common credo for early regional theaters. Jones's conceptions of for-profit and nonprofit theater were not so different from each other, as reflected in the early years of Arena Stage.

In 1956 Arena Stage moved to a larger space, the Old Vat Brewery, fitted with five hundred seats. But because that building was soon slated for destruction to make way for a new bridge across the Potomac, the company had to move again. This time the company sought permanence and nonprofit status. During a meeting with the board of directors in 1958, Fichandler "pointed out that we were at present in an anomalous position, being set up as a private-profit making venture, and yet by our aims and policy not seriously expecting to make any sizeable private profits, but rather attempting primarily to furnish the Washington area with high caliber theatre fare."[7] Part of gaining nonprofit status entailed Arena's assertion that it was already not in the business of making substantial economic profits but instead focused on profiting the community with professional theater.

At the same time, however, Arena did have a relationship with commercial theater. It gained a reputation for bringing to life shows that had flopped on Broadway, such as the acclaimed Australian drama *The Summer of the 17th Doll*. Its production, helmed by Alan Schneider, was so successful that producer Sidney Bernstein proposed that he transfer and coproduce the show with Arena Stage off-Broadway. After considering the potential high prestige and low financial risk, the board of directors voted unanimously to cover half of the capitalization.[8] The fact that the play had not done well at the Broadway box office and was moving to the less explicitly commercial clime of off-Broadway likely helped to justify this economic and symbolic capital-driven decision. Just a couple of years later, in "A Permanent Classical Repertory Theatre in the Nation's Capital," part of the application for Arena to obtain nonprofit status, Fichandler indicted Broadway and articulated the art versus commerce binary: "Broadway's objective is not culture at all. Its objective is commodity."[9] Regional theater and off-Broadway, though they occasionally produced the same plays that had premiered on Broadway, were considered distinct from Broadway at the time.

Raising a subscription audience was another tool to present Arena as less commercial. The theater could count on subscribers to pay for and fill seats whether or not the individual production was well liked, paralleling the audience model of other performing arts nonprofits. When speaking of subscriptions, Fichandler was fond of quoting Jean-Louis Barrault: "a theatre's duty was 'to strive unbendingly to attract the devoted adherent as opposed to the transient public interested only in the hits.'"[10] She attributed the theater's success in the 1959–60 season to subscribers and community-oriented programs, such as "preview performances for government workers" and "the teen ticket plan for high school students and teachers."[11] During these transitional years, she asserted the continued importance of ticket sales and "unpretentious entertainment": "success is the first law of the theatre, profit or non-profit."[12] According to Fichandler, "The reason we moved from 247 to 800 [seats] was because we weren't taking enough in to do what we wanted to do, and we were selling out. It was success that turned us into non-profit."[13]

The late fifties were financially the best years yet, though they did not grant structural stability. Reincorporation as a nonprofit was primarily about constructing and securing a home, which would be extremely expensive but worthwhile for Arena to establish itself as a durable institution and for Washington, D.C., to showcase a new cultural site. The South West Development Agency promised to sell land to Arena at a reduced cost if it were a nonprofit. Such status would also allow the company to receive grants, donations, and new tax breaks on income and tickets to help cover the tremendous cost. Zelda's husband, Thomas Fichandler, an economist who worked for the Twentieth Century Fund and served as the vice president of Arena's board as well as its executive director, undoubtedly played a huge part in researching these options and in financial planning, though it is sometimes difficult to determine which Fichandler was responsible for which fiscal policy. In 1959 Zelda and Thomas Fichandler persuaded the stockholders to dissolve the corporation and transfer its assets to the new nonprofit, Washington Drama Society. This change was a bold experiment because the Fichandlers and the new board knew they had to raise nearly $1 million for a permanent home, and they believed Washington, D.C., was a difficult city for fundraising. Still, they forged ahead and hoped their past success would guide their future.

NONPROFIT STABILITY

In 1961 the Arena Stage Theatre became the first theater built in Washington, D.C., since 1895, the first arena-style theater built for a U.S. company, and the largest theater for a resident U.S. professional company, with its more than eight hundred seats.[14] When Arena representatives first inquired into support from national and local foundations and corporations, they mostly failed to get contributions to what seemed a shaky venture. Once they developed more concrete plans, one foundation after another contributed to the capital campaign, often with matching grants. Arena also raised funds by taking donations, principally from loyal patrons and the stockholders, now members of the board of trustees, and selling bonds to the public, thereby making the theater more of a community-driven initiative. Although Arena was left with a mortgage of many hundreds of thousands of dollars, the press celebrated the financial security that the permanent home promised. Reporters hardly discussed potential artistic changes the new building and nonprofit status would make possible, reinforcing the notion that Arena had been behaving like a not-for-profit company and would continue business as usual.[15]

The Ford Foundation provided substantial economic security in 1962 when it gave Arena Stage $863,000. W. McNeil "Mac" Lowry, the head of the Humanities and the Arts Division of the Ford Foundation from 1957 to 1965 and later a vice president, had previously given grants to Fichandler as a director. In 1962 Zelda and Thomas Fichandler told the board of trustees that Lowry had consulted them on the state of regional theater and funding their own institution as part of a new project.[16] The resulting grant showed Lowry's faith in Arena's artistic and financial track record. It covered the mortgage, bonds, and site acquisition for the new theater and left more than $150,000 in reserve. For the Ford Foundation, the funding initiative was an opportunity to make a significant impact on the performing arts field. The funding also raises the issue that capitalism enabled the success of Ford and its subsequent philanthropy, which could then help the Ford brand, further complicating the relationship between for- and not-for-profit. Between 1962 and 1971 the foundation gave $2,659,450 to Arena, out of a total $16 million distributed among seventeen regional theaters.[17] The impact of this financial support cannot be overstated in giving the theater a permanent space and what Fichandler famously called the freedom to fail.

Sheila McNerney Anderson argues that "Lowry shaped arts policy and institutional development in the performing arts community in the United States more than any other single individual."[18] He was particularly interested in the development of European-inspired acting companies, "non-commercial theatre," "classics," and the "creation of a new body of American classics."[19] These interests translated into funding permanent acting ensembles, playwrights in residence, and new play productions at handpicked regional theaters. The funding of permanent acting ensembles was key to Arena retaining and training talented actors and cultivating ongoing relationships between the artists and audiences. Ford also funded playwrights in residence such as Herbert Boland, whose *Battle Dream* received its world premiere at Arena Stage in 1963, and Civil War novelist and historian Shelby Foote.

With financial and symbolic support from foundations, Fichandler chose more challenging plays. In 1961 she opened the new space with what was billed as the American premiere—although it was actually the premiere of John Holmstrom's translation and probably the first professional American production—of *The Caucasian Chalk Circle*. Directed by Alan Schneider, the play signified the kind of work Fichandler wanted to promote on her new stage. Fichandler uses the play and its subsequent revivals as a framing device for her introduction to the self-produced commemorative book *The Arena Adventure: The First 40 Years*. Reflecting on the 1961 production, she notes, "There was some consternation about picking this particular then-avant-garde play by this particular East German writer for so spotlighted an event," especially considering that the Berlin Wall had gone up a couple of months earlier.[20] In the week leading up to the launch of the new theater and *The Caucasian Chalk Circle*, the *Washington Post* printed several articles about Arena Stage, its new building, and Brecht, as well as a favorable review by Richard Coe. The production was a hit, but writing to Lowry, Fichandler claimed that audiences were coming to see the new theater, not necessarily the play.[21] This was probably true to an extent, yet it was likely a tactic to continue asking the Ford Foundation for targeted artistic grants.

In its first seasons at the new home, Arena earned more income from the box office than ever before, according to Tomoko Aono's thorough study "The Foundations of American Regional Theatre."[22] The company continued to produce eight-show seasons but now for more weeks and seats. The prestigious plays *The Caucasian Chalk Circle* and *The Threepenny Opera* had the highest ticket sales in the 1961–63 seasons.[23] Thomas Fichandler had interestingly recommended raising ticket prices for *Threepenny* because of the particularly high cost of hiring an orchestra. The board of trustees argued about the theater's duty as a nonprofit and ultimately defeated the motion.[24] According to Zelda Fichandler, maintaining low ticket prices was one of her greatest achievements because "everybody can come," opening up the possibility for dialogue and transformation.[25] Producing this kind of musical and providing greater access to it helped Arena articulate what it meant to be a nonprofit regional theater. Brecht and Brecht-inspired plays were incredibly popular in the 1960s, likely because their politics, cultural capital, and use of music attracted middlebrow audiences. *The Threepenny Opera* and *Oh! What a Lovely War*, as examples, were two of the most produced plays across the country in the midsixties.[26] Play selection was not a simple matter of choosing between high art and high box office receipts. Politically progressive yet popular, in several senses of the term, these plays linked Arena's artistic mission and commercial needs.

The theater's own narrative, as seen in *The Arena Adventure*, emphasizes its hard-hitting 1960s social dramas that "paralleled the turbulent decade in which they took place,"[27] but classics and comedies never left the repertoire. The theater continued to produce Renaissance comedies such as *Volpone* and *The Taming of the Shrew*. Before and after the move to the new building, some of

Arena's most commercially successful shows were comedies, especially those of George Bernard Shaw, and Washington premieres of contemporary plays, such as *The Wall* by Millard Lampell. Thus, in the early 1960s, Fichandler curated an eclectic repertory of classics and new plays that proved to be financially viable.

It was not until the midsixties that Fichandler moved the repertory toward more of the daring work she had long desired to produce. This included contemporary British plays in the vein of *Serjeant Musgrave's Dance* and *Oh! What a Lovely War*. The 1965–66 season subscription mailer advertised John Arden's play by citing *The Hostage*, which Arena had produced three seasons prior, and emphasizing the high literary quality. The description of *Oh! What a Lovely War* relied on knowledge of Joan Littlewood and emphasized entertainment: "The English musical review [*sic*] from Miss Littlewood's Theatre Workshop . . . a brightly inventive, caustic entertainment blending dramatic and humorous skits with songs of the First World War."[28]

Whereas the early marketing downplayed the antiwar messages of these works, the productions themselves seem to have been provocative, or they are remembered as such. Covering the 1965–66 season, *The Arena Adventure* spotlighted only these two plays and declared, "Arena kept pace with the country's growing skepticism about armed conflict in Indochina by offering two distinctly different anti-war plays."[29] The productions were particularly topical in the context of the nation's capital and Arena's elite audience. During the run of *Serjeant Musgrave's Dance*, Arena planned to put photographs of the Vietnam War and other wars in the lobby. *Washington Post* critic Geoffrey A. Wolff observed that Arden's play "obviously speaks to our moral dilemmas in Vietnam."[30] Meanwhile, Richard Coe bemoaned the absence of the irony he had appreciated so much in the original Theatre Workshop production of *Oh! What a Lovely War*, a "brilliant, black, bitter revue."[31] Programming these plays capitalized on the audience's mostly liberal politics, which were not limited to off- and off-off-Broadway but were very present in sixties regional theater.

DEALING WITH THE DEFICIT

After the 1965–66 season Arena Stage experienced its first deficit, which was approximately $50,000,[32] and then its first decrease in subscriptions.[33] In 1963 Thomas Fichandler explained that the company regularly lost half of its subscribers each season—one-quarter because of the transient nature of Washington, D.C., and one-quarter for no known reason.[34] But in an oft-repeated speech, Zelda Fichandler claimed that Arena lost half of its subscribers because conservative audiences disliked the year's experimental and politically charged repertory, which included short works by Ionesco and Pinter in addition to *Serjeant Mus-*

grave's Dance and *Oh! What a Lovely War*.[35] According to *The Arena Adventure*, including these antiwar plays in "this banquet gave some subscribers indigestion and they left the table. More traditional fare was added."[36] The food diction interestingly elevates this repertory as a "banquet" while stating that art is meant to be consumed. As noted earlier, this same commemorative book describes these antiwar plays as reflections of popular American sentiment. But here these plays are positioned as unpopular in a strictly commercial sense.

In total, Arena Stage had only four hundred fewer subscribers than the year before, totaling the still sizable sum of sixteen thousand in the 1966–67 season. Throughout the midsixties, the audience typically filled 90 percent of the house, suggesting the popularity of the left-leaning repertory among subscribers and individual ticket buyers.[37] *Oh! What a Lovely War* was actually the biggest box office draw of the season, bringing in more than $90,000, an amount second only to *The Threepenny Opera* years earlier.[38] Admittedly, because of the hired band and projections, *Oh! What a Lovely War* was probably more expensive to produce. It also had fewer available seats because Arena removed one section of seating, the first and only time the theater has done this, to create a thrust stage and area for projections. Still, *Oh! What a Lovely War* was the single production whose image graced the mailing for subscribers to renew for the next season—perhaps the reason why some subscribers "left the table." Despite the financial success and entertainment value of *Oh! What a Lovely War*, the widely held belief that challenging, high art could not also be commercial permitted Zelda Fichandler and others to blame the deficit on the experimental repertory and supposed audience rejection of that repertory. Following the deficit year, the 1966–67 season was more conservative, featuring several tried-and-true plays, including *Macbeth*, *The Crucible*, and *The Inspector General*, and fewer plays in total.

Accounts of this phase focus on Fichandler's speech to the American Educational Theatre Association, an audience likely receptive to praises of avant-garde and antiwar plays and to critiques of popular audiences. Fichandler disclosed that Richard Schechner admired most of Arena's productions, such as *Oh! What a Lovely War*, but derided what he called the "Marshmallow Theatre" movement and absence of working-class audiences. According to a study conducted in 1964, more than half of Arena Stage patrons had some graduate school education and their average family income was $15,000, approximately twice the Washington, D.C., average.[39] On the other hand, Fichandler had received complaints from her audience about the repertory becoming too "specialized" and not enough "fun." She asserted that to survive, "what we <u>had to do</u> was to acknowledge that the audience was our Master (oh oh oh six o'clock and the master's not home yet, pray God nothing's happened to him crossing the Potomac River. If anything happened to him we'd all be inconsolable and have to move to a less desireable [*sic*] residence district!).”[40] Although Fichandler acknowledged loyal subscribers as the backbone of her theater, she also resented their influence and critiqued their frankly white, middlebrow tastes.

This did not mean Fichandler produced more canonical fare necessarily against her own wishes. There was no conservative board of trustees constantly imposing its will, an accusation used against nonprofit theaters since the sixties.[41] According to regional theater scholar Joseph Zeigler, who interned at Arena Stage in 1962 and wrote on it in his invaluable study *Regional Theatre: The Revolutionary Stage*, the “board may technically employ Zelda and fix her salary, [but] she controls the board. Arena Stage is a ladylike autocracy.”[42] In her essay “Theatres or Institutions?,” among other speeches and publications, Fichandler actively advocated for classics that spoke to contemporary audiences, and she defended 1930s farces for their aesthetics as well as their box office appeal.[43] From the opening of the new building in 1961 to 1970, Arena produced four plays by Shakespeare and three each by Shaw and Chekhov. This period also included multiple productions of plays by Brecht, Feydeau, Pirandello, O’Neill, Sackler, Anouilh, and Kaufman and Hart. The more traditional season of 1966–67 attracted some audiences—the number of subscribers did increase that year—while remaining well within the bounds of Fichandler’s artistic preferences.

The theater still had to focus on selling tickets, because the foundation safety net was relatively small. Arena Stage’s contributed income accounted for 18 to 30 percent of expenditures, increasing throughout the decade. Studying these income trends, Tomoko Aono notes that Arena’s grant applications and appeals to donors in the early 1960s called for one-time capital funds, insisting the theater would support itself through ticket sales thereafter.[44] Artistic and foundation leaders, such as Lowry, frequently pointed to Arena’s financial stability in the 1950s as evidence of a theater not needing to raise constant unearned income—“unearned” being money from grants and donations, while “earned” income is from ticket sales, rentals, and the like, though of course both forms of capital are earned in a sense.

Many theaters used individual, foundation, and, later, government contributions to construct permanent homes, and as with Arena’s model, they established themselves as nonprofits in the sixties. According to the 1965 Rockefeller Fund study *The Performing Arts: Problems and Prospects*, “More than half the professional theatre projects outside New York—and almost all the major ones—have been created as nonprofit undertakings.”[45] Reversing earlier ideas about theater sustainability, the report concluded in bold italics, “*This panel believes that as a general principle the nonprofit performing arts organizations should not be expected to pay their way at the box office. Indeed, they cannot* do so and still fulfill their true cultural mission."[46] The "should not" to "cannot" move underscores the value seen in the "true cultural mission," viewed as somewhat at odds with hits at the box office.

The Rockefeller panel's beliefs and recommendations were supported by the publication of William Baumol and William Bowen's 1966 landmark study *Performing Arts: The Economic Dilemma*. The Princeton economists dispelled the 1960s cultural boom myth: Americans were not spending more on cultural activities with respect to percentage of income, and the percentage of people attending performing arts events had not increased. Moreover, Baumol and Bowen argued that the nonprofit theater's income gap would worsen over time. They reasoned that technology would not meaningfully improve productivity in theater, so production costs would continue to increase. Ticket prices could not keep up with inflation, production costs, and salaries while remaining low enough to attract diverse audiences.[47] Arena Stage and other nonprofit regional theaters subsequently cited Baumol and Bowen and changed the language of their grant requests to accept deficits as the natural condition of nonprofit theaters.[48] As a result, they created fundraising initiatives to maintain the operations of the theaters rather than asking for donations only for capital campaigns.

Many theaters also started or expanded public service projects. According to Zeigler, "The concept of public service is partly an insurance policy for the regional theatre institution. By serving, it hopes to provide for itself and its public an alternative to the 'hit-or-miss' psychology of the commercial theatre." He adds that "service had all the respectability that mere production of plays did not have."[49] Part of being a nonprofit theater is doing such service, often in the field of education. In the 1960s Arena added educational programs, including internships and the Living Stage, a company that performed for and with public school students. These educational initiatives did not directly make money, though they arguably helped to cultivate new audiences and symbolic capital. In addition, Arena regularly requested and received grant money from the Ford Foundation and later the National Endowment for the Arts to subsidize actor training. Such programs and applications for targeted grants to support those programs helped Arena to extend its community and artistic outreach and therefore gain greater legitimacy as a public-serving institution.

Zeigler further contends that Zelda Fichandler purposefully sought a deficit in order to secure more funding from foundations and install ambitious programs.[50] Aono echoes this claim when she charts the increasing expenditures of Arena Stage in the late 1960s.[51] Indeed, according to Fichandler, "Every time the box office caught up with our intentions, our intentions grew."[52] Since having a deficit was now acceptable, Fichandler could implement the artistic plans she had envisioned years earlier without needing to end the season in the black.

Like education, art could be positioned as having a higher calling than commerce. Nevertheless, funding concerns continued to help dictate the maintenance of programs and the installation of new ones.

EMBRACING THE DEFICIT

Modeling Arena Stage on European theaters, Zelda Fichandler argued throughout the sixties that a company of the highest achievement needed a resident acting ensemble and rotating repertory. Even in a recent interview, she asserted, "The hardest dimension of the theatre and the most central is the acting company."[53] In a letter to subscribers, she explained that the actors would build relationships with each other and the audience, while their taking on different roles each night would keep performances fresh with new insights. The rotating schedule would allow visitors to Washington, D.C., to see several shows and allow flexibility in scheduling. If one production proved more popular than others, then that play could have more performances.[54] In the late sixties Arena did experiment with rotating plays, producing, for instance, *The Tenth Man*, *Room Service*, and *The Iceman Cometh* in repertory. But the costs of frequently changing the sets proved too high. Arena returned to straight runs after 1969, though Fichandler produced a few two- and three-play rotating repertories in the 1970s, showing her commitment to this notion.

In 1968 Fichandler obtained a large grant from the Ford Foundation to hire and train African American actors for the resident ensemble. She observed a "profound aesthetic dislocation" between the whites on stage and in the audience of Arena versus the majority African American population of Washington, D.C.[55] Stories of sixties racial anxieties were not being told in her theater, yet they were staged in race riots and marches on the National Mall. In "Toward a Deepening Aesthetic," a lengthy essay in her funding application, Fichandler frames the multiracial ensemble in humanistic, aesthetic, and even political terms rather than economic ones (that is, as giving employment to nonwhite actors).[56] At times she championed "race-blind" casting, while at others she promoted deliberate multiracial casting to underscore thematic points.

Reactions to the multiracial casting were mixed. Richard Coe acknowledged the integrated ensemble near the end of his reviews of *The Threepenny Opera*—a new production—and *Six Characters in Search of an Author*, which ran in rotating repertory, but claimed the integration had zero effect on the productions.[57] In his review of *King Lear* later that season, he did not mention race, perhaps as a way to perform how he liberally sees past race.[58] On the other hand, some audience letters in the Arena Stage archives reveal discomfort and/or anger about the casting, particularly when family members in the plays were of differing races. Other letters accuse the black actors of being less talented, or at least less trained, criticizing their diction. In *No Safe Spaces*, Angela Pao observes these phenomena across her case studies of multiracial casting in American theater; the reactions to Arena were not unique, though Arena was one of the first U.S. companies to attempt a sustained commitment to such casting.[59]

The integrated ensemble folded at the end of the season. In a letter to the Ford Foundation, Fichandler called the program a temporary failure and reported that she thought black audiences were not interested "in our kind of repertory" but instead in the Black Arts Movement.[60] She did not implicate white audiences or invoke Arena's actual proximity to race riots but situated the failure as one of not attracting a sizeable black audience. At the annual membership meeting in 1969, Fichandler said that finding and keeping qualified black actors was difficult and that the integrated company was "several years ahead of its time" but she and the Ford Foundation "felt it was a worthwhile attempt and did not regret trying it."[61] Despite the discontinuation of the program, Arena's experiment with an integrated acting ensemble was historically significant, especially considering the racial climate of D.C., and it was contingent upon performance at the box office and possible only with foundation support.

Grants also sponsored world premieres, which were risky projects. As a for-profit in the 1950s, Arena had produced a handful of premieres, including Robert Anderson's *All Summer Long*, which subsequently moved to Broadway. As a nonprofit with targeted grants for new work, Arena produced one or two premieres each season to varying success. In the midsixties Fichandler secured funding from the Ford Foundation for Howard Sackler to write a new play based on the life of boxing champion Jack Johnson. Arena had previously produced another play by Sackler, and Fichandler admired this ambitious new play that offered commentary on contemporary race relations. *The Great White Hope*, famous for starring James Earl Jones, transferring to Broadway, and winning the Pulitzer Prize, was only the third-highest-grossing play for Arena in the 1967–68 season. In fact, Arena lost $50,000 on the production, and it lost half of its resident acting company to the Great White Way. The play's success in the commercial world—principally the payment of $1 million to Sackler for the movie rights—led to a public tussle in *Variety* over financial and artistic compensation for the regional theater.

Several of Arena's productions had moved to New York years before, but the success of *The Great White Hope* crystallized the idea that a regional theater could gain national attention and substantial profits from a Broadway transfer. Arena soon afterward produced the American premiere of *Indians*, by Arthur

Kopit, and transferred the play to Broadway. From 1969 to 1970, Zeigler notes, "15 percent of all plays on the main stages of theatres were new plays—triple the percentage in the two seasons before *The Great White Hope*," and more regional theater productions transferred to Broadway or off-Broadway.[62] These increases provoked some critics, such as Martin Gottfried, to accuse regional theater artistic directors of producing plays for their commercial rather than artistic potential.[63] Yet the overwhelming majority of these transfers did not turn a profit. Instead they offered regional theaters prestige. New York, specifically Broadway, was—and is—at the top of the theatrical hierarchy, in spite of attempts by the regional theaters to legitimize themselves through their nonprofit status and attendant community service.

Much like in the early sixties, Arena Stage in the late sixties produced edgy, contemporary plays alongside classics and comedies. Critic Julius Novick wrote in 1968, "More and more, the Arena is expanding beyond its old preoccupation with familiar plays for its contented middle-class audience."[64] *Marat/Sade* provoked hostile mail because of its explicit scenes, as did *No Place to Be Somebody* because of what some patrons viewed as its racist portrayal of whites. This was the first play by a black playwright, Charles Gordone, to win the Pulitzer Prize, and Gordone was the first black playwright produced at Arena Stage. *No Place*, *The Great White Hope*, and the integrated ensemble signaled Arena's growing interest in cultivating an African American audience.

On the apparently more commercial side, Fichandler looked to musicals. Because the first production of *The Threepenny Opera* was so successful, Arena produced the Brecht-Weill piece again in 1968. That season Fichandler also proposed hosting the tour of *Hair*: "*Hair* will take some explaining, but we can point to it and say, 'Look! We can't make it in the big theatre so we are using it commercially to subsidize our operation.'"[65] Her phrasing here is interesting because *Hair* is obviously tied to the nonprofit Public Theater and is essentially about liberal politics, yet Fichandler had to justify presenting the musical because of its financial success. But, adhering to the nonprofit mission, the board reeled at the idea of dramatically increasing the ticket prices, which would have been demanded by *Hair*'s producers, and did not host the tour. Instead, the company placed *Jacque Brel Is Alive and Well and Living in Paris* in its musical slot. In his study of American theater economics from 1968, Thomas Gale Moore did not perceive any decrease in ticket sales at the National Theatre when it reopened in 1952, implying that there was little competition between road shows and Arena's repertory.[66] This likely changed, however, when Arena Stage began to produce musicals more frequently and more theater companies opened, notably the Kennedy Center in 1971, but that history is outside the scope of this chapter.

CONCLUSION

From 1965 to 1969, Arena Stage ran a deficit, yet instead of scaling back artistic programs, it expanded its horizons. In 1970 the company literally expanded by opening the Kreeger Theater, a second stage with a flexible proscenium meant for more experimental work and named for a major donor. The program given to attendees of the theater's opening used *Serjeant Musgrave's Dance* as the primary example of the kind of play one could expect in the Kreeger, again suggesting the importance of that play and production, despite disavowals of its popularity. Meeting minutes reveal that Zelda Fichandler had been planning this new theater since the midsixties, precisely when her theater first moved toward a deficit model. She insisted, "We need to test the resources of the community vis-à-vis the major foundations' attitudes towards grants."[67] Such statements reflect Fichandler's use of the accepted deficit to execute her larger vision. In 1969 Thomas Fichandler wrote to W. McNeil Lowry for more funding and ultimately received a combined $900,000 from the Ford Foundation and NEA to help cover the cost of the new building. Lowry came to the rescue again, but these organizations demanded a stipulation that Arena could not ask for more money for several years. This was a problem, as Baumol and Bowen had shown that performing arts nonprofits would need increasing financial support. Foundations and the federal government had also learned this lesson, and they were trying to shift the source of unearned income to local communities.

And so Zelda Fichandler wrote "Theatres or Institutions?," calling for more federal funding of the arts. Concerned about "the hand that rocks the cradle," she felt uncomfortable about the audience donating to the theater and dictating the repertory.[68] In time, however, individual donors would mostly fill the financial gap created by foundation retreat. As seen with *Hair*, Fichandler was willing to make what she considered more ostensibly commercially driven decisions, so long as they did not jeopardize her artistic integrity. She also endorsed classics and comedies as vital to the repertory, the human spirit, the public, and the subsidizing of new work and other programs. She confessed, "I cling to European institutional models—the subsidized, well-staffed, anything-that-money-can-buy theatre," but she also recognized that "we have had to teach ourselves to be independent of European models . . . [to] be conceived more fluidly."[69]

In 1970 Arena Stage's income met its expenditures for the first time in years, not counting the new building-related costs. That year the theater also lost subscribers, increased ticket prices, and still lacked a development office. Arena had figured out the limits to its costly, adventurous artistic programs and new stages. While the integrated ensemble and rotating repertory did not last into the 1970s, other educational and creative programs, particularly the support of new work, persevered. All the while, Zelda Fichandler intelligently steered the repertory and leveraged the deficit to conduct artistic experiments and fortify her theater institution within the demands of show business. Negotiating the meaning and model of the viable nonprofit regional theater, she, along with her husband, Thomas Fichandler, and patron "Mac" Lowry, sustained Arena Stage with money and art.

The dozens of nonprofit regional theaters that followed in Arena's wake in the 1960s typically emulated its course. They frequently developed equivalent artistic programs and produced the same plays. After Arena opened its new building with *The Caucasian Chalk Circle* in 1961, for example, the Actor's Workshop in San Francisco produced it in 1963, and the Guthrie Theater did so in 1965. Other regional theaters likewise dealt with deficits and built institutions on economic and symbolic capital.

Fifty years later, nonprofit regional theater institutions wrestle with similar issues. In 2010 Arena Stage constructed a third stage and encased its theaters in a wall of glass, creating the Mead Center for American Theater and driving related financial and artistic decisions for the flagship to stay afloat. The new center launched with a multiracial production of *Oklahoma!* that was artistically and politically insightful as well as the highest-grossing show in Arena's history. Today some critics lament the state of the art as having gone commercial, while they romanticize the purer motives of theater companies and leaders of the past. It is true that there are new and more tangled relations between nonprofit and for-profit theater now. For example, commercial producers increasingly use enhancement money to test new products with subscription audiences at regional and off-Broadway theaters.

But it is crucial to remember that Arena Stage did not start out as—nor did it become—a totally avant-garde, anti-Broadway, nonprofit art house and that such classifications obscure the relations of capital in cultural production. Instead, Arena began as a for-profit corporation that behaved much like what would become the norm of a nonprofit theater, with its eclectic repertory of classics, comedies, and new work, its resident acting ensemble, and other innovative artistic programs alongside ties to commercial theater in New York. Its productions of experimental political theater were very profitable, and to think they were otherwise perpetuates oversimplified assumptions about the cultural values of art. Historicizing the apparently simplistic terms of profit is necessary for a more complex and complete understanding of theatrical economy. Too often, art and commerce are pitted against one another. Regional theaters, especially in the sixties, provide productive points of entry for scholars to destabilize the false dichotomy.

NOTES

1. Zelda Fichandler, "Theatres or Institutions?," *Theatre* 3 (September 1970): 110.

2. Vincent Landro, "The Mythologizing of American Regional Theatre," *Journal of American Drama and Theatre* 10 (Winter 1998): 82.

3. Edward Mangum qtd. in Bernard Coyne, "A History of Arena Stage, Washington, D.C." (PhD diss., Tulane University, 1964), 14.

4. Zelda Fichandler, "Report to the Stockholders of Arena Stage, Inc.," June 8, 1955, p. 1, box 1, fol. 32, Arena Stage Historical Documents 1950–1998, Special Collections and Archives, George Mason University Libraries, Fairfax, VA.

5. Ibid., 5.

6. Margo Jones, *Theatre-in-the-Round* (New York: Rinehart, 1951), 67–68.

7. Minutes of a Meeting of the Board of Directors of Arena Enterprises, May 8, 1958, box 30, fol. 1, Thomas C. Fichandler Papers 1950–1997, Special Collections and Archives, George Mason University Libraries.

8. Minutes of a Meeting of the Board of Directors of Arena Enterprises, Inc., June 29, 1959, box 30, fol. 1, Thomas C. Fichandler Papers.

9. Zelda Fichandler, "A Permanent Classical Repertory Theatre in the Nation's Capital," p. 27, box 2, fol. 11, J. Burke Knapp Papers, Special Collections and Archives, George Mason University Libraries.

10. Zelda Fichandler, remarks at the meeting of the Washington Drama Society, June 7, 1961, p. 4, box 108, fol. 1, Zelda Fichandler Papers 1950–2000, Special Collections and Archives, George Mason University Libraries.

11. Minutes of the First General Membership Meeting of the Washington Drama Society, Friday, June 10, 1960, box 30, fol. 2, Thomas C. Fichandler Papers.

12. Zelda Fichandler, remarks at the meeting of the Washington Drama Society, June 7, 1961, p. 10, Zelda Fichandler Papers.

13. Zelda Fichandler, interview with the author, December 29, 2012.

14. Dorothy B. Magnus, "Matriarchs of the Regional Theatre," in *Women in American Theatre*, 3rd ed., ed. Helen Krich Chinoy and Linda Walsh Jenkins (New York: Theatre Communications Group, 2006), 208.

15. "New, Modern, Permanent Home Is Assured Arena," an unsigned article from the *Sunday Star*, October 18, 1959, does acknowledge that the flexible stage would be suitable for classics.

16. Minutes of a Meeting of the Board of Trustees, Washington Drama Society, Inc., June 24, 1962, box 30, fol. 3, Thomas C. Fichandler Papers.

17. Joseph Wesley Zeigler, *Regional Theatre: The Revolutionary Stage* (Minneapolis: University of Minnesota, 1973), 185.

18. Sheila McNerney Anderson, "The Founding of Theater Arts Philanthropy in America: W. McNeil Lowry and the Ford Foundation, 1957–65," in *Angels in the American Theater: Patrons, Patronage, and Philanthropy*, ed. Robert A. Shanke (Carbondale: Southern Illinois University Press, 2007), 176.

19. Ibid., 180–83.

20. Zelda Fichandler, introduction to *The Arena Adventure: The First 40 Years*, by Laurence Maslon (Washington, D.C.: Arena Stage, 1990), 6.

21. Zelda Fichandler to Mac Lowry, March 30, 1962, box 154, Zelda Fichandler Papers.

22. "Financial Structure of Arena Stage," in Tomoko Aono, "The Foundations of American Regional Theatre," (PhD diss., CUNY Graduate Center, 2010), 82.

23. Box Office Receipts, 1961–62 and Subsequent Seasons, box 82, fol. 2, Zelda Fichandler Papers.

24. Minutes of a Meeting of the Board of Trustees, Washington Drama Society, Inc., February 28, 1963, box 30, fol. 3, Thomas C. Fichandler Papers.

25. Fichandler, interview.

26. Aono, "Foundations of American Regional Theatre," 27. Aono compiled this data using *The Best Plays*, local newspapers, and theaters' commemorative publications and internal records.

27. Maslon, *Arena Adventure*, 24.

28. 1965–66 Arena Stage subscription mailer, box 3, fol. 3, J. Burke Knapp Papers.

29. Maslon, *Arena Adventure*, 36.

30. Geoffrey A. Wolff, "Stark and Brutal Theme Is Found in 'Sergeant Musgrave's Dance,'" *Washington Post*, March 19, 1966.

31. Richard L. Coe, "Arena Creates a New Stage," *Washington Post*, June 4, 1966, http://search.proquest.com.ezproxy.cul.columbia.edu/docview/142695501?accountid=10226.

32. "Financial Structure of Arena Stage," in Aono, "Foundations of American Regional Theatre," 82.

33. "Arena Stage: Number of Subscribers," in ibid., 144.

34. Minutes of the Fourth General Membership Meeting of the Washington Drama Society, June 23, 1963, p. 1, box. 30, fol. 3, Thomas C. Fichandler Papers.

35. Zelda Fichandler, "The Future of the Resident Professional Theatre in America," August 22, 1967, pp. 5–6, box 108, fol. 24, Zelda Fichandler Papers. For a recent rehearsal of this myth, see Gerald M. Berkowitz, *New Broadways*, 2nd ed. (New York: Applause, 1997), 95.

36. Maslon, *Arena Adventure*, 24.

37. "Arena Stage: Attendance and Box Office Income, 1961–62 through 1970–71 Seasons," box 24, fol. 5, Thomas C. Fichandler Papers.

38. Box Office Receipts, 1961–62 and Subsequent Seasons, box 82, fol. 2, Zelda Fichandler Papers.

39. Susan Powers, press release, January 20, 1964, Arena Stage Records, Special Collections and Archives, George Mason University Libraries.

40. Fichandler, "Future of the Resident Professional Theatre in America," 7–8.

41. See, among others, "What Future for Lincoln Center Repertory?," *New York Times*, December 10, 1967, http://search.proquest.com/docview/118133144?accountid=7287, in which critic Michael Smith writes, "From the start the Repertory Theater has been burdened with too much advice. Mr. Irving is responsible to a board of directors concerned more with financing culture than creating theater."

42. Zeigler, *Regional Theatre*, 35.

43. Fichandler, "Theatres or Institutions?," 105–16.

44. Aono, "Foundations of American Regional Theatre," 85–89.

45. Rockefeller Brothers Fund, *The Performing Arts: Problems and Prospects, Rockefeller Panel Report on the Future of Theatre, Dance, Music in America* (New York: McGraw-Hill, 1965), 38.

46. Ibid., 54.

47. William J. Baumol and William G. Bowen, *Performing Arts: The Economic Dilemma* (Cambridge, MA: MIT Press, 1966), 35–70, 161–302.

48. Aono, "Foundations of American Regional Theatre," 137–42.

49. Zeigler, *Regional Theatre*, 4, 171.

50. Ibid., 35.

51. "Financial Structure of Arena Stage," in Aono, "Foundations of American Regional Theatre," 82.

52. Fichandler, interview.

53. Ibid.

54. Zelda Fichandler to Arena Stage subscribers, "Repertory . . . What is it? Why do it?," n.d. but likely 1967, Arena Stage Printed Materials 1950–2000, Special Collections and Archives, George Mason University Libraries.

55. Zelda Fichandler, "Arena to Create a New Inter-Racial Stage Force," *Sunday Star*, June 30, 1968, D-1.

56. Zelda Fichandler, "Toward a Deepening Aesthetic," box 108, fol. 27, Zelda Fichandler Papers.

57. Richard L. Coe, "'Threepenny Opera' Opens Arena Stage," *Washington Post*, November 28, 1968 http://search.proquest.com.ezproxy.cul.columbia.edu/docview/14339 4613?accountid=10226; Richard L. Coe, "Arena Puts New Note into Pirandello," *Washington Post*, November 29, 1968, http://search.proquest.com.ezproxy.cul.columbia.edu/ docview/143243006?accountid=10226.

58. Richard L. Coe, "Impulses," *Washington Post*, January 23, 1969, http://search.proquest.com.ezproxy.cul.columbia.edu/docview/147723744?accountid=10226.

59. Angela Pao, *No Safe Spaces: Re-casting Race, Ethnicity, and Nationality in American Theater* (Ann Arbor: University of Michigan Press, 2010).

60. Zelda Fichandler to Mac Lowry, July 8, 1969, box 154, Zelda Fichandler Papers.

61. Minutes of the Annual Meeting of the Membership of the Washington Drama Society, November 10, 1969, Thomas C. Fichandler Papers.

62. Zeigler, *Regional Theatre*, 196.

63. Martin Gottfried, "What Shall It Profit a Theatre If . . . ?," *New York Times*, August 23, 1970, http://search.proquest.com.ezproxy.gc.cuny.edu/docview/117965802?account id=7287.

64. Julius Novick, *Beyond Broadway: The Quest for Permanent Theatres* (New York: Hill and Wang, 1968), 50.

65. Minutes of a Meeting of the Board of Trustees, Washington Drama Society, Inc., November 6, 1969, pp. 1–2, box 30, Thomas C. Fichandler Papers.

66. Thomas Gale Moore, *The Economics of the American Theater* (Durham, NC: Duke University Press, 1968), 141.

67. Minutes of a Meeting of the Board of Trustees, Washington Drama Society, Inc., February 9, 1967, p. 2, box 30, fol. 3, Thomas C. Fichandler Papers.

68. Fichandler, "Theatres or Institutions?," 110.

69. Ibid., 108, 111.

PART V
POPULAR DEMONSTRATIONS AND INNOVATIVE PERFORMANCES

James M. Harding

The High Road, the Low Road, and the "Many Roads to Truth"

Richard Schechner, Peter Brook, and the Royal Shakespeare Company's 1966 Production of US

IN DEFENSE OF RICHARD

Over the course of almost forty years at the helm of *TDR* (1962–69, 1986–present), Richard Schechner has proven himself to be a bit of an intellectual chameleon. The common misconception about chameleons, of course, is that they change color to camouflage themselves, when in fact their spectacular transformations, among other things, have much more to do with communicating changes in mood or intention than with blending into the existing environment. With regard to Schechner and his involvement with *TDR*, communications of changes in mood or intention—particularly those expressed in his numerous *TDR* editorials—have more often been acts of provocation than of camouflage, and as is frequently the case with provocations more generally, Schechner's attempts to provoke the discipline into taking new directions have been followed by more tempered assessments that look to the middle ground of what he earlier characterized as a dichotomous terrain. Not long ago, Stephen Bottoms highlighted one of the more famous examples of this tendency. In an open letter to Richard Schechner on the occasion of Schechner's seventy-fifth birthday, a letter that was published under the title "In Defense of the String Quartet," Bottoms first recalls Schechner's somewhat infamous assertion in 1992 "that theatre as we have known and practiced it—the staging of written dramas—will be the string quartet of the 21st century: a beloved but extremely limited genre, a subdivision of performance."[1] Bottoms then follows this reminder by noting that Schechner candidly admitted in his first *TDR* editorial of the twenty-first century that he in fact had been wrong in his earlier assertion: "theatre" was, he acknowledged, very much "alive in the new millennium."[2]

Bottoms's major concern with this subsequent correction is that for all its seeming admission of error, it is actually, he argues, a bit of a ruse. He contends that the finer details of Schechner's admission ultimately reveal a tendency "to grant artistic license, autonomy, and validity to every theatre artist *except* the playwright."[3] From this, Bottoms concludes that beneath the surface of an admission of error Schechner "hadn't really revised [. . . his] opinion at all"[4] and that his comments "represent a continuation of a long, avant-gardist tradition of suspicion of dramatic conventions."[5] But on this note Bottoms is not entirely accurate. While Schechner readily acknowledges that from the very beginning of his involvement with *TDR* in 1962 he "wanted to make *TDR* more 'theatre' and less "drama,"[6] and, I might add, ultimately more performance and less theater, the question of a playwright's artistic license, autonomy, or validity has a lot more to do with the space and location of that autonomy or license—the creative space of the actual act of writing—than Bottoms implies, and he overlooks comments to this effect that come at the end of Schechner's editorial. "There is the text of plays," Schechner argues in that first editorial of the new millennium, "but," he continues, "there is also the text of behavior, of acting, of scenography, of blocking. Each of these," Schechner adds, "is autonomous, and can be developed on its own and/or in relation to the others" but they need not be "envisioned as a unity." They can equally be envisioned, he argues, "as disparity, contradiction, and the interplay of forces, a totality without the requirement of unity."[7]

In many respects, Schechner's argument here is a slightly modified refrain of sentiments that have been in circulation since the beginning of modernism itself, if not earlier. At the very least his embrace of an "interplay of forces" that, depending on the context, can be envisioned either as unity or as disparity is sufficiently broad enough in articulation to allow for the artistic license, autonomy, and validity of the playwright that Bottoms defends in his critique—even if this allowance may vary in degree from production to production. There is no imperative that one agree with Schechner on this point, and, based on his open letter, it is fairly clear that Bottoms doesn't agree with him. Perhaps that is because actual collaborations and negotiations are often lopsided and far from the balanced ideal they are in theory. Perhaps too it is because the decisive moment in any negotiation tends to occur prior to the negotiation itself: when the terms of that negotiation are set. In this respect, it is worth considering how the term *text* functions in Schechner's work as a theorist and in the subtle negotiations that his work has encouraged over nearly five decades of scholarship. For it actually functions somewhat contrary to expectation.

It is not text nor dramas nor playwrights per se that are delegitimized—as is the case in the kinds of overly simplistic binaries that privilege performance over text. In Schechner's work as a theorist, *text* often serves as a coded indicator or sign of theatrical practice that ultimately is labeled as conservative, mainstream, and/or commercial, and those designations are of greater concern than anything associated with text, drama, or playwrights. Beneath that sign—beneath the term *text*—the issue is not so much what Bottoms characterizes as the "avant-gardist tradition of suspicion of dramatic conventions." It is rather what one might more accurately describe as the regulation of an all-too-neatly-maintained conceptual distinction between supposedly progressive and conservative—or alternatively, between supposedly experimental and mainstream—theatrical practice: a distinction where *progressive* and *experimental* are privileged signifiers.

Whether conceptualized as a binary between the progressive and the conservative or between the experimental and the mainstream, the terms regulating the distinction between the two have remained relatively constant from the beginning of Schechner's career in the early 1960s up to the present, and they tend to draw their lines not in opposition to written dramas or playwrights themselves but rather according to the level of one's allegiance to the dramatic text as the center of artistic authority and thus as "the center of performance."[8] Here the issue is not "text" but rather one's relationship to it and whether that relationship can be said to defer to conservative and/or mainstream theatrical practice more generally and its commercial concerns in particular. As recently as his 2010 article "The Conservative Avant-Garde," for example, Schechner denounces contemporary experimental theaters whose "strong return to the text"[9] is, so he argues, a symptom of decidedly conservative inclinations in tune with processes of broad commercialization. In the contrast that Schechner makes with what he characterizes as the explosive and creative period of the 1950s and 1960s, he laments not the contemporary avant-garde's return to the text but the fact that this return is one among many symptoms suggesting a more fundamental problem: the unfortunate devolution of the avant-garde into a mere style and its consequent absorption into a conservative and popular cultural mainstream.

This lament is nothing new in Schechner's work, and in fact it echoes similar arguments articulated back in the early 1990s in *The Future of Ritual*. But it does serve as a reminder that, at some level, all of Bottoms's talk about the playwright and about Schechner's seeming "disregard" for a playwright's "own intentions"[10] really misses the deeper point and overlooks a far more influential polemical concern that has remained constant in Schechner's work for well over forty years. Much of that concern is discernable in the way that Schechner's reference to an "interplay of forces" echoes his long-standing commitment to the ensemble notion of the theater, a commitment that is traceable back to what was only the second editorial that Schechner wrote after becoming editor of the *Tulane Drama Review* in 1962 and that thus also places us at the founding scene of one of the most lasting and influential conceptual structures for how subsequent scholars have assessed the value of various forms of theatrical practice in the 1960s and beyond. In that early editorial from 1963, which was entitled "Intentions, Problems, Proposals," Schechner not only specifically called for a principled support of playwrights as theater practitioners, boldly asserting, for example, that "the playwright will be the cornerstone of our emerging theatres," so that he or she will once again create "in the theatre" rather than "merely [being] represented there."[11] He also and, more importantly, definitively embraced an "ensemble" notion of theater for the first time, and by "ensemble" he meant the notion of a theater company—which includes the playwright—devoted to an overarching idea that translates into what Schechner describes as "a commitment to a particular kind of theatre which the company leaders (and eventually every member) believe to be 'the best theatre.'"[12] As Schechner noted, "'Ensemble' is not a magic word," but a commitment to an "'ensemble company' is an idea-in-action with power and promise."[13] Moreover, Schechner argued, "We all know that ensembles have always been the most efficient generators of theatre art,"[14] and there is a "purity of intention" when "the company is committed to an idea, and each member of the company is committed to the ensemble."[15]

Over the years, Schechner's early embrace of this notion of an ensemble and its unwavering commitment to an idea of what constitutes "the best theatre" has echoed not only through Schechner's own work in the theater but also through his work as an editor and theorist. Moreover, his embrace of the "ensemble," combined with what Bottoms rightly cites as Schechner's interest "in 'guru' directors such as Grotowski,"[16] has had a lot to do with the kind of support that he extends to playwrights. It is not so much that Schechner has been unwilling to grant validity to playwrights or to the staging of written dramas. In his lengthy history with *TDR*, Schechner has lent his support to plenty of playwrights, not only by championing their work in published articles but by actually publishing their scripts in the pages of *TDR* as well, especially during the 1960s and 1970s. But within the American context, Schechner has a record of championing the work of specific kinds of playwrights: those affiliated with the traditions of modernist and postmodernist experimental theatrical practice where cultural value is centered not on the primacy of the playwright but on a collaboration and negotiation between artists each bringing their own political and aesthetic priorities to the stage. That—as one can see if one has followed Schechner closely through the years—is what he believes to constitute "the best theatre."

There is clearly a political agenda underlying this belief. That agenda is grounded in a dichotomy that, I would suggest, subsumes Bottoms's general concern with the artistic prerogatives of the playwright, if only because granting the playwright a privileged status is but one example of the kind of individualism that Schechner believes produces bad theater. At the most basic level, that agenda works against the "star system" and its privileging of individual performers—or, as the case may be, of individual playwrights—over the collective endeavors of the ensemble. That same agenda gives shape to the assertion Schechner made in 1963 that practitioners must bring the playwright into the theater as a fellow practitioner rather than having him or her "merely represented there."[17] For what emerges in this early editorial from Schechner is not so much an "avant-gardist tradition of suspicion of dramatic conventions"[18] or, more specifically, a proclivity on Schechner's part to grant artistic license to everyone "*except* the playwright."[19] It is rather a challenge to what, even at this early date, Schechner perceived as a problematic tendency in the United States to conceptualize theater in ways that play to the logic and individualistic values of the marketplace rather than in ways that pursue artistic goals. It is a challenge, in other words, to the kind of theater culture that privileges what Schechner describes as "personal success" and "individual rewards" over "long range communal goals."[20] Schechner's attitudes toward playwrights—or, for that matter, toward performers and directors— fall within the larger context of a more general call for a theater no longer subservient to commercial values, and hence to what I want to suggest has become a defining binary of how subsequent scholars have understood the theater of the sixties and much of experimental theater afterward: a binary between experimental and mainstream theaters.

That binary is evident in the limits that Schechner himself imposes on what he characterizes as the "best" theater. Experimentation and artistic license are certainly a part of this theater, but they are not tantamount to a willful, random disregard of a playwright's discernable intentions. In that same 1963 editorial where he embraces the ensemble notion of the theater, for example, Schechner also specifically castigates directors likes Elia Kazan for altering the text of Tennessee Williams's *Sweet Bird of Youth*, Maurice Valency for altering the text of Friedrich Dürrenmatt's *The Visit*, and Joseph Anthony for altering the text of Eugène Ionesco's *Rhinoceros*. Artistic license is not the issue here. Schechner castigates Kazan, Valency, and Anthony because the alterations they made to the dramatic texts were the result of kowtowing to the economic priorities of Broadway rather than adhering to aesthetic principles. On this note Schechner has remained constant throughout his career, and this brings us back to "string quartets."

PLOWING THROUGH THE FORKED PATH

A deep concern with the consequences of kowtowing to the economic priorities of commercial theater led Schechner in his 1963 editorial to complain that "while experimentation is encouraged among our young scientists, our theatre departments are infected by the idea of the commodity theatre." Their "goal," he continued, "is to succeed, not to experiment."[21] Read in their context—read, in fact, as they were clearly intended—Schechner's provocative 1992 comments likening "the staging of written dramas" to a "string quartet" were in fact a direct echo of the concerns he articulated thirty years earlier in "Intentions, Problems, Proposals." The underlying concerns in his allusion to "string quartets" were not really about playwrights, the antiquated quaintness of theater, or even, as his argument is commonly misconstrued, about privileging performance over theater. They were about the context of a specific kind of theater—mainstream commercial theater—and the cynical way that U.S. university theater programs cater to it rather than embracing a mission focused on artistic, intellectual, and academic rigor.

Regrettably, Schechner's comments, formulated as they were as a provocation, came across as a categorical assertion about theater more generally when in fact they were directed as a rebuke to the disingenuous promises that U.S. university programs make to undergraduates by preparing them "for the orthodox theatre"—and by *orthodox* Schechner meant "regional theatre," "Broadway," "television," and "film."[22] His argument was that such programs mislead students about the profoundly limited professional opportunities they will face after graduation while at the same time failing to provide them with the basic critical skills generally associated with a liberal arts education—skills that could be cultivated through a complex understanding of performance as a critical paradigm. Whatever misunderstandings might have resulted from the seemingly categorical nature of Schechner's reference to string quartets, one thing is certain. That reference fell well within the parameters of a more substantial and enduring polemic that has been a mainstay in Schechner's work for well over forty years. Rather than focusing on playwrights, that polemic has consistently taken the form of a stark dichotomy between artistic, intellectual, and academic rigor on the one hand and mainstream, commercial, and orthodox theater on the other.

If one is looking for the arc that bridges Schechner's forty-year tenure as editor of *TDR*, its structures are evident not in his reference to "string quartets" but rather in his dismissive reference to "orthodox theatre." The opposite end of that same arc is evident not in his admission of error about "string quartets" in "Theatre Alive in the New Millennium" but in his reference to those he identifies as "the experimentalists," who he claims have finally "won many of the battles over the 'future of theatre.'"[23] That same arc is also visible in Schechner's subsequent disillusionment with the experimentalists and his lament in "The Conservative Avant-Garde" that because of "branding and marketing," and because of "the touring circuit and overseas commissions," the "hype that nothing could be further from Broadway than the avant-garde" no longer rings true.[24] Indeed, from his early rebuke of Kazan, Valency, and Anthony in 1963, through his provocative allusion to the string quartet in 1992, all the way up to more recent editorials and polemical essays like "The Conservative Avant-Garde" in 2010, Schechner has conceptualized theater and performance not in opposition to the staging of written dramas but in opposition to the corrupting influence of the commercial logic of the marketplace—an influence that he has consistently characterized as being epitomized in mainstream commercial theater and its supposed profit-driven cannibalization of the innovations of experimental theater or of any other artistic expression it can appropriate. If that concern were limited to Schechner alone, it might be little more than an important footnote in theater history, but it is clearly a concern that has shaped the discipline significantly, particularly in the way that subsequent scholars have written histories of theater in the 1960s.

In one way or another, the contrasts mentioned above all arguably lead back to the stark polemical binary that Schechner formulated at the end of "Intentions, Problems, Proposals" in 1963. There, with a feel for the kind of rhetorical provocation that has had lasting reverberations not only across his own career but also across the profession more generally, Schechner famously threw down a gauntlet before his readers, telling them bluntly, "You choose Broadway and I'll choose an experimental theatre. There are many roads to truth. But neither of us can choose *both* Broadway and an experimental theatre. That's a contradiction in intention."[25] The broad rejection of commercial theater implicit in the either/or provocation that Schechner posited between Broadway and experimental theater in this early editorial established one of the most enduring paradigms in scholarship on theater in the 1960s: one that subordinates mainstream commercial theater to the presumably more innovative, artistic, and political engaged proclivities of experimental theater.

The contrasts here are well known but worth rehearsing. To this day, Schechner, like numerous other scholars, credits the avant-garde with "originality, innovation, and the rejection, if not outright destruction, of the past." He attributes to the vanguard a "clear intent (rhetorical if not actual) to destroy both the existing sociopolitical and aesthetic order."[26] His understanding of a progressive avant-garde is one that has a loose, experimental relationship not only to "the text" but also to performance. And all of these positive, progressive attributes stand, so the narrative goes, in stark contrast to the commodified values of mainstream theater. Whereas the avant-garde ostensibly lives up to its literal definition of being "in advance of," mainstream theater presumably adheres to the logic of the marketplace rather than heeding the call to aesthetic innovation or to radical political transformation. It siphons off innovation and originality from the vanguard, repackaging it in an innocuous, marketable form and then selling it secondhand to complacent, bourgeois audiences.

Although subsequent articulations may vary from scholar to scholar, the choice that Schechner gave his readers in 1963 codified a binary opposition that has proven to be one of the most enduring in the historiographies of theatrical practice in the 1960s. While conceptual binaries are not inherently bad or misleading, I want to suggest that this one laid the foundation for what has become one of the great myths of 1960s theater in the West, and while Schechner has hardly been alone in perpetuating that myth, it is one whose underlying assumptions, values, and cultural preferences he has so effectively maintained in his capacity as editor of *TDR* that even Bottoms ironically re-affirms them in his caustic suggestion that it was Schechner's "own most famous ensemble-based production, *Dionysus in 69* (1968), which first brought commercial values to bear on the alternative, downtown theatre scene" in New York and that he did so by shrewdly marketing a combination of what Bottoms calls "countercultural grunge" and the "time-honored appeal of sexual spectacle."[27] The problem with this argument, however, is that the lines between alternative and mainstream theater in the 1960s were never as clearly drawn as Schechner or Bottoms makes them out to be. The lines of history, I want to suggest, are a lot blurrier.

LOOKING FOR THE EXCLUDED MIDDLE

Rather than suggesting that the mainstream appropriated the aesthetics of the fringe or that the fringe was corrupted by the commercial values of the mainstream, we would do well to consider historical examples that fall between this neatly formulated dichotomy glorifying the experimental and dismissing the mainstream. And there are good examples to consider. One of the more important came roughly five years after Schechner had issued his provocative either/or proposition in "Intentions, Problems, Proposals." This was when Peter Brook published his now-classic vision for the theater *The Empty Space*, a work whose insightfulness is matched perhaps only by its accessibility. It is there, in the first section, entitled "The Deadly Theatre," that Brook argues, "If we try to simplify the problem by making tradition the main barrier between ourselves and a living theatre we will . . . miss the real issue. There is a deadly element everywhere."[28] It is there, in the section entitled "The Holy Theatre," that Brook argues, "All forms of sacred art have certainly been destroyed by bourgeois values but this sort of observation does not help our problem. . . . If the need for a true contact with a sacred invisibility through the theatre still exists, then all possible vehicles must be re-examined."[29] Similarly, in the final section, entitled "The Immediate Theatre," Brook argues once again, "It is foolish today to expect any single production, group, style or line of work to reveal what we're looking for. . . . All is not movement, all is not destruction, all is not restlessness, all is not fashion. There are pillars of affirmation. Those are the moments of achievement which do occur, suddenly, anywhere."[30] Such comments sweep across the spectrum of theatrical forms, calling for an assessment of the particular event rather than for categorical generalizations.

Even as he admits that his own categories of "the deadly," "the holy," "the rough," and "the immediate" theaters are themselves limited and at best provisional, Brook admonishes us to consider that stagnancy and deadliness can plague both the mainstream and the fringe and that transformative moments can occur equally in conventional or experimental theaters. Such arguments eliminate the need for proclamations that theater has become something akin to a string quartet, or for later concessions that the analogy was premature. So too do such comments admonish us to be wary of a sweeping pronouncement of "The Decline and Fall of the (American) Avant-Garde,"[31] of generalized denouncements of contemporary experimental theaters as a "conservative avant-garde," or, more to the point, of a categorical dismissal of established theatrical convention or of a general disregard of the possibilities available within mainstream theatrical venues.

While Schechner was arguing that we cannot "choose *both* Broadway and an experimental theatre," Brook maintained that if we are to keep theater viable as a cultural, social, and political form, we must be attentive to the full range of theatrical possibilities and choose the theater that is most suited to the situation. In the arguments that they formulated early in their careers, Schechner and Brook thus offered us strikingly different visions for theater in the 1960s and beyond. Following the logic of Brook's arguments, the conclusions are not difficult to find: there are many roads to truth, but different situations call for different paths and thus for different theaters, and at any given moment the most effective theater might very well be found where one least expects it. It is senseless, therefore, Brook maintains, to dismiss any one form of theater outright when we do not know whether new situations tomorrow will demand that practitioners take artistic paths that seemed counterproductive the day before. Although it is not packaged in the flourish of provocation, there is nonetheless something profoundly sensible in this approach as a viable alternative to

Schechner's either/or proposition. The choice, then, is not so much between Broadway and experimental theater but between two very different theatrical orientations, between starkly formulated and provocative dichotomies on the one hand and a cautious openness to the potential viability of diverse theatrical forms on the other.

Perhaps, too, this latter orientation might set a very different bearing for scholarship as well, particularly for scholarship on the period of the 1960s, in which it was articulated. Brook's monograph *The Empty Space* is certainly one of the key texts from the decade, and while Brook did not have an apparatus like *TDR* at his disposal to cultivate the agenda articulated in his important book, one could do far worse than to echo in scholarship his call for "all possible vehicles [. . . in theater to] be re-examined" and thus to use the agenda spelled out in his book as a conceptual frame for reexamining and for rewriting the histories of theatrical practice in the 1960s. Such an approach would plot a more inclusive if not altogether more accurate course. At the very least, it plots a course toward serious mainstream theater.

It is this last point, about reexamining the possibilities available within mainstream theatrical venues, that opens the doors to the Aldwych Theatre in London's West End in mid-October 1966, where after an internationally successful and highly acclaimed production of Peter Weiss's *Marat/Sade* two years earlier, Peter Brook ventured into uncharted territory with the Royal Shakespeare Company (RSC) in an ensemble production of a collaboratively created piece ambiguously entitled *US*. The piece, which was billed as a "group-happening-collaborative spectacle,"[32] had been in rehearsal for fifteen weeks prior to opening to mixed reviews on October 13. Despite those tepid reviews, it remained in the RSC's repertoire, having a run of some "fifty performances" over the next six months and playing to packed audiences at the Aldwych,[33] who responded to the production's urgent call for something approaching a "true and honest"[34] exploration of the global significance of the unfolding war in Vietnam—not just for the United States but for all of "us." "In the case of Vietnam," Brook opined, "it is reasonable to say that everyone is concerned, yet no one is concerned: if everyone could hold in his mind through one single day both the horror of Vietnam and the normal life he is leading, the tension between the two would be intolerable."[35] Hence the ambiguity in the title *US*: it was about the United States and the violent side of its foreign policy, but so too was it about how each and every one of "US" in the West is complicit in the death and destruction wrought by an unjust war.

One of the very first major antiwar pieces, *US* premiered a month before the Open Theatre's production of Megan Terry's *Viet Rock* in New York. In this particular instance, ironically, the West End was a step ahead of experimental theater's advance guard. Looking back on the production in his 1998 memoir, *Threads of Time*, Peter Brook recalls, for example,

> A number of friends, some from the original Theatre of Cruelty groups—the designer Sally Jacobs, the musician Richard Peaslee, and others involved in the Royal Shakespeare Company, Michael Kustow, Albert Hunt, Adrian Mitchell and Denis Cannan—were very disturbed to see that in the length and breadth of the English theatre there was hardly any reflection of this terrifying reality, for a play on the subject of the Vietnam War did not exist. This inexplicable fact shamed us into trying to make one collectively as quickly as possible.[36]

In this effort they were ahead of the curve, and though this puts a bit of a wrinkle in the edge-to-center narratives that glorify experimental theaters as the source of aesthetic and political innovation, the point here is not so much to suggest that it was the West End that was at the cutting edge of theater challenging the war. It is rather to highlight the fluidity between mainstream and experimental theater practitioners—a fluidity that gives the lie to the mythical binary separating mainstream and experimental theaters. At that moment, there was less of a rush to establish precedence than there was to respond to an emerging sense of common cause in the face of an unfolding moral outrage. *US* may have opened before *Viet Rock*, but neither opened in a vacuum. Indeed, following an invitation from Brook, the Open Theatre's Joe Chaikin had actually visited the ensemble and conducted workshops with them in rehearsal, and he was not the only visitor. "At the beginning of August, Jerzy Grotowski, with one of his actors, Ryszard Cieslak, came to work with the company for two weeks."[37]

It is worth pausing momentarily to consider the implications of Chaikin's and Grotowski's involvement in the rehearsals of *US*—particularly Grotowski's. For at that moment, if one follows the constructed mythology of sixties theater, Grotowski was where he did not belong: at the center of British commercial theater in London's West End. This was roughly a year before Grotowski traveled to New York and conducted that legendary "first American workshop, at NYU in November 1967"[38]—a workshop that counted both Chaikin and Schechner among its participants. As Schechner recalls in the deeply moving obituary that he wrote for Grotowski in *TDR* shortly after his death in 1999, "Grotowski could change the way a person experienced and understood the ground from which theatre grows."[39] Perhaps there is evidence of that ability to effect a ground change in one's understanding of theater even in the obituary that Schechner wrote paying tribute to his mentor and friend. For suddenly, in the midst of that moving homage, the strict dichotomy between the experimental and the mainstream falters and opens up to allow a middle ground, where, not surprisingly, we discover Peter Brook. Arguing essentially that Grotowski ultimately managed to transcend conventional divisions in the theater, Schechner contends,

> Grotowski scholars said that the Polish director had "left the theatre"—a domain roughly bounded by the Wooster Group, Robert Lepage, and Pina Bausch on one side, Peter Brook, Robert Wilson, and Ariane Mnouchkine in the middle, and Broadway, the Boulevard, and the West End on the other. Grotowski was no longer a part of that theatre.[40]

Here, beneath the vague, transcendent position that Schechner ascribes to a quasi-mystic Grotowski, we discover an acknowledged middle ground between the experimental and the mainstream that, in fact, has always been there despite the provocative dichotomies that scholars like Schechner have readily embraced in the years following the stark contrast that he laid out in his 1963 editorial. Discovering that unexpected acknowledgment is in and of itself something well worth reflection. Perhaps it is worth even more than his subsequent acknowledgment that he was wrong in likening theater to seemingly anachronistic string quartets. For in the case of the RSC's production of *US* in London's West End in 1967, the stakes—indeed, the costs—were substantially higher.

THE RADICALITY OF THE MAINSTREAM VENUE

The details of the work that Grotowski did with the cast of *US* always remained a guarded secret. Shortly after the production, Michael Kustow wrote, for example, that he would not describe the work that Grotowski did with those working on *US* because "such work is only free if it is in confidence, and confidence depends on its confidences not being disclosed."[41] But subsequent critics have suggested a close correspondence between "Grotowski's emphasis on the 'total act' of the actor sacrificing himself in front of the audience" and the central image of the production, "the sacrificial act of self-immolation."[42] This image, which recurred at strategic moments throughout the show—at the beginning of the first and second acts and scattered throughout the rest of the piece—took two forms. The first was a simulated act of self-immolation performed by the actor Mark Jones on what was supposed to be a representation of the streets of London. The image itself was a kind of composite of the actual acts of self-immolation by the Vietnamese Buddhist monk Thích Quảng Đức on the streets of Saigon in June 1963 and by the American Quaker Norman Morrison beneath the windows of the Pentagon in Washington, D.C., in November 1965. The second form came in the closing moments of the play when the actor Bob Lloyd released butterflies into the audience, then appeared to catch the last one and set it on fire with a lighter. Both images proved to be controversial among the cast and then with the audience, and yet they still have much to say about the middle ground that Brook's production occupied.

With regard to Mark Jones's simulated act of self-immolation, controversy centered not on the act itself but on the debate constructed around it, a debate that reached its apotheosis in the second act when Glenda Jackson challenged the actor Mark Jones as he prepared to simulate the act of self-immolation. Through her provisionally constructed character, she suggested that for all the depth of its motivation the act itself was an exercise in futility: "You think we'll change," she asked, "just like that, because among all the other accidents and horrors we read a little paragraph about you setting yourself alight?" Beyond the immediacy of this moment was the larger question being raised though the debate about the futility of an act of self-immolation as a gesture to stop the war. That larger question was not really about the Thích Quảng Đứcs or the Norman Morrisons of the world but about theater itself as an effective means of protest against the atrocities that made up the war in Vietnam and every war since then.

It is on this point that we come full circle and arrive at the profound significance of the mainstream venue in which Brook's production of *US* was performed. For the question about the efficacy of theater was a question about what kind of theater bourgeois audiences actually wanted, what kind of theater they could justify, and what kind of results they ought to expect from encountering theater. These were questions from which they themselves as members of the audience were not—and could not—be separated. As David Williams has noted, Brook had distilled the production down to "a burning question: 'If I say I care about Vietnam, how does that influence the way I spend my time?'"[43] Simply coming to the RSC's production of *US* entangled the audience in this question, since the piece itself was about the war in Vietnam. In this respect, the question pertained as much to going to theater as it did to the making of theater. Yet it was a question for which a ticket stub from the Aldwych ultimately could not count as a sufficient answer. If nothing else, the production of *US* underscored the view that attending theater— even theater that attempted to engage the war directly—was not enough. The production sought to disrupt theatergoing complacency and smugness and force audiences to confront the question of how their ostensible concern for Vietnam affected their day-to-day affairs.

On the critical side, Albert Hunt questioned the logic not only of placing the debate between Jackson and Jones at the centerpiece of the production's second act but also of leaving unresolved the question of how concern with the war affects the way performers and spectators spend their time. Hunt's concerns were echoed in the press by critics like Charles Marowitz. For his part, Hunt suggested that Glenda Jackson too easily received the clinching lines in the debate and that both Brook and Jackson thus seemed to "revel" in what they perceived to be the "futility" and "hopelessness of protest" and in "the inability of middle-class intellectuals in London to *do* anything about the war."[44] This suggestion struck at the heart of the production since much of the motivation came from a pronounced conviction that, as artists and intellectuals and as ordinary citizens, the members of the RSC had to do something. Marowitz expressed similar criticisms in his review of the production. He suggested that the danger of the show was that "the Bourgeois Public" might easily draw the conclusion that "these nice Royal Shakespeare intellectuals" shared their naively complacent view that "the situation in Vietnam" was "all terrible" but also "highly complicated and practicably insoluble."[45]

Most damning of all, however, was Marowitz's own sense of disappointment, not with the RSC's desire to take the issue of Vietnam to mainstream audiences but with Brook not having taken full advantage of the opportunity that he had. In the penultimate paragraph of his review, Marowitz complained,

> I had come to the theatre—as so many people will come—out of a hunger to do something, see something, say something which cuts a path out of the chaos. One doesn't need a theatrical performance to explain that we are at an impasse. The role of the theatre in times like today is to elucidate and give a positive lead. A conventional play may end up in a state of fascinating ambiguity, but a social document dealing with a red-hot contemporary crisis cannot."[46]

In many respects, Marowitz took the opportunity of his review to engage in a grand debate about theater, and it is not a matter of coincidence that Marowitz's review ultimately ended up in *TDR*. For Marowitz, if we may borrow from the language of Schechner, was engaged in a debate about what constitutes "the best theatre." Marowitz's disappointment came from a preconceived yet certainly legitimate notion that theater *can* make a difference and that in doing so it ought to lead the way for others. In putting theater in this kind of leadership role, he implicitly suggested that theater must literally be an avant-garde. Yet it is not so much that the RSC production of *US* refused to lead. It is that its leadership followed a very different logic. Ironically, that leadership employed the kind of audience participation that would increasingly become a signature trope of experimental theater in the late 1960s and early 1970s.

Nowhere was that logic of that leadership more evident than in the impatient responses that the production provoked among critics like Kenneth Tynan, who in a moment of exasperation with the vagueness of the show's ending shouted out from the audience at the performers on the stage, who had been directed to remain stationary until all the members of the audience decided to leave. Looking back on the opening performance thirty years later, Brook recalled that "Tynan . . . deeply impatient with what he considered our unclear political commitments, shouted at the immobile group onstage: 'Are you waiting for us, or are we waiting for you?'" Here, in that one decisive moment, the cutting edge and the mainstream blurred. Here was the result of a provocative experimental theatrical practice unfolding on the mainstream stage. "Far beyond what [. . . Tynan] intended," Brook later argued, "the question rang true. This was the uncomfortable moment of doubt that a political performance should arouse, one that needs to be carried away into the street, where hopefully it can continue to nag."[47] Well before the Living Theatre would tell audiences leaving *Paradise Now* that they were the revolution, and well before the members of The Performance Group would lead audiences out of the Performance Garage and on to Wooster Street, Brook's production of *US* embraced the notion that if anything was going to happen to stop the war, it was not the theater but the audiences who would have to act, and they would have to act from an irresistible conviction that the war was unjustifiable. Theater could raise the issue, yet when all was said and done it was the audience who would have to act if the war was to end.

There were instances where the audience did act, and even if those actions seemed to take the form of small measures, they often carried amazing resonance. Perhaps the most remarkable among them centered on the second controversial image of immolation: the burning of the butterfly in the final scene of the show. Given the production's attempt to address the bombs, the Agent Orange, the napalm, and the killing that resulted from the U.S. military's involvement in Vietnam, the burning of a butterfly might seem to be a relatively trivial matter. But in the larger context of efforts to stop unnecessary violence, Brook's proposal to set a butterfly aflame was deemed cruel and ignited "a furious argument [. . . among] the production team."[48] That argument was settled only when they opted to use a sleight of hand on the stage that, after releasing real butterflies in the theater, would allow them to conclude by lighting a paper butterfly on fire instead. A variation of this same argument played out among the audience as well, who, once the show was mounted, were caught by the illusion and presumed that the cast was burning real butterflies. Albert Hunt and Geoffrey Reeves note, for example, that on one occasion audience sentiments actually spilled over onto the stage when two Quaker women, having observed the burning of the butterfly from balcony seats at the Aldwych one night, purchased front-row seats for the next show in order to intervene. As Hunt and Reeves recall, "One night the butterfly did not burn: as Bob Lloyd took the lighter from his pocket a middle-aged [Quaker] woman climbed on to the stage from the front row and stopped him, saying 'You see, you can do something.' When she saw what he had in his hand she turned to her friend and said 'It's only paper.'"[49] Even though her sense that something could be done fell prey to a theatrical illusion, Hunt and Reeves emphasize that "the company, especially Bob Lloyd, greatly admired the courage of the action."[50] Understandably so! That action was consistent with the kinds of actions that the company hoped to cultivate among audience members more generally: acts small and large that would ultimately bring the war to an end.

Whether interventions like the self-immolation by Thích Quảng Đức in 1963 and Norman Morrison in 1965, like the disruption of *US* by the Quaker women from the audience, or even the production of *US* itself actually made the kind of difference that could cut the "path out of the chaos" that Marowitz expected was always debatable. But the underlying assumption of the production of *US* was that each act was a small part of a larger configuration of necessary actions that collectively could make a difference. In many respects, this assumption was directly tied to the image of the burning butterfly itself—an image that was a hybrid of different ideas that had emerged within the workshops leading to the performance at the Aldwych Theatre. Certainly, setting a butterfly aflame was a kind of poetic rendering of the deeply disturbing acts of self-immolation that had made international news and in the case of Thích Quảng Đức had radically transformed international attitudes toward the unfolding conflict in Vietnam. But the image and use of butterflies was by no means an original idea. It was borrowed from the work of the Fluxus artist La Monte Young, whose "Lecture 1960" (which was published in *TDR* in the winter of 1965) the ensemble had read in one of their workshops. Looking closely at that published lecture, one becomes quickly aware of how indebted *US* was to Young's work. There is a strong case to be made, for example, that the idea for the ensemble to remain on the stage until the entire audience had left was borrowed from Young's description of the ending of his piece "Din" (also called "clap piece"), which concluded by leaving the audience "in the dark and silence forever or at least until they decide to leave," since Young opted not to "prompt them with . . . any kind of please leave signal."[51] More important still was Young's discussion of "Composition 1960 #5."

"Composition 1960 #5" was a Cage-inspired musical composition that simply involved releasing one or more butterflies in an auditorium. In his lecture, Young recalls that the director of UCLA's noon concerts had once refused to allow the piece to be performed and that the poet Diane Wakoski suggested to Young that perhaps the reason was because the director thought the piece "wasn't music." In response to this speculation, Young asked Wakoski "if she thought the butterfly piece was music to any less degree than 'Composition 1960 #2,' which consists of simply building a fire in front of the audience." When Wakoski replied that "in the fire piece at least there are some sounds," Young recalls that he immediately told her that he "felt certain the butterfly made sounds . . . that unless one was going to dictate how loud or soft the sounds had to be before they could be allowed into the realms of music that the butterfly piece was music as much as the fire piece."[52] In this telling exchange was the core of an idea that Brook and the RSC took to heart: the point was not how loud or soft, or large or small; the point was to make a sound as opposed to remaining silent. Whether it was heard or not, whether it "cut through the chaos" or not, the point was to speak up about the war. The one significant difference was the venue. Whereas Young played to select audiences of avant-garde aficionados, Brook directed his performance to the general public.

In choosing a mainstream venue for this particular piece, Brook took his general question of how expressing concern about Vietnam actually influences the way that one spends his or her day and he addressed it to the audiences that really mattered: not to the bohemian intellectual coteries of New York's Greenwich Village or of London's Soho or even to the readers of *TDR* but to the mainstream, bourgeois audiences that frequented what Schechner lumped together as "Broadway, the Boulevard, and the West End." It was there that the real battles over the political ethics and moral justification of an indefensible war in Southeast Asia had to be waged, and must still be waged. There is no need to preach to the already converted in the small circles of the experimental theater community. Irrespective of whether the issue is the indiscriminate use of napalm or of unmanned drones, if the choice is really between Broadway and experimental theater, the moral, artistic, and radical imperative is to choose—indeed to invade—the Broadways, the Boulevards, and the West Ends of the world and to supplant their dinner fare with contemporary substance. This is in fact the bearing that Brook sets in his introduction to *US* when he notes that "commonsense is outraged by the supposition that old wars in old words are more living than new ones, that ancient atrocities make civilized after-dinner fare, whilst current atrocities are not worthy of attention."[53] If there are many roads to truth in times of moral, political crisis, then the choice that crisis behooves us to make is the road most traveled, for it is the road most in need of rerouting.

Returning as a point of conclusion to that influential dichotomy where Schechner drew a clear line between experimental theater and Broadway—a line that separated the practice of serious theater from the influence of the commercial interests that dominate the mainstream—one might question whether the desire to invade the Broadways, the Boulevards, and the West Ends of the world is an unrealistic ideal. Certainly, there is a legitimate question as to whether such invasions of the mainstream are capable of stepping over the powerful interests of what is commonly called "the bottom line." But perhaps here, too, the RSC production of *US* might provide a lesson in effective financial politics and in how an activist theater might function successfully in the mainstream. Some sense of that efficacy can be gleaned from the RSC's dealings with the Lord Chamberlain's office over the production of *US*.

Initially the plans to stage *US* ran into strong resistance from the Lord Chamberlain's Office, which in 1966 still wielded immense powers of censorship in the UK through its authority to grant or deny theaters a license for a performance. The Lord Chamberlain specifically targeted *US*. While the show was still in development, he called "George Farmer, the Chairman of the Governors of the RSC, about *US*," asking him to intervene and prevent the show, which the Lord Chamberlain characterized to Farmer as nothing short of "bestial, anti-American and communist"[54] and hence unsuitable for the British public. In the absence of a discreet behind-the-scenes intervention by Farmer, the Lord Chamberlain threatened to take the more public course of not issuing a license for the production. Proceeding without that license entailed substantial risk. At that time the penalties for mounting a production without a license would result in substantial fines that could be levied against everyone involved in the "performance, down to the stage-door-man."[55] Farmer was very much in support of Brook and the show and countered by weighing the possibility of moving the production from the Aldwych Theatre (which the RSC only rented) to Stratford, where the RSC as owners could carry full liability for defying the Lord Chamberlain's potential refusal to grant a license. As Michael Kustow recalls, "I shall not forget for a long time Peter Hall [founder of the Royal Shakespeare Company] sitting in the pub at lunchtime . . . weighing up whether, if we put on an unlicensed performance of *US* at Stratford-upon-Avon instead of the Aldwych, the authorities would risk the ridicule of taking our license away, and thus preventing the Stratford Shakespeare season."[56]

But it wasn't just ridicule that was at stake here. It was the center of a cultural tourist industry that in a decisive moment could be brought to bear as one source of power against another. The result was a standoff that allowed the production of *US* to proceed, for the Stratford Shakespeare season was ultimately immense cultural and commercial leverage that could be used to rescue *US* from censorship. In a manner of speaking, the performative cultural equivalent of a "string quartet" procured a secure place for an experimental political theater piece in the mainstream. Perhaps it was a unique combination of interests that allowed for this moment. Then again, perhaps this was a telling moment in the history of 1960s theater, the lessons of which we have not yet fully learned and applied.

NOTES

1. Qtd. in Stephen Bottoms, "In Defense of the String Quartet: An Open Letter to Richard Schechner," in *The Rise of Performance Studies: Rethinking Richard Schechner's Broad Spectrum*, ed. James M. Harding and Cindy Rosenthal (London: Palgrave Macmillan, 2011), 23. Schechner's comments were originally published in the essay "A New Paradigm for Theatre in the Academy," *TDR* Comment, *TDR* 36.4 (1992): 8.

2. See Richard Schechner, "Theatre Alive in the New Millennium," *TDR* Comment, *TDR* 44.1 (2000): 5–6.

3. Bottoms, "In Defense of the String Quartet," 25.

4. Ibid., 24.

5. Ibid., 25.

6. Richard Schechner, "*TDR* and Me," *TDR* 50.1 (2006): 7.

7. Schechner, "Theatre Alive in the New Millennium," 6.

8. Richard Schechner, "The Conservative Avant-Garde," *New Literary History* 41 (2010): 900.

9. Ibid.

10. Bottoms, "In Defense of the String Quartet," 25.

11. Richard Schechner, "Intentions, Problems, Proposals," *Tulane Drama Review* 7.4 (1963): 16–17.

12. Ibid., 16.

13. Ibid.

14. Ibid., 15.

15. Ibid., 16.

16. Bottoms, "In Defense of the String Quartet," 29.

17. Schechner, "Intentions, Problems, Proposals," 16–17.

18. Bottoms, "In Defense of the String Quartet," 25.

19. Ibid.

20. Schechner, "Intentions, Problems, Proposals," 8.

21. Ibid., 17.

22. Schechner, "New Paradigm for Theatre," 8.

23. Schechner, "Theatre Alive in the New Millennium," 5.

24. Schechner "Conservative Avant-Garde," 897–98.

25. Schechner, "Intentions, Problems, Proposals," 21.

26. Schechner, "Conservative Avant-Garde," 904.

27. Bottoms, "In Defense of the String Quartet," 29–30.

28. Peter Brook, *The Empty Space* (New York: Atheneum, 1968), 17.

29. Ibid., 48.

30. Ibid., 135.

31. See Richard Schechner, "The Decline and Fall of the (American) Avant-Garde," pts. 1 and 2, *Performing Arts Journal* 5.2 (1981): 48–63; 5.3 (1981): 9–19.

32. David Williams, *Peter Brook: A Theatrical Casebook* (London: Methuen, 1988), 74.

33. Albert Hunt and Geoffrey Reeves, *Directors in Perspective: Peter Brook* (Cambridge: Cambridge University Press, 1995), 112.

34. Albert Hunt, "Narrative One," in *The Book of US* (London: Calder and Boyars, 1968), 12.

35. Peter Brook, introduction to *The Book of US*, 9.

36. Peter Brook, *Threads of Time: A Memoir* (London: Methuen, 1998), 138.

37. Hunt and Reeves, *Directors in Perspective*, 102.

38. Richard Schechner, "Jerzy Grotowski 1933–1999," *TDR* Comment, *TDR* 43.2 (1999): 7

39. Ibid., 7.

40. Ibid., 5.

41. Michael Kustow, "Narrative Two," in *The Book of US*, 133.

42. D. Keith Peacock, *Changing Performance: Culture and Performance in the British Theatre since 1945* (Oxford: Lang, 2007), 191.

43. Williams, *Peter Brook*, 74.

44. Hunt, "Narrative One," 118.

45. Charles Marowitz, "The Royal Shakespeare's 'US,'" *Tulane Drama Review* 11.2 (1966): 173.

46. Ibid., 175.

47. Brook, *Threads of Time*, 142.

48. Hunt and Reeves, *Directors in Perspective*, 119.

49. Ibid., 112.

50. Ibid.

51. La Monte Young, "Lecture 1960," *Tulane Drama Review* 10.2 (1965): 74.

52. Ibid., 75.

53. Brook, introduction, 9.

54. Kustow, "Narrative Two," 143.

55. Ibid., 145–46.

56. Ibid., 146.

Graham White

Sixties Secrets

The Beatles, Yoko Ono, and the Borders of Experiment in 1960s Rock Music Performance

"INOVASION"

On November 18, 1963, NBC television's *Huntley-Brinkley Report* aired a segment on the phenomenon of Beatlemania in the UK. This report is the first filmed appearance of the band in the North American media. It is precise and focused in its presentation of the group as the product of tough, working-class Liverpool and of the era of the Blitz, but, as he presents footage of a concert in Southend, the serious tone of reporter Edwin Newman's feature shifts to a certain amused trepidation as he mentions their likely arrival in the United States. Newman concludes that the band may have become popular because it's "almost impossible to hear them," and he deftly opposes Shakespeare and modern pop culture to suggest that the quality of "Mersey" is strained in the deafening—due to the audience's screams—environment of the concert.[1] His air of arch dismissal is mirrored in his colleague's closing comment on the clip, the program's anchor Chet Huntley suggesting that "anyone hunting for some 'mute, inglorious Milton' will just have to go on looking." The report implies a wry "high" cultural concern with the dumbing-down potential of these British invaders, of rock and roll music, and of the unsophisticated enthusiasm of the mass of ten-to-sixteen-year-old female youth whom Newman identifies as the demographic of the Beatles' audience. It also implies that the band's impact on the United States will be of sociological rather than aesthetic interest and that while Beatlemania is a remarkable phenomenon, Beatlemusic is not art.

The Beatles' arrival in the United States certainly bore out Newman's anticipation of something remarkable. Their February 9, 1964, appearance on the New York–based *Ed Sullivan Show* was watched by a record North American television audience of seventy-three million. It marked the onset of North American Beatlemania, in which the mass appeal of mainstream popular music seemed to blend into something more like obsession for a significant proportion of the nation's youth.[2] The band followed the TV appearance with a first live show at the Washington, D.C., Coliseum, their besuited presentation of a restrained version of the rhythm and blues and rock and roll roots of their music laced with show tune melodicism (the first set featuring Meredith Wilson's show standard "'Til There Was You" prominently), all choreographed for maximum broad appeal. At the Coliseum they played in the round to accommodate the largest possible audience, and further live and television shows in the following fifteen days capitalized on the scale and success of these initial appearances. A quickly planned second tour of North America in August and September of the same year saw them playing twenty-four cities over thirty-three days to huge audiences and making the biggest financial return per date then recorded in U.S. popular entertainment. These early tours present the band in the context of accomplished and effectively marketed mainstream entertainment and do so to a chorus of media commentary on the nature of their audience's response. There is little in the performances to suggest that the aesthetic content or style of popular music or its codes and conventions were to be radically reordered, or indeed that the work might carry the weight of that transatlantic artistic legacy which Newman's report references.

It is, however, clear from the beginnings of Beatlemania that particular brands of literary and popular performance traditions—absurdism, cultural whimsy, lyrical and musical tropes from music hall and comedy—had a place in the register of the band's work. This could be seen in the wordplay, wit, and clowning that were part of both the songs and the on- and offstage performances of the band or in the kinds of visual, literary, and film cultures that the band engaged throughout the first stage of their fame. By the moment of the Beatles' final live concert in the United States, at Candlestick Park in San Francisco (only two and a half years after the Ed Sullivan appearance, in August 1966), encounters with a range of artistic influences appear to have further shifted the template of the material that the band produced. Paul Gleed characterizes this as the moment referenced in the commonplace question "when did the Beatles get all artsy?" He gives the answer as somewhere around the 1965 *Rubber Soul* and 1966 *Revolver* albums (and suggests that they had definitively made the transition by 1967's *Sergeant Pepper's Lonely Hearts Club Band*).[3] Notwithstanding this shift, the band's final set at Candlestick Park contained only two songs from the post–*Rubber Soul* era, and in the live stadium setting the band remained locked in the light entertainment template of their previous incarnation. It was after this concert that the band withdrew from touring, confining public appearances to television slots and the famous final rooftop gig in London in 1969—the tensions of maintaining this form of performance while exploring new artistic avenues finally proving too great. In doing so they began a period of composition and experimentation that ushered in the reconsideration of the band as a significant "serious" cultural force, one in a range of contributors to mid-decade shifts that forged new versions of the relation between popular and high cultural formations in the period.

Once they embraced it, the "artsy" was explored by the Beatles at full pace and in the intense public glare of their enormous popularity. By 1969 one band member had produced work in which he appeared naked (with a collaborator) on the cover of an album of experimental tape loops; another had released an album of entirely electronic sounds, and a third had constructed a piece of orchestral experimentation so radical—or perhaps ill-achieved—that it has yet to see the light of day since its one hearing as the soundtrack to a psychedelic rave in London in 1967.[4] The whole band contributed to the extraordinary mélange of styles, influences, and experiments that makes up the critically panned *Magical Mystery Tour*, which was laid before an unsuspecting British television audience at Christmas 1967, but in each band album that they released they explored a wide variety of styles and techniques, to contrasting critical acclaim and great commercial success. The retreat from physical performance opened a space in which the theatricality of sound performance, of media event, and of the emerging definitions of performance art permeated the language of the group and asked audiences to negotiate a range of unfamiliar territories in response. As a result the Beatles' mid- and late-sixties experimentation provided entry into—or a puzzled retreat from—the world of the avant-garde for much of its audience. It is in this late Beatles era that the work of Yoko Ono, the pioneering performance artist whose work became entwined with the band's through her involvement with John Lennon (she is the collaborator who appears naked with him on their album cover), intersects to provocative effect with their own explorations, problematizing the division between mainstream appeal and avant-garde experiment as it does so.

The Beatles' journey occurs within the broad landscape of experimentation in popular music through the mid- and late 1960s, and today the opening of archives of audio and visual material that makes Newman's report and the *Ed Sullivan* appearance instantly available for reconsideration brings with it a number of episodes that allow for reflection on the relationships between the mainstream and the experimental in the moment. The particular occasions that this essay explores illustrate the ways in which the appearance of hidden histories in and in parallel with the Beatles' paradigmatic journey might prompt reconsideration of the tensions, dialogues, and exchanges in which the broadly avant-garde collides with the broadly mainstream in 1960s music performance. Noting Alan Filewod's comment that "a truly critical approach to the vanguard requires attention to the problem of who's looking, where, and why," and as a result, that "questions of form and method—the traditional concerns of the avant-garde—give way to questions of effect,"[5] I will consider the complex nature of meetings on the binary border and examine the subsequent negotiation of cross-border relations that results. Questions of form and method remain, but the reconsideration of effect—of what happens to practices that collide with, abrade against, and flow into their apparent opposites, and what happens to practitioners and audiences who encounter the results—is brought into contemporary focus by the disruption of archival boundaries that has telescoped history in the recent past. The lost, rumored, or unfinished performance is now brought up for reconsideration alongside the official artifact. As a result the television shows, the unfinished tracks, the in-studio discussions became secret histories, documented, perhaps bootlegged, hard to find, difficult to verify. In the endless archive of the Internet the reappearance of these materials in the first decades of the twenty-first century forces a revision of established histories. In doing so, it also suggests the value in further consideration of the divergences and correspondences between the experimental and the mainstream in sixties rock music performance.

This essay does not seek to provide a comprehensive view of this landscape. It instead aims to look with a microhistorical eye at the relationship between mass popularity and experiment exemplified in the Beatles' "artsy" narrative, alongside the more focused and conventionally "avant-garde" practices and accommodations of the work of two other musicians of the moment whose experiments intersected with the mainstream in thought-provoking ways. In doing so it seeks to examine how the assumed bifurcation between the popular and the experimental reaches a pitch of complexity in these cases, which sit on the brink of deconstructing and disintegrating the mainstream, and to examine moments in which the commitment to art and artistic expression becomes entwined among and in conversation with the coopting and questioning of aspects of the mainstream.

SIXTIES SECRETS

In February 1963, the Beatles recorded "Do You Want to Know a Secret?," a piece of pop music to which even their most dedicated mythologizer fails to assign any grandeur or artistic significance. It is, according to Ian MacDonald, "the first Beatles original to outstay its welcome,"[6] and its principal writer, John

Lennon, claimed that its vocals used only three notes because George Harrison, who sang on the track, "wasn't the best singer in the world."[7] Its history, as a song awarded to the third, and at the time non-songwriting, vocalist in the band for inclusion on their hastily recorded second album, suggests that it occupied the space of "filler," music contrived to plug a gap on an album containing more interesting or marketable material and slated for speedy release. The albums it was featured on, *Please Please Me* in the UK, *Introducing the Beatles* in the United States, were both mixtures of cover versions and originals released in the era before Beatlemania, on the back of the band's first "number-one" single in the UK. The song appeared at a moment when their status as a besuited, industry-manufactured boy band plugged into the light entertainment circuit of the day was yet to be transmogrified by massive popular success into something more global, economically monstrous, and, in light of the vast body of commentary surrounding their later career, artistically significant. It represents a model of the cynically mainstream pop song, and at this stage of the band's career there was little to suggest that such binary oppositions of low and high culture, of the commercial against the artistic, or of the mainstream against the experimental would be troubled or problematized by their work.

The distance from "Do You Want to Know a Secret?" to later Beatle songs like "Strawberry Fields Forever" or "A Day in the Life" is often read as unarguably qualitative and as a marker of the gap between the mainstream of commercial entertainment and the emergence of popular music as a space for serious artistic experiment during the 1960s. "Secret" stands as a commerce-driven product forced out in the heat of the boy band's manufactured emergence, something lacking the originality, craft, artistic seriousness, and integrity to which the later work of the Beatles aspired and through which they were part of the renegotiation of the previously understood relationship between the mainstream and experimental, making pop music, and its offshoot later in the decade, "rock," the ground for this reworking. Somewhere around 1965 the steady emergence of experimental effects and motifs in the Beatles' recordings, whether that be a sitar on "Norwegian Wood," experiments in tape loops and text from the *Tibetan Book of the Dead* on "Tomorrow Never Knows," or the nonsense wordplay of "I Am The Walrus," suggested that the commercial was being reshaped by the avant-garde bleeding into it, through the influence of classical music, drugs, literature, and the consideration of religious, political, or philosophical concepts. It is another commonplace of Beatlemyth that the 1967 film and accompanying album *Magical Mystery Tour* represented a collision between artistic daring and self-indulgence that jeopardized this relationship, but in the subsequent period of their career the stakes raised by such experiments and the sense that the dominant commercial relationships between pop, the rock that seemed to claim more authenticity and integrity,[8] and the diverse audiences engaged by the Beatles' work grew higher and more resonant.

The Beatles are far from unique in their embrace of avant-garde experiment in the moment. During the latter half of the 1960s rock music played a wide and well-documented role in negotiating, blending, and reworking the boundaries and definitions between the mainstream and the experimental. In doing so, it frequently embraced the tropes and ambitions of avant-garde experiment, engaging with forms of language, musical structures, and visual culture from a mass of literature, visual art, performance, and media. In this era a broad range of pop and rock acts such as Captain Beefheart, Frank Zappa, and the West-Coast Pop-Art Experimental Band in the United States, David Bowie or Marc Bolan in the UK, the Plastic People of the Universe in post-68 Czechoslovakia, or Os Mutantes and other "Tropicália" performers in Brazil were exploring, blurring, and redefining the relationship between popularity and the desire to represent complex experience, challenging habituated modes of composing, listening to, or performing popular music through questioning and through provocative lyrics, musical structures, and performance styles. Scholarship focusing on the cultural role of music performance finds the presence of experiments in musical form, in the performative representation of identity, and in engagement with the social and political resonance of acts of aesthetic representation as key to understanding and articulating the significance of the exchange between the avant-garde and the mainstream in music performance in the period. Works such as Philip Auslander's *Performing Glam Rock* (locating the culture of rock music performance between the worlds of cultural and performance studies), Elizabeth L. Wollman's *The Theater Will Rock* (examining the challenge to the notion of the separated realms of rock music and theatrical cultures represented by the emergence of the rock musical), or Nicholas Cook and Richard Pettengill's *Taking It to the Bridge* (exploring the relationship between performance studies and musicology to consider the ways in which popular and rock performances might be studied with the same seriousness and focus as contemporary theater and live art performance) all identify in the late 1960s a blurring of boundaries between the experimental and the popular, the avant-garde and the mainstream, and the "authentic" and the self-consciously performative in art, culture, and popular entertainment that brings into being a new set of relations.[9] Yet in this wider cultural field the Beatles stand centrally as an example of a truly mainstream cultural phenomenon whose unprecedented popularity renders the embrace of a host of influences particularly significant, as what Gleed terms their "new style of borderless art"[10] enters a complex negotiation with questions of popularity, experiment, tradition, and cultural identity.

UNDERGROUND AND OVERGROUND

In September 1963, as "Do You Want to Know a Secret?" played across the UK and Europe as part of the Beatles' stage shows, an edition of the American light entertainment television show *I've Got A Secret*[11] reflected the apparent division between mainstream entertainment and experimental art practice through an encounter between a panel of celebrities seeking to guess the shared secret of two young men appearing alongside the host, Garry Moore. In fact, the encounter resonates with increasing significance as time passes and the legacy of the cultural actions at work plays out as a re-mediated presence—I stumbled across it on YouTube's endless archive—both because of how it speaks to that apparent gulf of intention between the experimenter and the mainstream performer and because of the legacy of the key figure involved.

One of the men is introduced as Karl Schenzer, the other as Mr. X. The audience is told what the connection between the two men is through a caption, and it appears obscure enough that the panel will struggle to identify it. In fact they work out the connection fairly quickly, showing a familiarity with recent news items that suggests they keep their ears to the cultural ground or that they have been prompted. Mr. X is revealed to be John Cale, a young Welsh musician and composer who had recently participated in a full-scale recital of Erik Satie's eighteen-hour piece *Vexations*, following John Cage as a part of the relay of pianists playing a three-line composition 840 times. Alongside him Schenzer is declared to be an off-Broadway performer, currently playing in a show called *The Brig*—the Living Theatre's piece, although the group is not named and there is no discussion of this particular avant-garde event. Schenzer's connection to Cale is that he was the only audience member to sit through the entire eighteen hours of the Satie piece. The secret out, Moore questions Cale about the work, holding it up to gentle ridicule. Cale then plays the piece, the camera panning across the panel, who are variously watching earnestly, looking bemused, or trying not to laugh. Moore notes that the piece doesn't resolve itself, suggests that there's no rule that says it should, and asks Cale why he used the music, rather than memorizing it. Cale suggests, straight-faced, that it's a difficult piece to remember, and Moore finally congratulates Cale on his participation, saying, "You have a will of iron"[12] (although the host appears to say "whim," a fitting slip).

In these exchanges, Cale's "secret" participation in an avant-garde ritual is read through the normalizing lens of light entertainment as something extraordinary, baffling, "vexatious," admirable, frivolous, but also as deeply serious, ritualistic, noteworthy. The tone of mild ridicule is both taken as a norm—guests suggesting that this is foolish—and undermined—guests hinting that it is their own comprehension that is at fault in their not grasping the majesty of the avant-garde ceremony. There is an air of distanced and skeptical respect for the initiates of strange art practices and the beginnings of a journalistic critical dialogue in the host's questions. Here the experimental is more prominent, more in dialogue, and more present in the landscape of the mainstream than we might now expect. It is also difficult to decide who is in charge in this exchange—the stony-faced Cale and his associate Schenzer, bringing avant-garde practice to the mass audience, or the program's makers, maintaining the norm by highlighting otherness.[13] Cale's "iron will" would be tested later in the decade through his collaboration with Lou Reed in the cofounding of and then expulsion from the experimental rock band the Velvet Underground, in part, at least in its early days, a pop-art project curated by Andy Warhol.

Schooled in avant-garde experimentation with Cage and La Monte Young, Cale went on to work both with the Velvet Underground's marriage of pop and experiment and with various forms of experimental music making, including collaboration with Terry Riley. His later solo career has mixed classical, rock, and baroque pop composition in a variety of styles and collaboration as performer, producer, and musician with an extraordinary range of artists, including Patti Smith, the Stooges, Nick Drake, Jonathan Richman, Nico, Brian Eno, Squeeze, and Happy Mondays, among many others. As an artist he has always been ready to negotiate the fluid boundaries between experiment and mainstream, in the sixties and after, and perhaps is an illustration of the degree to which the reinscription of a form of mass entertainment—popular music—as a space in which artistic experiment, seriousness, and integrity might be read challenges the maintenance of a definitional boundary between the experimental and the mainstream.

Nineteen sixty-three is also the year that another young British musician, Roger "Syd" Barrett, was interviewed for a place at the Camberwell School of Art in London. For Barrett, as for Cale and Lennon, the influence of an education in the world of artistic experiment and creativity was crucial to the nature of the popular music he was later to produce, and the creative histories of all three provide further instructive illustration of the intersecting trunk roads of the era. By 1968 the English rock band Pink Floyd, coformed by Barrett and for which he was the songwriter, lead singer, and guitarist, were releasing their second album, *A Saucerful of Secrets*. The band had emerged as the free-form house band of a particular psychedelic underground in London in 1967, playing lengthy sets at UFO, a pioneering hippy club on London's Tottenham Court Road and embracing both sonic and visual experimentation as well as a brand of whimsy and nonsense embodied in Barrett's lyrical and musical stylings. Barrett's was a quirky, original presence for a blues-rock band, and it was his lead that took this group of architecture students into uncharted territory, at the head of a countercultural wave and then into the clinical, white-coated session territory of Abbey Road studios. Alongside the Beatles, they recorded albums and singles for EMI and watched their experimentation collide with the commercial expectations of the pop market, which few acts had transcended. Package tours, *Top of the Pops*, breaking America, and marketable singles to be written, recorded, and released in dizzying profusion were the labors expected of the rock band of the day. Somewhere in this maelstrom, Barrett seems to have decided to stage a resistance to the terms of the pop music encounter.

There are many accounts of what it was that led to Barrett's rapid mental decline from the golden-egg-laying mind behind the band's "See Emily Play" and "Arnold Layne" to the point in 1968 where the band quietly replaced him as guitarist and reconstructed the album that he had originally intended to write, retaining only one of his tracks. The much-bootlegged songs written by Barrett that did not appear on the album—"Vegetable Man" and "Scream Thy Last Scream" (along with the tantalizingly titled but only rumored track "John Latham"—Latham being a highly influential English experimental artist of the day)—seem to bear witness to a deliberate, satiric confrontation with the narrative structures and concerns of the musical mainstream of the day. The one song retained by the band, "Jugband Blues," shares some of these qualities. Barrett went on to record two semicoherent solo albums before withdrawing from music and becoming the reclusive and much pursued quarry of fans and press alike. It is likely that drug abuse contributed to serious mental illness and that the remainder of Barrett's life (he died in 2006) was spent mastering and maintaining some kind of equilibrium. The band went on to become the model of the rock band behemoth, their music remaining serious and artistically driven, often expressive of broadly countercultural sympathies and critiques of power while leading the band to immense fame and wealth. The wilder edge of Barrett's surrealist imaginings and vivid engagement with immersive performance was arguably tamed in their later music. In the emergent cultural archive of the Web, this relatively hidden history is brought to light by the appearance of sound and photographic illustrations of the moment, with the songs, still officially unreleased, easily available in a way that bootlegging of the 1970s could never hope to emulate. A strand of the surreal remains in Pink Floyd's aesthetic, but it's tamed, managed, more A-level art exam than disruptive embrace of the destabilizing, the avant-garde present as an element of radicalism sprinkled into the smoothed-out melodic rock surface.

In his 2010 biography of the singer, Rob Chapman suggests that the recovered archive now reveals Barrett's decline not as the sudden descent into drug-induced madness conventionally represented but as in large part a deliberate response to the limitations and expectations of the music industry culture of the day. Rumors of catatonic stage show appearances or refusals to play more than a single note onstage are painstakingly reinvestigated and matched against available video and audio material of the band's appearances during 1967, when Barrett's decline is said to have occurred with alarming rapidity, to show an engaged but resistant presence throughout the period of supposed collapse. This is a figure whose recalcitrance was dogged, but whose radical detuning of a guitar onstage, for example, becomes an act consistent with previous, lauded experimentation. That Barrett became ill is undisputed, but the terms on which his behavior was judged are shown by Chapman to be flawed. Barrett's interest in the models of avant-garde experimentation found in the work of artists like Latham created a culture of inspiration and attitude.

Latham was famous for destroying a St Martin's College of Art library copy of Clement Greenberg's 1961 *Art and Culture* by chewing it up and then returning it in an acid-filled vial for a piece called *Still and Chew*.[14] Chapman sees Barrett's engagement with the mainstream as being on his own terms, as a refusal to compromise his own vision of creativity in order to participate in the process through which creativity can be "chopped up into convenient little sausages which can be marketed," as one of Chapman's interviewees puts it.[15] This stance would seem to be of a piece with the setting of a binary between the mainstream and the experimental, but in Chapman's reading the pathways the band took as they edged Barrett out of creative involvement were not only a matter of their decision to embrace careerism—Barrett's work representing a negotiation, an entryist journey into the mainstream that appears to shift, reorganize, and disturb that mainstream's precepts.

In these cases the strand of experiment brought into close proximity to the mainstream is initially brought there on terms dictated by the mainstream, but the forms its appearance takes suggest that the mainstream is forced into some kind of reconsideration of those terms, both because of the values posited and because of the commercial transaction involved. In Cale's case the experimental is also presented as the artistic and reinscribes the significance of art, in part through its radical form. Barrett's sidelining in the process of creating the Pink Floyd album represents a recognition of experimental sound as an element in popular music's changing aesthetics, but it does so in part as an engagement with the commercial imperative—it is a shrewd business decision by the band to refocus their music and to step aside from the Artaudian derangement of the sonic world present in the dropped songs.

It's perhaps useful to consider where, in the playing out of the scenes of the sixties, such examples of conformity or challenge go, and how their elements might be revealing of a complex series of interactions and transactions between experimental impulses and mainstream accommodations. In the binary of experimental versus mainstream the challenge of experimental art is often impossible to disentangle from the challenge of the category of art itself, and the recognition of an artistic seriousness of intent in popular culture is a strategy that necessarily begins to destabilize this in the period after 1963 (in fact, John Cage had preempted Cale's TV intervention in a 1960 appearance on the same show, performing *Water Walk*).[16] However, it is the Beatles' journey from immensely successful pop mainstream toward an experimental strand of art-pop that contains perhaps the most clear-cut and well-documented example of a reciprocal breakdown of the barrier between experimental and mainstream. It's in the replaying of the secret past of this encounter that the YouTube archive now permits that we begin to see this most strongly, in particular in the episodes surrounding the band's encounter with the radicalism of Yoko Ono's performance art.

BEATLEMYTHS AND THE ONOVERSE

The appearance of Yoko Ono in the Beatles' playing out of the originary myth of a rock band's growth and disintegration is a signal example of 1960s mainstream arts practice becoming engaged with and challenged by avant-garde actions. It is the moment when this band comes to exemplify the collision between experimental and avant-garde practices and those indicative of the mainstream. Prior to her involvement with the band through a relationship with John Lennon, Ono was associated with a range of significant figures in the international avant-garde, including the Fluxus group, John Cage, George Maciunas, and La Monte Young, and was already noted for her own artistic practices, which engaged with music, Dadaist performance, happenings, conceptual formulations, and writings in the experimental art worlds of New York in the mid-1960s (John Cale was also involved with these circles and created a Fluxus film piece, *Police Car*, alongside his involvement with music performance).

Maciunas's propositions on neo-Dadaist arts practice rejected illusionism for actions rooted in realities. The propositions outline, among other things a model of "concrete sound" that is closely related to the object producing it and is unmoderated by tone, pitch, or harmony and another model of "indeterminate form," which rejects the shaping of the artwork to, in his words, "perceive the reality of nature," something "which is largely indeterminate and unpredictable."[17] Maciunas propounded forms of artistic work that claimed a primary truthfulness in their registering of the reality from which they emerged. These ideas informed the interest in live, kinetic, indeterminate, and audience-participatory work that Ono pursued as part of the arts scene in which she first encountered Lennon, at a show of her work at London's Indica Gallery in 1967.[18]

To an international avant-garde, Ono's radicalism, most influentially and enduringly instanced by her 1964–65 *Cut-Piece*, which was restaged in London during Gustav Metzger's historically significant Destruction in Art Symposium in 1966 (an event to which John Latham also contributed), was proportionately as innovative and challenging as the Beatles' midsixties experiments in rock music were in their own field. At this point the group (which had been through two significant stylistic phases, as a club covers band and as besuited pioneers in the mainstreaming of the cultural dominance of rock and roll), was passing through a period of apparently progressive innovation, in which their music was increasingly tinged with the formalist experiments of modernist pioneers, literary nonsense games, and the lysergic adoption of tropes from Beat poetry, surrealism, and Hindu mysticism. Theirs had become an influential, if always warily commercial, exploration and adoption of many avant-garde strategies. The band's interest in complicating and challenging the palate of rock performance was particularly influenced by Lennon and McCartney's involvement in the underground art scene in sixties London, by Lennon's political sympathy for aspects of the wider counterculture, and by Harrison's interest in Hindu mysticism and the musical traditions of the Indian subcontinent.

Ian MacDonald,[19] among others, points to the ways in which the legacy of the modernist avant-garde made an appearance in the Beatles' work on the 1968 double White Album. By this stage Lennon and Ono were lovers and MacDonald notes the clear influence of Ono's own practices on Lennon's tape-loop collage "Revolution 9" from that album. Indeed, MacDonald claims the track as a truly significant avant-garde experiment in its moment, stating that "one need only compare Lennon's work with Luigi Nono's similar 'Non consumiamo Marx' (1969) to see how much more aesthetically and politically acute Lennon was than most of the vaunted avant-garde composers of the time."[20] This acuteness runs for MacDonald not only into a consideration with form but also with effect, amplifying the impact and influence of these experiments, placing the moment of the Christmas Day 1967 broadcast of the band's collaborative *Magical Mystery Tour* as the instant when the Beatles' tension with the mainstream became apparent and "parents began to part company with their sons and daughters over the group, rightly suspecting a drug-induced pretension setting in."[21] MacDonald is particularly concerned with the effect of the experimentation of "Revolution 9," suggesting that the context in which it happened amplified its impact and influence and that "Revolution 9" was particularly effective because of its appearance in a mainstream setting. Describing the track as Lennon's "sensory attack on the citadel of the intellect: a revolution in the head aimed, as he stressed at the time, at each individual listener,"[22] MacDonald points to the entryist achievement of the piece: "Merely to be exposed to it was (in theory), to disperse the stale, institutionalised consciousness which class-stratified society supposedly exuded like a cognitive smog." He adds that "around a million households owned copies if it within days of its release and, a quarter of a century later, its hearers number in the hundreds of millions."[23] What MacDonald suggests here is that the slippage between mainstream and experimental in the moment of the late-1960s media landscape had the potential to profoundly disorder the terms on which such a mainstream might operate and exist.

If this is indeed the case, then the immediate next steps in the Beatles' and Ono's aesthetic progress are worth examining to consider what happens to the mainstream when the experimental is deliberately engaged with, faced up to, and embraced—when the cultural citadel opens its doors and MacDonald's "revolution in the head" becomes externalized. While the Beatles might be interested in adopting avant-garde postures and forms, what might be the effect on the commercial and industrial imperatives surrounding their aesthetic choices if they should follow the logic of "Revolution 9" and begin to break down the definitional boundaries of their own previous practice? Barrett's maneuvers ended in failure; Cale's remained commercially, though not culturally, marginal. At the moment of their engagement with Ono, the Beatles were still a globally significant force.

THE BOOTLEG BEATLES

During early 1969 the issue of just how far experimental practices might operate in the mainstream came to the fore for the Beatles as the band tried to put together a new album prior to a return to live performance, the whole to be captured on film for cinema release. The abortive recordings came to be known as the *Get Back* sessions and could be heard for many years in a series of bootlegs, a form of samizdat popular culture in the 1970s and 1980s that steadily became more widely available as the Internet developed, leading to the official release of sections of the recordings in the "official" *Anthology* and *Let It Be Naked* CDs in the late 1990s and early 2000s. This partial release was then further built upon in the unlicensed release on the Web of sound recordings and video made by the film crew recording the project, containing hours of studio banter and conversation alongside footage of rehearsals.

As Simon Reynolds suggests in his *Retromania: Pop Culture's Addiction to Its Own Past*, that segue between the traditional obscurity of the analog archive—so hard to source, so costly to amass and preserve, so daunting to transcribe—and the digital—easy to compile, store, and index, so simple to protect—has swiftly rearranged the relationship between present and past: "old stuff either directly permeates the present, or lurks just beneath the surface of the current, in the form of on-screen windows to other times," making it difficult to recall that prior to this "one lived most of the time in a cultural present tense, with the past confined to specific zones, trapped in particular objects and locations."[24] What ought to be added here is that particular symbolic relations, readings, and interpretations, based in large part on sequentiality—on how something appeared then, how it spoke in its moment—have also undergone a reworking. Reynolds remarks on the remodeling of what it is to make art in a present where the past is always available to act on the present. Yet he is concerned primarily with the availability of the past now. If we look at how the presence of this past inflects our reading of the Beatles, we can see it changing the meaning of *then*.

In the Beatles' case, three taped sessions in particular, all emerging from the period of January 1969, capture some of the tension of the interplay between the band as purveyors of mainstream entertainment, as innovators who are at odds with their past and yet still caught up in it, and as representatives of a mainstream culture that is being questioned, challenged, and threatened by the arrival of the avant-garde in its contemporary formulation. One, filmed in the Beatles' Saville Row headquarters in January 1969 and available on YouTube for some time in the earlier part of the decade, then blocked by Apple Corps Ltd. due to copyright infringement, although the clip remerges frequently, records a moment of routine rehearsal.[25] The band awaits a take, the camera focused on Paul McCartney. He rises to begin the song "Get Back," cued in by the film crew, clearly aware of the camera. The take soon breaks down, but the camera still rolls. McCartney and Lennon slide into a parody of the working musician, mocking their own superstar status at the interruption and comically abusing those in the control room. The tape then cuts to a rehearsal of a second song, "I've Got a Feeling," at the moment where it again breaks down. At this point Lennon starts a parody version of an earlier Beatles song, "Help," his own, at the time groundbreaking, composition. His parody suggests a stilted, childish, show band version of the earlier incarnation of the group. McCartney joins in, mocking the call-and-response backing vocals, both singing a "piss-take" recognizable as the kind of *Goon Show*-influenced comedy exaggeration that the band is shot through with. They do the same with a brief burst of "Please Please Me," an even earlier hit. The previous, suited, light-entertainment-group formula of the band appears to be mocked here. The rehearsal then breaks, the musicians set down their instruments, chat, leave the room. As they do so the camera pulls back and it becomes clear that Yoko Ono has been sitting, silent, with her back to the camera throughout the take. While McCartney works with guest keyboardist Billy Preston on another song John and Yoko stand silently at the other end of the studio, hugging.

The video clip, dragged from the past by YouTube's existence, re-visions a set of familiar tropes from Beatles mythology—the band's look, beards, long hair, a sense of dazed, claustrophobic disengagement—that is captured in the parallel studio-shot film sessions included in the film *Let It Be*. The personalities and tensions conventionally ascribed to the band members are present, as is the existence of Ono as a focus for those tensions. The readiness of the band to undermine themselves, their break with past styles indicated in the mocking of old work, the sense of Lennon being in charge of the parody dynamic, with McCartney joining in but perhaps not quite getting the joke, are all also familiar from accounts of the band's internal dynamic. However, the film also resonates with a hidden history of "Beatlemyth," interweaving with exterior mythologizing of the meanings, methods, and achievements of the band and with the symbolic orders of rock music, youth, radicalism, corporate identity and globalization, innovation, and tradition that circulate around it. In particular, the silent, seated presence of Ono brings into the rehearsal a raft of ideas and energies that highlight the particular difficulties of unpicking the radical and the conventional, the experimental and the mainstream, in this moment. Seated among the laddish camaraderie of a group of young Englishmen renowned for the deflating brand of humor known as "taking the piss" sits a representative of a knowing, serious yet playful cosmopolitan avant-garde, whose radicalism consists of a deliberate rejection of the boundaries of mainstream arts practice, its definitions of value, its relationships to temporality and commodity, its negotiation of the relation between performer and spectator.[26] Above all, Yoko Ono's presence brings the forceful impact of issues of gender and ethnicity into the previously monocultural space of Beatles performance, as does, at this moment, the cooption, as a short-term fifth member, of the talents of the young African American keyboard player, Billy Preston.

What is perhaps most significant in considering the reframing of the then in the now that arises from this is the way in which the historically inscribed impasse between Beatlenorms and Onovations shifts as one examines the tapes. In other footage the tense coexistence between Ono and the band for a time seems to move toward something else. Another scene from the same session shows the band seated in the same positions in the studio and jamming on a free-form piece while Ono ululates wordlessly over the top of it.[27] Here the whole band apart from Harrison appears to be involved, with Starr drumming intensely and McCartney dragging feedback out of his guitar. Seated next to Ono, Lennon hammers the back of his guitar, then waves it in front of a microphone to set up a feedback loop. Another, heavily edited, recording exists of the band jamming with Ono as they rehearse in Teddington film studios for the final version of *Let It Be*.[28] Ono, wearing a black hat, stands before a microphone—a performer and a collaborator in her own right, her vocalizing Maciunas's concrete sound exemplified—while the band members improvise on a blues-rock riff. McCartney plays the accompanying iconoclast for this deconstruction, setting up feedback by holding his guitar in front of his amplifier. This is the Beatles with Ono somehow, unexpectedly, a part of their aesthetic experiment, apparently accepted into engagement with the whole group rather than standing to the side as Lennon's mentor. It appears that Ono's contribution contradicts the dominant existing categories of rock, of singing, composition, technique, tradition, in a moment where avant-garde experiment, driven by any of these participants, begins to clash with the dynamics and the aesthetic and commercial demands, of the conventional band. However, it is as bootleg that the film survives, the footage not included in the final edit of the *Let It Be* film.[29] Ono is present in that film, but as the conventional interloper of "Beatlemyth," the companion to John Lennon whose hostility broke up the band rather than the artist with an independent international reputation. The limitations of the injection of Dadaist innovations into the existing form of the music are clear, both musically, as McCartney and Lennon seem to resort, in the face of Ono's performance, to attempts to break the confines of blues rock, but find themselves repeating familiar riffs or breakdowns, and institutionally, as the official archive glosses over her involvement. Some online fansite commentaries suggest that the whole performance was a muddled, irritated reaction to Harrison walking out on the band earlier in the day—a hiatus that lasted for a period and led the band to relocate from the film studios to their Apple basement recording suite.[30]

If the experiment of "Revolution 9" were to lead somewhere, we might expect it to be at this point that we see the band's aesthetic change, shift, mutate. In fact, in the setting of the *Get Back* rehearsals, as the band members find themselves circling around jams on their own influences and roots material, the essential conservatism of the form they have become exponents of seems to have taken hold once again. Close analysis of the multifarious bootlegs and fragments of the sessions suggests that the Twickenham jam predates the Saville Row videos and that Ono's collaborative involvement generally provoked the diplomatic, or petulant, disappearance of one or another of the group from the sessions (George Harrison, in the case of the Teddington jam).[31] There is little from these recordings that carries any of the charge of those underground, experimental influences. There is also little on the official releases from these or the associated sessions—1969's *Abbey Road* and 1970's *Let It Be*—that makes anything like the same claim to experimentalism.

Notwithstanding the official release pattern, a strand of defiantly playful experiment emerges from this meeting and becomes a challenging confrontation with the mainstream of commercial pop culture represented by the cutups of Lennon's "Revolution 9" or the vocal experiments of Lennon and Ono's "Cambridge 1969" from the album *Unfinished Music No 2: Life with the Lions* or their earlier *Two Virgins* album from 1968. Ono's introduction of the extremes of Dadaist performance into the rehearsals of the band is a signature of the blurring of the boundaries between the mainstream and the experimental that the moment of the late 1960s seems to have opened up. In its aftermath, as the relationship between countercultures and dominant cultures changed, and as the commercial landscape of art and mass entertainment also mutated, both of the traditions that the band and the artist represent can be seen to be interweaving. The shock of Ono's aesthetic as a revolution not only of the head but of the body, voice, and social being is registered and embraced.

In the moment of these recordings it is Lennon who seems to be placed in dialogue with a general radicalism, being persuaded to fund causes and publications and, over a period, being drawn into the world of U.S. radicalism on one of the albums most written out of the group's iconography, his and Ono's *Sometime in New York City*. It is in the later period that McCartney seems to become more concerned with his reputation in relation to experimentalism, almost as though this represents a harder corrective to his own perceived sentimentalism and concern for melody and relatively tame lyrical concepts above social commentary. For Ono, the commitment to avant-garde artistic event and publishing practices continues through the early stages of her involvement with the Beatles and into the period after the group's split, but then becomes increasingly focused on a hard-edged musical experiment that seems to echo the work done at these sessions and that, despite some diversions, forms as influential a strand of precedent and influence as that of the band themselves, one that resurfaces repeatedly in a range of movements—punk, riot grrl, dance, and rave—into the contemporary period. Her solo albums, such as *Yoko Ono/Plastic One Band*, at one point derided as the unlistenable counterpoint to Lennon's own and as a form of millionaire vanity publishing, have grown increasingly in reputation, in part as explorations of the Dadaist approach that Maciunas might have recognized.

REREADING THE ARCHIVE

This relatively "hidden" evidence of Ono's Dadaist rehearsals with the Beatles, as well as the parallel engagement with artistic experiment in the works of John Cale and Syd Barrett where the experimental remains the less prominent, less supported B-side to the A-side of their groups' catalogs, perhaps suggests a reinforcing of an experimental/mainstream binary. The irreconcilable nature of the collaboration appears clear, as each road to truth threatens to tarmac over the other. However, if we consider the ways in which the archive now represents these experiments, it also suggests that such a dichotomy is perhaps a misrecognition of the mechanism of cultural transformations, one that might become clear only when read with hindsight, through consideration of the relational nature of its terms, their conceptual basis, and, crucially, the effects of avant-garde practice. The *Get Back* moment, along with Barrett's solo albums and Cale's TV show and subsequent slippery pop career, perhaps illustrates that roads to truth were being rerouted during the 1960s.

In 1994 Doug Sulpy and Ray Schweighardt's *Drugs, Divorce and a Slipping Image: The Unauthorized Story of the Beatles' "Get Back" Sessions* put together a painstaking reading of what the audio tapes gathered during the *Get Back* filming appear to mean. The book contains an exhaustive transcription of each available session, of the music and the context in which it is made and heard, of the chat, and of the inflections of voice and tone. It is a dogged and strangely touching act of detective work, pushing toward a comprehensive microhistorical reading of the moment, and its appearance in 1994 reflects the fact that a vast range of material recording the events existed but was not officially in the public domain nor widely available at the time of the sessions. In the subsequent period the analog archive has been supplemented by the digital. The appearance of the Cale TV show tape on the Web is of a piece with the ongoing mining of his own hidden, lost, or neglected works, from a set of experimental classical compositions and collaborations to the 2015 compilation of his production work with a range of iconic figures. Barrett's own history as a Pink Floyd band member, solo artist, and recluse has led to official and bootleg releases, along with a plethora of unlicensed Web material containing everything from stalker videos of his later life in Cambridge—a shambling figure ghosted onto the recirculating images of his younger self—and interviews with Cambridge characters who claim a connection with him to an official site containing pictures of his artwork and his "craft"—a range of eccentrically colored furniture with which he furnished his semidetached house in his later years. There is much that is ethically suspect about some of this material, yet it is the rediscovery of mediations from the 1960s on the Web that has allowed a writer like Chapman to reassess the mythologies surrounding Barrett's retreat.

While the official film of the *Get Back* sessions, *Let It Be*, remains unavailable on DVD, the digitization and circulation of the archive has flung up footage of the work of the Plastic Ono Band, Lennon and Ono's attempt to stage some of the potential of experiment that could not find a place in the Beatles' output. Some of that work was released as *Live Peace in Toronto*, the soundtrack to a 1969 concert by the band at a rock and roll revival festival. For it, the hurriedly assembled group of musicians rehearsed on the plane over, and the album was released in a beautiful light-blue sleeve with a cloud in the corner, which was of a piece with the strand of utopian imagery in Ono's visual artworks at the time. Side one (vinyl divide noted) contained a mixture of Lennon's homages to his rock and roll roots, in keeping with the festival's plans and notable for the degree of fear recognizable in Lennon's voice. The second side of the original vinyl LP contained Ono's contribution, a disconcerting collision of the surreal with the pedestrian that simultaneously showed quite how far the Dionysian drive of "rock" was tempered and restrained by the moment of the pop song. Having occupied a bag next to Lennon during the rock and roll set, Ono then adds vocalizations to two of Lennon's numbers before becoming lead singer on two of her own extended songs, "Don't Worry Kyoko, Mummy's Only Looking for Her Hand in the Snow" and "John, John, Let's Hope for Peace." Her intervention is truly remarkable, a cacophonic presentation of the human voice as Artaudian vehicle of free expression, a texture rather than a tune, a radical contrast with what has gone before. As with "Revolution 9," this was entryism, and to my teenage mind it was a revelation—if not one that I wished to revisit frequently. Upon first encounter as audio, the event seemed to my imagination to be a tightrope walk of agonized rock expressionism from its protagonists, blasted into the darkness of a vast hall and electric with the intensity of confrontation. In later years I began to read side 1 a little differently. It wasn't very good. Arty postpunk replaced blues rock, and the album was sold. The DVD of the festival, filmed by D. A. Pennebaker and featuring footage of the other acts but repackaged with an interview by Yoko as a Lennon artifact, reawakened my interest—the past brought into the present.[32]

The film of the event reawakens a sense of the entryist dynamics of Ono's art. A stadium, a crowd steeped in Bo Diddley's, Chuck Berry's, and Little Richard's appearances, some period rigging and facilities presage the collision of the avant-garde and the conventional in a ritual of mutual incomprehension. This is an audience of rock and roll traditionalists, Teddy Boys, and rockers with a devotion to the acts that formed the core of the crossover explosion of rock and roll in the mid-1950s. Undoubtedly for the figures in the Toronto stadium, the point of the Plastic Ono Band was to present Lennon's homage to his urban rocker roots, and not to his suburban middle-class art school heritage, the place from which his sympathies for the experiment and audacity of Ono's work may be seen to emerge. Perhaps the nervousness in Lennon's voice, at the time expressed as a fear of performing live onstage again after a three-year absence, was as much a fear of the situationist-style intervention that he was about to perform as Ono became the counterpoint to his mainstream harnessing of the audience's goodwill and attention. Certainly the strategy seems like an avant-garde theatrical coup—give the audience what they want and then, as J. L. Styan said of the purposes of the Dada exhibition, create the "utmost degree of misunderstanding between the performer and the audience."[33] The impression that the album recording leaves behind is of the band exiting the stage, amplifiers screaming, to an audience response of baffled uncertainty. The DVD version presents a less confident retrospective playing out of avant-garde practice, Lennon managing Ono's appearance with a mixture of humor and unease, Ono even seeming to seek the approval of the audience as singer, not as hardened provocateur.

At this historical remove the event as a whole remains fascinatingly awkward to categorize—not tired commercial art seeking revitalization nor hard-core avant-garde provocation—not interventionist prank, nor entirely straight-faced immersion in the avant-garde aesthetic on show. Philip Auslander discusses the concert in the context of delineating the self-conscious playing with performance identities of a series of late-sixties acts in the "glamticipations" chapter of his *Performing Glam Rock*. In this case he reads Lennon's band's performance as grounded in a deliberately "serious, musicianly image favoured by psychedelic rockers," which locates it both as continuous with the rock and roll acts he followed and with the counterculture's anticipated rock rituals—low on show, high on serious engagement in a musical ritual. In this reading he places Ono's contribution as interestingly "grounded in and continuous with the rock-and-roll tradition" due to its emergence from an opening chord sequence based on an Everly Brothers song.[34] The film gives little evidence of the reception of Ono's appearance—there is no audience footage, and little can be heard of applause, acclaim, or derision—and contemporary accounts are contradictory. However, one of the foundational observations regarding the binary divide between modernist arts practices and the traditions they assault is that made by Ortega y Gassett in 1927: "Modern art will always have the masses against it. It is essentially unpopular, indeed, it is antipopular."[35] It is unlikely that the worship of a Beatle's live appearance extended to an embrace of Dadaist provocation in this case.

AVANT-GARDES, MEN, AND 1960S MAINSTREAMS

The landscape of artistic production into which Ono intrudes through her relationship with Lennon is an elaborately homosocial one, defined by the codes and habits of a close-knit crew who have developed their working and interpersonal practices over many years, often through enforced close proximity. The tapes and videos seem to illustrate an awareness of this particularity. The physical presence of Ono as Lennon's companion appears to be jarring to the cultural codes of the room. It's clear that the challenge of her and Lennon's combined positioning, the suggestion that Ono is part of the rehearsal, that her word is to be considered, and that, if strong opinions are expressed, they're shared between the couple is confrontational. The admittance of Ono into rehearsal suggests that Lennon is deliberately forcing the band to accept an avant-garde edge not within their conceptual frame and that this edge is not just about the nature of music but about the degree of openness to the ethical, cultural, psychological, sexual, ideological positions that the assumed norms of the band represent.

What happens in the aftermath of the period when the Beatles meet Ono is fascinating primarily for what doesn't result. Lennon and Ono go further than "Revolution 9" and the filmed jams, into material such as *The Wedding Album*. Harrison produces his own record of experimental music, *Electronic Sound*, but the band stays focused on pop-rock, and when it finally performs a rooftop concert for the *Let It Be* film, it does so as a four piece. Whatever happened in the rehearsals, some of them containing Ono as part not of the Plastic Ono Band but of the Beatles themselves, the band identity remained mainstream, suggesting that while Ian MacDonald is right to identify the shifted consciousness—the revolution in the head—of the moment as something that such avant-garde practices helped to create, its challenge was to be accommodated within conventional frames. Indeed, while the radicalism of Ono's contribution to the Beatles' sessions is significant, it is not a long temporal journey from them to her 1972 appearance, again available on YouTube, as a saccharine soft-rock balladeer, singing "Winter Song" from her *Approximately Infinite Universe* album, a record made with Lennon's assistance and suggesting that her experimental aesthetic might be infinitely adjustable. It may be that in the case of the Beatles the appearance of the experimental in the citadel of the conventional calls into question the terms on which the conventional operates, and in doing so has the potential—and actual—effect of breaking up the band, because the terms on which it operates are no longer valid. This would suggest that unsettling experimental radicalism may be powerful and efficacious in its provoking of aesthetic or social change. Yet it may also be that the entryism into the cultural citadel is the step that begins the reverse process, effecting the smoothing out of the jagged aggression of the avant-garde and its transformation into something more consoling to the mainstream.

Simon Reynolds presents a persuasive account of where the slow fade of modernist ambitions leads in popular music during the post-1960s era when he suggests that pop and rock as art forms are no longer places to look for oppositions. In his analysis what remains of the sixties in the contemporary picture is a space where works such as "Revolution 9" and "Octopus's Garden"—or "Do You Want to Know a Secret?"—coexist in the same massive library of materials. From here they surface in the works of the magpie Web-browsing musical innovators he cites, such as Hudson Mohawke, Nico Muhly, and Daniel Lopatin,[36] whose innovation is a form of never-ending collage that both the Schwitters and the Russolos of the high modernist age might admire and celebrate for its creative juxtapositions, if not its interventionist rigor.

An anecdote that surrounds Syd Barrett and is confirmed in Chapman's book as being basically true has him leading the other members of Pink Floyd through a rehearsal of a new song during the sessions for ". . . Secrets." The song, centered on Barrett's shouted chorus of "have you got it yet," seemed impossible to follow, the structure and chords changing as Barrett played it and the band trailed along—until the moment they realized they'd been had and that the title was the conceptual joke of the whole piece. In that story, and perhaps in the Beatles' awkward, uncertain adoption of aesthetic innovation around Ono or in Cale's straight-faced seriousness, we see at work the dynamic that emerges as the key modulating factor between the mainstream and the experimental, undermining the conventional and defusing the radical in ways that point forward to the flattening effects of the postmodern era. The playing out, in this space, of the role of "taking the piss" anticipates a burgeoning ironization characteristic of the subsequent era. Perhaps what is most clearly illustrated in these episodes is a "classically" postmodern illustration of the ways in which such ironization effects a renegotiation of the border agreements between the experimental and the mainstream, reinscribing the radicalism of the experiment as a matter of effect rather than form and illustrating that such effects may only, as in the case of Cale and Barrett, be judged with close attention to the microhistorical complexity of the moment.

POSTSCRIPT: WHO'S LOOKING, WHERE, AND WHY?

In the summer of 2003 Paul McCartney played a concert in Moscow's Red Square. The concert was an event that drew together the swirling iconographies surrounding what might be termed "late rock" in a mélange of free-market, celebrity, mediation, technological, national, and cultural identities, fashions, and aesthetics and that referenced two eras, both the sixties as a nostalgic reference point for an idealized freedom and the same moment in the past of the Soviet Union, in which rock music functioned as a form of samizdat underground culture. The ironies of postsixties history were jumbled together as the event progressed—the former GUM department store alongside the square was carpeted in real grass for the invitation-only reception; the sharpshooters on the roof watched over an introductory piece of musical theater choreographed by Heather Mills, including a Magritte figure with an apple suspended in front of his face, a pierrot, a Marie Antoinette circling to the techno authored by McCartney's late rave era alter ego The Fireman. I found myself part of the "support group," in the well of the stage where only the hardened fans could wave and shout, themselves not the golden circle of seated ultrarich who filled the first fifty yards of the space beyond the stage before the people crowded into the rear. Halfway through an early song the diminutive figure of Putin took his seat, passing behind where I stood, a smile of embarrassed satisfaction flickering as he took the rapturous applause of the golden circle, Gorbachev's presence a few feet away seemingly ignored by all. Onstage, McCartney's band of slightly less youthful than they played it rockers performed as if they'd hit the session musician's jackpot, ranging from early sixties Liverpudlian rewrites of American rock and roll to late-sixties internationally inflected versions of the same, from the strange, Northern kitchen sink melancholy of "Eleanor Rigby" to the indefinable auto rock of McCartney's later years in which there seems to be no clear set of roots or reference points. The whole was a relentlessly engineered spectacle of commodified gestures toward archetypes of freedom, individuality, sentiment, and the corporate promise of transcendence offered by big rock.

And yet, standing next to a man in his sixties holding a St. Petersburg Beatles Fan Club banner, I found it impossible to remain divorced from the fact that this event held, nurtured, and celebrated some potent and resonant values. Its postmodern plurality did not flatten but in fact attenuated a concoction of affects. It did so in a manner that reflects some of the key ways in which rock music performance emerging from the 1960s problematizes the boundaries between entertainment and art, between the obscure and the popular, and between the conventional and the radical. Built into its subsequent mythologizing are a series of negotiations across the values we might associate with the commercial, the mainstream, the dominant, and the conservative in arts practices as well as the drives, desires, and energies of the radical, the avant-garde, and the subversive: the challenging, in other words, often reflected in moments where the appearance of rock music as an aesthetically conservative, simplistic, commodified, and trivial form in one context might be reflected back through its appearance as the opposite of all of these in another. For the St. Petersburg branch of the Beatles Fan Club, for the left-wing Spanish activist under Franco who once described to me the group as the "kind of cultural imperialism of which I approve," for the young John Cale as he enters the world of the American game show, or for the young Syd Barrett faced with the music machine's demands, the context of the encounter operates as radical, and as experimental. It challenges accepted binaries and categorizations, and it answers to the NBC anchor's suggestion that one should keep looking, in the face of the Beatles approaching America, for that "mute, inglorious Milton." It also seems to me that it does so on the fault line between commodified fiction and resilient, absorbent, energized actuality. That actuality relates directly to the explorable and documented effects of artistic and cultural strategies of engagement. Their secret histories are increasingly represented and available as the accessibility of the archive grows and grows. In the rock music of the 1960s the experimental raises the same question as the besuited Beatles of 1963, "Do You Want to Know a Secret?" But it presents a different answer: that the world is more complex, less representable, more mysterious than habituated forms might allow and that to acknowledge this is to be bound up in constant, engaged, and provocative process and exchange.

NOTES

1. The audio soundtrack of the now lost film can be heard at "Historic NBC Beatles TV Find Was First to Show Group in Concert, Author Says," Examiner.com, November 20, 2013, http://www.examiner.com/article/historic-nbc-beatles-tv-find-was-first-to-show-group-concert-author-says.

2. To watch the performance now is to notice some interesting inflections in the presentation of the group's music, the setting provoking a careful choreography of sound and image to achieve popular mainstream appeal. The besuited band are well drilled and "professional" in their presentation. Their repertoire references American rhythm and blues and rock and roll roots, but with the energy and abrasiveness of those forms restrained and balanced in a repertoire that also embraces show tunes. The first set of the evening consisted of four numbers, all featuring Paul McCartney's lead vocals and including a middle-of-the-road standard, Peggy Lee's "'Til There Was You." At one point the band members chat with Sullivan and appear to be about to be introduced to their audience, but the conversation is kept off mike and the much-remarked-upon—and unpredictable—cheek and charm of the band's wit is held at bay.

3. Paul Gleed, "'The Rest of You, If You'll Just Rattle Your Jewelry': The Beatles and Questions of Mass and High Culture," in *The Beatles: Cultural Studies, Literary Criticism and the Fab Four*, ed. Kenneth Womack and Todd F. Davis (Albany: State University of New York Press, 2006), 164.

4. John Lennon and Yoko Ono, *Unfinished Music No 1: Two Virgins* (London: Apple, 1968); George Harrison, *Electronic Sound* (Zapple: London, 1969); John Lennon and Paul McCartney, "Carnival of Light," unreleased, 1967.

5. Alan Filewod, "Part III: Introduction," in *Avant-Garde Exchange and Material Cultures: Vectors of the Radical*, ed. Michael Sell (Basingstoke, UK: Palgrave Macmillan, 2010), 145–46.

6. Ian MacDonald, *Revolution in the Head: The Beatles' Records and the Sixties*, 2nd ed. (London: Pimlico, 1995), 51.

7. David Sheff, *All We Are Saying: The Last Major Interview with John Lennon and Yoko Ono* (New York: St Martin's Press, 2000), 165.

8. For an articulation of this perspective, see Elizabeth L. Wollman, "Rock 'Authenticity' and the Reception of the Staged Rock Musical," in *The Theater Will Rock: A History of the Rock Musical, from Hair to Hedwig* (Ann Arbor, University of Michigan Press, 2006), 24–41.

9. Philip Auslander, *Performing Glam Rock: Gender and Theatricality in Popular Music* (Ann Arbor, University of Michigan Press, 2006); Wollman, *Theater Will Rock*; Nicholas Cook and Richard Pettengill, eds. *Taking It to the Bridge: Music as Performance* (Ann Arbor, University of Michigan Press, 2013).

10. Gleed, "The Rest of You," 163.

11. *I've Got A Secret*, broadcast September 16, 1963, http://www.youtube.com/watch?v=TYHIqMmtS-0.

12. Ibid., 19:51.

13. In fact, Cage himself had already appeared on the same show, in 1960, to perform *Water Walk*. In 1963 the young rock musician and classical composer Frank Zappa also performed a similar crossover, making an appearance on the *Steve Allen Show* and playing a bicycle with the host.

14. Robert Chapman, *Syd Barrett: A Very Irregular Head* (London: Faber, 2010), 196.

15. Ibid., 195.

16. *I've Got A Secret*, broadcast January 1960, http://www.youtube.com/watch?v=SSulycqZH-U.

17. George Maciunas, "Neo-Dada in Music, Theater, Poetry, Art," in *Art in Theory 1900–2000: An Anthology of Changing Ideas*, 2nd ed., ed. Charles Harrison and Paul J. Wood (Oxford: Blackwell, 2003), 729.

18. Chris Stephens and Katherine Stout, *Art and the Sixties: This Was Tomorrow* (London: Tate, 2004), 41.

19. MacDonald, *Revolution in the Head*.

20. Ibid., 204. Lennon and Ono collaborated on a series of experimental side projects during the period in which many of the techniques Maciunas outlines were employed.

21. Ibid.

22. Ibid., 231.

23. Ibid., 230.

24. Simon Reynolds, *Retromania: Pop Culture's Addiction to Its Own Past* (London: Faber, 2011), 57.

25. Beatles rehearsal, January 23, 1969, Apple headquarters, Saville Row, London, previously available at http://www.youtube.com/watch?v=Bg9TyUVHXPk&feature=related; this video was withdrawn for copyright reasons, but it has resurfaced recently at https://www.youtube.com/watch?v=29Fpi2FAeik.

26. This ironic and ambivalent response rose tellingly when Paul McCartney sought to release his sound experiment "Carnival of Light" for the Beatles *Anthology* project in the 1990s. By this stage George Harrison was in full retreat from the experimental and

vetoed the release; McCartney suggested that Harrison's attitude toward this kind of experiment could be summed up as "avant-garde a clue." Vanessa Thorpe, "Forty Years on McCartney Wants the World to Hear 'Lost' Beatles' Epic," *The Guardian*, November 16, 2008, http://www.theguardian.com/music/2008/nov/16/paul-mccartney-carnival-of-light.

27. Beatles rehearsal, January 23, 1969, 2:43 onward.

28. Beatles rehearsal, 1969, outtake from *Let It Be* sessions, Twickenham Studios, opening to 2:43. This video is no longer available online, although currently a compilation of scenes featuring Ono jamming with the Beatles from both the Saville Row (3:10–7:54) and Twickenham Studios sessions (opening to 2:53; n.b., the sound recording here is out of sync with the video) can be found at https://www.youtube.com/watch?v=4FcW7v9Txkw.

29. Though sections of it appear in a later Ono documentary, *Yoko Ono, Then and Now* (1984).

30. For example, see the detailed commentary on the contents of a bootleg version of the session, "The Beatles—Twelve Days at Twickenham," Collectors Music Reviews, October 4, 2011, at www.collectorsmusicreviews.com/beatles/the-beatles-twelve-days-at-twickenham-unicorn-records-uc.

31. Doug Sulpy and Ray Schweighardt, *Drugs, Divorce and a Slipping Image: The Unauthorized Story of the Beatles' "Get Back" Sessions* (Princeton Junction, NJ: The 910, 1994), 10.4.

32. D. A. Pennebaker, *John Lennon and the Plastic Ono Band: Sweet Toronto* (N.p.: Slam Dunk Media, 2010), DVD.

33. J. L. Styan, *Modern Drama in Theory and Practice*, vol. 2, *Symbolism, Surrealism and the Absurd* (Cambridge: Cambridge University Press, 1981), 51.

34. Auslander, *Performing Glam Rock*, 27.

35. José Ortega y Gassett, "The Dehumanization of Art" (1927), trans. Helene Weyl, in *Art in Theory 1900–2000: An Anthology of Changing Ideas*, 2nd ed., ed. Charles Harrison and Paul J. Wood (Oxford: Blackwell, 2003), 324.

36. Reynolds, *Retromania*, 78–79.

Kimberly Jannarone

Mass Performance, outside and inside the Democratic National Convention, August 1968

Mayor Richard Daley is on his feet, shaking his fist. The camera does not record the sound, but the words he forms with his mouth are clear: "Fuck you," he yells to Senator Abraham Ribicoff of Connecticut, "Fuck you." Images of police brutally beating young men and women are playing on television screens in front of horrified delegates. A cheerful white balloon floats in front of the mayor's face. He swats it away. Ribicoff speaks into the microphone, underneath the roars now rising in the auditorium. "How hard it is," the senator says. "How hard it is to accept the truth."[1]

The "truth" Ribicoff had just asserted was that there were "Gestapo tactics" at work that night "in the streets of Chicago."[2] The date is August 28, 1968, the place is Chicago's International Amphitheater, and the event is the Democratic National Convention. Its significance, for this volume, is the fact that the tactics of experimental mass performance have just infiltrated the mainstream, with dramatic and devastating results.

This essay reads three major events surrounding the Chicago convention—street violence outside the Hilton Hotel, the peace debate, and the nominating procedure—as moments when outside, experimental, participatory mass performance clashed with the inside, orderly, commercial performance. Flag burners—unkempt, bohemian, and chaotic—confronted the flag wavers—well dressed, well funded, and bureaucratic.[3] Both groups used mass performance to fight for the hearts and minds of the people. Both claimed to embody participatory democracy. Outside and inside, drama and politics ran on parallel tracks, in a violent, dizzying circulation of performance tactics. The results of August 1968? The media's role as a defining force in political conventions was catapulted to a new level.[4] The Republicans—unscathed by any comparable internal division—won the presidency. The Vietnam War—the reason for the protests—continued well into the next decade.

The riots on the outside are well known, the orchestration of the inside event less so. This essay is not the place to rehearse the protest events in Grant and Lincoln Parks in detail: those have been discussed well in book-length studies such as those of David Farber and Norman Mailer and also in the excellent Chana Gazit documentary.[5] Critical works have tended to focus primarily on the protestors, highlighting how their fervent protest was brutally punished by the forces of law and order. What is crucial for our purposes here, however, is the violent exchange of performance tactics outside and inside the amphitheater. This fraught confrontation gives us a lens through which to view how, in 1968, two influential social bodies tried to use mass performance to manifest different conceptions of "the people."

The outside's and inside's two performance strategies reflect, to a large degree, a conservative/experimental divide, but the impact of the week comes from their convergence. The streets were experimental, but experiment was the norm for youth culture in 1968. The cult figures, musicians, performers, and authors on the scene at the Chicago protests were part of popular culture for young women and young men—especially those threatened with being sent off to die in Vietnam. The Democratic National Committee (DNC) delegates and Mayor Daley were shielded by their age and careers against the immediate pressures bearing down on the younger generation. Outside was primarily youth; inside was the older generation. (The protestors, though not all young, represented youthful idealism and inclusiveness. This is a fact emphasized in the detailed coverage by Norman Mailer, who consistently uses the word *kids* to describe the protestors.) It was when the people attending the convention realized that it was their sons and daughters who were outside that the appeals of the outside popular culture finally made themselves known inside the amphitheater and the convention hotels.

Representative Wayne Hays reflected a common way of parsing the sixties when he yelled into a microphone at the Democratic convention on Wednesday, "There's a minority among us, represented over in Grant Park, who would substitute beards for brains, license for liberty, . . . riots for reason."[6] His angry dualism established this familiar opposition: passionate, embodied, youthful protest on one side, expressed through "cursing, anger, and fury";[7] on the other side, orderly, administratively cool, middle-aged enforcement of power, expressing its force through a sheen of polite decorum. The week in Chicago manifests this opposition in the two different approaches to mass performance. The outside creates and welcomes experimental artists—Beats, Yippies, activist theater troupes; the inside houses the commercial mainstream, where seats are bought, programs are followed, the audience behaves according to prescribed rules, and spectators are coaxed to demonstrate how much they are enjoying themselves. In Chicago both sides created a mise en scène appropriate to their ideals, as we will see, and both attempted to stage their beliefs by directing the bodies of as many people as they could.

We will examine the two sides' approaches to performance—what I will call the Internal Machine and the Street Theater—and then follow three major dramatic scenes where those approaches clashed and crossed over. My argument is that the tidy binaries established by both sides broke down over the course of five days (August 25–29), with a third system—anchored in the media—establishing itself. By tracing how methods of mass performance shifted hands and changed meaning, we can gain clearer insight into the turbulent circulation of ideas that marked culture in the sixties.

THE INTERNAL MACHINE

Considering the convention planners' performance as a machine—political, traditional, mainstream—allows us to analyze their production strategies as distinct from those of the protestors. The DNC leaders strove to write a strong narrative, cast key political figures in leading roles, reduce the rest of the players to supporting parts, design the space, manage the house, and control technologies in ways that would force focus on a unified event. Jamming the amphitheater with more people than it was meant to hold (6,511 delegates on a floor meant to hold 4,850),[8] they strove to use coordinated masses to enact an ideal "body politic."

Inside the amphitheater where the convention was held, the leading Democrats—mostly middle-aged and older—advanced an "us versus them" narrative, employing a binary framework to establish themselves as the stable party fighting off an unruly challenger. "We have no flag-burners at this Democratic National Convention," Mayor Daley shouted on Monday, "and I don't think any of them would belong here." "We," the delegates, are not "they," the masses threatening to intrude on the peaceful unfurling of the democratic process. The convention would host not passionate, embodied debate but carefully orchestrated displays of unity, national pride, and parliamentary procedure. Control and decorum were the rules for this performance, organized with a mind to the mainstream audience who would be watching it on television. The organizers carefully stage-managed the event, following traditional convention scripts.

President Lyndon B. Johnson did not attend the convention, but he was essentially coproducing it with Daley. When analyzing the DNC's performance, we must keep in mind that Johnson was the man behind the curtain who wrote much of the script and cast most of the roles. His control over the party included not only the choice of nominee and the location of the event but also—crucially, disastrously—the majority party position on Vietnam. Just days before the convention, Vice President Hubert Humphrey had put forward a war policy that included concessions to peace advocates, but Johnson unequivocally rejected it, leaving Humphrey with nothing to offer the voices of dissent.[9] The convention thus began with a clear display of the president's power: When asked how he would differentiate his position on Vietnam from Johnson's, Humphrey declined to answer. "Would you mind if I just stated my position?" he asked, answered by a chorus of no's—"I did not come here to repudiate the President of the United States."[10] This supervised position, stated and taped in a controlled fashion, reflects how Johnson, who had a negative attitude toward the press, coordinated the media in an unprecedented manner for a convention.

By 1968 national conventions had to be staged with a mass audience in mind. No longer events staged primarily for the few thousand attendees, conventions responded to what Stephen J. Wayne refers to as "democratizing pressures" after World War II, "aided by developments in communications technology. The advent of television provided a medium through which people could now see and hear the political campaigns in their own living rooms."[11] Media historian David Culbert argues that "changes in television's format and scope [have] made it easy to see what the medium contributed to the 'meaning' of the 1968 convention. In 1968 nearly half of all Americans watched the convention—some 90 million viewers."[12] To control the medium appeared to be the route to dictating the message. Johnson and Daley fought hard for this control, but, as we will see, they overestimated the importance of the living crowds in the convention hall, underestimated the power of the crowd outside, and totally misjudged the media's persistence and adaptability.

The setting was crucial to advancing their narrative, and this was decided by the top producers of the event. The Democrats had chosen Chicago for their convention because of the power and visibility of the city and also because of Daley's influence and Johnson's desired narrative. Moves had been made in June of that year to relocate the convention to Miami, when the DNC learned not only that the Yippies and the Mobe (the National Mobilization Committee to End the War in Vietnam) were planning a protest in Chicago but also that the Chicago electrical workers were on strike that week, which would cause major problems for press and media coverage. After the Republicans hosted a very successful convention in Miami, Democratic pleas to move the convention intensified, but they were shut down by Daley and Johnson.[13] Daley threatened to withdraw his support from the presumptive presidential nominee, Humphrey, if the convention were moved. Johnson, when approached, reportedly rejected the idea with, "Miami Beach is not an American city."[14] Johnson knew what story he wanted to tell which audience, and that narrative did not involve economically and ethnically diverse Miami.

The worried delegates' fears were well founded in immediate social and political contexts. Leading up to the convention, events of shocking violence had galvanized activists, and Chicago was, infamously, no friend to peaceful protests. On April 4 of that year, Martin Luther King Jr. had been shot and killed in Memphis. Fires, beatings, and looting consequently broke out in several major cities, and Mayor Daley's reaction to the threat of violence in his hometown was to order his police to "shoot to kill" anyone who looked like they were about to engage in mass violence. On June 3 Andy Warhol was shot in New York City. On June 4, in Los Angeles, the leading Democratic candidate for president, Robert Kennedy, was assassinated. His votes went, under the helping hand of President Johnson, to Humphrey. The atmosphere was palpably foreboding, so Daley attempted to manage the event in as controlled a way as possible, leading to production strategies that forced focus on the staged event, including control of media, sets, and sound; house management; the mise en scène; and timing.

The electricians' strike that frustrated the media seemed, at first, to play into the DNC's hands to control production technologies. While camera crews could tape and broadcast live inside the auditorium and the main convention hotel (the Hilton), there was no way for them to broadcast from outside—there were no operative lines, and Daley wouldn't allow them to run cables from outside generators. So, when the protests heated up, the press was forced to record outside on film, rush the film across town to be developed, then run it back to the amphitheater to broadcast it, creating a delay of between one and four hours. Ultimately, this delay created the most sensational juxtaposition of the entire week, as we'll see, when the film was finally broadcast on Wednesday night just as the nominating process was beginning.

The DNC attempted to house manage the events, limiting who could see what and who could be heard. This management included severe restrictions on media access to the event. Plastic press passes with magnetic squares had to be swiped on both leaving and entering the amphitheater, and the number of passes issued was "drastically restricted."[15] Norman Mailer, covering the events, wrote on Monday, "Whenever the convention came alive, it was next to impossible to reach the floor, so the amount of damage which could be done by keen press coverage was limited."[16] Mailer's use of the word *damage* points toward the threat to the convention posed by both the media and, later, by the peace delegates themselves, who mounted an aggressive assault against these house rules. Daley's and Johnson's attempts to control the media eventually backfired, as the press became increasingly incensed at their restrictions and television crews developed strategies for circumventing the mainstream power of the planners.

Another production strategy to contain dissent and show a united front to the viewers involved the use of seating banks. With access to the amphitheater already tightly restricted to delegates and press, further divisions among the audience were strategically implemented via assigned seating. The person in charge of the seating arrangements was John Criswell, a Johnson man and DNC treasurer. Featured directly next to the podium: Daley and Texas governor John B. Connally, who held down Humphrey support in one of the most populous states in the nation. In front of the podium: majority whip, majority leader. All around the podium: delegates from Texas, Tennessee, Pennsylvania, Florida, Illinois, and other states, where the combined total of votes for Humphrey was 730 out of 834. Farther back, as far away from the podium as possible: the delegates from California, Puerto Rico, New York, Oregon, and others, where the total of Humphrey votes was only 297 out of a possible 720.[17]

This arrangement represented more than cronies giving cronies the best seats in the house. It was a stage management strategy that attempted to monopolize focus on the spectators most willing to support the show. Delegates in the front could directly boo or cheer the speakers, leading the tone of the events. Delegates in the back were less visible and less audible. In fact, Mailer reports an astonishing ploy (also picked up by others in the press): the microphones for the front-row Humphrey delegations were strong and clear, but the microphones for the back-of-the-house delegations were weak in volume. "In an emergency, in any attempt to gain the attention of the Chair, how much more difficult to yell from the rear, how much more futile to wave the standard. In any total emergency when all the mikes were dead—one hand on the switch could accomplish that—who would ever be heard in the rear if the front was demanding the floor?"[18] The producers of the event used technology to stack the deck in favor of a polished presentation of unanimity, a narrative of untroubled cohesion.

The amphitheater itself was architecturally conducive to ordering the movements of thousands of people. An impressive space with low-hanging balconies, now decked out in red, white, blue, and black, it could be accessed only by narrow tunnels well patrolled by security guards. Entrances and exits were stringently monitored, and several reporters and non-Humphrey supporters described being hassled and detained on flimsy pretexts. The outside of the building was plugged into another deterrence system: generator trucks stationed outside were "ready to send voltage down [a] line of barbed wire."[19] If there were to be crowds performing their beliefs at this convention, the planners worked to ensure they would be supporters, not the chaotic masses, not unruly in any way.

So this was the physical arrangement of the indoor performance space: a tightly controlled stage and audience with sound and visual focus favoring, exclusively, supporters of the event. Attendees had all "purchased" the seats according to their rank—through either their votes or their financial contributions. House management had worked to ensure that any activity that did not celebrate the performance could be minimized or even simply cut off.

The unfolding of the event in real time was also uncompromisingly stage-managed. During any debate, the length, order, and response time for statements were restricted: for example, fifteen minutes for one speaker, five minutes for a response, fifteen minutes for the next, and so on. With alternating sides speaking for brief periods of time, the format was regulated against the unfolding of any drama. As Mailer notes, "No massive presentation of argument nor avalanche of emotion would ever result" from such a timed arrangement.[20] The speakers took their cues (at least, at first; we will soon see how this broke down on Wednesday) and spoke according to prescribed rules of order. Dispassionate, reasonable, bureaucratic speeches skimmed lightly over seething topics—one million American soldiers at war, the impassioned protests outside. Trained in placid oratory, committed to making a good impression on the television watchers, the speakers—in the beginning days of the convention—stuck to the script and tone the DNC had directed.

STREET THEATER

On the outside, things could not have been more different. Whereas inside, the orderly audience was stage-managed by hidden forces with an eye toward pleasing the mainstream media, outside, the antiwar protestors were enacting their ideals in plain sight, visibly embodying passionate debate, inviting participation, and trying out new methods to achieve their somewhat disparate goals. Camping out, playing music, smoking, and meditating, the protestors shunned the respectable appearance favored by the delegates, decried the convention's neat authority, and enlisted onlookers, residents, and the press to join their cause. Charisma, not polish, was the allure of the outside; dynamism, not self-congratulatory satisfaction, was the motor of performance. They, too, hoped to embody their ideals with the thousands of people they had gathered, but the protestors advocated a different set of strategies than the convention planners had. Their ideals counter the convention's in every point of performance: the protestors advocated spontaneity instead of preplanned events, creativity instead of strict organization, emotionality instead of reason, immediacy and authenticity instead of the exercise of established power. The heart of their differences is this: whereas the planners sought one result, to represent themselves well, the protestors had two agendas: to represent themselves *and* to expose others. Their performance involved revealing a heretofore hidden element—the coercion, violence, and unrepresentative power of the established politicians.

The narrative advanced by the activists was thus less binary. "We are not outside the mainstream of the Democratic Party," insisted a peace activist.[21] The protestors declared they *were* the people, in all their diversity, and they wanted to force the powerful leading Democrats to recognize their valid claim to represent the will of the people.[22] Their approach to mass performance reflects their inclusionary ideals: varied protest approaches and splinter groups were welcomed. Their protests included pacifist strategies as well as more aggressive ones—they were not all strict "doves." The National Mobilization Committee to End the War in Vietnam (the Mobe), led by Rennie Davis, with experience in organizing large demonstrations, spearheaded the events. Throughout the week, Allen Ginsberg led a circle of people in meditation, his "Oms" rasping and cracked as each day damaged his throat with more tear gas. David Dellinger, a longtime activist, advocated peaceful protest, attempting to lead a respectful march from Lincoln Park to the convention center, stopping to try to politely convince the police they should be let through.[23] The Yippies (a moniker invented specifically for this event), organized by Jerry Rubin, Paul Krassner, and Abbie Hoffman, encouraged small groups to break off and make their own way to the convention hall. Bobby Seale, representing the Black Panthers, gave an inflammatory speech advocating violence against the police. Norman Mailer encouraged the crowds on a stage in the park, flanked by two young men rocking out on electric guitars. Hippies were present en masse, preaching and practicing free love and the use of psychedelics. Literary heavyweights Jean Genet, Terry Southern, Richard Seaver, and William Burroughs worked their way through the events. Phil Ochs sang populist songs. Men of the cloth erected crosses on the lawn. The crowds were defined by divergent ideas and tactics, with the common denominator being that they were all participating, they were all trying to create a new reality by being together, as free agents, in time and space.

The Yippies were versed in Happenings, in new approaches to language that moved away from polished reason and toward free-flowing images, and in improvisatory street theater via the Diggers, a street theater group grown from the San Francisco Mime Troupe.[24] The outside's whole approach was antithetical to the one being espoused indoors: in their minds, young people "had to create a situation in which people would participate and so become, in a real sense, their own leaders."[25] The way to do this, according to Abbie Hoffman, was to "create a series of imageries that conflict,"[26] to push interpretation and agency back on the individual—a goal that treats the spectators as differently as conceivable from the delegates as imagined by Daley and Johnson.

The inclusive nature of the protest activities was part of the plan to ensure a large number of protestors. As David Farber explains, "They would have to allow for a number of different protest options, ranging from militant confrontation to passive resistance to peaceful, legal assembly. Each demonstrator would decide for him or herself which tactic best suited his or her needs. . . . Decisions would be made spontaneously by all the participants."[27] Fliers distributed to advertise the protest extended the invitation to everyone. After listing a number of ways to participate, the flier reads, "Who says these are the only categories? God? Make up your own—set up your own thing—fill in the blanks, read the white space. Participate. Initiate."[28] Fliers were signed by Arlo Guthrie, Timothy Leary, The Pageant Players, and the Bread and Puppet Theatre, representing literature, music, and theater conceived as ways of liberating spectatorial imagination and empowering individual participants.

As opposed to the decorum directive being issued at the convention, the protestors issued the directive to be passionate. Jerry Rubin stated, "We communicate to the public many emotions. . . . The expressions of these emotions across the nation are the real external goals of the demonstration. We feel deeper than those who support the war. We are shown to be alive."[29] Protestors were encouraged to feel, to emote, to internalize, to externalize, to fly off the handle, to speak off-the-cuff, to love, hate, and yell—everything in opposition to the propriety wielded by their political leaders.

As far from wanting to control their protest event as possible, the activists denounced order, reason, and stability as inherently opposed to their goals. As Keith Lampe said, "We understand that logic and proportion and consistency, often even perspective are part of the old control system and we're done with the old and done with the control systems."[30] Any gathering had to combine, in Hoffman's words, "a high element of risk, drama, excitement, and bullshit."[31] Theorizing these elements as their property, the protestors would find, before the convention was over, that risk, drama, excitement, and bullshit would ultimately infiltrate the amphitheater itself. Their production strategy treated individual engagement and unscripted action as a sine qua non of spectatorial response.

A more mainstream element was also present in the protests, a slight counterpoint to the innovative performance practices just mentioned. Inclusionary ideals extended to a more traditional tactic for orchestrating crowds in the fight for power and public sympathies. The peace activist Tom Hayden wrote, in 1962, a statement of participatory democracy that was to be known as the Port Huron Statement. His vision included the idea that "decision making of basic and social sequences be carried on by public groups; that politics be seen positively, as the art of collectively creating an acceptable pattern of social relations; that politics has the function of bringing people out of isolation and into community."[32] In planning the Chicago protests, this idea was taken up by David Dellinger and others, who wanted to dramatize how far the current government had strayed from representing the people. Their diverse protestors—*the* people—would emphasize, in all their variety and eagerness to engage, that the well-dressed, homogenous, order-loving bureaucrats inside the amphitheater only used the veneer of civility as a shield against true participation. They hoped to expose how the delegates were following the orders of a few and not representing the many. The battle had to be fought with coordinated crowds—how effectively each side could harness thousands of people would show how well they could embody their ideals. However, Dellinger's orderly march never got permission to approach the amphitheater, and the protestors' effect was made solely through their more innovative street tactics.

The protestors comprehended better than the DNC the power of the media and the press's attraction to a dynamic story. And the media quickly perceived that the protestors would stage the real news event. Hampered by a lack of live feed, the camera crews still filmed as much as they could, even though they were pulled into the fray, bullied, beaten, their equipment attacked. Outside, the media hung on to the dramatic story that was unfolding in the parks and the streets, waiting for the moment to exact their revenge on the controlling bureaucrats inside who had so severely restricted their freedom. The press was literally mediating a clash of two live performances, eventually asserting a production power beyond and in contradiction to what the DNC had allotted them.

I've outlined the two approaches to the week's events in terms of mass performance because to coordinate a unified action with others on such a scale delivers a specific message, distinct from other modes of activism and performance. To orchestrate the bodies of thousands of people is to form an image of the ideal world you are proposing. Moving together, physically, en masse, toward a common goal, with the stage set with the symbols, music, and focal points that summarize your ideology—this is a powerful mise en scène, engineered to simultaneously train the people engaged in the performance and impress your viewers.

The Yippies and the Mobe knew the power of mass performance, understood the emotional and ideological power of numbers, and recruited as many bodies as they could to demonstrate their ideals. Inclusionary, pacifist, unfettered by oppressive systems, their mass protest would ideally reflect to the United States an image of itself that could be peaceful, diverse, and open. But their challenge lay in preserving a unified image while orchestrating a coherent mass performance. To straddle harmony and chaos, integration and diversity, experimentation and consistency: this was the impossible task they set for themselves in Chicago. Splinter groups naturally formed, contradictory messages were delivered, disagreements about the exact level of required "peacefulness" inevitably arose, adversarial stances turned violent, and this lent an element of instability to their performance of a better world.

Inside the amphitheater, the convention's challenge lay in its resistance to change, its inability to alter production methods when new pressures demanded it. The Democrats wanted to remount the conservative mass performance of the Republicans in Miami, eager for the accompanying audience acclaim. Videos of that Republican convention show a unified front: delegates move together in time, they wave their banners on cue, the media follow the planners' prompts, people sing along with the band, and all balloons are treated with the joy and appreciation for Republican values they invite. To wish for such a convention shows how unable the Democrat's producers were to respond to change. Their lack of innovation, their stubborn belief in the established convention format, led them to try to orchestrate their thousands of bodies as if there were no influx of new performance methods about to invade their stage.

What we see, then, in Chicago is a clash of mass performance, and that clash is why this event had the far-reaching impact it did. Two views of the future of the Democratic Party—and, by extension, of the United States—tried to find articulation and to gain political power through the arrangement of bodies, signs, music, symbols, and narratives. What we will now follow is how the inside found itself—willingly and unwillingly—drawn into the methods of the outside, and how this dramatic infiltration ultimately secured a victory not for the peace activists, nor for Humphrey, but for the media, on one hand, and for the Republicans, on the other, who had already, in Miami, mastered the contemporary, media-supported art of mass performance.

THREE SCENES OF PERFORMANCE

We will now focus on three major scenes from the week, where the differing performance methods clashed in revealing and dramatic ways. The scenes are the Tuesday late-night breakdown of the DNC at the Hilton Hotel, the Wednesday morning musical standoff following the peace debate, and the Wednesday evening farce of a nominating procedure. To give readers some context as to where these scenes take place in the overall week, the timeline of the events is as follows.[33] Sunday, August 28, a Festival of Life is held in Lincoln Park, the protests begin, violence and arrests. Monday, occupation of Lincoln Park, police fire tear gas and smoke grenades, violence and arrests, the convention begins. Tuesday, press conferences, occupation of Lincoln and Grant Parks, tear gas, violence and arrests, the National Guard brought in with shotguns, bayonets, and barbed-wire-covered jeeps.[34] Wednesday, a rally and march at Grant Park with ten thousand to fifteen thousand people, the peace plank defeated in the convention, tear gas, mace, violence and arrests, broadcasting of what would be known as the Massacre of Michigan Avenue, the voting in of Humphrey as the presidential candidate. Most days involve several thousand protestors.[35] The three scenes we will examine resulted from the clash of two opposing views of society, enacted in the microcosm of mass performance.

The Hilton Hotel: Set and Lights

The Hilton Hotel became the dramatic scene for a direct confrontation of tactics on Tuesday night and the early hours of Wednesday morning. Tuesday morning had begun with a preplanned, corporate performance inside the convention: a highly mediated presidential "debate" in which Humphrey, Eugene McCarthy, and George McGovern were each given ten minutes to speak.[36] The debate's careful stage management ensured that nothing inflammatory or disruptive occurred. But throughout the day, the delegates were watching the protests, learning of the events in more detail, and by the evening that early morning's orderly debate had become a performance style of the past. The peace delegates had gotten ideas from the protestors on how to bring emotion into staged conversations. The DNC had originally planned to hold a debate on the party's war position—the one last attempt to pass a "peace plank"—on Tuesday night. But the contagious energy from outside changed the schedule. During the evening, peace plank delegates began conversations about what was happening outside and adopted strategies they had been witnessing. During the hours originally allotted for the debate, the erstwhile "doves" disrupted the performance of the convention and broke the unified binary narrative. They fought for control of attention, of the media, of volume, of energy. They flouted order, yelled over their weak microphones, and took long detours from procedure in an attempt to keep the floor open as long as possible. "When we weren't recognized being our polite, adult selves," McCarthy delegate Jean Wallin recalled, "then we started to yell,"[37] a remark that echoes the sentiments and strategies of the protestors outside.

Daley, in his role as producer of the events, tried to adapt to the disruption of order. His first strategy to direct the chaos was to let the doves run on until midnight, which would enable him to hold the debate at 1:00 a.m. New York time—when no one would watch it. In this way, he would be able to keep the debates under his control, while allowing the peace delegates to appear unreasonable on camera. He underestimated, however, the fervor of his newly unruly peace delegates, who were becoming less peaceful and no longer sticking to the script. He also underestimated the anxiety their new tactics would produce among the conservative elements of his production staff. His security guards, unnerved by the unleashed energies, grabbed a newsman and threw him to the floor. This was filmed on live camera, shocking television viewers. Unable to adapt to the new tone, Daley then appealed to a sense of decorum that, in the wake of the events outside, was simply no longer credible: "Let's act like ladies and gentlemen," he exhorted the noisy crowd, hoping to win the admiration of the millions of television viewers, "and let people be heard."[38] This came off looking stiff, "mainstream" in the worst possible way, as the doves inside were just capturing and channeling the energy of the outside. Fearing that insistence on an after-midnight debate would make them look terrible, the convention organizers realized the best they could do would be to cut off discussion for the night, at least getting the increasingly aggressive doves off television. The way they did this was defiantly undemocratic, a stagey gesture taken from an imperial narrative: a signal was passed to Mayor Daley by an administration spokesman, and Daley "drew his finger across his throat," twice, to signal an adjournment.[39] This was caught on camera.

Following the adjournment, the delegates participated as immediate spectators of the street theater, as they returned to their hotels and then watched the riots through their hotel windows. We can read this spectatorship as the turning point in the peace delegates' approach to mass performance. The protests had moved directly in front of the Hilton Hotel, where hundreds of convention attendees were staying and where the Humphrey and McCarthy delegations had their headquarters. This was the only spot outside of the amphitheater where live news cameras were positioned. Minutes after adjourning the delegates, Daley ordered in the National Guard to reinforce the Chicago police. The Guard brought out what Mailer described as "evil-looking jeeps with barbed-wire gratings."[40] Seeing these, the crowd added to its ongoing shouts of "pig" a chant of "Sieg Heil Sieg Heil!" All the delegates staying at the Hilton observed this as they returned to their rooms, and then they heard and watched it through their windows. What they saw is easy for us to imagine: a juxtaposition of uniformed, armed, military officers alongside long-haired, exhausted youth. The delegates saw a killing machine, backed by established power, squaring off against the "kids," their own sons and daughters.

The hotel provides an extraordinarily apt mise en scène for this shifting point. The Hilton had no laundry service because of the bus strike; the elevators did not work; the phone lines were overloaded, underserviced, and often dead; and outside, people clamored incessantly, "Join us! Join us!"[41] Tear gas floated in through the windows, stink bombs clogged up the lobby, and a mysterious ventilation malfunction caused the hotel to smell like vomit. Delegates walked around with smarting eyes, opened their windows, and leaned out, literally forced to witness the chaos below. As Mailer describes it, "The Hilton heaved and staggered through a variety of attacks and breakdowns. Like an old fort, like the old fort of the old Democratic Party, about to fall forever beneath the ministrations of its high shaman, . . . derided by the young . . . the old Hilton had become artifact of the party and the nation."[42] Inside the hotel, delegates watched as the very functioning of the planners' convention gave way under the assault of the energetic, chaotic protestors, who clamored for participation and hurled invective against their leaders, their fathers, their security forces, their "delegates."

From their windows, many delegates signaled that they were drawn to the outside performance of freedom, emotion, unruliness. That was their family out there, and that "us versus them" divide was a fiction. The binary that had kept them separate was—they could see through their windows as youth were being clubbed and gassed—artificial, a product of power divisions, not of inherent ideals. In a remarkable moment, the creaking building, bastion of the Democratic production company, itself became a signifier of the switch. Mailer narrates it vividly:

> The kids were singing. . . . An hour could not go by without . . . "We Shall Overcome" and "This Land Is Your Land." . . . They cheered with wild enthusiasm when one speaker, a delegate, had the inspiration to call out to the delegates and workers listening in the hundreds of rooms at the Hilton with a view of the park: "Turn on your lights, and blink them if you are with us. If you are with us, if you are sympathetic to us, blink your lights, blink your lights." And to the delight of the crowd, lights began to blink in the Hilton, ten, then twenty, perhaps so many as fifty lights were blinking at once, and a whole bank of lights on the fifteenth floor and the twenty-third floor went off and on at once. . . . The McCarthy headquarters . . . were blinking, and the crowd cheered. Now they had become an audience to watch the actors in the hotel. So two audiences regarded each other, like ships signaling across a gulf of water in the night, and delegates came down from the hotel. . . . And the Hilton, sinking in its foundation, twinkled like a birthday cake.[43]

Sympathetic delegates took the cue: blinking their lights, leaning out of the windows of their crumbling, smoke-filled set, learning the new lines offered up by the "kids," they signaled that they were ready to join forces and try out the new methods.

The Peace Debate: A Musical Showdown

Wednesday morning immediately reflected the solidarity of 3:00 a.m. The calls to "Join us!" were heeded when members of the convention adopted even more of the Yippie, Panther, and activist tactics. Peace delegates began yelling, breaking the rules, defying order. The first salvo was fired by Lester Maddox, the fourth presidential candidate, who began the morning by resigning. In a news conference inside the Hilton, with his wife crying beside him, Maddox called the politicians misinformed and power-mad. The Democrats, he announced, were the party of "looting, burning, killing. . . . What's more, I denounce them all."[44] The inflammatory language previously heard at Lincoln and Grant Parks—and in front of his hotel room at 3:00 a.m.—was hitting the mainstream.

When the long-awaited debate on the war arrived, the cracks in the well-planned convention showed immediately, revealing the influence of the language of Hoffman and the protestors. Wayne Hays got up and made his "beards for brains, riots for reason" attack, to hearty applause from the Humphrey delegates. And then, through a gargantuan mustering of conservative stage management powers, the forces of scripted procedure prevailed for two hours longer. The planners had instituted tightly regulated speeches: for this momentous debate, a maximum of only one hour for each position was allotted, with each side alternating. The speakers, especially the pro-war delegates, carefully restrained from passionate engagement and imagistic language about Vietnam, not evoking the thousands dead, the thousands more to die. Following this nondebate, the peace plank was voted down, with the majority plank winning by a substantial but not landslide margin.[45]

And then, immediately following the vote, the second-most-extraordinary instance of the protestors' tactics infiltrating the convention occurred. Furious with the vote, inspired by the events of the previous evening, adopting the strategies of the street performance they had been watching from their hotel windows, the peace plank advocates pulled the outside in, and the mainstream convention planners fought back. What happened next was a fight, as clear as day, between two competing modes of staging a show for the masses. As we follow the unfolding of this increasingly aggressive event inside the amphitheater, we will see how the convention stood by its tried-and-true methods of controlling live bodies and how the peace delegates employed diverse innovations from outside.

Mailer provides a vivid description of the end of the war debate—notice how music, staging, sound cues, blocking, and lines all derive from outside performance methods:

> The floor would not rest. The New York and California delegations began to sing "We Shall Overcome." Quickly, the Platform was passed; still the New York delegation sang. Now Wisconsin stood on its seats. The rear of the floor booed the front of the floor. A few hundred posters, STOP THE WAR, quickly printed a couple of hours earlier for this occasion, were held up. Defeated delegates yelled, "Stop the War" . . . The convention recessed. Still the New York delegation sang "We Shall Overcome," standing on their seats.[46]

The delegates picked up the songs ("We Shall Overcome") and tactics (yelling over the prescribed order of events) of the protestors. They were standing on their assigned seats, throwing up hastily printed posters with large letters. They attempted to gain control of the spectators, both those on the floor and those watching the live feed on their televisions. Finally, they got out of their chairs and started marching around the podium, commanding the attention of not only the hall but also the cameras.

The strategies the Yippies and the Mobe had advocated were being deployed here in the amphitheater by the peace delegates, who had come scripted and dressed for a mainstream convention and who were now following street theater dictums, as if enacting the protest fliers: "Make up your own categories—Set up your own thing—Participate. Initiate." Yelling from the back of the floor, they projected what Jerry Rubin had announced: "We communicate to the public many emotions. . . . We feel deeper than those who support the war." Holding their makeshift posters high, singing, marching, they embodied what Lampe had said: "We're done with the old, and done with the control systems." They embodied the spontaneity advocated by the street protestors. As one delegate recalled, "I don't remember if it was day or night. . . . There was a group of people marching in a circle in front of the podium, and they had flags, and I got up, and I started to march with them. . . . It was just a tremendous, emotional outlet, I don't think anyone said anything, we just did it."[47] As far from orderly, rehearsed performance as possible, that protestor was engaging in street theater, grabbing the stage and channeling emotion into song and action.

The majority party fought back with its own performance, leading to the most ludicrous battle waged the whole week: a standoff between mainstream and street theater, fought through music. The convention band, trying to drown out the protests, struck up a cheerful tune to enforce some good, orderly humor. It played "We Got a Lot of Living to Do," a hit song from the Broadway musical *Bye Bye Birdie*, getting louder as the singing on the floor continued.[48] The protestors kept singing "We Shall Overcome," and the fight was on. Notice how, in the following description, the showdown between musical styles crystallizes Hoffman's directive, cited earlier, to "create a series of imageries that conflict":

> In disgust the hawks left the floor. The doves continued to sing "We Shall Overcome." Now, the orchestra played "Happy Days Are Here Again." The demonstrators chanted, "We want peace! We want peace!" "I'm Looking Over a Four-Leaf Clover," the orchestra offered, then rejected, then switched over to "If You Knew Suzy," then they gave up. The demonstrators began to sing "The Battle Hymn of the Republic." New York, California, Oregon, Wisconsin, South Dakota and other delegations marched across the empty floor. It was half an hour after the convention had recessed. Still they sang.[49]

Emphasizing conflicting imageries, the peace delegates left their assigned seats, making themselves unavoidably visible to the cameras and television viewers. They sang increasingly militant songs as the band played ever more insipid tunes. The result is a drama recorded by the news crews, still striking today, of a uniformed orchestra battling a tattered group of delegates marching in shirtsleeves, perky popular tunes clashing with strident populist anthems. The cacophony clearly symbolized to all viewers the terrible disunity, the conflicting ideals, of the Democratic Party.

Music was not the only strategy the DNC leaders employed to try to win this showdown. Note how, during the musical confrontation, the planners deployed their preset performance and media technologies in an attempt to force focus on their performers:

> The managers of the convention turned the New York microphones down, and amplified the public address system for the band. So on the floor of the convention, the doves were drowned in hostile sound, but on the television sets, the reception was opposite, for the networks had put their own microphones under the voices of the delegates, and they sang in force across the continent. Thus a few thousand people on the floor and the gallery heard little of the doves—all the rest of American heard them well.[50]

Daley's production team hadn't anticipated the infectious power of the protest tactics. Nor had they foreseen the willingness of the outraged media to give the new type of drama every advantage it could. The media, placing their microphones next to the doves, created a third dimension right at the scene, outside anyone's anticipating. "Small wonder the old party hands hated the networks—it was agitating to have mastered the locks and keys in the house of politics and discover that there was a new door they could not quite shut," Mailer observes.[51] Small wonder the old party lost this battle: it remained inflexible in the face of vibrant new performance strategies, resistant to dialogue, and not strong enough to win a fight with its established methods. The image it wanted to convey through performance—people singing together, thousands of delegates enjoying the same speeches and music, a mise en scène of cheerfulness and harmony, a show of strength through unity—this image was destroyed when they lost the musical standoff on live television.

The Nominating Procedure: From Drama to Farce

After the peace plank defeat that afternoon, many delegates had left the convention to join the protests outside. The party did not miss them. Daley was trying to get the performance back under his control. But his production methods were not innovative, flexible, or powerful enough to direct the energy of all those unruly bodies, of the raging energies, and of the media's lust for the most dramatic performance.

Outside, protestors continued their singing, marching, and fighting with the police. The worst of the clashes on Michigan Avenue began at 8:00 p.m. The protestors were beaten with clubs, gassed, dragged into police vans. Bloodied and outnumbered, they shouted, "The whole world is watching!" They were being brutalized in front of cameras, but the "whole world" had to wait over an hour to watch: the news crews didn't get their film developed and aired until 9:30 p.m., at which point the delegates had reassembled in the amphitheater. The convention convened for its nominating process as the police rioted outside.

Experimental street performance brings with it an attendant rise in anxiety among the keepers of the peace. Just as the police outside were agitated, excitable, and angry, the security forces on the inside were now experiencing the same energy. The peace-delegates-turned-agitators embodied the aggressively adversarial role of the street protestors, with the attendant consequences. One delegate was dragged from the floor when he refused to return to his seat after a sergeant commanded him to. Another delegate hung on to him, and he was dragged out, too. The mainstream media were roped into the same roles: Mike Wallace of CBS took a hit to the jaw from the police, and they were all removed from the floor in a violent flurry.

The press brought the outside fighting directly into the amphitheater: news channels were showing the footage as fast as their staff could develop it. With it, they unleashed the individualism, passion, and immediacy that the convention had been trying so hard to keep at bay. As the film was broadcast, order broke down. Name calling, violence, participation—all of this was aided by the media, whose superior production machine and keen sense of an engaging theatrical spectacle undermined Daley's convention narrative of unity and wholesomeness.

The nominating procedure began at 11:30 p.m., with delegates leaving continually to get a better view of the footage of America's youth getting clubbed. As the Gazit documentary puts it, "Hubert Humphrey sat helpless, as the American people watched his nomination through a prism of violence and turmoil." Humphrey acted the role of happy delegate, in another ludicrous juxtaposition between the performance the convention wanted to stage and the real drama unfolding: shots of him smiling, clapping his hands, and forcing himself to make expressions of pleasure jar painfully with the commotion, brutality, and disorder happening all around. Continuing to stick to his script, his painful inflexibility shows even more strongly in the face of illogic, unreason, disorder—everything advocated by the Mobe, the Yippies, and the hippies.

When Senator Ribicoff came out with his shocker (which we encountered at the beginning of this essay)—"Gestapo tactics on the streets of Chicago"[52]—it was captured on live television. What had been chanted the previous night in front of the Hilton—"Sieg Heil Sieg Heil!"—had made it, with all its performative power to shock, command attention, and disrupt, inside. Accusations of Nazism, emotional outbursts of mistrust and hatred, and the fervent desire to expose, to give the lie to a narrative—all of this commanded the attention of a viewing audience of ninety million people.

Daley's "Fuck you," then—uttered in the midst of this late-night farce of a nominating procedure—this "Fuck you" was to Ribicoff, of course, but also to the doves, to the protestors, to the media, to the street theater. They interrupted his performance, undermined his direction, and destroyed the collective, unified, self-congratulatory event he had worked so hard to produce. He yells "Fuck you" to a new mode of performance he doesn't understand and hasn't mastered. On Thursday, showing how clearly he still didn't get it, he persisted in his old-fashioned mode: "We Love Mayor Daley" signs popped up all over downtown Chicago, their corny facades attempting, like the convention orchestra, to simply drown out the noise of the new voices with volume, scale, and money.

The nominating procedure, staged late at night for a viewing audience of millions, can be charted as veering from a scripted mass performance of unified, flag-waving patriots to a melee of live-projected violence, swearing, accusations of fascism, and cheerful convention balloons being swatted away like the incongruous reminders of the failed mainstream convention that they, in fact, were.

STAGE AND SCREEN

In the clash between the outside protests and the inside's organizational efforts, neither party won. A third kind of performance emerged victorious, one that would continue to prevail for decades. That victor was the way the media captures, interprets, and projects live events into the minds and vision of millions of viewers.

The convention's end, the moment of total infiltration of the mainstream by street performers, carries the exaltation of activist victory with it, when looked at through a very narrow lens. The street has invaded the citadel of government, police brutality has been exposed, and the tightly controlled convention has burst into passionate, spontaneous performances of individual dissent and fervor. It could seem as though the protestors channeled their ideas of diversity, youthful idealism, and anticorporate performance methods into a performance enacted by thousands of bodies and appreciated by millions more spectators.

However, many historians of the moment read the results of the event with less optimism. The protestors, choosing to undermine the DNC, not the RNC (which had a unified and successful convention in Miami), ultimately ensured the DNC's demise for a painful period of time. Indeed, one could say that the peace delegates successfully, yet unfortunately for their long-term goals, adopted Hoffman's strategy, bringing "a high element of risk, drama, excitement, and bullshit" into the convention. As a Humphrey staff member put it, the protestors' "victory" made it look like "we Democrats could not run a convention, much less a country."[53] The disunity and fury of the evening lost the presidential election for the Democrats, and with it, any hope of a less hawkish administration. The Vietnam War went on for seven more years.[54]

The consequences of introducing "risk, drama, excitement, and bullshit" into the convention have been far-reaching. Much like the security guards inside the amphitheater, who quickly became anxious and violent when threatened with the instability of hundreds of agitated bodies, convention planners subsequently cracked down even harder on future unscripted elements. The outside violence ultimately created an atmosphere of mistrust toward the protestors among the population, and it generated a need to appear more unified than ever among political parties.[55] Afterward, conventions went even beyond Daley's strategies, throwing all their energy into the scripted, televised nature of the event. No longer a participatory event in which live bodies would make decisions, conventions became thoroughly mediated performances of unity, crafted for static self-congratulation and increasingly bored television audiences.

"Liveness," in August 1968, was at a turning point for national conventions. The mass performance inside in the amphitheater was staged with an eye toward the media, but Daley's direction still allowed (in spite of itself) for elements of immediate, unscripted performance to infiltrate. These unstaged bodies are what made the events so interesting. Their elimination has enabled conventions to stage their ideologies more perfectly, but at a cost to both viewer interest and public dialogue. Peggy Phelan wrote in 1993, "Presidential campaigns are, above all, elaborate performances of state culture,"[56] and her argument holds true today:

> Since the campaign is staged almost exclusively on and for television, the campaign performance employs the tropes (and traps) of television narrative. This creates a certain critical problem for performance scholars who continue to insist that the live body or live ("staged") event is the crucial atom which defines "performance" as such. The distinction between live body and the re-presented body seems to me no longer valid.[57]

With the advent of total media control, campaign performances must now be evaluated "through the grammar and syntax of television. There is, literally, no other way to 'see' the campaign."[58] The Democratic National Convention of August 1968 marks the turning point in this transformation. Convention planners have figured out how to manipulate the seeing eye of television far better than they had in 1968, and thanks to the Democratic disaster in Chicago, they have learned that the suppression of unruly live bodies is a sine qua non for success. It is a dubious honor for this dramatic moment.

The infiltration of street performance into state performance was violent, heady, theatrical, showing the drama that results when two approaches to performing a body politic clash. Its legacy is one exhilarating battle, won by the street performers who effectively infiltrated the mainstream, and one major war lost, with Democrats losing the election and the possibility to end the war and the national convention system being turned, once and for all, into a static, mainstream, scripted performance whose producers learned the hard way how to perform their mass unity and completely lock their doors against the unruly body politic outside.

NOTES

1. Chana Gazit, "Chicago 1968," *American Experience*, season 8, ep. 3, aired November 13, 1995 (New York: E1 Entertainment, 1995), http://www.youtube.com/watch?v=1Iye1NQy1NY.

2. Qtd. in ibid., among other sources.

3. "By and large, the majority of the delegates were the kind of men and women who had always come to American conventions—middle-aged, established in their parties, their unions, in civic responsibility, in high office. For such people, conventions have always been part carnival, part family reunion, part business. But among them was an entirely new leaven, the delegates of the new mood of 1968, for whom the convention was not only business, but crusade. . . . The insurgents had come to Chicago to bring an end to old politics; they were crusaders playing a new convention game called St. George and the Dragon; and the Dragon was Hubert Humphrey." Theodore H. White, *The Making of the President 1968* (New York: Atheneum, 1969), 319.

4. See Zachary Karabell, "The Rise and Fall of the Televised Political Convention," Discussion Paper D-33, Joan Shorenstein Center for Press, Politics, and Public Policy, John F. Kennedy School of Government, October 1998.

5. See Gazit, "Chicago 1968"; David Farber, *Chicago 68* (Chicago: University of Chicago Press, 1988); and Norman Mailer, *Miami and the Siege of Chicago* (New York: Signet Books, 1968).

6. Lewis Chester, Godfrey Hodgson, and Bruce Page, *American Melodrama: The Presidential Campaign of 1968* (New York: Viking Press, 1969), 646–47, cited in Farber, *Chicago 68*, 195.

7. As stated by David Ginsberg, former Humphrey staff, in Gazit, "Chicago 1968."

8. White, *Making of the President*, 318.

9. George Rising, *Clean for Gene: Eugene McCarthy's 1968 Presidential Campaign* (Westport, CT: Praeger, 1997), 83.

10. Mailer, *Miami and the Siege of Chicago*, 123.

11. Stephen J. Wayne, "Presidential Nominations and American Democracy," U.S. Diplomatic Mission to Germany, Public Affairs/Information Resource Centers, March 2004, http://usa.usembassy.de/elections04/wayne.htm.

12. David Culbert, "Television's Visual Impact on Decision-Making in the USA, 1968: The Tet Offensive and Chicago's Democratic National Convention," *Journal of Contemporary History* 33.3 (July 1998): 446.

13. "Although the television networks wanted to ease their expenses by having both parties meet in Miami, and though security would be easier in the Florida city, Johnson went with Daley and decided to hold the convention in Chicago in late August." Lewis Gould, *1968: The Election That Changed America*, (Chicago: Ivan R. Dee, 1993), 105; also see Mailer, *Miami and the Siege of Chicago*, 103.

14. Mailer, *Miami and the Siege of Chicago*, 103.

15. Ibid., 116.

16. Ibid.

17. Ibid., 114. See also White, *Making of the President*, 318: "There remains then only the chorus to the drama—the delegates, all 6511 of them to be squeezed onto a floor that normally held only 4850, delegates arriving by bus, auto and airplane, delegates finding themselves isolated by lack of telephones, delegates arriving to be told that there were no

seats in the galleries for their wives, delegates whose hearts belonged to Robert Kennedy and found no balm in Gilead. Confused and uncertain, they milled about. Normally, the two largest delegations—California (174) and New York (190)—set the convention tone. But the majority of these had belonged to Robert Kennedy, and, as the two largest blocs at the convention, they now found themselves orphaned, with no political home from which to operate. Upon them, also, was heaped humiliation—they had been separated by the Johnson design of the convention and given the furthest rear seats of the convention floor, separated from each other as far as physically possible. Sensing themselves abused, they were to become pockets of bitterness."

18. Mailer, *Miami and the Siege of Chicago*, 115.

19. Ibid., 114.

20. Ibid., 161.

21. Gazit, "Chicago 1968."

22. The protests began in Grant Park for Mobe's "Meet the Delegates" march. The Festival of Life, featuring MC5, was in Lincoln Park. Both happened on Sunday, August 25.

23. "Dellinger and others yelled into bullhorns that the march was to be nonviolent and that anyone who could not abide by such a rule should leave the march." Farber, *Chicago 68*, 197.

24. Ibid., 8.

25. Ibid., 13.

26. Qtd. in ibid., 13.

27. Ibid., 13, describing strategies first put into place for the march on the Pentagon the previous year.

28. Ibid., 18.

29. Qtd. in ibid., 19.

30. Qtd. in ibid., 24.

31. Qtd. in ibid., 45.

32. Qtd. in ibid., 77.

33. The events are described in detail in ibid., 167–207.

34. Paul J Scheips, *The Role of Federal Military Forces in Domestic Disorders, 1945–1992* (St Louis: Center of Military History, United States Army, 2005): "With not more than 11,000 protesters and onlookers altogether, there appears to have been about one agent for every dozen demonstrators" (360). "The weapons used by the radicals among the demonstrators consisted mainly of 'rocks, bricks, and sticks,' while the police used tear gas, mace, and billy clubs" (361).

35. The reported numbers on the first three days range from two thousand to ten thousand. See Farber, *Chicago 68*, 180.

36. Mailer, *Miami and the Siege of Chicago*, 119.

37. Gazit, "Chicago 1968."

38. Mailer, *Miami and the Siege of Chicago*, 160.

39. Gazit, "Chicago 1968."

40. Mailer, *Miami and the Siege of Chicago*, 55.

41. Ibid., 156–57.

42. Ibid., 156.

43. Ibid., 159.

44. Walter Rugaber, reporting for the *New York Times*, qtd. in ibid., 160.

45. 1,567 3/4 voted for the majority plank; 1,041 1/2 voted for the peace plank. Ibid., 164.

46. Ibid.

47. Gazit, "Chicago 1968."

48. Mailer, *Miami and the Siege of Chicago*, 164–65.

49. Ibid., 165.

50. Ibid.

51. Ibid.

52. Gazit, "Chicago 1968."

53. Ibid.

54. "April 30[, 1975]: The last American personnel in Vietnam leave via helicopter from the roof of the U.S. Embassy as Saigon becomes Ho Chi Minh City. Three million Americans served in the war; nearly 58,000 were killed, 150,000 seriously wounded, and over 1,000 are missing in action." Dean Blobaum, Chicago '68: A Chronology, http://chicago68.com/c68chron.html updated August 27, 2014.

55. As Candace J. Nelson argues, "As early as 1960 the networks had begun to work with the Democratic and Republican parties to shape the convention to the needs of television. The unfavorable coverage of the Democratic Convention in 1968 heightened the desire for the parties to stage conventions to show the party and its nominee in a favorable light." *Grant Park: The Democratization of Presidential Elections, 1968–2008* (Washington, D.C.: Brookings Institution Press, 2011), 56.

56. Peggy Phelan, "The Rats and the Democrats," *TDR* 37.3 (Autumn 1993): 171.

57. Ibid.

58. Ibid.,172.

AFTERWORD

James M. Harding

Looking Back at a Funhouse Mirror

Reflections on Experimental Theater in the Sixties

By the mid-1970s, critics, historians, and practitioners were already taking stock of the much-celebrated explosion of experimental theater in the 1960s. Though many historians would later begin to speak of "the sixties" as a long decade that carried over well into the seventies, that critical sensibility had not yet taken hold in the theater community, which, by the end of the Vietnam War, already had a sense that something had changed and that a moment of reflection on the previous decade was in order. In the fall of 1977, for example, the editors of *Performing Arts Journal* (*PAJ*) published a special section dedicated specifically to such reflection. Under the heading "American Experimental Theatre: Then and Now," they asked invited contributors—playwrights, practitioners, critics, and scholars—to reflect on how, in the transition from the sixties to the seventies, "experimental theatre" had changed "in its relationship with the press, the university, foundations, theatrical institutions, the audience, and the other arts."[1] At some level, this publication was itself a signal that the sixties were over and that the constructed history of "the sixties" had begun.

Barely a year old at the time, *PAJ* had literally emerged on the far side of the Vietnam War, and the commission that the editors gave to their contributors, to reflect on experimental theater "then and now," was as much a moment of historicizing the sixties as it was of staking out territory in an new era. While there is much in this special section of *PAJ* that is worth examining in closer detail, two things in particular stand out almost immediately. First and foremost, there is the focus on experimental theater itself, and in this respect, it was not only the contributors—all of whom had been active as practitioners or critics in the previous decade—who encouraged subsequent scholars to historicize the sixties in terms of experimental theater. The commission to which the contributors responded had already set an agenda that reflected a growing consensus among theater critics and historians that the definitive moments of the previous decade were to be found in the experimental arts, and the implied expectation of the commission was that the history of seventies theater would follow suit. In light of later publications like the anthology *The Drama Review: Thirty Years of Commentary on the Avant-Garde*, edited by Brooks McNamara and Jill Dolan, which was published in 1986 and plots *TDR*'s long history of championing experimental performance, it becomes clear that Bonnie Marranca and Gautam Dasgupta (the editors of *PAJ*) were very much within the mainstream of emerging scholarly assessments of the period when they asked contributors to consider experimental theater "then and now." But while the commission that they gave to their contributors reflected an emerging consensus about the sixties, the results of that commission were anything but uniform, and this brings us to the second and perhaps most noticeable quality of *PAJ*'s special section on "American Experimental Theatre: Then and Now."

What is amazing about this fleeting moment of concerted reflection is the lack of consensus among the contributors about what actually constitutes experimental theater, regardless of whether the point of reference was the sixties, the seventies, or later. At one end of the spectrum, Richard Kostelanetz simply dismissed experimental theater in the sixties and seventies as being derivative of Allan Kaprow's *18 Happenings in Six Parts*, the Living Theatre's production of *The Connection*, or John Cage's legendary 1952 untitled piece at Black Mountain College—all of which were products of the fifties.[2] At perhaps the opposite end of the spectrum, the critic Stanley Kaufmann noted that one bit of continuity between the sixties and the seventies was that a "monist doctrine continues to be a burden" and that the idea that "the theatre 'is' This; or 'is' That" was not for him.[3] So if the 1960s began on a dichotomous note with a fabricated choice between experimental and mainstream theaters, here they ended with an unanswered question about what experimental theater was or is in the first place. Of course, the temptation is to see in this lack of consensus what one might call the perennial elusiveness of experimental theater: its Houdini-like tendency to break the constraints of any definition imposed upon it. But that tendency really comes into play only in response to categorical definitions that would delimit future performances rather than in response to definitions that would characterize past ones—even past performances that were in close enough proximity that Marranca and Dasgupta could solicit responses from practitioners and critics who had firsthand knowledge of the experimental performance scene in the sixties. Given that close proximity, the lack of consensus among their contributors is all the more surprising. They were there; they should know; and however different their aesthetic tastes, some consensus about experimental theater as a scene or movement ought not to be beyond the contributors' grasp. On the other hand, there is an important lesson here. The lack of consensus is a critical reminder of what lies beneath the surface of dichotomies that critics have long taken for granted in subsequent scholarship on theater and performance from the period.

Among the more pronounced assumptions about experimental theater in the 1960s is the notion that experimentation with form was intertwined with a radical or progressive political agenda and that innovative experimentation was thus part of a unique aesthetic strategy for reorienting political and ideological sensibilities within the social order. In many instances, this was certainly the case. But as the essays in this volume demonstrate, such strategies were neither an exclusive nor a distinctive signature of experimental theater. They were in fact writ across many mainstream and popular performances as well. In this respect it should come as no surprise that one of the more important points to emerge from *PAJ*'s special issue on experimental theater is that experimental theater in the 1960s had no exclusive claim on a progressive political agenda. Two of the more prominent critics contributing to *PAJ* emphasize this very point. Addressing the perception that experimental theater in the seventies was "less political" than experimental theater in the sixties, Stanley Kaufmann, for example, notes that the obvious explanation for the declining interest in politics among experimental theater practitioners in the seventies was the end of the Vietnam War in 1974. Yet for all its obviousness, Kaufmann is not entirely satisfied with this explanation. He suggests that if, with regard to politics, opposition to the Vietnam War is what distinguishes experimental theater in the sixties from experimental theater in the seventies, then the distinction "throws some retroactive doubt on the legitimacy of sixties politics" more generally since it suggests "that most anti-Viet Nam war action" was motivated by "self-preservation" rather than politics. "If all the groups who were doing anti-war pieces had been motivated by political conviction rather than by immediate political disgust or the wish to preserve self and/or friends," Kaufmann reasons, "political theatre would not have dwindled."[4] Following this logic, the larger question about politically inflected "experimental" theater is really a question of whose political interests or whose class interests it serves. If the political undercurrent of experimental theater in the sixties was really about self-preservation, then there are, as Kaufmann suggests, legitimate arguments to be made that experimental theater was ultimately catering to a privileged elite.

Kaufmann concedes that he has "caught some hell from students"[5] for questioning the depth and scope of political commitments among theater practitioners who allied themselves with the antiwar movement, and even today his argument is an inconvenient alternative to basic narratives of the transition from the sixties to the seventies or, more specifically, from what Elizabeth Wollman in *The Theater Will Rock* describes as the transition from "the 'can-do' 1960s" to the "me-decade" of the 1970s.[6] For it suggests that the "can-do" of the 1960s was deeply committed to "me" well before the 1970s arrived. But even on this note, the notion of a "me" is always embedded in class interests. Inasmuch as Kaufmann's reading of the politics of experimental theater "then and now" suggests a narrow class focus in terms of the theater's constituency, it is very much in sync with Michael Feingold's reflections on "then and now" in the same issue of *PAJ*—only Feingold is less evasive with regard to class. Rather than suggesting that in the seventies experimental theater had become less political, he suggests that the politics of seventies theater were all too evident, and he argues that in the shift from the sixties to the seventies, experimental theater underwent a "steady retrenchment and retreat," becoming more and more conservative because "the wealthy elite which patronizes the avant-garde" had become "increasingly selective" in the theater that they would subsidize and support.[7] The subtle reminder in Feingold's reference to wealthy elite patrons is that one cannot speak of experimental theater without considering the material economies in which it circulates or without considering how those economies shape its aesthetics and its politics. So long as the children of the affluent are potential cannon fodder, a politically inflected experimental theater serves its purpose in building opposition to an unpopular war, but once the war is over and the draft has ended, wealthy patrons can turn their attention and their purses elsewhere.

The question is not so much whether experimental theater practitioners are more or less political, but whether the patrons who finance their theater projects are, and whether in the absence of war those same patrons look for a different return on their investments in the arts. The director Lawrence Kornfeld voices a similar sentiment in his reflections on "then and now," noting that after the sixties, foundations tended to offer only "token" support to experimental work—especially showing interest in supporting work "that can appeal generically to a large audience"—so that they (corporations and foundations) "can legitimately claim to develop the arts."[8] For theater practitioners, the consequence of this shift was clear: in the interests of their own survival, financially strapped theaters began tailoring their work to available funds and thus tended to experiment within already established parameters that might have brought stylistic innovation but that ultimately left the political status quo intact. In the post–Vietnam War era of the midseventies, this dynamic may have been temporarily more visible, but it would be naïve to imagine that this same dynamic was not in place earlier in the sixties. One notable exception to this dynamic may be the Living Theatre, but even with the Living one has to wonder—amid the still unexplored larger implications of Jack Gelber's provocative 1986 *TDR* essay "Julian Beck, Businessman"[9]—about the extent to which the Living catered its "radical" experimental theater to the liberal sensibilities of the patrons from whom it sought support, patrons who—like the bourgeois audiences in Paris cited in Kate Bredeson's contribution to this volume—enjoyed the aura of radical chic. And radical chic is rebelliousness always already contained.

At the point where the radical politics of experimental theater become suspect—the point where they become the vanguard not of change but of its spectacle—the moniker of "experimental theater" itself begins to lose much of its luster, at least as a point of contrast with mainstream theater. Interestingly enough, in 1981, just as the Wooster Group was embarking on what would become a two-decade reign as New York's premier experimental theater, its director expressed similar sentiments in an essay that she wrote for *PAJ*. Reflecting on the experimental theater that unfolded against the backdrop of the Vietnam War, Elizabeth LeCompte writes,

> Audience [members] as well as people working in the theatre, who wanted no part of money that was made at the expense of dead Vietnamese babies . . . brought an inflated sense of importance to an ongoing movement. It gave some people—including Richard Schechner—the feeling that they were reshaping the world, when in reality, they were only inventing new techniques to be absorbed into the mainstream of commercial theatre. And a lot of "experimental" work that looked good against a different political background paled without its context.[10]

Beyond the political background to which LeCompte refers, what remains is experimentation with form, style, and technique, and at some level, all practitioners are involved and interested in the innovation that results from such experimentation. This is perhaps Feingold's most important argument earlier in the essay that he contributed to *PAJ*'s special section on "Experimental Theatre: Then and Now."

Looking back on the sixties, Feingold maintains that despite all of the hype about the experimental theater of the era, it did not provoke "the great change in the nature of theatre that a miniscule group of academics would like to believe" but merely marked the introduction of "new stage techniques to an ongoing theatrical tradition that [. . . did] not change in any substantive way." Indeed, Feingold argues, as would LeCompte a few years later, that rather than transforming the foundations of theater, the celebrated innovations of experimental theater were "assimilated easily and with gratitude . . . by serious professional theatre people, who, practical as always, simply borrowed what they could use and jettisoned the rest."[11] While Feingold does lament the fact that the innovations of experimental theater could so easily be separated from "the principles and ideals that made [. . . them] significant in the first place"—and it is important to read political engagement as one of those "principles and ideals"—the practical reality he acknowledges is that there is nothing inherent in the techniques and styles of experimental theater that would wed it to anything other than theater itself, let alone to specific political principles or ideals. Nonetheless, some of Feingold's more conservative contemporaries argued that the practical innovations forged by experimental theater practitioners in the 1960s came at a cost and fostered a cultural shift that compromised theater's artistic promise. There is no shortage of irony in such arguments by conservatives, given that those who defended experimental theater actually positioned it as a bastion of artistic practice resisting the compromising onslaught of commercialism. Yet it was with arguments against experimental theater that the decade literally ended.

If experimental theater had no inherent tie to political activism, it certainly was caught up in cultural politics, or at least that was the perception in more traditional and culturally conservative quarters, where critics viewed sixties experimentation with alarm and argued that it trafficked in a trivial countercultural sensationalism and gimmickry that threatened the sanctity of art. There is perhaps no better example of this view than the polemic against "experimental theatre" that Oscar Mandel published in the *Massachusetts Review* in 1970, just as the sixties ended. If for no other reason, Mandel's now largely forgotten essay entitled "Drama: Reactionary Notes on the Experimental Theatre" is worth recalling because often the clearest image of what a given art form is or does emerges from those who most vehemently react against it and who in their resistance to an emergent artistic form help others to identify its most significant particulars. In short, what a conservative critic points to in his or her cry of "Foul!" has a good chance of being central to what makes a given art form significant in the first place. At some level, then, Mandel's essay is worth reading with an eye toward teasing out its mirror image, and in fact this happened almost immediately after it was published.

The negative response to experimental theater in Mandel's "Reactionary Notes" was vehement enough that it provoked a rebuttal from Richard Schechner, who felt that Mandel's conclusions, "if accepted," would "retard the growth and development of theatre."[12] In that explanation, Schechner placed experimental theater at the forefront of theater more generally and attributed to it the task of sustaining theater's continued viability. Flawed though many of Mandel's arguments themselves might have been—and his rather bizarre equation of the "thrust stage" with "environmental theatre" is just one example of his questionable arguments[13]—it is worth pausing to consider the image of experimental theater that emerges from Schechner's rebuttal. Surprisingly, it is an image that with its references to "growth and development" inscribes experimental theater into the market logic of the very commercialism that it ostensibly opposes.

The most striking aspect of Schechner's positioning of experimental theater within a linear continuum of theater's growth and development is that this move tends to place experimental theater in the service of, rather than as an alternative to, the theatrical mainstream. The image that emerges here is of experimental theater as the research and development wing of that mainstream. In short, Schechner gives credence to Feingold's assertion in *PAJ* just a few years later that beneath the hype experimental theater in the sixties was always already contained as an integral part of the processes of an evolving or "ongoing theatrical tradition," although in referencing this tradition Feingold makes no distinction between the principles of experimental theater and those of mainstream commercial theater. Both are interested in what we might call "the next new," as are all market-oriented enterprises. Both the experimental and the mainstream participate in the same general processes that seek theater's continued viability. Indeed, Schechner's emphasis on theater's evolution through experimentation implicitly acknowledges this very point and collapses the experimental/commercial divide by conceptualizing experimental theater through the basic logic of market capitalism, in which growth and development are essential strategies for sustaining viability.

In the absence of inherent ties to an explicit political agenda, experimental theater thus begins to look a lot like a marketplace of the new that is dominated by a struggle over who gets credit for what innovation and by debates over where and when an innovation first occurred. There is obvious cultural cachet at stake in those debates, but at some point the debates begin to resemble old-fashioned struggles over intellectual property rights. At some level, Richard Kostelanetz is engaged in precisely such a struggle when, calling himself "a sometime cultural historian, who has written critically about advanced tendencies in all the arts," he maintains that he sees "little difference between the sixties and the seventies" and argues that the only real innovation in the latter half of the twentieth century occurred in the late 1950s with the work of Cage, Kaprow, and the Living Theatre.[14] By implication, then, the celebrated explorations of theatrical form in the 1960s and early 1970s (the fully immersive "environmental theatre" of The Performance Group or, alternatively, what Bonnie Marranca calls the "theatre of images"[15] of Richard Foreman, Robert Wilson, and Lee Breuer, to cite only a couple of prominent examples) were derivative of, indeed were *indebted* to, the precedents cited by Kostelanetz, and were thus somehow less significant because they were less original or new.

What potentially gets lost in those struggles over debt and indebtedness is not only clarity about when actual innovation occurs or, alternatively, about when the rush toward "the next new"—a rush that is itself a product of market logic—produces merely the semblance or spectacle of innovation rather than innovation itself. In those struggles, other criteria of assessment and value are given a backseat to a socially cultivated sense of urgency to brand one's own work as the experimental edge or as the radical forefront of an emerging new form. Consider, for example, the Wooster Group's rise to prominence. Despite having been one of the pivotal players in The Performance Group's development of the techniques of environmental theater, LeCompte—at the time when the Wooster Group was really beginning to stand on its own and had broken with The Performance Group—felt compelled to argue that "the most radical thing to happen in theatre over the last ten to fifteen years was not 'new staging options'" (or for that matter, "'political theatre' or the 'theatre of images'") but rather "the combining of the playwright, director and designer in one person."[16] The special pleading of this assertion notwithstanding, one has to question not only whether the example of a playwright, director, and designer rolled into one person was really as radical or new as LeCompte claimed (Brecht and Piscator come immediately to mind) but also whether it is worth considering what prompted such a claim in the first place. Indeed, there is a strong case to be made that LeCompte's claim is a prime example of the requisite tropes of "newness" to which one must pay lip service in the marketplace of the culture industry.

An argument about similar issues was at the crux of the debate between Schechner and Mandel in 1970, as the sixties closed. In simplest terms, theirs was a debate over whether experimental theater produces actual innovation or mere gimmickry. It was a debate about whether experimental theater in the sixties produced art or cheap commercial tricks. In the context of that debate, Schechner's embrace of "the growth and development of theatre" responded to Mandel's far more pessimistic sense of theater's demise and devolution under the influence of experimental theater practitioners who, impatient with what Mandel calls an increasingly exhausted and "dreary naturalism," replaced conventional dramatic theater with a "mindless formalistic gimmickry," which in Mandel's opinion was typified in the work performed at "La MaMa Café."[17] This debate was and, I would suggest, still is well worth the price of admission, if one will pardon the expression. But it is also a debate that has a bit of a familiar ring to it, particularly on Mandel's part. For in many respects, Mandel's "Drama: Reactionary Notes on the Experimental Theatre" is arguably a poorly cribbed adaptation of Michael Fried's infamous conservative bombshell, the essay "Art and Objecthood," which he first published in *Artforum* in June 1967, three years prior to Mandel's essay.

Structurally at least, the parallels between Mandel's argument and Fried's are striking. As is well known, Fried's essay is a polemic against minimalist art, which he preferred to call "literalist art" and which he argues emerged as a response by minimalist artists to the belief that "pictorial illusion" was as a form of artistic expression "on the verge of exhaustion."[18] This argument is echoed in adapted form in Mandel's assertion that experimental theater is a response to what he describes as a fifty-year tradition of "dreary naturalism." The echoes of Fried in Mandel's essay are even stronger with regard to Fried's main argument about the aesthetic price that minimalist artists pay in their rejection of "illusionism." Citing interviews with Donald Judd and Robert Morris, Fried argues that minimalist artists attempt to get "rid of the problem of illusionism"[19] by replacing it with a calculated nonrepresentational "presence,"[20] which Fried dismisses as a celebration of "objecthood," a dismissal that ultimately culminates in his infamous assertion, "The literalist espousal of objecthood amounts to nothing other than a plea for a new genre of theatre; and theatre is now the negation of art."[21] Fried's reference in this assertion to a theater that "is now the negation of art" is, it is important to note, not so much a reference to theater in general as it is to "a new genre of theatre," a genre that in the 1960s was allied with—and was a part of—the experimental theater community. Indeed, Mandel underscores that connection in his own argument that art in theater consists not "in showing the object but in expressing the idea"[22]—an argument that, conceptually at least, is indebted to Fried's polemic against "objecthood" in the graphic arts.

If Fried's intent was a spirited defense of high modernist painting against the staging of presence, immediacy, or "objecthood" by minimalist artists, Mandel attacked from the opposite flank, targeting roughly the same enemy. Indeed, one could easily cite Fried and Mandel as the reluctant critical voices supporting the historical genealogy of performance that Noël Carroll mapped out in his vastly underrated 1986 essay "Performance." Plotting the rise of late twentieth-century experimental performance, Carroll argues,

I see contemporary performance emerging from two dominant sources. On the one hand, it was a reaction by certain painters and sculptors to what they believed to be the fundamental, theoretical problem of gallery aesthetics in the sixties. Call this dimension of performance *art performance*. On the other hand, at roughly the same time, practitioners of the theatre initiated a revolt against the dominant and prevailing forms of drama. Theatre that was preeminently literary in its orientation was displaced by spectacle. The conventional separations of the audience and the actor and that of the actor and the character were assaulted in an attempt to dissolve them. Call this dimension of performance *performance art*. However, though art performance and performance art arose in reaction against distinctly different artforms, the two movements have at times crossed with important effects.[23]

What we find in the work of Fried and Mandel, then, are two critics from opposite ends of the disciplinary spectrum later described by Carroll who were working against the convergence at the intersection of what might be characterized as "art performance art"—which Carroll shortens to "performance"—one crucial dimension of which is experimental theater. Just as Fried argues that minimalists were dissatisfied with "illusionism," Mandel argues that experimental theater practitioners were dissatisfied "with theatre" itself, which he equates with being dissatisfied "with fiction" and dramatic literature.[24] "Theatre," Mandel maintains, "is fiction," and he claims that "when fiction ceases, we stand before a life-event: a lecture, a sermon, a revival meeting, a session of group therapy, a political rally." Call these events whatever one will, for Mandel they were not art, even when shrouded in the aura of experimental theater or performance.

Mandel's embrace of drama and fiction, which as Schechner points out could easily be attributed to the fact that Mandel was also a playwright,[25] is consistent with Fried's argument that the survival of all of the arts "has come increasingly to depend on their ability to defeat theatre."[26] Echoing this same line, Mandel's main argument in "Reactionary Notes" positions experimental theater in an antagonistic relation to dramatic literature. In doing so, he reinforces Fried's antitheatrical bias and characterizes experimental theater as a sophomoric assault on a presumably more substantive playwright's theater, where everything is subordinate to the artistry of the dramatic text and to high literary form. Whereas Fried defended the presumed artistic integrity of high modernist painting, Mandel defended the presumed artistic integrity of high modernist literature. Both sought to keep the experimental theater that they found in the middle in its place and contained.

Almost fifty years later, it is safe to say that both Fried and Mandel were premature in their arguments that minimalist art and experimental theater spelled the end of art. Not only is Schechner correct in his observation that one of the crucial problems with Mandel's argument is that it is stated in "absolute terms,"[27] but at some level the same is true of Fried's arguments as well. Although Fried characterizes minimalist art as "a new genre of theatre," he conceptualizes that new genre in an either/or proposition with art itself. Supposedly, it is only possible to choose one at the expense of the other. If there are many roads to art, apparently that new genre of theater was not one that Fried or Mandel were willing to travel. But it was never the dead end that they presumed it to be for art.

By 1974 Michael Kirby, for example, writing a review of the first Invitational

Festival of Experimental Theatre, which was held at the University of Michigan in late February of that year, noted that "experimental theatre" had neither spelled the end of art nor brought about a fundamental change in theater as such—despite the alarmist proclamations to the contrary by critics like Fried and Mandel. It was Kirby, of course, who a decade earlier in his 1965 *TDR* essay "The New Theatre" had championed the very movements that sparked the ire of Fried and Mandel, celebrating what he called experimental theater's use of "non-matrixed performance,"[28] in other words celebrating its objecthood, its focus on presence, and its embrace of life events. But what Kirby saw at the first Invitational Festival was that the much-celebrated experimental theater of the 1960s had ultimately emerged as little more than "the name of another genre"[29]—not a genre that marked a radical negation of art or the transformation of theater as such but merely one genre among other theatrical forms. The question is whether this is what it had become or whether, beneath the heady countercultural idealism of the 1960s, this is what it always was.

The myth of that genre—the notion that experimental theater was "a new theatre" in some categorical sense that rendered previous theater somehow no longer significant—has proven difficult to dispel. But perhaps Kirby was already pointing the way beyond that myth in his 1974 review of the Invitational Festival of Experimental Theatre at the University of Michigan. There Kirby initially expresses disappointment that "experimental theatre" at the festival "appeared not as a term indicating innovation—or even an attempt at innovation—but as the name of another genre," as something "readily understood" and as an "available category on which to base a festival."[30] As a genre, it was something that could be branded and marketed. This sense of disappointment echoes similar sentiments expressed by the critics Richard Schechner, Robert Corrigan, and Martin Esslin—all of whom had been invited as panelists to offer commentary on the festival and all of whom, as Kirby notes, "made clear [in their public comments] that none of the work they saw at the festival was truly experimental or innovative."[31] But looking back after the festival was over, Kirby believed that perhaps he and the other critics had subscribed to a problematic "absolute" notion of "innovation," a notion that understood innovation, and by extension experimental theater, in universal terms.

Kirby suggests that a more contextual understanding of experimental theater is in order. "A work may be obviously derivative in certain respects" or contexts, Kirby argues, "while offering significant innovation in others." But more important still, "innovation may occur on an intuitive rather than a conceptual level."[32] Following this line of thought, it was not so much the conceptual, technical, or stylistic originality that mattered as it was the uniqueness of its contextual setting. Kirby's intent here was to cultivate a more regionally diverse sense of innovation, suggesting that what may not be new to a New York or cosmopolitan critic may in fact have a unique innovative resonance within a regional setting like Ann Arbor, Michigan, for example. Indeed, Kirby reasons: "After all, what is 'old' to cosmopolitan judges may be 'new' in Michigan. This kind of newness may also be important."[33] Inasmuch as Kirby never really explores how that kind of newness may be important, I would suggest that there is much beneath the surface of Kirby's argument that remains unexplored.

While Kirby's reflections merit more consideration than they have received heretofore, they also merit consideration beyond the geographical framework in which he conceptualized them. Beyond regional differences, it is worth considering how the concept of "innovation" varies within different performance communities—in fact, within different kinds of communities: social, political, cultural, ethnic, and religious communities. At a more fundamental level, it is also is worth questioning the underlying assumption in Kirby's review that to speak of experimental theater is somehow automatically to speak of innovation, as if innovation is somehow the exclusive domain of those associated with the experimental theater community or is somehow inherent to the very definition of what distinguishes experimental theater from other theatrical forms. If we are to break from what Kirby calls the concept of "absolute innovation," then it also behooves us to break the mythical spell that falsely binds innovation and experimental theater within the same fabricated concept and finally to recognize, as the essays in this volume have made abundantly clear, that innovation occurs across the spectrum of theatrical practice—at least as far as one can legitimately speak of innovation at all.

One is reminded here of the arguments that Rosalind Krauss famously offers in *The Originality of the Avant-Garde and Other Modernist Myths*, that "originality"—and here I would add "innovation," as originality's cognate—"is a working assumption that itself emerges from a ground of repetition and recurrence."[34] Looking back at the sixties "then and now," Krauss's reminder about the myth of originality puts experimental theater in an awkward situation. With neither inherent ties to politics nor exclusive claims to innovation—with innovation itself a questionable category, at least in absolute terms—experimental theater begins to look a lot like what it appeared to Kirby to be in 1974 and to Fried in 1968: a genre of theater, one genre among many. Beneath the branding, it works in some contexts and for some audiences but not in all contexts or for all audiences.

NOTES

1. *Performing Arts Journal* 2.2 (1977): 13
2. Richard Kostelanetz, "American Experimental Theatre: Then and Now," *Performing Arts Journal* 2.2 (1977): 19.

3. Stanley Kaufmann, "American Experimental Theatre: Then and Now," *Performing Arts Journal* 2.2 (1977): 14.

4. Ibid.

5. Ibid.

6. Elizabeth Wollman, *The Theatre Will Rock: A History of the Rock Musical, from Hair to Hedwig* (Ann Arbor: University of Michigan Press, 2006), 73.

7. Michael Feingold, "American Experimental Theatre: Then and Now," *Performing Arts Journal* 2.2 (1977): 23.

8. Lawrence Kornfeld, "American Experimental Theatre: Then and Now," *Performing Arts Journal* 2.2 (1977): 16.

9. Jack Gelber, "Julian Beck, Businessman," *TDR* 30.2 (1986): 6–29.

10. Elizabeth LeCompte, "Who Owns History?," *Performing Arts Journal* 6.1 (1981): 51.

11. Feingold, "American Experimental Theatre," 22–23.

12. Richard Schechner, "Commentary on Mandel's 'Reactionary Notes on the Experimental Theatre,'" *Massachusetts Review* 11.3 (1970): 578.

13. See Schechner, "Commentary on Mandel's 'Reactionary Notes,'" 579–80, for a critique of Mandel's equation.

14. Kostelanetz, "American Experimental," 19.

15. Bonnie Marranca, *Theatre of Images* (Baltimore: Johns Hopkins University Press, 1996), X.

16. LeCompte, "Who Owns History?," 50.

17. Oscar Mandel, "Drama: Reactionary Notes on the Experimental Theatre," *Massachusetts Review* 11.1 (1970): 101.

18. Michael Fried, "Art and Objecthood," in *Minimal Art: A Critical Anthology*, ed. Gregory Battcock (New York: Dutton, 1968 117–18.

19. Donald Judd cited in ibid., 118.

20. Ibid., 120.

21. Ibid., 125.

22. Mandel, "Drama: Reactionary Notes," 112.

23. Noël Carroll, "Performance," *Formations* 3.1 (1986): 65–66.

24. Mandel, "Drama: Reactionary Notes," 105.

25. Schechner, "Commentary on Mandel's 'Reactionary Notes,'" 582.

26. Fried, "Art and Objecthood," 139.

27. Schechner, "Commentary on Manel's 'Reactionary Notes,'" 578.

28. Michael Kirby, "The New Theatre," *Tulane Drama Review* 10.2 (1965): 26

29. Michael Kirby, "College Experimentation?" *TDR* 18.2 (1974): 4.

30. Ibid.

31. Ibid.

32. Ibid., 5.

33. Ibid., 4.

34. Rosiland Krauss, *The Originality of the Avant-Garde and Other Modernist Myths* (Boston, MA: MIT Press, 1986), 158.

Contributors

Neil Blackadder is the author of *Performing Opposition: Modern Theater and the Scandalized Audience* (Praeger, 2003). He also translates contemporary drama from German and French; his translations of the works of playwrights such as Lukas Bärfuss and Ewald Palmetshofer have been staged in London, New York, Chicago, and other cities. He teaches theater at Knox College.

Stephen Bottoms is a professor of contemporary theater and performance at the University of Manchester, United Kingdom. His books include *Playing Underground: A Critical History of the 1960s Off-Off-Broadway Movement* (University of Michigan Press, 2004), *Small Acts of Repair: Performance, Ecology and Goat Island* (with Matthew Goulish; Routledge, 2007), and *Sex, Drag and Male Roles: Investigating Gender as Performance* (with Diane Torr; University of Michigan Press, 2010).

Kate Bredeson is a theater historian, a director, and a dramaturg. Recent publications include essays in *PAJ, Theater,* and *Modern and Contemporary France.* She is currently editing Judith Malina's lifetime diaries, and finishing her book *Occupying the Stage: Theater of May '68.* She is an associate professor of theater at Reed College.

Marvin Carlson is the Sidney E. Cohn Distinguished Professor of Theatre, Comparative Literature, and Middle Eastern Studies at the Graduate Center of the City University of New York. His recent book is *Shattering Hamlet's Mirror: Theatre and Reality* (Michigan, 2016).

Dorothy Chansky is the director of the Humanities Center at Texas Tech University, where she also teaches history, theory, and criticism in the School of Theatre and Dance. She is the author of *Kitchen Sink Realisms: Domestic Labor, Dining, and Drama in American Theatre* (Iowa, 2015) and *Composing Ourselves: The Little Theatre Movement and the American Audience* (Southern Illinois, 2004) and coeditor of *Food and Theatre on the World Stage* (Routledge, 2015). Her articles have appeared in *Theatre Journal, TDR, Text and Performance Quarterly*, and the *Journal of American Drama and Theatre*, among other places.

David A. Crespy is a professor of playwriting, acting, and dramatic literature at the University of Missouri. He founded MU's Writing for Performance Program and serves as its codirector. He is the founding artistic director of MU's Missouri Playwrights Workshop, and he is president of the Edward Albee Society. His publications include *Off-Off Broadway Explosion* (Watson-Guptill, 2003) and *Richard Barr: The Playwright's Producer* (SIU Press, 2013), both with a foreword by Edward Albee.

Susannah Engstrom received her Ph.D. in U.S. history from the University of Chicago in 2016. Her dissertation examines the development of professional arts institutions in the 1950s and 1960s, focusing on the rise of the nonprofit regional theater and the effect of this new framework for cultural production on the urban landscape of Minneapolis and St. Paul.

Donatella Galella is an assistant professor of theater at the University of California, Riverside. She researches economies and racial dynamics of regional theater, musicals, casting, and African American and Asian American performance. Her work has been published in *Theatre Journal, Continuum, Theatre Survey*, and *PAJ*.

James M. Harding is an associate professor of theater and performance studies at the University of Maryland, College Park. He is the author of *The Ghosts of the Avant-Garde(s): Exorcising Experimental Theater and Performance* (Michigan, 2013) and *Cutting Performances: Collage Events, Feminist Artists, and the American Avant-Garde* (Michigan, 2011). He coedited *The Rise of Performance Studies: Rethinking Richard Schechner's Broad Spectrum* (Palgrave, 2011) and *Restaging the Sixties: Radical Theaters and Their Legacies* (Michigan, 2006) with Cindy Rosenthal.

Kimberly Jannarone is a professor of theater arts at UC Santa Cruz, where she holds the Gary D. Licker Memorial Chair. In 2015–16, she was a visiting professor of dramaturgy and dramatic criticism at the Yale School of Drama and a Beinecke fellow at Yale Repertory Theater. She is the author of *Artaud and His Doubles* (winner of honorable mention for the Joe Callaway Prize for best book in drama) and the editor of *Vanguard Performance beyond Left and Right* (both University of Michigan Press).

Cindy Rosenthal is a professor of drama at Hofstra University and a performer and director. She has published essays in *TDR, Theatre Survey,* the *New York Times, Women & Performance,* and *Women: A Cultural Review* and is the author of *Ellen Stewart Presents: Fifty Years of La MaMa Experimental Theatre* (Michigan, forthcoming,). She coedited *The Rise of Performance Studies: Rethinking Richard Schechner's Broad Spectrum* (Palgrave, 2011) and *Restaging the Sixties: Radical Theaters and Their Legacies* (Michigan, 2006) with James Harding. She is also coeditor with Hanon Reznikov of *Living on Third Street: Plays of the Living Theatre 1989–1992* (Autonomedia, 2008).

Alisa Solomon is a professor at Columbia University's Graduate School of Journalism, where she directs the arts and culture concentration in the MA program. A longtime theater critic, dramaturg, and political journalist, she is the author of the award-winning books *Re-dressing the Canon: Essays on Theater and Gender* and *Wonder of Wonders: A Cultural History of "Fiddler on the Roof."*

Graham White is a professor of drama in the Department of Drama, Theatre and Performance at the University of Roehampton, London. He works on modern drama and the politics of the avant-garde and on the "play" of performance in legal settings and its role in the construction of narratives of history. He is also a playwright, most recently contributing a 12-part dramatization of Primo Levi's *The Periodic Table* to BBC Radio 4. His favorite Beatles album is the White Album.

Stacy Wolf is a professor of theater, the director of the Program in Music Theater, and the director of the Princeton Arts fellows in the Lewis Center for the Arts at Princeton University. She is the author of *Changed for Good: A Feminist History of the Broadway Musical* (Oxford, 2011) and *A Problem Like Maria: Gender and Sexuality in the American Musical* (Michigan, 2002) and is working on "Beyond Broadway: Four Seasons of Amateur Musical Theatre in the U.S."

Harvey Young is a professor of theater, performance studies, and African American studies at Northwestern University. He is the chair of Northwestern

University's Theatre Program. He is the author of *Theatre and Race* (Palgrave MacMillan, 2013) and *Embodying Black Experience* (Michigan, 2010); coauthor with Queen Meccasia Zabriskie, of *Black Theater Is Black Life: An Oral History of Chicago Theater and Dance, 1970–2010* (Northwestern, 2014); editor of *The Cambridge Companion to African American Theatre* (Cambridge, 2013); and coeditor of *Suzan-Lori Parks in Person* (Routledge, 2014), *Reimagining A Raisin in the Sun* (Northwestern 2012), and *Performance in the Borderlands* (Palgrave MacMillan, 2011).

Index